D1047680

*O God, make us hungry to learn what your love
makes you so ardent to teach!*

(Augustine, Sermon 80)

OCT 06 2016

248
Oden. T

# THE GOOD WORKS READER

*Thomas C. Oden*

WILLIAM B. EERDMANS PUBLISHING COMPANY
GRAND RAPIDS, MICHIGAN / CAMBRIDGE, U.K.

© 2007 Thomas C. Oden
All rights reserved

Published 2007 by
Wm. B. Eerdmans Publishing Co.
2140 Oak Industrial Drive N.E., Grand Rapids, Michigan 49505 /
P.O. Box 163, Cambridge CB3 9PU U.K.

Printed in the United States of America

12  11  10  09  08  07      7  6  5  4  3  2  1


Library of Congress Cataloging-in-Publication Data

Oden, Thomas C.
The good works reader / Thomas C. Oden.
p.      cm.      — (Classic Christian readers)
ISBN 978-0-8028-4031-8 (pbk.: alk. paper)
1. Good works (Theology)   I. Title.

BT773.O34   2007
248 — dc22
2007004949


www.eerdmans.com

# Contents

CONTENTS

**PART FOUR**

# THE IMPRISONED AND THE PERSECUTED    201

## PART FIVE
## THE LEAST OF THESE

# Preface

The Reader Series presents classic Christian texts on vital contemporary issues.

This volume of the Reader Series is designed to be read either separately or in sequence with the previous volume — *The Justification Reader*. The two themes (justification by faith alone and good works) are best kept in constant tension.

*The Good Works Reader* probes both the faith that becomes active in love, and the grace by which faith lives. These are inseparable. Yet it is still possible that some who might see this book independently, apart from the previous volume — *The Justification Reader* — might conclude that good works may be somehow detachable from justifying grace. Those who may be inclined to draw this conclusion are referred to the last Part of this volume and to the previous Reader. There is no way to reverse the order. Good works are born in grace, and live breathing the air of grace.

To anyone who might imagine that Christianity begins with good works, we can only say that the great classic exegetes all rejected this assumption. Christian teaching on good works is at every point correlated with the Gospel itself, the good news of God's coming into human history.

## The Surprising Relevance of the Fathers

Nowhere in the modern literature on the poor, to my knowledge, has extensive attention been paid to patristic writers. Here they speak for themselves. If your special interest is in the study of nursing or health care or social ethics or psychotherapy or philanthropy or ministries of compassion, relief, and advocacy, the spiritual resources you will find in classic Christianity are stunning. This is especially true if you wish to relate your practical concerns to historic Christian wisdom.

Even if you are not Christian, you will find their challenge formidable. No special background knowledge is required to probe this Reader. Its subjects are down-to-earth. Its proposals are non-speculative.

It is surprising to realize that the ancient Christian writers were socially engaged long before modern forms of social activism. It is easier to push them aside than to listen. Even to take them seriously as agents of social change, we must set aside some of our intuitions and modern predispositions. Our biases are often corrupted by the pretensions of a modernity that imagines that all good ideas must be modern ideas.

We come with inordinately low expectations of the patristic writers, expecting them to be sexist, authoritarian, chauvinist, dated, or anti-democratic. We are surprised when they turn out to be gentle, humane, highly educated, and very much in tune with many of our present social and moral dilemmas. We expected them to be just old dead white Europeans. They turn out to be nothing like this. Most were African or Asian, not white, and far from dead.

Anyone today involved in a ministry to the poor, hungry, sick, or imprisoned will find ancient Christian teaching intriguing and thought-provoking, even though some aspects may cause discomfort. They speak to persons from all points on the modern political spectrum.

# Authors Quoted

*Early African Writers Designated by Asterisk*

Ambrose (Bishop of Milan, c. 333-397, teacher of Augustine, first of four great Latin "doctors of the church")

Ambrosiaster (pseudonymous author of fourth-century commentaries attributed to Ambrose, fl. c. 366-384)

*Ammonius (Alexandrian biblical commentator, c. fifth century)

Andrew of Crete, or Andreas (seventh-century catenist, hymnographer, and homilist)

Apollinaris of Laodicea (Bishop of Laodicea, c. 310-c. 392)

*Athanasius (Bishop of Alexandria, c. 295-373, theologian of Nicene orthodoxy)

*Augustine (Bishop of Hippo, 354-430, leading theologian of western Christianity)

Basil the Great (Bishop of Caesarea in Cappadocia, b. ca. 330, fl. 357-379)

Bede the Venerable (Northumbrian Benedictine, father of English history, c. 672-735)

Caesarius of Arles (Bishop of Arles, homilist, c. 470-543)

Cassian, John (conveyed eastern monastic traditions to the west, founded monastery in Marseilles, 360-432)

Cassiodorus (statesman, translator, monk, founded Vivarium, scriptorium in Calabria, c. 485-c. 580)

Chromatius of Aquileia (Bishop of Aquileia, scholar, homilist, fl. 400)

*Clement of Alexandria (head of Alexandrian catechetical school, c. 150-215)

Clement of Rome (Bishop of Rome, fl. c. 92-101)

*Cyprian (Bishop of Carthage, martyr, fl. 248-258)

*Cyril of Alexandria (Patriarch of Alexandria, exegete, theologian, 375-444)

Cyril of Jerusalem (Bishop of Jerusalem, catechist, c. 315-386)

*Didymus the Blind (Nicene theologian and exegete, head of Alexandrian catechetical school, c. 313-398)

Diodore (Bishop of Tarsus, exegete, d. 394)

Egeria (nun, pilgrim, diarist, probably of Galicia, Spain, fl. 381-384)

Ephrem the Syrian (deacon of Nisibis and Edessa, hymnist, exegete, theologian, c. 306-373)

Epiphanius the Latin (Bishop of Benevento or Seville, late fifth/early sixth century)

Epiphanius Scholasticus (monk, Cassiodorus' secretary, late fifth/early sixth century)

Eusebius (Bishop of Caesarea, church historian, c. 260/263-340)

*Fulgentius of Ruspe (Bishop of Ruspe in North Africa, c. 467-532)

Gennadius of Constantinople (Patriarch of Constantinople, d. 471)

Gregory the Great (Bishop of Rome, fourth and last of Latin "doctors of the church," c. 540-604)

Gregory of Nazianzus (the Theologian, Cappadocian father, Bishop of Constantinople, b. 329/330, fl. 372-389)

Gregory of Nyssa (Bishop of Nyssa, Cappadocian, c. 335-394)

Hesychius of Jerusalem (monk, presbyter, biblical commentator, fl. 412-451)

Hilary of Arles (monk at Lérins, Archbishop of Arles, c. 401-449)

Hilary of Poitiers (Bishop of Poitiers, exegete, "Athanasius of the West," c. 315-367)

Hippolytus (presbyter, theologian of Rome, exiled to Sardinia, fl. 222-245)

Irenaeus (Bishop of Lyons, theologian, c. 135-c. 202)

Jerome (ascetic biblical scholar, exegete, translator of Latin Vulgate Bible, c. 347-420)

John Chrysostom ("Golden Mouth," Antiochene homilist, Bishop of Constantinople, 344/354-407)

Justin Martyr (Palestinian apologist, taught at Ephesus, Rome, beheaded, c. 100/110-165, fl. c. 148-161)

*Lactantius (African Christian rhetorician and apologist at Nicomedia, c. 260-c. 330)

Leo the Great (Bishop of Rome, theologian, fl. 440-461)

Maximus of Turin (Bishop of Turin, homilist, d. 408/423)

Maximus the Confessor (Byzantine theologian, exegete, ascetic writer, c. 580-662)

*Minucius Felix (African Christian apologist, advocate in Rome, late second or early third century)

Oecumenius (catenist from Isauria, wrote earliest extant Greek commentary on John's Apocalypse, early sixth century)

*Origen of Alexandria (commentator on the whole Bible, systematic theologian, 185-c. 254)

*Pachomius (founder of cenobitic monasticism, author of first monastic rule, c. 292-347)

Paterius (biblical commentator, disciple of Gregory the Great, c. sixth/seventh century)

Paulinus of Nola (Roman senator, Latin poet, 355-431)

Peter Chrysologus (Latin archbishop of Ravenna, homilist, c. 380-450)

Polycarp (Bishop of Smyrna, martyr, c. 69-155)

Prudentius (Latin poet, hymn writer, c. 348-c. 410)

Pseudo-Basil, works attributed to Basil whose authorship remains disputed

Quodvultdeus (anti-Pelagian Bishop of Carthage, exiled to Naples, fl. 430)

Salvian the Presbyter (historian of Marseilles, c. 400-480)

Severian of Gabala (Bishop and exegete of Gabala, Syria, fl. c. 400)

Severus of Antioch (Bishop of Antioch, fl. 488-538)

Shepherd of Hermas (compilation of visions, precepts, parables, second century)

Symeon the New Theologian (abbot in Constantinople, leading Byzantine mystic, c. 949-1022)

*Tertullian (Carthaginian apologist and polemicist, c. 155/160-225/250, fl. c. 197-222)

Theodore of Heraclea (biblical commentator, Bishop of Heraclea in Thrace, d. c. 355)

Theodore of Mopsuestia (Bishop of Mopsuestia, founder of Antiochene school of exegesis, c. 350-428)

Theodoret of Cyr (Bishop of Cyrrhus, Antiochene exegete, c. 393-466)

Theophylact of Ohrid (Byzantine archbishop, Bulgaria, exegete, c. 1050–c. 1108)

Valerian of Cimiez (monk of Lérins, homilist, Bishop of Cimiez, fl. c. 422-439)

*Victorinus, Marius (former imperial rhetor, apologist, early Latin commentator on Pauline epistles, b. ca. 300, fl. 355-363)

# Abbreviations

| | |
|---|---|
| ACCS | Thomas C. Oden, ed. *Ancient Christian Commentary on Scripture.* 24 vols. to date. Downers Grove, IL: InterVarsity Press, 1998-. |
| ACD | Augustine. *On Christian Doctrine.* D. W. Robertson, Jr., ed. and trans. (*Library of Liberal Arts,* v. 80) Indianapolis: Bobbs-Merrill, 1977, c1958. |
| ACG | Augustine. *Concerning the City of God Against the Pagans.* H. Bettenson, trans. Harmondsworth, Middlesex: Penguin, 1972. |
| ACWCa | Cassiodorus. *Explanation of the Psalms.* P. G. Walsh, ed. and trans. 3 vols. (*Ancient Christian Writers,* v. 51-53) New York: Paulist Press, 1990-1991. |
| ACWCas | John Cassian. *John Cassian, The Conferences.* B. Ramsey, ed. and trans. (*Ancient Christian Writers,* v. 57) New York: Paulist Press, 1997. |
| ACWCh | John Chrysostom. *Baptismal Instructions.* P. W. Harkins, ed. and trans. (*Ancient Christian Writers,* v. 31) New York: Paulist Press, 1963. |
| ACWG | Gregory the Great. *Pastoral Care.* H. Davis, ed. and trans. (*Ancient Christian Writers,* v. 11) Westminster, MD: Newman Press, 1950. |
| ACWM | Maximus of Turin. *The Sermons of Maximus of Turin.* B. Ramsey, ed. and trans. (*Ancient Christian Writers,* v. 50) New York: Newman Press, 1989. |
| ACWOp | Origen. *Prayer; Exhortation to Martyrdom.* J. J. O'Meara, ed. and trans. (*Ancient Christian Writers,* v. 19) Westminster, MD: Newman Press, 1954. |
| ACWOs | Origen. *The Song of Songs: Commentary and Homilies.* R. P. Lawson, ed. and trans. (*Ancient Christian Writers,* v. 26) Westminster, MD: Newman Press, 1957. |

AEG      H. D. Smith, ed. *Ante-Nicene Exegesis of the Gospels.* 6 vols. London: SPCK, 1925.

AF      J. B. Lightfoot and J. R. Harmer, trans. *The Apostolic Fathers.* M. W. Holmes, ed. 2nd ed. Grand Rapids: Baker, 1989.

AMA      Augustine. *Miscellanea Agostiniana.* G. Morin and A. Casamassa, eds. 2 vols. Rome: Tipografia Poliglotta Vaticana, 1930-1931.

ANF      A. Roberts and J. Donaldson, eds. *Ante-Nicene Fathers.* American reprint of the Edinburgh ed. 10 vols. Buffalo, NY: Christian Literature, 1885-1896. Reprint, Grand Rapids: Eerdmans, 1951-1956. Reprint, 1978-1980.

AOR      Augustine. *Augustine on Romans: Propositions from the Epistle to the Romans, Unfinished Commentary on the Epistle to the Romans.* P. F. Landes, trans. (*Texts and Translations,* v. 23) Chico, CA: Scholars Press, 1982.

ARL      Athanasius. *The Resurrection Letters.* J. N. Sparks, ed. Nashville: Thomas Nelson, 1979.

BTMV      Marius Victorinus. *Commentarii in Epistolas Pauli ad Galatas ad Philippenses ad Ephesios.* (*Bibliotheca Scriptorum Graecorum et Romanorum Teubneriana*) Leipzig: Teubner, 1972.

CASL      Cyril of Alexandria. *Select Letters.* L. R. Wickham, ed. and trans. (*Oxford Early Christian Texts*) Oxford: Oxford University Press, 1983.

CCL      *Corpus Christianorum. Series Latina.* 175+ vols. to date. Turnhout [Belgium]: Brepols, 1954-.

CEC      J. A. Cramer, ed. *Catena in Epistolas Catholicas.* (*Catenae Graecorum Patrum in Novum Testamentum,* v. 8) Oxford: E. Typographeo Academico, 1840.

CER      Origen. *Commentarii in Epistulam ad Romanos* (Commentary on the Epistle to the Romans). T. Heither, ed. 5 vols. Freiburg im Breisgau: Herder, 1990-1995.

Cetedoc      Centre de Traitement Électronique des Documents. *Cetedoc Library of Christian Latin Texts.* 5 CD-ROMs. Turnhout [Belgium]: Brepols, 1991-2000.

CGSL      Cyril of Alexandria. *Commentary on the Gospel of St. Luke.* R. Payne Smith, trans. Long Island, NY: Studion Publishers, Inc., 1983.

COV      Chrysostom. *On Virginity, Against Remarriage.* S. R. Shore, trans. (*Studies in Women and Religion,* v. 9) New York and Toronto: Edwin Mellen Press, 1983.

COWP      Chrysostom. *On Wealth and Poverty.* C. P. Roth, trans. Crestwood, NY: St. Vladimir's Seminary Press, 1984.

CSBH      Bede the Venerable. *Homilies on the Gospels.* L. T. Martin and D. Hurst, trans. 2 vols. (*Cistercian Studies Series,* v. 110-11) Kalamazoo, MI: Cistercian Publications, 1991.

| | |
|---|---|
| CSEL | *Corpus Scriptorum Ecclesiasticorum Latinorum.* 90+ vols. Vienna: Hoelder-Pichler-Tempsky, 1866-. |
| CSGF | Gregory the Great. *Forty Gospel Homilies.* D. Hurst, trans. (*Cistercian Studies Series,* v. 123) Kalamazoo, MI: Cistercian Publications, 1990. |
| CSPE | J. A. Cramer, ed. *Catenae in Sancti Pauli Epistolas ad Galatas, Ephesios, Philippenses, Colossenses, Thessalonicenses.* (*Catenae Graecorum Patrum in Novum Testamentum,* v. 6) Oxford: E. Typographeo Academico, 1842. |
| CSPK | Pachomius. *Pachomian Koinonia.* A. Veilleux, trans. 3 vols. (*Cistercian Studies Series,* v. 45-47) Kalamazoo, MI: Cistercian Publications, 1980-1982. |
| CWSO | Origen. *Origen.* [*Selections.*] R. A. Greer, trans. (*Classics of Western Spirituality*) New York: Paulist Press, 1979. |
| CWSS | Symeon the New Theologian. *The Discourses.* C. J. de Catanzaro, trans. (*Classics of Western Spirituality*) New York: Paulist Press, 1980. |
| ECTD | Ephrem the Syrian. *Saint Ephrem's Commentary on Tatian's Diatessaron: An English Translation of Chester Beatty Syriac MS 709.* C. McCarthy, trans. and ed. (*Journal of Semitic Studies,* Supplement 2) Oxford: Oxford University Press for the University of Manchester, 1993. |
| EDP | Egeria. *Egeria: Diary of a Pilgrimage.* G. E. Gingras, trans. (*Ancient Christian Writers,* v. 38) New York: Newman Press, 1970. |
| EHG | Ambrose of Milan. *Exposition of the Holy Gospel According to Saint Luke with Fragments on the Prophecy of Isaias.* T. Tomkinson, trans. Etna, CA: Center for Traditionalist Orthodox Studies, 1998. |
| FC | R. J. Deferrari, ed. *Fathers of the Church: A New Translation.* 100+ vols. to date. Washington, DC: Catholic University of America Press, 1947-. |
| FGNK | T. Zahn. *Forschungen zur Geschichte des Neutestamentlichen Kanons und der Altkirchlichen Literatur.* 10 vols. Erlangen and Leipzig: A. Deichert, 1881-1929. |
| GCSO | Origen. *Origenes Werke.* P. Koetschau et al., eds. 12 vols. (*Die Griechischen Christlichen Schriftsteller der Ersten Drei Jahrhunderte,* v. 2-3, 6, 10, 22, 29-30, 33, 35, 38, 40-41) Leipzig: Hinrichs, 1899-1955. |
| GMI | J. Ford. *The Gospel According to S. Mark: Illustrated (Chiefly in the Doctrinal and Moral Sense) from Ancient and Modern Authors.* 2nd ed. London: J. Masters, 1864. |
| GNF | Gregory Nazianzus. *Faith Gives Fullness to Reasoning: The Five Theological Orations of Gregory Nazianzus.* F. W. Norris, ed. Leiden and New York: E. J. Brill, 1990. |
| HOP | Ephrem the Syrian. *Hymns on Paradise.* S. Brock, trans. Crestwood, NY: St. Vladimir's Seminary Press, 1990. |

| | |
|---|---|
| IOEP | John Chrysostom. *Interpretatio omnium Epistolarum Paulinarum per Homilias Facta.* F. Field, ed. 7 vols. Oxford: J. H. Parker, 1845-1862. |
| JF B | E. Barnecut, ed. *Journey with the Fathers: Commentaries on the Sunday Gospels, Year B.* Hyde Park, NY: New City Press, 1995. |
| JTS | *Journal of Theological Studies.* London, 1899-. |
| KJV | King James Version (1611). |
| LCC | J. Baillie et al., eds. *The Library of Christian Classics.* 26 vols. Philadelphia: Westminster, 1953-1966. |
| LCLJ | Jerome. *Select Letters of St. Jerome.* F. A. Wright, trans. *(Loeb Classical Library)* London: Heinemann and Cambridge, MA: Harvard University Press, 1954, c1933. |
| LXX | Septuagint |
| MKGK | J. Reuss, ed. *Matthäus-Kommentare aus der griechischen Kirche.* Berlin: Akademie-Verlag, 1957. |
| NASB | New American Standard Bible |
| NIV | New International Version |
| NPNF | P. Schaff et al., eds. *A Select Library of the Nicene and Post-Nicene Fathers of the Christian Church,* Series 1 and 2 (14 vols. each). Buffalo, NY: Christian Literature, 1887-1894. Reprint, Edinburgh: T. & T. Clark, and Grand Rapids: Eerdmans, 1952-1956. Reprint, 1971-1979. |
| NRSV | New Revised Standard Version |
| NT | New Testament |
| NTA 15 | K. Staab, ed. *Pauluskommentare aus der griechischen Kirche: Aus Katenenhandschriften gesammelt und herausgegeben* [Pauline Commentary from the Greek Church: Collected and Edited Catena Writings] (*Neutestamentliche Abhandlungen,* v. 15) Münster in Westfalen: Aschendorff, 1933. |
| OFP | Origen. *On First Principles: Being Koetschau's Text of the De Principiis.* G. W. Butterworth, trans. Gloucester, MA: Peter Smith, 1973, c1936. |
| OT | Old Testament |
| PG | J.-P. Migne, ed. *Patrologia Graeca.* 166 vols. Paris: Migne, 1857-1886. |
| PL | J.-P. Migne, ed. *Patrologia Latina.* 221 vols. Paris: Migne, 1844-1864. |
| PL *Suppl.* | A. Hamman, ed. *Patrologiae Latinae Supplementum.* 5 vols. in 6. Paris: Garnier Frères, 1958-1974. |
| POG | Eusebius. *The Proof of the Gospel.* W. J. Ferrar, trans. London: SPCK, 1920. Reprint, Grand Rapids: Baker, 1981. |
| RSV | Revised Standard Version |
| SCC | Chromatius of Aquileia. *Sermons.* J. Lemarie, ed. H. Tardif, trans. 2 vols. (*Sources Chrétiennes,* v. 154, 164) Paris: Editions du Cerf, 1969-1971. |
| SCH | Hilary of Poitiers. *Sur Matthieu.* J. Doignon, ed. 2 vols. (*Sources Chrétiennes,* v. 254, 258) Paris: Editions du Cerf, 1978-1979. |

SCQ      Quodvultdeus. *Livre des Promesses et des Predictions de Dieu.*
R. Braun, ed. and trans. 2 vols. (*Sources Chrétiennes*, v. 101-2) Paris: Editions du Cerf, 1964.

SSGF      M. F. Toal, ed. and trans. *Sunday Sermons of the Great Fathers: A Manual of Preaching, Spiritual Reading and Meditation.* 4 vols. Chicago: Regnery, 1958. Reprint, Swedesboro, NJ: Preservation Press, 1996.

TCPE      Theodoret. *Commentarius in Omnes B. Paula Epistolas.* C. Marriott, ed. 2 vols. Oxford: J. H. Parker, 1852, c1870.

TEM      Theodore of Mopsuestia. *Theodori Episcopi Mopsuesteni in Epistolas B. Pauli Commentarii: The Latin Version with the Greek Fragments.* H. B. Swete, ed. 2 vols. Cambridge: Cambridge University Press, 1880-1882.

TLG      L. Berkowitz and K. Squitier, eds. *Thesaurus Linguae Graecae: Canon of Greek Authors and Works.* 2nd ed. Oxford: Oxford University Press, 1986.

TTHB      Bede the Venerable. *Bede: On the Tabernacle.* A. G. Holder, ed. (*Translated Texts for Historians*, v. 18) Liverpool: Liverpool University Press, 1994.

WSA      Augustine. *Works of St. Augustine: A Translation for the Twenty-First Century.* J. E. Rotelle, ed. 29 vols. to date. Hyde Park, NY: New City Press, 1990-.

# Introduction

## A. The Purpose

### 1. An Opening Caveat

*The good works discussed here are those that follow from God's own good work of grace on the cross, received by faith, as attested in scripture.* Hence the heart cry of the Reformation — grace alone, faith alone, scripture alone — stands as the central premise of this inquiry. It would be premature to conclude that good works can be considered apart from grace. All talk of good works assumes a due consideration of justifying grace, in classic Christian teaching.

My major purpose is not to display how relevant to contemporary society are classic Christian teachings of good works. Rather it is to allow the ancients to speak for themselves, and let their relevance be judged by those who wish to put their vision into actual practice. The aim of this exercise is changed behavior, not theoretical insight alone. Only so far as behavioral changes occur will this project have reached its mark.

The decisive sacred text for uniting justification and good works is Paul's concise phrase: "The only thing that counts is *faith working through love*" (Gal. 5:6, NRSV). Faith is most truly faith when it is becoming active in love. The Letter to Titus asks: "In all things [show] yourself to be a pattern of good works" (Tit. 2:7, NKJV).

1

## 2. *The Purpose*

My purpose is simple: to set forth nothing more or less than *the classic Christian teaching of good works* grounded in salvation by grace through faith. I will focus on those texts on which there is substantial agreement between traditions of east and west — Catholic, Protestant, and Orthodox — with regard to both their importance and ecumenical authority.

We learn from these texts to think deeply about the poor, their hunger and thirst, their vulnerability. Here we hear the cry of the needy, the widow, the fatherless, the sick, and the imprisoned. These teachings are not simply about political acts or policies or ideologies, but rather about God's own way of mercifully coming in the flesh to care for humanity in its pain, sorrow, and suffering. Thus the question of good works brings us into the realm of concrete responsiveness to the incarnation, the messianic miracles, the binding up of demonic powers, the cross, and the glory of the eternal city.

Some will reduce the question to practical outcomes alone, missing their motivation and meaning. Some will come to the question of good works with their eyes fixed only on their political implications, not their expression of life with God. Some will see good works only as human actions, missing their placement within the history of salvation. Some will see good works only in relation to moral choices, not in relation to God's holiness. Some will come to the question of good works having in mind only the physical needs of the needy, not the deeper human need at its tragic sweep. Some will come to the question of good works having in mind only the horizontal dimension of practical service and applicability, not the vertical dimension of standing before God now and on the last day.

All these partial approaches stand to be corrected by the wholeness of the teaching of the Fathers of the whole faith for the whole world. It is the whole that matters in theology. That is what is meant by *cath 'olou*, according to the whole, and hence *catholikos,* which means — the whole faith for the whole world held fast by the whole world of believers.

Jesus prayed for the unity of the body of believers. Through cooperative acts of relief and mercy, Christians of all sorts are today being brought together. They range from mainline liberal Protestants to Evangelicals, from Catholics to Orthodox to Baptists and Pentecostals. This unity is especially being demonstrated in the works of love for the needy. All these traditions are poised to relearn from the classic scriptural interpreters of the earliest Christian centuries.

### 3. Classic Christianity

Long before the divisions of the church in the second millennium, these classic Christians of the first millennium were drawing the diverse accounts of scripture toward a consensus on good works. That is what we will show textually.

While Protestants still rightly protest the vestiges of the abuses of late medieval scholasticism, they generally agree that scripture provides the basis for judging all issues of Christian teaching, including the practice of good works. The early biblical interpreters that prevailed most widely in ancient Christianity are themselves consonant with the received Protestant teaching (of Luther, Calvin, and Wesley) on the necessity and urgency of good works. This imperfect but real consensus is first expressed in the writings of the Fathers of the east and west. Today it is extending to embrace liturgical and charismatic traditions, both high and low church traditions of all sorts. They may disagree on polity, ministry, sacraments, and church order, but hardly at all on good works.

When congregations hold passive views of human responsibility, the evidence is that they are not growing. If some teaching claims to be the Gospel but does nothing in response, does not elicit any compassionate action, then it is surely not the Gospel. The fantasy of a gospel that does nothing is not the good news of the New Testament.

The heart of the Gospel is God's good work for us. What we do in response is a story every believer lives out. It is the story of *faith becoming active in love.*

My promise to the reader is as before — to make no new contribution to theology — nothing creative or imaginative, only classic Christianity. I will not set before you anything new or innovative. As a former addict of fad theology, I have returned to ancient ecumenical Christianity to center my work in classic Christian teaching, letting these teachers speak for themselves in their own way without my interference insofar as possible. My only desire is to report the truth of the early apostolic tradition as it was generally received east and west, without changes or distortions. If something here should inadvertently seem to be novel or avant-garde or personally creative, it would constitute a serious lapse of attentiveness. Meanwhile the Gospel itself is ever new, ever creative, full of truth to be rediscovered.

### 4. If the Reader Is Not a Christian Believer

If the reader is not a Christian believer, there is still much to learn by observing good works of Christian believers. You may wish to regard this exercise as an act of historical or sociological or psychological *empathy*. Ask yourself: Suppose I risk engaging in this simple empathic exercise: What do Christianity's own classic texts teach about good works? This is an exercise that can be broached without any entanglements or commitments — at least at first. But be forewarned that it might change your life.

### 5. The Primary Audience: Those Eager to Mine the Wisdom of Classic Christian Teaching

This Reader is mainly for those who already relish the true taste of the earliest apostolic teaching as it was being freshly remembered in its first centuries. You may already know how to recognize its tonality, its rhythms. If so you will not mind taking unhurried time listening to the divine address speaking through scripture, as seen through the eyes of the earliest interpreters of the written Word. This is the meat Paul distinguished from the milk. The target audience is the hungriest whose taste buds are already salivating.

What do Christians of all times and places believe about the good works that are elicited by faith? This Reader shows that there is a stable, central core of substantial agreement. The cumulative witness of the Fathers themselves will point unmistakably to that core. If after having read their testimony, you do not grasp that core, check to see if you have been fully awake. Such an exercise must be a meditation on the whole range of the Bible, yet focused on a single theme: the acts of love elicited by God's love made known in history.

The means by which we seek to rediscover Christian teaching in this series is by re-examining those ancient texts of Christian scripture and scriptural interpreters that express the good works that follow from faith. These texts, written prior to the divisions of Christianity, remain the patrimony of all Christians today of all continents and races and cultures.

These texts are often called the Fathers of the church. They are by general consent the consensus-bearing teachers of the earliest centuries of scriptural interpretation. The wisdom of the Fathers was prematurely discarded by fad theology. The terms "patristic" and "classic exegetes" and "Fathers" are used equally to refer to the first millennium of ecumenical biblical exposition.

## 6. The Principal Sources

The texts offer the exposition of scripture by the most representative voices in widely different Christian cultures of the earliest Christian centuries. A wide consensus on moral teaching emerges in the central stream of ancient Christian teaching.

Who are these principal sources? They are those who have gradually gained the most general consent in the east and west, and between early African and Asian traditions, as universally esteemed. They include the eight great doctors of the church — especially (by long tradition) Athanasius, Basil, Gregory Nazianzus, and John Chrysostom in the east, and Ambrose, Jerome, Augustine, and Gregory the Great in the west. All were avid biblical expositors immersed in the whole range of scriptures.

Among these Chrysostom and Augustine were the most influential voices on the relation of saving faith to good works. In addition to these eight, there are a number of widely respected classic Christian teachers cited by various ecumenical councils as most generally reliable to the church in all its eastern, western, and African varieties — notable among them are Cyprian of Carthage, Cyril of Jerusalem, Gregory of Nyssa, Ambrosiaster, Cyril of Alexandria, Leo, and John of Damascus.

None of these voices became consensual by modern consent. Their status as consensual teachers was well established a thousand years before modernity. The ancient general councils cite them specifically as reliable and consensual. Those who might wish to add the Gospel of Thomas or Arius or Pelagius to the list would do well to look at the ecumenical council canons to see if they are affirmed.

## 7. For the Laity

Any layperson can think with the whole church about the whole range of scripture texts relating to the theme of good works. Any layperson can then validate its meaning according to his or her own Spirit-guided conscience.

This time-tested approach has admittedly been neglected in recent

5

decades, but it is making an amazing comeback. It has been neglected for about two hundred years, but is now proving its worth once again. The result of this neglect is that in our time we do not even have many of these classic texts readily available to us in any modern language. With all our publishing skills we still remain text-deprived and translation-hungry, and thus argument-deficient. But this is not an irreversible dilemma. It is being reversed, and you hold in your hands one of the signs of reversal.

## B. The Texts

### 1. Getting Acquainted with the Fathers

Some may think it daunting to face texts written more than a thousand years ago. We have tried to make this less dreadful by providing non-technical terms in the translation of these ancient texts. These writers are not so intimidating. They want to be easily accessible. Good works are not difficult to understand conceptually. They do not require a professional vocabulary.

This Reader seeks to simplify the layperson's access to these teachings by providing a dynamic equivalency translation in ordinary English. We will try to remove obstacles without dumbing-down the substance of the meaning of the ancient text, whether originally written in Hebrew, Greek, Latin, or Syriac.

We hope to hear scripture addressing us personally. This listening occurs, according to the ancients' testimony, through the guidance of the Holy Spirit.

The blessings to be received are abundant. In the few hours it takes to examine this Reader, the heart and mind will be bathed in scripture in an unforgettable way, and in the early tradition's memory of scripture. The main reason we read the ancient Christian writers is that they teach us anew what scripture taught them. None of the classic Christian writers taught apart from scripture.

### 2. Learning to Read Scripture with the Ancient Church

The ancient Christian writers give us a model for reading scripture under the guidance of the Holy Spirit. To ignore that wisdom is foolish. Classic

Christian teaching provides a reliable pattern for the spiritual formation of our active life, our deeds, our actions.

The freedom to love, which is enabled by grace, energizes the act of mercy in unexpected ways. If we read only contemporary sources, we give ourselves less of a chance to understand this than if we read scripture along with the *consensus fidelium,* the mind of the believing church of all times and places. We are not the first generation to ask about good works that are honoring to God while being helpful to the neighbor. Our convoluted efforts to do good works may end in despair if we are not being freed to love the neighbor.

This Reader provides a pattern for laypersons to think with the historic community of faith about simple daily acts of mercy and kindness. The Holy Spirit promises to make that happen. God the Spirit has promised to accompany the faithful in seeing what is to be done for others and why.

### 3. Why a Good Works Reader?

*The Justification Reader* dealt with the error of desperately seeking righteousness *through* our own works. *The Good Works Reader* deals with the opposite error: desperately pretending righteousness *without* good works. Together the two fit hand in glove to resist opposite temptations: faith without works of love, and works of love without faith.

Together they provide equilibrium for both an exaggerated legalism and an exaggerated antinomianism. Legalism forgets grace. Antinomianism forgets the moral requirement of grace (where the Gospel is viewed as if against moral requirement, so that good works have no place in the Christian life). Thus these two Readers (Justification and Good Works) are seeking to give balance in the correction of a single error: the displacement of faith by works or works by faith. This balance is expressed in the scriptural teaching of *faith active in love.*

Reliable Christian teaching is based on canonical scripture. Each text of scripture has gone through twenty centuries of memory, application, and reflection. The earliest layers of this memory, in the earliest centuries of Christian teaching (first through the eighth centuries), provide the texts that give us the most dependable instruction.

Why more dependable? Four reasons: Because

- they were closer to the events of the Gospel narrative,
- the church they served was less divided, more cohesive,
- they were closely attentive to the Spirit,
- and they were not corrupted by either medieval or modern cultural assumptions.

Those who have most reliably remembered and understood scriptural teaching have provided succeeding generations with a seamless account of good works. This account has survived centuries of historic change. We will listen chiefly to those most widely trusted by the historic circle of believers of all generations.

### 4. Why Good Works Require Careful Study

But why *read* about good works — why not just go out and *do* them? To learn to do good works, we do well first to understand what constitutes and motivates a good work. Doing good works in the Christian sense requires understanding the good work God has done for us.

The Christian life calls for decisive behavioral outcomes. These texts will describe these behaviors so anyone can recognize them easily. Faith's power will be misspent if they are not clearly seen.

No one who fairly reads the ancient Christian writers can come away with the impression that these acts and behaviors are socially irrelevant, intellectually thin, unfair to certain people, outdated, or downright wrong. They avoid all these errors. Those who persist in seeing them in these ways have not read them with empathy. So read carefully and meditatively, and you will enter into a sweaty, energetic, active exercise room of biblical, theological, and moral reflection, with treadmills, weights, and hot tubs. Like aerobic and weights training, you cannot rush it.

### 5. Why the Fathers Are a "Must-Read" for Both Liberals and Conservatives

The Fathers are a "must-read" for both liberals and conservatives. Why? Because they provide arguments that all modern ideologies do well to examine.

Pragmatically, they show an achievable way to human improvement.

8

Intellectually, the Fathers give plausible arguments for their conclusions. Emotively, they move the soul to follow that way. It is no accident that they have been viewed as profound and authoritative for almost two millennia. I make no claim that this book is a must-read, but the Fathers indeed are a must-read amid our contemporary dilemmas.

It is possible to think about *how faith works* in a way that is shared by intergenerational Christians of all times and cultures. We begin to sense how the Spirit is at work to bring Christians of very different sorts together through coordinated systems of acts of mercy for the benefit of humanity. We learn how the Spirit is overcoming our tragic divisions and uniting our competing historical memories. Orthodox Christians, Protestants, and Catholics are all invited to the feast at this table. All belong. Through the lens of these common ancient interpreters these diverse traditions are newly vivified.

When Protestants discover what the classical ecumenical writers have to say about faith's good works, it is clear that these ancient biblical expositors are very close to the best of their own Protestant tradition. When Pentecostal and charismatic believers discover how the Spirit has been working in history to bring Spirit-led Christians (whether Orthodox, Catholic, or Protestant) to identical conclusions on good works, they often glimpse a work of the Spirit in history that has not been strongly emphasized in their own recent traditions. As Catholic and Orthodox believers are rediscovering their own classic texts, they are coming into a wider awareness of catholic and orthodox faith.

## 6. Cross-Cultural Wisdom

The languages and cultures in which the teaching of good works first emerged and later developed were amazingly multicultural: Jewish, Greco-Roman, North African, Byzantine, and later further developed in European, medieval, Reformation, and modern cultures. Though expressed in different languages and cultures, the core of the teaching remains remarkably consistent.

This core is what we want to reveal textually. It was well understood in the early centuries of Christianity, never better articulated than in the first four centuries. In it we find a set of arguments that still have powerful ramifications for our torn society — for the health of our families and our personal lives.

### 7. On the Genre of the "Reader"

This book is a Reader — more like a collection of poetry than a history. It is more like an attempt to introduce you personally to the poets, their cadences, their actual writings, than to seek a formal conclusion. It presents readings or extracts from classic sources woven into a cohesive pattern. It is not a work of originality, not an imaginative story, not a philosophical proof, but an album.

We limit ourselves to a single issue: How does faith come alive in active good works? Put differently: What deeds and actions characterize the life of faith? Can they be described? Are they feasible? Can they be lived out?

You *are* the reader. This printed Reader in your hands is only a fragile vehicle for the important part that you will do: read. It is you alone whom the ancient Christian writers want now to address. They want to convey to you these treasures in language that touches you. They want you to understand every sentence. They want you to understand what they wrote in the same way that they understood it. They thought that how they understood it was largely the same way that Christians everywhere and always have understood it. They had no desire to improve on apostolic teaching. Where their reasoning may seem odd, bear with them. If at one point they may seem to cause stumbling, they hope that this will be corrected and brought to balance by your patience and empathy.

### 8. A Lay Reader

This is a Lay Reader. It does not pretend to be a detailed technical commentary on all of its excerpts, or any of them. It aims at economy and coherence. Its task is not to place each text in its historical, social, or political context — that could require a shelf of books.

This Reader is intended for anyone who is hungry for the Word, whose faith has matured to the point of wanting to live a godly life, whose time is too valuable to be impressed by scholarly pedantry, who yearns for clarity. We will not often resort to a paraphrase of a text, unless some rhetorical freedom is required to bring the text into fuller contemporary expression, yet all the while seeking to hold to its original authorial meaning. Those who want a detailed discussion of the historical or social context of these texts will want to consult scholarly historical studies on particular scripture or patristic texts.

## 9. *The Usefulness of Careful Selection*

There may be a few purists who doubt the value of any effort at presenting excerpts in any form whatever. If you are such, ask yourself whether you ever make use of anthologies or collections of aphorisms or incisive prose. Surely collections of photographs or sculpture or art or political wisdom are not to be thrown out of the library just because they are excerpts. Anyone who reads poetry or prose collections reads carefully culled excerpts of the artist's work. Those who love poetry do not demean the labor of careful text selection in the design of anthologies and primary source collections, provided they are good selections.

## C. The Consensus Established

### 1. *A Simple Thesis*

My thesis is straightforward: There is indeed a textually defined consensual classic Christian teaching on faith's good works, on the deeds that flow from salvation by grace through faith. This can be demonstrated by presenting the evidences of the classic consensual interpreters concerning the exposition of those key biblical texts upon which all agree that a Christian doctrine of good works is most fruitfully grounded. So what follows is a highly textual evidentiary presentation.

My intent is simple: I will show by citations how the classic Christian exegetes mostly of the first half of the first millennium understood and commended simple ordinary works of mercy. In doing so I will ask whether there is already formed in early Christianity a reliable, clear, central core of the classic Christian teaching of those common actions and attitudes that manifest salvation by grace through faith.

## 2. A Modest, Inductive Approach to an Alleged Consensus

Please make note: I am not approaching the question *deductively* by attempting first to define what the Christian teaching of good works is, and only then to see if that teaching is indeed found in scripture and consensual scriptural interpretation. Rather I proceed oppositely. I seek *inductively* to discern what the earliest Christian scriptural commentators in fact explicitly wrote concerning these good works.

They were commenting on canonical scripture read every Sunday in churches of all the world's languages everywhere, and have been read over the last two millennia. There has never been any doubt about the canonical status of the Torah or Paul's letters or the four Gospels, to which many of these patristic reflections appear as a commentary. There is little doubt that the commentators we quote here are widely revered in the whole of Christendom.

By this means we ponder whether there is indeed an orthodox consensual Christian teaching of good works to which Protestants, Catholics, Orthodox, and charismatics can all confidently appeal, without denying the distinctive gifts of their varied historical memories. All these traditions are free to claim legitimate ownership of this rich patristic patrimony. It belongs to them all. All have a right to honor and cherish and learn from these pre-European, pre-modern, pre-medieval classic expositors of scripture. All were written long before the quarrels began between Eastern Orthodox, Western Catholics, and all shades of Protestants. Most of those quarrels did not emerge until close to the end of the first millennium — after our time frame.

## 3. Whether There Is a Pre-European (Ancient Afro-Asian) Christian Consensus

Millions of Christians in Africa and Asia are looking toward pre-European exegesis to guide them in fresh, sound, plausible insights not dominated by tainted colonial, modern western premises. These familiar modern premises tend to be biased, exploitative, victimizing, westernized, and manipulative, when viewed from the perspective of non-western Christianity. This makes ancient Christian (pre-European) classic ecumenical teaching more readily hearable in the two-thirds world.

The Church Fathers are largely (almost entirely) *pre*-European. I did not say European, but pre-European. By pre-European we mean before Charlemagne, especially during most of the first half of the first millennium when most of what we today call Europe (especially central and northern Europe, as distinguished from the edges of the Mediterranean coast) was largely without a distinguished written culture, not yet having a cohesive cultural identity or literary tradition. Remember that *Beowulf* was not written down until the eighth century. By pre-European we refer to a literary culture, not merely a geographical continent.

Is Irenaeus European? Remember he was born in present-day Turkey, in Smyrna, and only later immigrated to the Rhône Valley. He would hardly think of himself as an advocate of European culture, but rather as a voice of catholic Christianity. Is Tertullian European? No, African. Is Didymus the Blind of Alexandria or Antony of the Desert European? Only by a massive stretch of imagination and language. Is Cyril of Jerusalem or Eusebius European? Not at all. They belong to the ancient near-eastern world. How about the Cappadocian Fathers and John Chrysostom? They are from the near east, which was called Asia long before the Romans. These are not incidental voices, but central to the classic pre-European tradition. Augustine lived most of his life in North Africa, and Jerome in Palestine. Ephrem the Syrian and Nemesius of Emesa had few if any European connections or sympathies.

## 4. The Consenting Community

Classical Christian teaching does not appeal to early consensual exegesis on the modern democratic premise that a majority of scholars or exegetes today might vote up or down on a particular idea. It is rather the whole church, the worshiping community worldwide, deciding and freely consenting over many generations to commonly agreed good actions and widely received interpretations of scripture.

The leaders (*episcopoi* and *presbuteroi* and governing authorities) of ancient Christianity had to rely on general lay consent over the generations for their actions to be accepted and to stand over a long period of time. *It was not particular scholars but the whole laity, the worldwide worshiping communities, who were the true agents of this consent.* Classic Christian scholarship is revalidating this perennial and venerable tradition of lay consent. The subsequent consent of bishops and ecclesiastical leaders has always depended on the efficacy of general lay consent in the worshiping community. It is upon this lay premise, this populist basis, that we set forth the time-tested confidence in ecumenical consent — not on a few bishops but on the many laity who were willing to die for the faith.

### 5. The Ancient Ecumenical Consensus and the Hunger for Unity

There is the deep and urgent hunger among many believing Protestants, Orthodox, and Catholics for rediscovering their unity in the one body of Christ as attested in scripture. This yearning is accompanied by a gnawing sense of disappointment with modern ideological biases. The actual useful outcomes of modern scriptural studies are to many disappointing. They are too often shaped by modern political agendas and the skewed assumptions of naturalism, narcissism, and relativism.

There is an emerging post-critical orthodox awareness, which is being recognized and honored equally among Protestants, Orthodox, and Catholics. This empirical fact has been chronicled in my study of *The Rebirth of Orthodoxy* (HarperSanFrancisco, 2002). Vital preaching and moral teaching now seek bearings that go deeper than the fads of modern university and academic biblical criticism. Recent critical styles have become captive to the upward-mobility patterns of modern university elites, and can no longer be thought authoritative or normative for Christian teaching.

Meanwhile the models and examples of ancient Christian teaching remain shockingly unfamiliar to modern worshipers, and even more so to educated pastors and academics. They are unfairly caricatured by ill-informed biblical scholars who have not yet bothered to read the ancient Christian writers with any empathy or depth. They are beginning to do so, but there is a long way to go.

The sources quoted here often stood in the rabbinic tradition, which valued typology, symbolic interpretation, and the nuances of sacred numbers. The reader is asked to be patient with these interpretive processes, and not to impose on the scriptural texts narrowly modern assumptions about what the text can or cannot teach.

## 6. The Spirit's Guidance through Persecution

General ecumenical consent proceeds on the premise that the whole church is being actively guided by the Holy Spirit into the truth amid whatever hazards that emerge through the vicissitudes of history. This providence is especially tested when the truth of apostolic testimony is directly on trial, in dispute — and especially where martyrdom is required to defend it. All classic Christian exegetes from Ignatius and Justin through Cyprian to Chrysostom were willing to die for the truth. They were confident of the providential guidance of the Holy Spirit to lead the church into all truth. None of these were European.

The exegetes most widely remembered and received by Christians of many different languages and cultural assumptions are those whose writings have been most assiduously preserved through persecutions and trials, both before and after Constantine. They have been preserved against the odds as counter-cultural artifacts. This is the patrimony of ancient Christianity. These patristic writers are assumed in this worldwide transgenerational consenting community to be the most dependable guides to the witness of the Holy Spirit and the truth of the Gospel. These are the sources largely quoted in these extracts.

It is poignant that our own era is the generation that has suffered the most widespread martyrdom in the history of Christianity. This is one reason why these ancient sources are being reread.

## 7. The Good News and the Bad News

The good news: Most ancient Christian views of good works can conscientiously be confessed by very different Christians who speak out of a catholic memory of Christian teaching, out of vastly dissimilar histories and liturgical practices: Russian Orthodox, South American Pentecostals, Chinese Roman Catholics, Ugandan Anglicans.

The bad news: Denominational self-interests still have deep-seated polemical resistances even to examining this shared ancient textual history. They would prefer to reinforce modern denominationalism, or refight the battles of sixteenth- or eighteenth-century Protestantism. By textual evidence we would hope to counterbalance these forms of resistance.

The Reader Series provides evidence for arguments that run contrary to this modern ideological consensus, whether of the religious left or right. As ecumenical teaching, it stands in tension with nationalistic, ethnocentric, or parochial partisanship.

## 8. The Reformers as Models of Patristic Learning

Many of the early church sources that were available to Luther, Calvin, and Wesley in Greek and Latin have remained untranslated into English for centuries. The Reformers could read these languages readily. Few can today. The irony is that modern Christianity has had to await the twenty-first century to read sources that were more available in the sixteenth than the twentieth.

These ancient Christian writers have been largely ignored by biblical scholars in the last century, even in the "best universities." The palpable evidence of this is that many of the most crucial sources of patristic biblical studies have remained wholly inaccessible in any modern language! Think of the absence in libraries of scriptural exegesis in English by such pivotal writers as Cyril of Alexandria, Jerome, Theodoret, Theodore of Mopsuestia, Isho'dad of Merv, and John of Damascus. This lacuna exists despite vast publication enterprises in biblical studies, innumerable scholarly journals, and stacks of historical monographs. This situation of neglect cries out for corrective texts written in the first millennium that can challenge the modern assumptions of biblical scholarship. This disaster might have been averted if the great classical languages of early Christian preaching and worship (Hebrew, Greek, Latin) had been more seriously studied.

## 9. Grasping Consensus

Those who have decided in advance that there can be no consensus in orthodoxy will obviously not be able to grasp the consensus on good works. No counter-arguments are persuasive to those who have already decided that all consensus is impossible. These polemics that deny consensus have regrettably prevailed for a century of liberal historicism, enamored as it was more by dissent than consent. Those efforts became narrowly fixated on quarrels based on political or economic differences.

The academic arena in which questions of good works are normally considered is ethics. Search the literature of contemporary ethics (on poverty, war, life and death, etc.) and you will find almost no reference whatever to the patristic writers. Why this dearth of reflection on good works among moderns about the key figures of the western ethical tradition? Read the journals in Christian ethics and you will find them filled with contemporary sources, but almost totally negligent of classic Christian sources. We leave speculation to speculators, but this Reader hopes to redress that weakness.

Unfortunately, it is an all-too-familiar assumption among some Protestants that the ancient Christian writers of the first millennium knew little or nothing about good works as specifically flowing from unmerited grace through faith active in love, as understood following the Reformation. The texts of this Reader, together with the Justification Reader, make that assumption very hard to defend. We will show that this common Reformation teaching was learned by the Reformers from Paul, who taught it to the Church Fathers, who passed it on without diminution.

## D. The Ancient Christian Writers on Good Works

### 1. The Modern Feeding-Frenzy for Novelty

Intellectual elites of all ideological stripes are still desperately feeding on modernity's tired illusions. This applies to evangelicals and Catholics, as well as the religious left and the religious right. The feeding-frenzy for novelty has resulted in the neglect of classic wisdom. Philosophical and critical fads are like dope for those modernizing junkies who are trying frenetically to accommodate to a dying modernity. Many are desperately trying to find some level of acceptability within a cultural and university ethos that itself is growing ever more untenable.

Optimistic modern fantasies often proceed as if there were no serious history of sin. The voices of the religious left of the last hundred years have viewed good works as easily acquired by human freedom, as if there were no obstacle of sin to stand as a durable and recalcitrant impediment to our natively good intentions. They seldom speak of God's judgment of sin, and much prefer to talk about the love of God on the assumption that it does not need to be placed in the context of God's holiness and the just judgment of sin.

## 2. Premature Dismissals by the Religious Right and Left

Both the religious left and right are still prone to caricature the ancient Christian writers as allegorists or naïve supernaturalists or legalists or reactionaries or uncritical minds misled by the superstitious. These familiar diatribes tempt modern readers to succumb to the ideological traps of social idealism, humanistic faddism, and narcissistic egocentricity. The ancient Christian writers avoided all these traps. They knew nothing of them. They were not tempted by ideologies not yet invented.

The religious right is at least as forgetful of ancient Christian wisdom as the left. Their caricature was that the patristic writers were ignorant of scripture, weighed down by traditions, entrenched in superstitions, tainted by political collusion.

Despite an avid interest in ethics, the religious left did not bother to study carefully ancient Christian writers on good works. Protestant writers from Strauss and Harnack to Tillich and Spong were far more interested in imposing their own modern ideological programs upon these texts than allowing them to speak for themselves. They have often construed good works finally as human virtues voluntarily and humanistically achieved by free moral agents, quite apart from grace in salvation history. Sadly wrong, from the viewpoint of classic Christianity.

The views of good works of the religious left, whether Protestant or Catholic, are inordinately caught up in a universalistic assumption of the original capacity of humanity to do good naturally, apart from grace. In their universalistic optimism, the religious left assumes, contrary to scripture, that all humanity is finally absolutely and unconditionally deserving of the forgiveness of God and divine clemency, regardless of what deeds are done by human freedom in this life. They then reduce good works to a political agenda of deliverance of the oppressed from social and political bondage. The modern intellectual tradition has rejected the Fathers wholesale, because they perceive them as challenging to their preferred, less critical, modern assumptions. The patristic sources have not seemed worthy of considering in their wholeness and complexity by the religious left. The religious left sees good works as little more than the human emulation of the moral teachings and ideals of Jesus. This, of course, forgets both sin and grace, hence the heart of scriptural and patristic teaching.

The modern intellectual tradition has shown itself appallingly ignorant of what the Fathers actually wrote and believed about the body, the poor, sexuality, slavery, and human equality. Having systematically neglected to read the Fathers, they have felt quite confident in speaking for and about them on these subjects. The heart of their confusion is that they have been reacting less to the actual texts of patristic teaching than to modern imaginings of what they said on equality and fairness.

Contrary to prevailing assumptions, the texts will show that the Fathers in fact had a well-crafted, balanced, highly nuanced teaching of caring for the poor, healing the sick, protecting the unprotected in society, ransoming slaves, freeing prisoners. All these are acts that define good works grounded in faith's response to God's grace.

This Reader shows how both these left- and right-wing caricatures are indefensible textually. These false assumptions, still repeated by polemicists, are still widely held by many sincere, uninformed Protestants, despite compelling contrary evidence. This evidence we will set forth.

### 3. The Proximate Unity of the First Five Centuries Compared with the Radical Disunity of the Last Five

This technical point must be conceded: This Reader acknowledges that among patristic exegetes there were admittedly many discrete differences in cultural assumptions, literary style, idiomatic language, and symbol systems. This is also true of the Reformers. But there is a remarkable level of general consensus, especially on the subject of faith's good works. Our thesis is so simple and clear that we are amazed that we can find so little about it in the literature. The intriguing contrast is between the *unity of the first five centuries* on good works teachings, and the *disunity of the last five centuries* on those teachings.

By "consensual" I do not imply that there were no varieties of interpretation under the vast umbrella of orthodox lay consent. Rather I mean that a worldwide consenting community freely received these ancient scripture scholars as standing faithfully within the east-west consensus defined by the early ecumenical councils, excepting those rare instances where even these leading exegetes failed to gain general consent.

The Fathers subjected to thorough critical examination virtually all of the key sacred texts on good works. In doing so, they were understood in much the same way that gracious works were to be later rediscovered by the Reformation writers. I am not arguing that there are no problematic patristic passages on good works. It is not difficult to find aberrations and exceptions. But I do argue that the consensus overwhelms the exceptions.

The evidence of this Reader shows that there is a stable, explicit, consensual tradition of exposition of the biblical teaching of those good works that stem from justification by grace alone through faith alone. This tradition was firmly established long before Luther or Calvin or the divisive debates of Augsburg and Trent, which were more fixated upon medieval scholastic distortions than patristic teaching.

### 4. The Mothers

If these were all "Fathers," where are the "Mothers"? Among the truly great early Christian teachers were Macrina, Egeria, Paula, Melania, Pelagia, Matrona, Theodora, Syncletica, Sarah, the voices of the Matericon, the Philokalia, and numerous named and unnamed desert mothers. Their sayings were remembered in ascetic communities long after they were gone, and they left an impressive tradition both oral and written. So the term "patristic" could honestly have been hyphenated as "patristic-matristic."

Many women decisively shaped the early Christian tradition of teaching through witness, and all too often by martyrdom. The frequent presence of women in the history of Christian martyrdom is astonishing. Regrettably, however, although there were many women of enormous influence, all too few of their written sources have survived. That we regret.

## E. The Evidence

### 1. A Fair Assessment

As a Protestant I am ready to see these sources assessed and judged by rigorous confessional Protestant teaching standards on justification, atonement, and grace. I am convinced that the leading patristic advocates of good works are profoundly in accord with the central Lutheran and Reformed teachings on good works from Luther and Calvin and Bucer to Gerhard and Owen to Hodge — but that is just the hypothesis that we must fairly and openly argue textually.

The only way to establish and confirm this thesis is to present the evidence. The evidence is concrete and textual. I will present the evidence without the intrusion of my own editorial commentary. I want to allow the patristic texts on good works to speak for themselves. I invite Protestant colleagues to show me what is substantively missing in patristic exegesis of passages on good work that is found in the Reformation. Some evangelical critics of the Justification Reader have complained that there is not consensus, but failed to present any plausible evidence against the consensus. They have only asserted that the consensus is not visible to them. I invite them to show me textually where the Reformers differ with the patristic writers. That has not occurred. I welcome attempts to do so.

## 2. The Fathers' Deep Immersion in the Written Word

According to patristic teaching, the scripture is the judge of all controversies concerning contested Christian teaching. On questions about good works, *sola scriptura* is a fixed premise of all ancient Christian teaching. If there is doubt about this, it can be corrected by reading the ecumenical council canons to discover that all the debates of all parties were appeals to scripture.

Protestants think of themselves as the guardians of the scripture texts on good works. It is a too-easy and facile charge that the patristic writers ignored scripture. Some assume that if they did not ignore scripture altogether, they read alien meanings into it that were not in line with authorial intent. And even if they recognized scriptural truth, they still did not manifest it in their actual lives. These texts provide powerful evidence to the contrary.

The Protestant fantasy that patristic writers paid little attention to scripture is easily corrected simply by reading their probing scriptural exposition. Every issue classically contested was settled by appeal to scripture. Every pertinent passage of scripture received careful critical examination on philological, linguistic, moral, philosophical, and liturgical grounds.

Many early Christian teachers memorized vast passages of the Psalms, the Prophets, and the New Testament. The whole range and flow of the scriptures were assessed in order to help solve particular dilemmas of interpretation. Those who may doubt the seriousness of the Fathers about scripture would do well simply to read their commentaries on scripture (starting with Origen, Jerome, Ambrose, Basil, Augustine, Cyril of Alexandria, and on to Gregory the Great and Bede).

## 3. The Same Patrimony

Classic Protestants, Catholics, Orthodox, charismatics, and the heirs of pietistic revivalism today all have a right to appeal to these same early scriptural interpreters. This is especially evident on questions of good works, where conjoint ecumenical ministries of compassion are so socially significant.

The divided church does not have to remain forever fixated on the polemics of defensiveness. The Holy Spirit today is leading the body of Christ toward greater awareness and ownership of first-millennium texts on the works of love. What is emerging from this is what might be called a postcritical orthodox consensus on Christian action. Consensus-bearing interpreters of the four Gospels and of Paul's letters give contemporary Protestants (whether Baptists, Calvinists, Wesleyans, Lutherans, holiness tradition faithful, or Pentecostals) a fresh opportunity to focus anew on the underlying thread of agreement on what constitutes the good life and good works.

It is distressing to note that recent Orthodox and Catholic scholars, from whom we might have expected a more sustained and active scholarly, moral, and homiletic interest in these patristic texts, have also neglected them, although not as wide of the mark as Protestants. The fixation of Roman Catholics upon modern Vatican II teaching has led to the inadvertent neglect of ancient ecumenical teaching, despite Vatican II appeals to the contrary. The Orthodox literature shows that they have seldom paid serious attention to western (Latin) patristic texts. Protestants have until recently doubly neglected both east and west prior to Luther. Lack of access to these sources has stood as a formidable block to the unity of the body of Christ.

## 4. Chipping Away at the Polemics Industry

Regrettably there is an ongoing polemics industry that nurtures distrust between Protestants and Catholics, and between Orthodox and all supposed latecomers. This industry has money, presses, airtime, sentimental momentum, attractive spokespersons, and a defensive audience to count upon.

All this provides an excuse for classical Christian believers not to coordinate their attempts to embody relief work. This imagination feeds on exaggerated misunderstandings of the others. This Reader hopes to show that these dreaded "enemies" are much more akin to ourselves than we might at first be willing to acknowledge. Meanwhile we possess together a shared history with these ancient voices. We are inheritors of the same traditions of orthodox, ancient ecumenical interpretation that is based on rigorous expositions of scripture.

In places like Cuba and China these polemics have disastrously weakened Christian witness. The Communist politicians of Cuba and China would much prefer to see Christians fighting each other than uniting. The restudy of the patristic writers provides leverage for rethinking intolerant and tendentious assumptions that are found equally among Catholics, Orthodox, charismatics, evangelicals, and liberals, not only in Havana and Moscow but also in Kinshasa, Mumbai, and Quito.

## 5. Believers Seek Integration

This lay Reader provides a model for integrating biblical, historical, theological, and ethical inquiry. The model provided by the ancient Christian writers never splits these disciplines into departmental segments. This segmenting now regrettably predominates in the competing methods of contemporary religious studies.

Anyone can think cohesively about a particular point of theology in an orthodox manner by reference to key scripture texts through the history of their interpretation. The study of the Fathers shows how by examining what the history of interpretation says about those sacred texts, it is possible to point the way toward that unifying classic Christian consensus that has shaped all subsequent centuries of Christianity.

## 6. Balanced Selectivity

I have tried to strike a balance between offering too much or too little evidence. It is understandable that some will wish more and some less. My academic critics will probably think that I have written too little, and my lay readers may think that I have written too much. So be it.

I have been duly cautioned that I may be writing too long a book for an impatient, practical lay reader, and too short a book for the professional scholar. I answer: I can only pray that providential grace will lead the ordinary lay reader to these pages, and thus to the voices of the ancient Christian writers. I am especially reaching out for laity who already sense the practical importance of this issue — how grace works through faith. These laypersons do not have to be convinced that such a study requires a serious immersion in the whole Word of God.

This book is not for the casual layperson who wants an easy, cheap answer. It seeks no "best-seller" status in book marketing. It seeks out the maturing lay believer who loves the Word, delights in meditating on it, and cannot get enough of bathing in the mystery of the Gospel. Many of these extracts are available only in highly scattered, often antiquated sources and translations.

It would require of a reader a great deal of patience and effort to bring these sources together into a single cohesive argument on classic Christian teaching of good works. It is the reader's valuable time that we are attempting to conserve. Such a book does not exist, and to my knowledge has never existed. So I have felt called upon to gather this source material in a Reader or catena format and develop a unified argument that draws into a sequence of reasoning these widely different texts on good works.

## 7. The Reference System

In each reference following a patristic extract there will be found the title of the work from which the selection is taken, usually followed by section or subsection numbers, and then a biblical reference. In each extract the author's name will appear either in the preceding paragraph or in the parenthesized reference. In some cases the reader may wish to correlate these extracts with further selections from the Ancient Christian Commentary on Scripture (ACCS), to whose publisher we are duly grateful for permission to utilize these texts that we ourselves have researched and selected. The key to making these ACCS correlations is the final biblical reference within the parentheses. Hence, if you wish to see more patristic comment on a given biblical passage, you may go to the last scripture reference within the parentheses, and then to the pertinent volume of the Ancient Christian Commentary on Scripture. The parenthesis reference is followed by a footnote number, which identifies the original source of the classical reference, either in its original language or in an English translation.

The text translation here is not necessarily identical with the ACCS rendering. In some cases syntax has been clarified, problematic terms omitted, and archaic translations stated in simpler street English, with some additions and some omissions. Where identical with the ACCS version, they are reprinted by the permission of InterVarsity Press. In each instance I have asked whether the translation available is the most fitting for a lay readership in ordinary English idiom. Some sentences or phrases have been retranslated in accord with the purpose of this series. A single asterisk indicates a slight change, a double asterisk a substantial change. ACCS translations were supervised by the volume editor and approved by the general editor. In this volume, the author has found further refinements that fit the specific purposes of the Reader Series. Some of the textual renderings and paraphrases are my own. The footnote itself, which follows the parenthesis, provides the primary reference, whether in the original language or English, or both.

Most patristic writers quoted scripture out of the Septuagint or Old Latin Bible, or provided their own translations from Greek or Hebrew. This is why there is significant variability in their Greek or Latin scripture quotations as distinguished from modern translations. Furthermore, since modern translations of the patristic writers are taken from different periods and styles of biblical translation, I have not sought to make them conform to one single modern translation. I have included extracts that have utilized various versions: King James Version, the Douay-Rheims Bible, the (L. C. L. Brenton) Septuagint, New American Standard, New English Bible, Confraternity Version, Today's English Version, Anchor Bible, the New Jerusalem Bible, the Jewish Publication Society, and translations by R. Knox, J. Moffatt, R. F. Weymouth, and others, without extensively burdening the footnotes by differential indicators. The translations most often used were the RSV, NIV, NRSV, and NASB. Where these are quoted directly, we have sought and received permission for direct quotations. Where the Fathers paraphrased scripture in their original language, we have sought to reflect the contours of their paraphrases. The appendix of brief biographical identifications indicates each patristic author quoted.

Non-professional readers who want to know more about these patristic figures are well advised to go to the *Encyclopedia of the Early Church* (New York: Oxford University Press, 1992), edited by Angelo DiBerardino.

### 8. Looking Ahead

The first five parts set forth good works in relation to those most in need: the poor, the hungry, the stranger, the imprisoned, the persecuted, and the child — the least of these. The last two parts discuss the good works of the rich, and the good works of those justified by grace through faith, apart from merit.

## PART ONE

# THE POOR

It is surprising that the ancient Christian writers were advocates for the poorest of the poor long before the modern notions of a "preferential option for the poor." Many had been slaves. Most were themselves poor. If they had acquired property, they often gave it away.

## A. "Come, O Blessed of My Father"

### 1. The Pattern

The pattern in the Christian life for caring for the poor is seen in the way in which Jesus himself, being poor, identified with the poor, giving them not only food but hope.

When we meet a beggar, we are to remember that we ourselves are beggars, according to Augustine: "'Blessed are the compassionate, for God will have compassion for them' [Matt. 5:7]. Do this, and it will be done to you. Do it in regard to another that it might be done in regard to you. Even when you have abundance, you remain in need, for even if you are overflowing with temporal things, you still stand in need of eternal life. So when you hear the voice of a beggar, remember that before God you are yourself a beggar. When someone begs from you, remember that you yourself are begging. *As you treat your beggar, so will God treat his.* You who are empty are being filled. Out of your fullness fill an empty person in need, so that your own emptiness may be again filled by the fullness of God" (Augustine, Sermon 53.5, italics added; Matt. 5:7).[1] As God has shown compassion on your destitution, so show your compassion for the destitute.

The biblical understanding of responsibility to the poor hinges on the recollection that we as the people of God were in poverty and slavery in Egypt. Ever since Israel served in bondage in Egypt, the delivering God has made special provisions for the poor and oppressed (see Exod. 23:6; Lev. 19:9-10; Deut. 15:11).

Listen carefully to the Fathers, and you will discover the richness of classic Christian reflection on the care of the poor and needy. It is about more than beans and socks in care packages.

## 2. Blessed Are the Poor in Spirit

The anonymous fifth-century Latin author of Opus Imperfectum had a sharp eye for anomalies in the text: "Luke simply said 'you poor' [Luke 6:20], whereas Matthew said 'poor in spirit.' One who is poor in spirit and humble of heart has a meek spirit and does not think great things of himself. On the other hand, one who imagines himself to be rich in spirit will pretend great things of himself. He is proud and does not fulfill the commandment of Christ that, 'Unless you turn and become like children, you will never enter the kingdom of heaven' [Matt. 18:3]. Only one who has repented and become like a child is poor in spirit" (Opus Imperfectum in Matthaeum, Homily 9; Matt. 5:3).[2]

These are the words with which Jesus began his Sermon on the Mount: "Blessed are the poor in spirit, for theirs is the kingdom of heaven" (Matt. 5:3a). The poor in spirit are those who have a humble character and attitude, who depend on God. They live profoundly blessed lives. Hilary of Poitiers commented that Jesus taught us humility by his voluntarily becoming poor. He "announced through the prophets that he would choose a people humble and in awe of his words [cf. Isa. 66:2]. In doing so, he introduced the first beatitude: humility in spirit. Those who are aware that they possess the heavenly kingdom are free to be inspired with humble things" (Hilary of Poitiers, On Matthew 4.2; Matt. 5:3).[3] They are deeply

1. PL 38:366; cf. FC 11:213-14; ACCS NT 1a:85-86*.
2. PG 56:680; ACCS NT 1a:80-81*.
3. SCH 1:120-22; ACCS NT 1a:81**.

conscious of having been united to each other by squalid and feeble roots. The poor in spirit are vulnerable, like children.

### 3. Does God Prefer the Poor?

It might seem from this as if the poor have a decisive advantage over the rich in God's presence. Caesarius of Arles provided balance: "The rich man 'went away sad,' as you have heard, and the Lord says: 'With what difficulty will they who have riches enter the kingdom of God!' [Matt. 19:22-23; Mark 10:22-23; Luke 18:23-24] At length the disciples became very sad when they heard this and they said: 'If this is so, who then can be saved?' [Matt. 19:25; Mark 10:26; Luke 18:26] Rich and poor, listen to Christ: I am speaking to God's people. Most of you are poor, but you too must listen carefully to understand. And you had best listen even more intently if you glory in your poverty. Beware of pride, lest the humble rich surpass you. Beware of wickedness, lest the pious rich confound you. Beware of drunkenness, lest the sober excel you" (Caesarius of Arles, Sermons 153.2; Mark 10:23).[4] Both the rich and poor are tempted to abuse either their possessions or lack of them.

God promises to exercise special care for the poor. They are more in need of protection (Job 24:3-10), as are children, widows, and the least of these. God's grace awakens the rich faith of the poor in order to show forth his unmerited generosity. "There is no difference between rich and poor in Christ," wrote John Chrysostom. "Pay no attention to the outward appearance, but look for the inner faith instead" (Chrysostom, quoted in Cramer, Catena in Epistolas Catholicas; James 2:3).[5] God has chosen the poor of this world to be rich in faith (Jas. 2:5). The poor may come to depend more on God because they do not have resources. It is in this sense that they came to be viewed in a special way as God's own people (Pss. 9:9-10; 14:4-6; Hab. 3:13-14). The hope of spiritual blessing in eternal life is of deeper poignancy to the poor, who do not have the hopes of this world, the fruits of this economy, the advantages of this political order. The poor are more ready to have the Gospel preached to them than are the rich (Matt. 11:5). They are not intrinsically better. They

---

4. FC 47:338*; ACCS NT 2:145.
5. CEC 10; ACCS NT 11:22.

are more humbled, meek, and ready for service in the kingdom of love (Matt. 5:3).

In God's own time, God provides for the poor (Ps. 68:10), lifting them up from the depths (Ps. 113:7). God stands at their right hand (Ps. 109:31), maintaining justice on their behalf (Ps. 140:12). In some measure this care is provided in this world by the compassion of the faithful, but in a longer view it will be provided by God in eternity. "One who is gracious to a poor man lends to the Lord" (Prov. 19:17, NAS). Let the poor eat the tithe (Deut. 14:28-29; 26:11-12). Welcome the poor into your house (Isa. 58:7). When you give a feast, invite them (Luke 14:13). To those who have nothing, send something (Neh. 8:10, 12). Remember the poor (Gal. 2:10). Visit them (Jas. 1:27). This is what it means to care for the poor.

### 4. The Poor Have Responsibilities

The Proverbs do not exalt the righteousness of the poor in such a way as to exempt them from responsibility. Those who love sleep inordinately will soon grow poor (Prov. 20:13). Stay awake and you will have food to spare. The drunkard and the glutton will come to poverty and their drowsiness will clothe them in rags (Prov. 23:21). An attitude of neglect and placing blame on others may cause poverty (Prov. 10:14). "Better one hand full with tranquility than two handfuls with toil and chasing after the wind" (Eccles. 4:6, NIV). It is better to do with less if you are inwardly tranquil, than to chase after the wind with excessive toil. Seek balance. Work but not excessively. Rest but not excessively.

### 5. Show No Partiality

While the poor are much beloved of God, they are not simplistically preferred so as to be invited to manipulate divine fairness to their own benefit. Jerome made this important point, still relevant in political life today: "'You shall not be partial to the poor' [Lev. 19:15, NAS], a precept given lest under a pretext of showing pity we should make an unjust judgment. For each individual is to be judged not by his status, high or low, but by the merits of his case. His wealth need not stand in the way of the rich man, if he makes a good use of it. And poverty of itself cannot serve as a recommendation for the poor, as if squalor itself keeps one out of wrongdoing" (Jerome, Letter 79.1; Lev. 19:15).[6] The poor are due justice in the court, which implies neither favorable nor unfavorable treatment (Exod. 23:3-7).

Concerning the scripture that says, "Blessed are the poor," Ambrose wanted to make the discrete distinction that

> not all the poor are blessed, for poverty is neutral. The poor can be either good or evil, unless, perhaps, the blessed pauper is to be understood as he whom the prophet described, saying, "A righteous poor man is better than a rich liar" [Prov. 19:22 LXX]. Blessed is the poor man who cried and whom the Lord heard [cf. Ps. 34:6 (33:7 LXX)]. Blessed is the man poor in offense. Blessed is the man poor in vices. Blessed is the poor man in whom the prince of this world finds nothing [John 14:30]. Blessed is the poor man who is like the incarnate Lord who, although he was rich, became poor for our sake [see 2 Cor. 8:9]. Matthew fully revealed this when he said, "Blessed are the poor in spirit" [Matt. 5:3]. One poor in spirit is not puffed up, is not exalted in the mind of his own flesh. This beatitude comes first in sequence. It is addressed to those who have laid aside every sin and put away all malice. If poor in spirit, only then am I content with simplicity, and destitute of evil. All that remains is that I regulate my conduct. For what good does it do me to lack worldly goods, unless I am meek and gentle? (Ambrose, Exposition of the Gospel of Luke 5.53-54; Luke 6:20-26)[7]

It is not upon poverty as such that God's blessing is promised, but upon the humility we may learn from our poverty.

The law teaches in Exodus 23:3 that we should bring no hint of partiality to a poor person, in order that equal justice not be corrupted. John Chrysostom commented: "'You shall not favor a poor man in his lawsuit,' Scripture says. What therefore is the meaning of these words? It means: Do not be overcome by pity or unduly influenced if the wrongdoer happens to be a poor man. And if we must not show favor to the poor man, much more must we not do so for the rich. Moreover, I address these words not only to judges but also to all men, so that justice may nowhere be corrupted but everywhere kept inviolate" (Chrysostom, Homilies on the Gos-

6. NPNF 2 6:163; ACCS OT 3:189*.
7. EHG 166-67*; ACCS NT 3:104-5*.

pel of John 49; Exod. 23:3).[8] Neither rich nor poor are due preferential treatment under the law.

No reasonable person can assume that the prayers of the rich receive God's attention any more than those of the poor, according to Augustine commenting on James 2:4: "Who could bear to see a rich man chosen to occupy a seat of honor in the church when a more learned and holier man is passed over because he is poor? Is it not a sin to judge by appearances that a rich man is a better man?" (Augustine, Letters 167.18; Jas. 2:4).[9] Rich and poor are equally corrupted by the history of sin.

## 6. Penury as Such Not Commended

It is not penury as such, but humility under grace that scripture blesses, according to Jerome: "Do not imagine that poverty bred by necessity was preached by the Lord. For he added 'in spirit' so you would understand blessedness to be humility and not penury. 'Blessed are the poor in spirit' who on account of the Holy Spirit are poor by willing freely to be so. Hence, concerning this type of the poor, the Savior speaks also through Isaiah: 'The Lord has anointed me to preach good tidings to the poor' [Isa. 61:1]" (Jerome, Commentary on Matthew 1.5.3; Matt. 5:3).[10]

Chromatius of Aquileia added: "We know many poor people indeed who are not merely poor but blessed. For the straits of poverty as such do not make any one of us blessed. But a devout trust that is sustained even through poverty does bless us. Some who have no worldly resources continue in sin and live without faith in God. It is evident that these people cannot be called blessed. Hence we must inquire just who are these blessed of whom the Lord says: 'Blessed are the poor in spirit, for theirs is the kingdom of heaven.' It means that those persons are truly blessed who, having spurned the riches and resources of the world to become rich in God, are willing to be poor in the world. Though they indeed may be poor in the sight of the world, they are rich in God. They are needy in the world but wealthy in Christ" (Chromatius, Tractate on Matthew 17.2.1-2; Matt. 5:3).[11]

---

8. FC 41:22; ACCS OT 3:117*.
9. FC 30:47; ACCS NT 11:22-23.
10. CCL 77:24; ACCS NT 1a:81.
11. CCL 9A:269*; ACCS NT 1a:81*.

## 7. Why the Poor Are More Likely to Be Rich in Faith

God has chosen to give the poor the opportunity to be especially rich in faith in order to put the mystery of his mercy in stark relief. "It is by choosing the poor that God makes them rich in faith, just as he makes them heirs of the kingdom" (Augustine, On the Predestination of the Saints 17 (34); Jas. 2:5).[12]

We should not be surprised when poor people contribute more than the rich. This Oecumenius observed: "When poor people are not preoccupied with the things of the world, when they come to faith, they often become more energetic and more determined to work at it than rich people do" (Oecumenius, Commentary on James; Jas. 2:5).[13] "Even if they are poor in material things, they may be more rich in faith" (Hilary of Arles, Introductory Tractate on the Letter of James; Jas. 2:5).[14]

Scarcity is not inimical to the human spirit. Rather, it may challenge the best in us. It was scarcity of food that urged Abraham to leave home and travel to find resources: "The scarcity of the necessities of life threw everyone into great apprehension, compelled them to leave their own home, and travel to those places where it was possible to find an abundance of resources" (Chrysostom, Homilies on Genesis 51.5-6; Gen. 26:1).[15]

According to Deuteronomy 28:48, the Lord, when necessary, does not hesitate to chastise us by sending us hunger, thirst, nakedness, want, and servitude. It is through this that we may become all the more ready to hear the good news of God's becoming poor on our behalf.

## 8. How to Love the Needy Is No Great Mystery

The royal law of scripture is "Love your neighbor as yourself" (Jas. 2:8, NAS). We are not called to love just with words or with our tongue, but with practical actions and in truth (1 John 3:17). This is how we know that we belong to the truth and how we set our hearts at rest in his presence, enacting — not just talking about — the love of God.

12. FC 86:260; ACCS NT 11:23.
13. PG 119:473; ACCS NT 11:23.
14. PL *Suppl.* 3:70; ACCS NT 11:23*.
15. FC 87:58-59; ACCS OT 2:153.

Rescue the poor from those who are too strong for them, from those who rob them (Ps. 25:10). Satisfy the thirsty. Fill the hungry with good things (Ps. 107:9). Lift the needy out of their affliction (Ps. 107:41). Raise the poor from the dust (Ps. 113:7). Satisfy them with food (Ps. 132:15). Seek justice for the poor. Uphold the cause of the needy (Ps. 140:12). This is what it means for faith to do good works.

If you plunder the poor, it may be that you yourself are in the perspective of eternity being plundered and deprived of your future (Prov. 22:22). Do not exploit the poor. Do not crush the needy (Isa. 25:4).

What is faith to do for those who have needs? Do as God does. Be a refuge for the poor. Take care of the needy in distress. Give shelter in the storm. Give shade from the heat. For those who are searching for water, whose tongues are parched with thirst, give them something to drink (Isa. 41:17). Love your enemies. Do well to them. Lend to them, without expecting to get anything back (Luke 6:35). Make the widow's heart to sing (Job 29:11). Rescue those who cry for help. Become a father to the fatherless. Be like eyes to the blind and feet to the lame (Job 29:15).

Do what is needed for those who lack shelter, who are drenched by rains, who spend the night cold and naked, who have nothing with which to cover themselves (Job 24:9). If you gloat over someone else's disaster, you will not go unpunished. If you mock the poor, you insult the maker (Prov. 17:5). You are a fool if you leave empty the hungry and withhold water from the thirsty (Isa. 32:6). If you make up evil schemes to destroy the poor with lies, this will ultimately backfire on you, as it did the "cows" of Bashan (Amos 4:1), and the women who oppressed the poor (Amos 5:11). Those who trample the poor are like those who have built mansions in which they will never live, or plant lush vineyards and never drink their wine. They are racing toward judgment.

Yet in giving a helping hand to the poor, do not show preferential favoritism for the poor. Treat each one case by case — fairly, justly, and equally. The faithful are not to have prejudices with respect to classes of persons (Jas. 2:9).

Do not be indebted to other people, except in love (Rom. 13:8). You are to forgive debts as your debts are forgiven (Matt. 6:12). Since God has canceled the bill of debt against us, we are to cancel the bill of debt toward others (Col. 2:14). Paul, in Philemon 18 (NIV), was willing to take responsibility himself for the debts of Onesimus. "If he owes you anything, charge it to me," he says. When we do good works for the poor and for others in need, whatever good we do, we ultimately receive it back from the Lord (Eph. 6:8). We will be repaid at the resurrection (Luke 14:14). There everyone will be rendered according to his deeds (Rom. 2:6).

There is very little of this that is hard to understand. It is all too clear. We might wish by further study to make it more ambiguous. We know who the least of these is. We meet them every day. The time to do something to help them is now.

## B. "Inherit the Kingdom Prepared for You from the Foundation of the World"

The coming kingdom is prepared for those ready to receive it. The poor and needy, knowing from experience of their human vulnerability, are more ready to receive it.

The kingdom is portrayed as an end-time feast, a wedding banquet. Those whose poverty of spirit has led them to repent and trust in the incarnate Lord, who have known hunger and thirst, and who have borne fruits worthy of their repentance, are invited to the feast.

### 1. Good News to the Poor

When Jesus announced his ministry in Nazareth by reading in the synagogue the text from Isaiah, the focus was upon the poor. Let Eusebius tell the story: "Our Savior, after reading this prophecy through in the synagogue one day to a multitude of Jews, shut the book and said, 'This day is this Scripture fulfilled in your ears.' He began his own teaching from that point. He began to preach the Gospel to the poor, putting in the forefront of his blessings: 'Blessed are the poor in spirit, for theirs is the kingdom of heaven' [Matt. 5:3]. He proclaimed forgiveness to those who were hampered by evil spirits and bound for a long time like slaves by demons. He invited all to be free and to escape from the bonds of sin, when he said, 'Come to me, all you that labor, and are heavy laden, and I will refresh you' [Matt. 11:28]" (Eusebius, The Proof of the Gospel 3.1.88c-89a; Luke 4:16-21).[16]

16. POG 1:102**; ACCS NT 3:80*.

## 2. *The Incarnate Lord, Though Rich, Became Poor for Us*

If God had not highly valued the poor, he would not have honored them by himself becoming a poor man in a lowly family in his incarnate life. God the Son chose to become poor that we might become rich (2 Cor. 8:9). On this text John Chrysostom commented: "If you do not believe that poverty is productive of great wealth, think of the poverty of Jesus and you will be persuaded otherwise. For if he had not become poor, you would not have become rich. By riches, Paul means the knowledge of godliness, the cleansing away of sins, justification, sanctification, the countless good things which God bestowed upon us and which he intends even further to bestow" (Chrysostom, Homilies on the Epistles of Paul to the Corinthians II.17.1; 2 Cor. 8:9).[17]

The Son freely willed to become poor for us. Bede the Venerable observed: "The Lord, mindful in everything of our salvation, not only stooped for our sake to become a human being, though he was God, but also he freely willed to become poor for us, though he was rich, so that by his poverty along with his humanity he might grant us to become sharers in his riches and his divinity" (Bede the Venerable, Homily 18; Lev. 12:8).[18]

The power of the almighty was temporarily obscured by the voluntary renunciation of God the Son to exercise this power during much of his incarnate life. Ambrosiaster commented: "Paul is saying that Christ was made poor because God deigned to be born as man, *temporarily obscuring the power of his might* so that he might obtain for men the riches of divinity and thus permit humanity to share in his divine nature, as Peter says. He was made man in order to allow human participation in the Godhead. Therefore Christ was made poor, not for his sake but for ours, but we are made poor for our own benefit" (Ambrosiaster, On Paul's Epistles to the Corinthians, italics added; 2 Cor. 8:9).[19] Jesus "came into this world a poor man. Yet he abounds in all things. He has filled all people. How mighty is he in riches. For he has made all rich by his poverty!" In this way Ambrose preached: "His poverty enriches, the fringe of his garment heals [Matt. 9:20-22; 14:34-36], his hunger satisfies, his death gives life, his burial gives resurrection. Therefore he is a rich treasure, for

17. NPNF 1 12:360; ACCS NT 7:272*.
18. CSBH 1:181; ACCS OT 3:179*.
19. CSEL 81:259; ACCS NT 7:272*.

his bread is rich. And 'rich' is apt, for one who has eaten this bread will be unable to feel hunger [John 6:35]. He gave it to the apostles to distribute to a believing people [Matt. 15:36]. And today Christ gives it to us. As our high priest, he daily consecrates it with his own words. Therefore this bread has become the food of the saints" (Ambrose, The Patriarchs 9.38; Gen. 49:20).[20]

### 3. The Poor at God's End-Time Banquet

God goes to the byroads when those who are fully satisfied reject the invitation to the banquet of his love. The poor will be abundantly present at God's end-time banquet, according to Irenaeus: "Where are the hundredfold rewards in this age for the dinners offered to the poor? These things will occur during the times of the kingdom on the seventh day that is sanctified when God rested from all his works that he made. This is the true Sabbath of the just, in which they will have no earthly work to do, but will have a table prepared before them by God, who will feed them with all delicious food" (Irenaeus, Against Heresies 5.33.2; Luke 14:7-14).[21] No works are required to qualify for this banquet, for all things are already provided. God has worked six days. Now God rests.

Some who were invited "paid no attention" to the invitation to God's end-time banquet, "and went off, one to his farm, another to his business," wrote Gregory the Great. "Neither takes notice of the mystery of the Lord's incarnation. They are unwilling to live in accordance with it. They are proceeding to their farm or business, refusing to come to the marriage feast of the king. More seriously, some not only decline the gift of the one calling them but even persecute those who accept it" (Gregory the Great, Forty Gospel Homilies 38; Matt. 22:5-7).[22] Workaholics who know business but do not know how to rest or enjoy life, wanting others to be like themselves, may be harsh toward those who come to the banquet.

God chooses a different way — go to the byways. The first invitation refused, the second is drastic: "The one who sees himself despised when he issues the invitations will not permit the marriage feast of his son the king

20. FC 65:263; ACCS OT 2:341*.
21. LCC 1:394*; ACCS NT 3:237*.
22. PL 76:1284-85; CSGF 343; ACCS NT 1b:145*.

to remain empty. He sends for others, because although God's word is in danger from some, it will find a place to come to rest. Then he said to his servants, 'The marriage feast is ready, but those invited were not worthy. Go therefore into the byroads, and call to the marriage feast everyone you find.' In holy scripture the road means our way of life, our actions, and a byroad is a sidetracked way, a failed action. Often those who have not been successful in their earthly actions come most readily to God. So the king's servants went out into the byroads and gathered all whom they found, bad and good, and the marriage feast was filled with guests" (Gregory the Great, Forty Gospel Homilies 38; Matt. 22:5-7).[23] Those on byroads, who have failed, now become the special object of God's grace.

The church remains a called-together collection of various real people, ordinary characters, not all pure. "Note that the mixed character of those at the banquet reveals clearly that the king's marriage feast represents the church of this present age, in which the bad are present along with the good. The church is a thorough mixture of various offspring. It brings them all to the faith but does not lead them all to the liberty of spiritual grace by which their lives are changed, since their sins prevent it. As long as we are living in this world we have to proceed along the road of the present age thoroughly mixed together. We shall be separated when we reach our goal" (Gregory the Great, Forty Gospel Homilies 38; Matt. 22:5-7).[24] However mixed the church may be in time, believers in eternity will be made ready to stand before God's holiness clothed in Christ's righteousness, aware of their own moral poverty.

What are we to do with the poor? Invite them to our banquet. Invite them along with the crippled, lame, and blind. Why particularly invite the poor? Because they cannot repay you, says Jesus in Luke 14:12, but you will be repaid at the Resurrection.

### 4. Look Who Came to the Wedding

Take note of who shows up at the wedding: "This wedding pictures the marriage of the church to the Word. . . . A failure to be on the alert prevents those who are invited from attending. . . . But grace is then given to the re-

---

23. PL 76:1284-85; CSGF 344; ACCS NT 1b:145*.
24. PL 76:1284-85; CSGF 344; ACCS NT 1b:145*.

jected and outcasts, 'to the wise and to the foolish' [Rom. 1:14], as Paul says, or to the evil and to the good, as the parable teaches" (Apollinaris, Fragment 111, quoted in Reuss, *Matthäus-Kommentare aus der griechischen Kirche;* Matt. 22:9-10).[25]

The garment we are called to wear to the end-time wedding feast is love, responding to God's own love. In commenting on the parable of the wedding garment, Gregory the Great wrote:

> Since you have already come into the house of the marriage feast, our holy church, as a result of God's generosity, be careful, my friends, lest when the King enters he find fault with some aspect of your heart's clothing. We must consider what comes next with great awe. The king came in to meet the guests and saw there a person not clothed in a wedding garment. What do we think is meant by the wedding garment, dearly beloved? For if we say it is baptism or faith, is there anyone who has entered this marriage feast without them? No, all at the feast have come to believe. What then must we understand by the wedding garment but love? The person in the parable wishes to enter the marriage feast, but without wearing a wedding garment — love. He may have faith, but he does not have love. We are correct when we say that love is the wedding garment because this is what our Creator himself possessed when he came to the marriage feast to join the church to himself. Only God's love brought it about that his only begotten Son united the hearts of his chosen to himself. John says that "God so loved the world that he gave his only begotten Son for us" [John 3:16]. (Gregory the Great, Forty Gospel Homilies 38; Matt. 22:11)[26]

One lacking love is not ready for this feast. Not even dressed for it.

The great banquet celebrates the works of love — God's love and all human responses to it. Our good works within time and space anticipate this banquet, awaiting Christ's return, according to Ambrose: "Truly, one for whom his own virtue suffices for pleasure, who receives Christ in his own home, prepares a great feast. It is a spiritual banquet of good works" (Ambrose, Exposition of the Gospel of Luke 5.19; Luke 5:29-32).[27] The

---

25. MKGK 37-38; ACCS NT 1b:146*.
26. PL 76:1287; CSGF 346-7; ACCS NT 1b:146*.
27. EHG 153; ACCS NT 3:96.

good works that flow from faith constitute the feast. To receive Christ in our own home means to attend that feast already in ordinary time.

## C. Where Your Treasure Is

All who come to the wedding feast of the Lord of glory come with the wedding garment of love. This is what the rich fool lacked. With a closet full of clothes, he lacked that garment.

### 1. *The Parable of the Rich Fool*

Jesus told the parable of the rich fool who stored his wealth in barns just before his death. Augustine commented on what makes for riches: "'The redemption of a man's soul is his riches' [Prov. 13:8]. This silly fool of a man did not have that kind of riches. Obviously he was not enlarging his soul by giving relief to the poor. He was hoarding perishable crops. He did this precisely while he himself was on the point of perishing! For he had handed out nothing to the Lord before whom he was soon due to appear. How will he know where to look when at that trial he starts hearing the words 'I was hungry and you did not give me anything to eat'? [Matt. 25:42] He was planning to fill his soul with excessive and unnecessary feasting. Meanwhile he was heedlessly disregarding all those empty bellies of the poor. He did not realize that the bellies of the poor were much safer storerooms than his barns. What he was stowing away in those barns was perhaps even then being stolen away by thieves" (Augustine, Sermon 36.9; Luke 12:16-20).[28] The rich fool was poor in soul.

However full his barns, the rich fool was empty in love. "What does the rich man do, surrounded by a great supply of many blessings beyond all numbering?" asked Cyril of Alexandria. "He does not raise his eyes to God. He does not count it worth his while to gain for his soul those treasures that are above in heaven. He does not cherish love for the poor. He does not even desire the value it gains. He does not sympathize with suffering. It neither gives him pain nor awakens his pity. Still more irrationally, he settles himself into a comfortable pattern of life, and pretends that he

28. WSA 3 2:180**; ACCS NT 3:208*.

owns his life. He says, 'I will say to myself, Self, you have goods laid up for many years. Eat, drink, and enjoy yourself.' Then it is said: 'O rich man, you have storehouses to receive your fruits, but where will you find time to receive your own soul? By the decree of God, your life is shortened.' God said: 'You fool, this night will require of you your soul. Who will then own all these things that you have prepared for yourself?'" (Cyril of Alexandria, Commentary on Luke, Homily 89; Luke 12:16-20).[29] Worldly riches may come to an abrupt end just at that point when imagined to be most secure.

## 2. Give to the Poor That You May Be Truly Rich

The economics of eternity are puzzling to earthly economics. Cyril of Alexandria urged his churches: "Give that which you must leave, even against your will, that you may not lose all these things later. Offer your wealth to God, that you may be more truly rich. Jesus showed the way: 'Sell your possessions, and give to the poor. Provide yourselves with purses that do not grow old, with a treasure in the heavens that does not fail' [Luke 12:33]. The blessed David teaches us the same wisdom in the Psalms, where divine inspiration says of every merciful and good man, 'He has distributed freely. He has given to the poor. His righteousness endures forever' [Ps. 112:9]. Worldly wealth has many foes. There are numerous thieves. This world of ours is full of potential oppressors. Some plunder by secret means, while others use violence and tear it away even from those who resist. But no one can do damage to the wealth that is laid up above in heaven. God is its keeper, and he does not sleep" (Cyril of Alexandria, Commentary on Luke, Homily 91; Luke 12:29-33).[30] They store treasures in heaven who care for the poor as God does, with compassion.

Jesus said: "For where your treasure is, there will your heart be also" (Luke 12:34, KJV). Augustine reflected: "If you lack earthly riches, do not seek them in the world by evil deeds. If they fall to your lot, let them be yielded up to heaven in good works. A steadfast Christian soul should neither be overjoyed at acquiring them nor cast down when they are gone. Let us instead reflect on what the Lord says: 'Where your treasure is, there will your heart be also.' Surely when we hear in worship that we should 'lift up

---

29. CGSL 361**; ACCS NT 3:207-8*.
30. CGSL 368**; ACCS NT 3:211*.

our hearts,' the familiar answer that we make [we lift them up, O Lord] should not be a lie" (Augustine, Letter 189; Luke 12:34).[31] To acquire or lose earthly treasure counts less in the divine economy than to love the neighbor.

Those who would regain what is most truly their own — their souls — must give to others what is finally not their own, but only temporarily in their charge. Cyril of Alexandria had a brilliant way of reminding his hearers of what the Savior said: "'If you have not been faithful in what is another's, who will give you what is your own?' [Luke 16:12]. We again say that what is another's is the wealth we seem to possess. We were not born with riches, but on the contrary, naked. Scripture confirms that 'we neither brought anything into the world, nor can carry anything out' [1 Tim. 6:7]." Cyril continued: "Let those of us who possess earthly wealth thus open our hearts to those who are in need. Let us show ourselves faithful and obedient to the commands of God. Let us be followers of our Lord's will in those earthly things that are temporarily made available to our souls, and hence finally not our own. Let us do this so that we may receive more truly what is our own — that holy and admirable beauty that God forms in people's souls, making them like himself, according to what we originally were" (Cyril of Alexandria, Commentary on Luke, Homily 109; Luke 16:9-13).[32] We do not possess wealth in the same way we possess our souls, the soul being "that which makes us alive." We do not have wealth in the same sense that we have life. Wealth is outside ourselves. The soul is ourselves. In sharing the wealth of the soul, the soul is not diminished. Let other needy people share in the possession of that which makes us alive.

### 3. Storing Up

What we learn from famine is to store food, as Joseph did in Egypt (Gen. 41:35-49). Yet, we are not inordinately to store up treasures on earth (Matt. 6:19). Rather, as faith is becoming active in love, we are already storing up treasures in heaven (Matt. 6:20). God is richly supplying us with everything we need (1 Tim. 6:17), equipping us with everything good in order to do his will (Heb. 13:21), through the ongoing provision of the Spirit (Phil. 1:19). In our earthly journey, God will be providing for us, as he provided a

31. FC 30:270**; ACCS NT 3:212*.
32. CGSL 444**; ACCS NT 3:256*.

lamb for Abraham (Gen. 22:8). He will be giving us everything pertaining to true life and godliness (2 Pet. 1:3). Consider the ravens, for they neither sow nor reap, neither do they have storehouses nor barns, but God feeds them (Luke 12:24).

In the light of God's provision, it is a moral claim that able-bodied persons provide for their families. If they fail to do this, it is like denying their faith (1 Tim. 5:8). There is a continuum of accountability in the balance between storing enough and storing too much. Joseph stored in due proportion.

Whether we are greedy or give provisions to the poor is our decision. We make that decision in time, and its consequences echo to eternity. Almsgiving raises our hearts toward God in eternity. Peter Chrysologus preached: "All this is what that treasure brings about. Either through almsgiving it raises the heart of a man into heaven, or through greed it buries it in the earth. That is why he said, 'For where your treasure is, there your heart will be also.' O man, send your treasure on, send it ahead into heaven, or else your God-given soul will be buried in the earth. Gold comes from the depth of the earth — the soul, from the highest heaven. Clearly it is *better to carry the gold to where the soul resides than to bury the soul in the mine of the gold.* That is why God orders those who will serve in his army here below to fight as men stripped of concern for riches and unencumbered by anything. To these he has granted the privilege of reigning in heaven" (Peter Chrysologus, Sermon 22, italics added; Luke 12:34).[33]

## 4. Relief of Suffering Not Based on Merit

Augustine shifted the focus of works of love from the weakness of the neighbor to the power of the One who died for him: "If you love the weak person less because of the moral failing that makes him weak, consider the One who died on his behalf" (Augustine, Questions 71; 1 Cor. 8:11).[34]

Do not be selective in acts of generosity. "It is easy, of course, to understand that we must give alms and a helping hand to the needy, because Christ himself receives these alms through them," wrote Augustine. "We can understand that we have to give alms and that we must not really pick

33. FC 17:67*; ACCS NT 3:211-12.
34. FC 70:185; ACCS NT 7:78.

and choose to whom we give them, because we are unable to sift through people's hearts. When you give alms to *all* different types of people, then you will reach a *few* who deserve them. If you are hospitable, you will keep your house ready for strangers" (Augustine, Sermon 359a.11, italics added; Luke 16:9-13).[35] Do not try to read the heart or motive of the person assisted. Alms are not based on merit. Give to all. Some will be deserving.

Jesus sought to elicit generosity toward the poor (Luke 14:13-24). The earliest Christians were quick to find practical ways of providing for the needs of the poor (Acts 6:1-6). Even though Paul's mission churches may have remained in great poverty, out of this poverty there welled up a rich generosity (2 Cor. 8:2). They gave as much as they were able and even beyond their ability. "They urgently pleaded with us for the privilege of sharing in this service to the saints" (2 Cor. 8:4, NIV).

### 5. Why Alms?

Jesus' disciples performed deeds of almsgiving (Matt. 6:4; Luke 11:41; 12:43). In doing so they were not to let the left hand know what the right hand was doing. Giving is without calculation, without pretense, without seeking an accompanying reward. Jesus criticized almsgiving if it is done for the notice of men (Matt. 6:2-3).

Alms, almsdeeds, or almsgiving is the practice of generous giving to the poor. It refers to any righteous or compassionate deed especially as directed to the poor. Alms (Greek *eleemosune*, Hebrew *tsedika*) imply taking care of any needy person, especially widows and the fatherless. Job showed his willingness to become a "father to the poor" (Job 29:16, KJV). Alms are not to be grudgingly given, as if a loan were being tracked, later requiring legal repayment. They are freely given. Failure to comply is a sin under Deuteronomic law (Deut. 15:9-10). You are not to harden your heart or close your hand to your poor brother (Deut. 13:7; 15:11). Relieve the one who has fallen into poverty and defenselessness, though he might be a stranger or sojourner. Welcome him (Lev. 25:35).

Especially those who are tempted to make a god of money are required to sell all that they have and give it to the poor, so they will have treasures in heaven (Luke 18:22). Yet, even those who give all to feed the

---

35. WSA 3 10:216*; ACCS NT 3:255*.

poor, but do it without love, find that it is all fruitless (1 Cor. 13). To give simply as a duty without responding to the overflowing love of God is to remain bereft of the motivating energy that prompts genuine almsgiving.

Alms are to be given without public show (Matt. 6:1-4; Rom. 12:8), freely (2 Cor. 9:6-7), tenderly (1 John 3:17). The faithful are taught not to delay giving alms when asked, but to give quickly. Examples in the New Testament are Zacchaeus (Luke 19:8), Dorcas (Acts 9:36), and Cornelius, the centurion of Caesarea who immediately gave alms as an expression of gratitude (Acts 10:12; 4:31).

Due to the recalcitrance of human sin, there will always be poor in the land. This is why God commands the faithful to be always open-handed toward the needy (Deut. 15:7-18). "You shall give to him freely, and your heart shall not be grudging when you give to him; because for this the Lord your God will bless you in all your work and in all that you undertake" (Deut. 15:10, RSV). Whoever sows sparingly will reap sparingly; whoever sows generously will also reap generously. Everyone is invited to give what he has decided in his heart to give, not reluctantly or under compulsion, for God loves a cheerful giver (2 Cor. 9:6-7).

## 6. Do Not Reinforce Slothfulness by Rewarding It

In giving alms, however, take care not to reinforce the idleness of the sluggard who does not plow, and therefore begs in harvest when he has nothing (Prov. 20:4). Scripture warns against rewarding idleness, sloth, gluttony, and drunkenness. The able-bodied do not get a free ticket just because they are poor. "If any will not work, neither shall he eat" (2 Thess. 3:10b, NKJV). "If a man is lazy, the rafters sag; if his hands are idle, the house leaks" (Eccles. 10:18, NIV). Those responsible for others are not to "eat the bread of idleness" (Prov. 31:27b, NIV). Those who do not work at all often become disorderly busybodies (2 Thess. 3:11). The slothful man refuses to work. What does him in is inordinate desire (Prov. 21:25).

This is a balance that must be fairly reviewed. We do not want to reinforce sloth and laziness in the poor by making them dependent, or tempting them to dependency, for sloth has a tendency to cast you "into a deep sleep," and cause the idle soul to suffer hunger (Prov. 19:15, RSV). A just parent is more likely to leave an inheritance to his children's children (Prov. 13:22), so they can receive a "goodly heritage" (Ps. 16:6b, KJV).

Work with your own hands so you will have something to share with those in need. If you are a believer who has a widow, or a needy or poor person in your family, do not let that person become a burden on the church or society, because that person is one who by kinship is closely connected with you. In doing so it will enable the church to help others who do not have the family connection, who are really in even more need, who do not have any family to protect and provide for them (1 Tim. 5:16).

## D. The Law and the Poor

The poor are vulnerable. They are most quickly deserted by those upon whom they have most depended (Prov. 19:4). Even if their fields in one season may produce foods, they may be next swept away due to injustices that unexpectedly overtake them (Prov. 13:23). This is why they must be equally protected by the law.

### 1. The Law Requires Justice for the Poor

In scripture, the law paid explicit attention to the duty of the people of God to the poor: "If there is among you a poor man, one of your brethren, in any of your towns within your land which the Lord your God gives you, you shall not harden your heart or shut your hand against your poor brother, but you shall open your hand to him, and lend him sufficiently for his need, whatever it may be" (Deut. 15:7-8, RSV). Helping the poor was not limited to emotive affinity or personal sympathy. It was the concern of the whole community. Those who grind the faces of the poor, who beat God's people into pieces, come under God's sure judgment (Isa. 3:15).

There would be no poor if all obeyed God. "There should be no poor among you, for in the land the Lord your God is giving you to possess as your inheritance, he will richly bless you, if only you fully obey the Lord" (Deut. 15:4-5, NIV). If only. A principal reason for the captivity of Israel was because they oppressed the poor (Amos 2:6-9; 4:1-3; 8:4-6). God brings judgment upon those who neglect the poor (Ezek. 16:49-50).

If Israel treats the poor fairly, they will lend to many nations, but borrow from none (Deut. 15:6; 28:12). If you are a king and you judge the poor with fairness, your throne will be secure (Prov. 29:14).

Yet under the conditions of sin that prevail in human history, the poor are always the first to be vulnerable. So to provide for the poor, the law of God allows them to glean the remains of the fields and vineyards, and harvest the corners. The just are called to leave the edges of their fields unharvested. Leave them as gleanings for the poor (Lev. 19:9). Under the law it was "unlawful to gather the sheaves left after the harvest, or to glean the vines after the vintage or to gather up the olives that remain after the trees were picked, because these things were to be left for the poor. Now if this was commanded those who were under the law, what shall we say of those who are in Christ? To them the Lord says, 'Unless your justice abounds more than that of the scribes and Pharisees, you shall not enter into the kingdom of heaven' [Matt. 5:20]" (Pseudo-Basil, On Mercy and Justice; Deut. 24:19).[36]

Mosaic law protected the poor by forbidding usury. "The law does not deem it right to collect interest on capital. It seeks to enable free giving to those in need, with hands and minds wide open. God is the creator of this free gift. It is he who shares his goods, exacting as the only reasonable interest the most precious things human beings possess: gentleness, goodness, high-mindedness, repute, glory" (Clement of Alexandria, Stromateis 2.84; Exod. 22:25).[37]

The law can convict us of sin, and make sin known to our conscience, but it cannot overcome sin. Marius Victorinus commented on Paul: "We have said that the law given by Moses teaches nothing but sins, admonishing us what sins are and how they are to be avoided. . . . The law is given not so that life may be sought from it but that by its written requirement it may both include all sins in its teaching and show that they should be avoided. Therefore righteousness is not from the law. Justification and salvation come not from the law but from faith, as is promised" (Marius Victorinus, Epistle to the Galatians 2; Gal. 3:21b).[38] We may learn from the law how poor in spirit we are, but the law as such does not give us freedom to love.

---

36. FC 9:510-11; ACCS OT 3:317.
37. FC 85:214; ACCS OT 3:116*.
38. BTMV 36-37; ACCS NT 8:48*.

## 2. The Jubilee

There was a cycle of remembrance of the poor in ancient Israel, integrated with Sabbath observation and the seasons of celebration of the Jewish year. "And you shall count seven weeks of years, seven times seven years, so that the time of the seven weeks of years shall be forty-nine years. Then you shall send abroad the loud trumpet on the tenth day of the seventh month; on the day of atonement you shall send abroad the trumpet throughout all your land. And you shall hallow the fiftieth year, and proclaim liberty through the land to all its inhabitants; it shall be a jubilee for you ... it shall be holy to you; you shall eat what it yields out of the field" (Lev. 25:8-12, RSV). The jubilee year broke the cycle of poverty. It was a time for experiencing dependence upon God who gives the land. "And if your brother becomes poor, and cannot maintain himself with you, you shall maintain him; as a stranger and as a sojourner he shall live with you" (Lev. 25:35, RSV).

Origen thought that much of the deeper meaning of the jubilee year would always remain a mystery: "Who is there who has grasped the mind of Christ so well that he knows the meaning of the seventh year of freedom of Hebrew slaves (Exodus 21:2), and the remission of debts, and the intermission of the cultivation of the holy land? Over and above the feast of every seventh year is the feast called the Jubilee. No one can ever come near divining its precise meaning or the true import of the prescriptions enjoined by it, except him who knows the Father's will and his disposition for every age according to 'his incomprehensible judgments and unsearchable ways' [Rom. 11:33]" (Origen, On Prayer 27.14; Lev. 25:10).[39] Worshipers stand in awe as they hear read the written Word concerning the jubilee.

What happened for the poor and for slaves on the fiftieth year? According to Basil the Great, "Seven weeks of years in ancient times produced the celebrated jubilee, in which the earth kept the Sabbath, debts were canceled, slaves were set free, and, as it were, a new life was established again, the old one in a certain way attaining its fulfillment in the number seven. These things are figures of this present age which revolves through the seven days and passes us by; an age in which the penalties for the lesser sins are paid according to the loving care of the good Lord, so that we may not be handed over for punishment in the age without end"

39. ACWOp 19:103-4; ACCS OT 3:198.

48

(Basil, Letter 260; Lev. 25:10).[40] The jubilee is a foreshadowed picture of the forgiveness all would be offered on the cross.

Jubilee means remission of debts, as seen prototypically in Psalm 50: "The number of this psalm, fifty, is not otiose," wrote Cassiodorus. "It has reference to the year of the jubilee, which among the Jews dissolved old contracts and obligations, and which in Leviticus the Lord ordered all dwellers on earth to call the year of remission. The number also refers to Pentecost, when after the Lord's ascension the Holy Spirit came on the apostles, working miracles and imparting the gift of charisms. So too this psalm, which is given the number fifty, if recited with a pure heart, looses sins, cancels the bond of our debt, and like the year of remission frees us through the Lord's kindness of the debts of our sins" (Cassiodorus, Exposition of the Psalms 50, Conclusion; Lev. 25:10).[41]

The jubilee is the anticipation of eternal tranquility, according to Bede:

> In the law, the fiftieth year was ordered to be called [the year] of jubilee, that is, "forgiving" or "changed." During it the people were to remain at rest from all work, the debts of all were to be canceled, slaves were to go free, [and] the year itself was to be more notable than other years because of its greater solemnities and divine praises. Therefore, by this number is rightly indicated that tranquility which provides the greatest peace. Then "the dead will rise and we shall be changed" [1 Cor. 15:52] into glory. Then, when the labors and hardships of this age come to an end, and our debts, [that is] all our faults, have been forgiven, the entire people of the elect will rejoice eternally in the sole contemplation of the divine vision, and that most longed-for command of our Lord and Savior will be fulfilled: "Be still and see that I am God" [Ps. 46:10]. (Bede, Homily 17; Lev. 25:10)[42]

The number fifty, designating the year of jubilee, is the number associated with the coming of the Holy Spirit on Pentecost. "We read in the law that the fiftieth year was ordered to be designated as a jubilee (that is, a [year for] releasing or exchanging), in which the whole people should rest

40. FC 28:224; ACCS OT 3:198.
41. ACWCa 51:512; ACCS OT 3:198*.
42. CSBH 2:174; ACCS OT 3:198.

from all cultivation of the land and everyone's debts should be canceled, and we know that in the New Testament the grace of the Holy Spirit came upon the apostles on the day of Pentecost (that is, the fiftieth day of the Lord's resurrection) and hallowed the beginnings of the Church that was being brought into existence by its coming [Acts 2:1-2]. It is agreed, then, that by this number can rightly be figured either the grace of the Holy Spirit or the joy of future blessedness to which one is brought through the gift of the same Spirit and in the perception of which alone is true rest and joy" (Bede the Venerable, On the Tabernacle 2.2; Lev. 25:10).[43] In this way early Christianity connected and interfused the jubilee acts of liberating of the poor from debt with the mission of the Holy Spirit following Pentecost.

### 3. Time and Atonement

Time was to be ordered around the atonement in Israel. On every day of every year you shall relieve the oppressed, be fair to the fatherless, plead for the widow (Isa. 1:17). But every seventh year all debts are to be canceled (Deut. 15:1-3). On the seventh year, let the land lie fallow so that the poor may use it, and that even the wild animals can eat from it. Do the same with your vineyard and olive trees — every seventh year let them rest, as God rests (Exod. 23:11). And on the seventh year, when you are letting your servants go free, don't send them away empty-handed (Deut. 15:12-13). Supply them liberally from your flock, your threshing floor, and your wine presses. Give to them as the Lord your God has blessed you (15:14).

At the end of every three years, bring all the tithes into town and let the widows and the fatherless eat and be satisfied (Deut. 14:28). When you give to the poor, give generously without a grumbling heart (15:10). If somebody makes a pledge to you of some of his possessions, like his coat, return it before sunset so that he may use it (24:12-13). Do not take advantage of one who is poor. Pay him his wages on the day that he works, before sunset, since he is desperately counting on it (24:14-15).

43. TTHB 18:54; ACCS OT 3:198-99.

## E. The Rich Man and Lazarus

The basic pattern for a Christian understanding of the relation of rich and poor is made clear in the parable Jesus told of the rich man and Lazarus. This parable has occupied the imagination of Christian scripture scholars ever since.

The parable teaches that the way we treat the poor impinges on our eternal destiny. After death there is an unbridgeable gulf between heaven and hell, with no possibility of later revisions of decisions once made. The poor who were once ignored by the rich as if invisible are now inheritors of the kingdom. The rich who gathered their treasures around themselves are now thirsting in a very hot place, and envy those poor who are safely in Abraham's bosom. Their problem is not wealth as such, but avarice.

### 1. How You Treat the Poor Impinges on Your Eternal Destiny

If the rich man would give to the poor only what he threw away for trash, thought Jerome, he would be doing himself a favor. Commenting on Jesus' parable (Luke 16:19-22), Jerome wrote: "The rich man, in purple splendor, is not accused of being greedy or of carrying off the property of another, or of committing adultery, or, in fact, of any wrongdoing. The evil alone of which he is guilty is pride. Most wretched of men, you can see there lying outside your gate a member of your own body, in torment. Have you no compassion? If the requirement of God means nothing to you, *at least take pity on your own human destiny, and stand in awe — for perhaps you might become like him.* Give what you would waste to your own neighbor, a member of the human family. I am not telling you to throw away your wealth. What you throw out, the crumbs from your table, at least offer as alms" (Jerome, On Lazarus and Dives, italics added; Luke 16:19-22).[44] Pride may blind the rich to even any slight recognition of the poor.

The personae who appear in the parable are one rich man (sometimes called Dives), one poor man, and Abraham, and the dogs. The rich man treated the poor man worse than the dogs, noticed Cyril of Alexandria: "Cut off from compassion and care, Lazarus would have gladly gath-

---

44. FC 57:201*; ACCS NT 3:260-61*.

ered the worthless morsels that fell from the rich man's table to satisfy his hunger. A severe and incurable disease also tormented Lazarus. Yes, it says that even the dogs licked his sores and did not injure him yet sympathized with him and cared for him. Animals relieve their own sufferings with their tongues, as they remove what pains them and gently soothe the sores. The rich man was even crueler than the dogs, because he felt no sympathy or compassion for Lazarus, but was completely unmerciful" (Cyril of Alexandria, Commentary on Luke III; Luke 16:19-22).[45] The dogs relieved his suffering. The rich man did not even recognize it.

It is only in eternity that the balance of the scales of justice will be determined and executed. Therefore do not be surprised if the final judge "assigns pain in return for riches, refreshment in return for poverty, flames in return for purple and joy in return for nakedness. The equal balance of the scales will be maintained. The standard of measurement will not be proved false that says, 'the measure you give will be the measure you get' [Matt. 7:2]. The reason he refuses to show mercy to the rich man in his pain is that while he lived the rich man neglected to show mercy. *The reason why he ignored the rich man's pleas in his torment is that he himself ignored the poor man's pleas on earth*" (Augustine, Sermon 367.2, italics added; Luke 16:23-26).[46] This is correctable by a change of heart.

## 2. The Unbridgeable Distance to Abraham's Bosom

Sister Macrina, speaking through the pen of her brother, Gregory of Nyssa, interpreted "the gulf" in the parable as voluntary, decisive, and eternal in its consequences: "This, in my opinion, is the gulf. It is not an earthly or visible abyss. It is the judgment between the *two opposite choices given us in this life*. Once one has fundamentally chosen the pleasure of this life and has not remedied this bad choice by a change of heart, he produces for himself a place empty of good thereafter. He digs this unavoidable necessity for himself like some deep and trackless pit." Macrina added that it is only in the "bosom of Abraham," the final destiny of the righteous, that "the patient sufferer finds rest . . . This patriarch [Abraham] was the first person recorded to have chosen the hope of things to come in preference

---

45. CGSL 453-54; ACCS NT 3:261*.
46. WSA 3 10:297**; ACCS NT 3:263*.

to the enjoyment of the moment. Deprived of everything he had in the beginning of his life, living among strangers, he searched for a future prosperity through present affliction" (Gregory of Nyssa, quoting Macrina, On the Soul and the Resurrection, italics added; Luke 16:23-26).[47] Abraham is the model for a relation with eternity that trumps a relation with time.

Those who hope for pardon at the end of history would be wise to show forth fruits of pardon here and now. Ephrem the Syrian wrote: "Why should the Lord have seen Abraham above all the just, and Lazarus comforted in his bosom? He saw him because Abraham loved the poor, and so that we might learn that we *cannot hope for pardon at the end unless the fruits of pardon are seen in us*. If Abraham, who was friendly to strangers and had mercy on Sodom, did not have mercy on the rich man who showed no pity to Lazarus, how can we hope that there will be pardon for us?" (Ephrem the Syrian, Commentary on Tatian's Diatessaron 15.12-13, italics added; Luke 16:23-26).[48] Those unwilling to pardon now cannot hope for God's pardon at the end.

Peter Chrysologus saw three levels of irony in this parable: "First, the rich man's pleas do not spring from new pain but from an ancient envy. Second, this hell does not kindle his jealousy as much as Lazarus's possession of heaven. People find it a serious evil and unbearable fire to see in happiness those whom they once held in contempt. Third, the rich man's ill will is never cured. It is by his own will that he is punished. He does not ask to be led to Lazarus but wants Lazarus to be led to him! *O rich man, beloved Abraham cannot send to the bed of your tortures Lazarus whom you did not condescend to admit to your table.* Your respective fortunes have now been reversed. You look at the glory of him whose misery you once spurned. He who wondered at you in your glory now sees your tortures" (Peter Chrysologus, Sermon 122, italics added; Luke 16:23-26).[49] The rich man is eternally incurable because uncured within time by his own willing.

It is not wealth as such that is demeaning, but the temptations it brings, according to Augustine: "I think that we have proved that Christ did not object to the riches of the rich man but to his impiety, infidelity, pride and cruelty. . . . When people hear about the rich man hurled into the pains of hell, they stand in awe. I have reassured them: They do not need to fear

---

47. FC 58:234**; ACCS NT 3:261-62*.
48. ECTD 235-36**; ACCS NT 3:263*.
49. FC 17:210-11**; ACCS NT 3:263*.

riches, but vices. They should not fear wealth, but avarice. They should not be afraid of creaturely goods, but of greed. Let them possess wealth like Abraham. Let them possess it with faith. Let them have it, and possess it, and not be possessed by it" (Augustine, Sermon 299e.5; Luke 16:23-26).[50]

### 3. The Invisibility of the Poor

The proud do not even see the poor. They are invisible to their eyes. Jerome commented on the strange invisibility of the poor: "Lazarus was lying at the gate in order to draw attention to the cruelty paid to his body and to prevent the rich man from saying, 'I did not notice him. He was in a corner. *I could not see him.* No one announced him to me.' He lay at the gate. You saw him every time you went out and every time you came in. When your crowds of servants and clients were attending you, he lay there full of ulcers" (Jerome, On Lazarus and Dives, italics added; Luke 16:19-22).[51] Even in the most visible location — the gate — the poor remain invisible to avarice.

Augustine commented on the irony that we know the name of the poor man — Lazarus — but not that of the rich man. Why? "You see, God who lives in heaven kept quiet about the rich man's name, because he did not find it written in heaven. He spoke the poor man's name, because he found it written there, indeed he gave instructions for it to be written there" (Augustine, Sermon 33a.4; Luke 16:19-22).[52] In God's economy, the one who is ignored on earth is recognized and known in heaven. On earth, nobody remembers the poor man (Eccles. 9:15).

The poor man's wisdom is often despised and his words are no longer heeded (Eccles. 9:16). Yet there may be great discernment in the soul of the poor. The poor see through the rich who think themselves wise (Prov. 28:11). It is better to be a poor man who tells the truth than a fool who tells lies (Prov. 19:1).

Do not steal from the sacrifice of the poor when you come to the Lord's table. Cyprian observed: "You that are rich cannot do good works in the church, because your eyes, saturated with blackness and covered with the shadows of night, do not see the needy and the poor. Do you who are

---

50. WSA 3 8:268**; ACCS NT 3:262*.
51. FC 57:201*; ACCS NT 3:261.
52. WSA 3 2:163**; ACCS NT 3:261.

rich and wealthy think that you celebrate the Lord's feast? You do not at all consider the offering. You come to the Lord's feast without a sacrificial offering and take a part of the sacrifice that the poor have offered" (Cyprian, Works and Almsgiving 15; Luke 21:1-4).[53] In the Eucharist the faithful, rich and poor, take part in a sacrifice in remembrance of the lamb of God. To come to that table without generosity is like stealing from the poor.

### 4. Consider the Poor

Do not turn your eyes away from the hungry or the wanderer (Isa. 58:7). Body language tells the tale of our unloving responses to the poor: the closed hand, the turned back, the upturned jaw. No. When you see him naked, look upon him with compassion, clothe him, be attentive to him.

The first duty to the poor is simply to open your own eyes. When Psalm 41:1 calls the faithful to "have regard" for the poor, it means: Wake up. Pry open your drowsy eyes. See them. Invite. Welcome. Draw near. Do not let them remain invisible to you. Consider the poor.

Give to him who asks (Matt. 5:42). Do not turn aside (Luke 3:11). Suppose one man has two tunics and another has none. Share with the needy what you have (Luke 12:33). Thereby you will provide purses for yourself that will not wear out, a treasure in heaven that will not be exhausted, where no thief comes near and no moth destroys.

We are blessed when we remember the poor. We are to remember the poor as if we were poor, behold those who are being mistreated as if we ourselves were being mistreated (Heb. 13:3). The Lord blesses us, and sustains us, and restores us, especially when we sustain and bless and restore others. "Let the outcasts of Moab sojourn among you; be a refuge to them from the destroyer" (Isa. 16:4, RSV).

### 5. Fire and Water

The story of Lazarus was celebrated by two of Christianity's greatest poets, Prudentius and Ephrem.

Prudentius retold Jesus' parable (Luke 16:19-31) in these Latin meters:

53. FC 36:240-41*; ACCS NT 3:316*.

But until the perishable body
You will raise up, O God, and refashion,
What mansion of rest is made ready
For the soul that is pure and unsullied?
It shall rest in the patriarch's bosom
As did Lazarus, hedged round with flowers,
Whom Dives beheld from a distance
While he burned in the fires everlasting.

(Prudentius, Hymns for Every Day
10.149-56; Luke 16:23-26)[54]

Before him Ephrem had written this hymn in Syriac about the thirst of the rich man in torment:

This place, despised and spurned
By the denizens of paradise,
Those who burn in Gehenna
Hungrily desire;
Their torment doubles
At the sight of its fountains,
They quiver violently
As they stand on the opposite side;
The rich man, too, begs for succor
But there is no one to wet his tongue,
For fire is within them,
While the water is opposite them.

(Ephrem the Syrian,
Hymns on Paradise 1.17; Luke 16:23-26)[55]

## F. Relief for the Needy

### 1. The Pattern

Where there are emergency situations of dire need, the pattern of Christian response is active relief, immediate attentiveness, compassionate obe-

54. FC 43:76*; ACCS NT 3:262.
55. HOP 84; ACCS NT 3:262.

dience within the urgency of the moment. Jesus did not delay in offering food to the multitudes in the desert. With relief he brought hope.

We are to give relief to the fatherless and widows, lighten the burden of those who are oppressed, plead for the widow (Ps. 146:9; Isa. 1:17), give alms freely out of whatever stores we have (Luke 11:41). The destitute are not only poor but powerless to change their poverty. The Lord listens to the prayers of the destitute (Ps. 102:17).

## 2. Actively Seeking Out the Needy

We are called actively to seek out the needy, according to Andrew of Crete: "John teaches us that we should not wait for needy people to come to us but should rather go out and look for them. That is what Lot and Abraham did" (Andrew of Crete, quoted in Cramer, Catena in Epistolas Catholicas; 3 John 8).[56]

Similarly in Chrysostom: "Paul urges that they not wait for those who are needy to come to them but that they seek out those who need their assistance. Thus the considerate man shows his concern, and with great zeal will perform his duty. For in acts of mercy it is not those who receive the kindness who are benefited, so much as those who do the kindness. They make the greater gain. For it gives them confidence toward God" (Chrysostom, Homilies on Titus 6; Tit. 3:13-14).[57] The giver becomes the unexpected recipient of a greater gift.

Augustine defended the hard-working poor who may still remain in serious need: "Nevertheless, after the apostle had said in such instruction and advice: 'Now such persons we charge and exhort in the Lord Jesus Christ that they work quietly and eat their own bread' [2 Thess. 3:12], he was mindful of such needs of the saints who, although they would obey his commands to work quietly and eat their own bread, would, for many reasons, lack some provision of necessary commodities. Hence, with foresight he added immediately: 'But you, brothers, *do not grow tired of well-doing*' [3:13], so that those who had the means of furnishing sustenance to the servants of God would not grow careless in this responsibility." He then made this general instruction specific: "Furthermore, when in writing to Titus, he

---

56. CEC 150; ACCS NT 11:241*.
57. NPNF 1 13:541; ACCS NT 9:307*.

THE GOOD WORKS READER

said: 'Help Zenas the lawyer and Apollos on their way, taking care that nothing is wanting to them' [Tit. 3:13]. He continued in this way in order to show why nothing should be lacking to them: 'And let the people also learn to excel in good works, in order to meet cases of necessity, that they may not be unfruitful' [3:14]" (Augustine, The Work of Monks 15.16; Tit. 3:13-14).[58]

### 3. Prioritizing Services according to Need

There is a process of mutual caring within this worshiping community by which needs of varying intensity are being addressed so that the whole body is working on behalf of the most needy, under the assumption that God supplies all of our needs (Phil. 4:19). The disciples sent relief to the brothers in Judea, "every man according to his ability" (Acts 11:29, KJV). The principle is stated in Acts 4:35: Distribute to each one "according as he has need."

The economy of providence will be fair in the long run. "At the present time your plenty will supply what they need, so that in turn their plenty will supply what you need. Then there will be equality, as it is written, 'He that gathered much did not have too much, and he that gathered little did not have too little'" (2 Cor. 8:14-15, NIV).

Those in urgent need cannot live long without meeting such basic requirements as breathing, nourishment, and proper body temperature.

The calculus of relief is obvious: Offer the most basic necessities first to the most needy. Like medical triage, apply remedies in relation to the urgency of the need.

Remember that all needs are not physical, even in the most urgent situations. Vary the remedy, whether physical or spiritual, to fit the particular need, as Bede made clear: "If a brother or sister has nothing and cannot even find enough to eat, we ought to give them the basic necessities of life. Likewise if we notice that they are deficient in spiritual things, we ought to guide them in whatever way we can." Our demeanor and attitude are factors in delivering care, Bede continues: "Of course we must be sincere in doing this, not looking for praise from other people, not boasting, and not pointing out that others who are richer than we are have not done nearly as much. For someone who thinks like that is full of deceit, and the gift of truth does not dwell in him, even if it appears on the surface that he

58. FC 16:356; ACCS NT 9:308*.

is showing love to others" (Bede, On 1 John; 1 John 3:18).[59] Subtle temptations to pride threaten truthful acts.

Paul asked for prayers for the poor that God may supply them according to their need. Chrysostom's description is poignant of the generosity of the needy of Philippi: "They were artisans and paupers. They had wives, reared children and owned houses. They had given these gifts freely from their small means. There was nothing absurd in praying that such people so situated should have sufficiency and plenty. Paul does not ask God to make them rich or affluent. He asks only that God may supply their every need — so they will not be in want but will have what they need" (Chrysostom, Homily on Philippians 16; Phil. 4.19b).[60]

### 4. Quit Making Excuses

We are not to make excuses (as was the case in Luke 14:18: Don't bother me, I am buying something). We are not permitted by the Good News to neglect the vulnerable and the needy (such as the widows mentioned in Acts 6:1). We are not to neglect the exercise of whatever gifts that happen to be given to each one of us (1 Tim. 4:14). "Much more is required from the person to whom much more is given" (Luke 12:48, TEV).

Ezekiel presents a litany of neglects and evasions: The people have not strengthened those who are sick, not healed those who are diseased, not bound up the broken, not tried to restore again the ones who have been driven away, not sought out those who are lost (Ezek. 34:4). Our evasions are as clever as they are constant. Avoid making excuses. All who neglect the needs of the poor are finally without excuse, according to John Chrysostom: "There are two arguments that deprive you of any excuse in this mischief. The first excuse is that the neighbor is weak, the second excuse is that he is your relative. I should add a third excuse also, one which is even worse than the others. What is this? That Christ died for him. But meanwhile you are not ready even to lift a finger to help him in the slightest" (Chrysostom, Homilies on the Epistles of Paul to the Corinthians I.20.10; 1 Cor. 8:11).[61]

59. PL 93:103-4; ACCS NT 11:204*.
60. IOEP 5:165; ACCS NT 8:288*.
61. NPNF 1 12:116; ACCS NT 7:78*.

By neglecting the poor, by failing to provide relief, we neglect our own salvation that calls us to embody the love we have received. How will we escape judgment if we neglect so great salvation (Heb. 2:3)? For one who knows the good and does not do it, to him it is a sin (Jas. 4:17).

## 5. Remember the Saints

"Paul calls believers 'saints' because they have been called to be holy" (Gennadius of Constantinople, quoted in Staab, Pauline Commentary from the Greek Church; Rom. 12:13).[62] The faithful are called especially to contribute to the needs of the saints.

Theodore of Mopsuestia wrote: "Paul says that it is right for us always to remember the saints, to regard their needs as our own, and thus to lighten their suffering" (cf. 1 Pet. 4:8-9) (Theodore of Mopsuestia, quoted in Staab, Pauline Commentary from the Greek Church; Rom. 12:13).[63]

Theodoret adds: "It is not just guests that Paul calls saints but also those (wherever they may come from) who are in any kind of need" (Theodoret, Interpretation of the Letter to the Romans; Rom. 12:13).[64] Relieve the needy without asking about their moral credentials. For Christ comes to us and meets us incognito through them. We may be entertaining angels unawares.

Giving to the saints is itself a special gift. "If the righteousness of a man who gives to the poor [Ps. 112:9] endures forever, how much more will this be true of a man who gives to the saints. For the poor are obvious to all, but the saints are known only to the mind that can discern them, for they are servants of God who are constant in prayer and fasting, and who lead a pure life" (Ambrosiaster, On Paul's Epistles to the Corinthians; 2 Cor. 9:9).[65]

---

62. NTA 15:405; ACCS NT 6:317.
63. NTA 15:162; ACCS NT 6:316-17.
64. PG 82:192; ACCS NT 6:317.
65. CSEL 81:268-69; ACCS NT 7:281*.

## G. The Fatherless

It is too easy for us to make the assumption that the ancient Fathers would more likely be insensitive to those who are the seed of broken marriages, children of split-up families, the children of those who have abused covenant sexual fidelity. The historical fact is this: The ancient Christian teachers were actively engaged in ministries to children bereft of fathers long before Victorian orphanages existed. When we learn of their abiding concern for lost children we are surprised. This is counter-intuitive because our intuition is corrupted by the pretensions of modernity so as to imagine that all good things must be recent.

### 1. The Plight of the Fatherless

The fatherless lack someone who was intended to be in their lives. They lack a kind hand to guide and point the way, to look ahead, and make provisions. They lack a father, and everything that implies. They lack resources. They learn to do without. They do with less love, less instruction, less discipline, less food, less money, less joy. They are less able to defend themselves, to provide for their own needs, to hold steady through periods of crisis. The smaller they are as children, the more they need the protection and guidance of a good father. The fatherless are those who lack someone to provide for and guide them and prevent harm coming to them.

The faithful community is called especially to care for these most vulnerable people who have little or no resources, no family to lean upon, no backup wealth, no place in the world. Lacking the protection parents bring, they need help.

### 2. The Pattern

According to the early Christian writers, the pattern in the Christian life for caring for the fatherless is most fully revealed in the Father-Son relationship reflected in the holy trinity. The Father has sent the Son on a lengthy and dangerous mission: to die for the sins of humanity. The eternal Son has a human mother, but no biological father. The incarnate Son knows by experience what it means to be lacking in status in this world, lacking in power, lacking in resources, lacking in food, lacking in reliable friends, indeed lacking a place in the world. This very incarnate Son himself reached out for those who were most vulnerable and least able to defend themselves.

The ancient Christian writers pondered fatherlessness, on doing without, on being alone in the world, on learning obedience through suffering. They meditated deeply on the mystery of fatherhood, both human and divine, and the risks of sonship in a fallen world — all this in the light of the incarnation and crucifixion.

### 3. Without a Father

The needs of the neediest are epitomized in the fatherless, the widow, and the single mother. Women and children who do not have protection, who lack husbands and fathers, are among those most vulnerable (Exod. 22:22; Deut. 10:18). Why are men so important? They are assigned by nature a protective role, without which both the mate and the offspring suffer. They are best fitted to find provisions for the family, protect from danger, and radiate hope and love in a safe environment.

Child without father and mother without husband are due special consideration and protection by the caring community. So it has been since the Day of Pentecost. They have no protector, no caregiver, no ablebodied physical father there to defend them against abuse. Societies, both ancient and modern, can be cruel to the defenseless.

In early Christianity, true religious character is measured by how a community cares for the orphan and the widow. To offer worship acceptable to God is to first meet the needs of orphans and widows (Jas. 1:27).

The fatherless are especially vulnerable to being overpowered by any who wish to exercise arbitrary power. The law seeks to protect the fatherless, but always does so imperfectly, and without the personal touch. Hence they may be forced to beg for food (Ps. 109:9-10). They are forever subject to abuse and acts of violence (Job 22:9). At times they were treated as property to be gambled for (Job 6:27). The fatherless may suffer the loss of their homes, their dignity, their just due (Prov. 23:10; Job 24:3).

## 4. Without Inheritance

The law of Israel sought to be especially protective of the fatherless who did not have a home, and hence did not have a visible inheritance (Lam. 5:2-3). The people of Israel had themselves been homeless, without inheritance, and slaves in Egypt. This revealed to them how they should treat those without inheritance.

On this premise, the law required that the fatherless should be cared for so they would be able to eat and be satisfied (Deut. 14:29). The righteous Job did not keep his bread for himself, but shared it with the fatherless (Job 31:16). The law required that no one afflict any fatherless child (Exod. 22:22). The law required that the tithe be brought in due season so that the needs of the fatherless would be provided by the people of God (Isa. 1:17). The law guaranteed that ancient boundary stones not be removed so as to allow others to take advantage of the property of the fatherless, the defenseless (Prov. 23:10).

The prophets pronounced woe upon those who rob the fatherless (Isa. 10:1), who deprive the poor of their rights, who oppress the people, who make widows their prey. Jesus came to promise his disciples that they would not be orphans (John 14:18), that they would have an inheritance.

## 5. Mending the Broken Father-Relation

Note in biblical texts how tragic is the *absence* of the father. The father is the one who protects and provides. Fewer abuses happen when the conscientious father is present. When the father is not present he does not provide, and that leaves the child and the mother more vulnerable. The government cannot substitute sufficiently. So it is today when the father is absent from accountability in the family.

John Chrysostom explained how our salvation is analogous to an orphan being adopted: "God has done the same as if a person were to take an orphan who had been carried away by savages into their own country, and not only to free him from captivity but become a kind father to him and raise him to a very great dignity. This is what has happened in our case" (Chrysostom, Homilies on Romans 11; Rom. 6:18).[66]

66. NPNF 1 11:412-13; ACCS NT 6:170*.

The decisive analogy of the prodigal son shows this: I am a child of God the father. Because of my self-assertive sin, I have lost my inheritance. Hence like a fatherless child, I go abroad and wander in the far country. Only belatedly do I decide to return to my father's house, but even then only hoping to be accepted as a servant. My father receives me as a son, and welcomes me back into the family. The redeemed life is like this. I am like a fatherless child who has just been received by a caring Father and offered a great inheritance that rust cannot corrupt nor thieves break in and steal.

## H. Protecting the Widow

Along with the fatherless, the widow is frequently cited in scripture as among the most needy. Both Old Testament law and evangelical charity are especially attentive to the widow.

Listen carefully to the ancient Christian writers, and you will discover the richness of classic Christian reflection on the care of the widow. It comes to more than a comforting glance or a safety net.

### 1. The Vulnerability of the Widow

It is a premise of scripture that a woman alone is more vulnerable to abuse than a man. She is more at risk than the woman who enjoys the protection of a caring husband. The lonely woman is due the protection of strong and caring people, both men and women, who may be better able to defend their vital interests than they by themselves.

Jesus decried the hypocrisy of those who make long prayers, yet devour widows' houses (Mark 12:38-40). According to an early commentary on Matthew, the Opus Imperfectum, Jesus described the psychological dynamics of intimidation by those who would take advantage of widows, as "imposters of holiness," who would "loiter especially with widowed ladies for two reasons. First, because a woman under the protection of a man is less able to be exploited, and less subject to deception. Lacking that protection, widows are in a position to be more easily intimidated. Second, they more easily involve themselves in things not subject to anyone else's authority, so as to make them more vulnerable to deceivers. Jesus here confronts the priests and warns Christian leaders against these temptations" (Opus Imperfectum in Matthaeum, Homily 44; Matt. 23:12).[67]

## 2. The Law and the Widow

The Mosaic Law offered special provisions to protect the needy widow (Lev. 22:13; Deut. 14:28-29). The people must not pervert or circumvent the justice due to a widow (Deut. 27:19). They are to plead for the widow's case (Isa. 1:17), and not take advantage of her vulnerabilities (Exod. 22:22; Deut. 24:17).

On the care of widows, the law became very specific: Do not forget to invite the widow to the feast (Deut. 16:14). Do not forget to leave gleanings in the field (24:19). When you are harvesting olives or grapes, leave something for the widow (14:28). This is what people do if they have been given their land and their very breath by God: "If you do not oppress the alien, the fatherless, or the widow, . . . then I will let you live in this place, in the land I gave your forefathers" (Jer. 7:6, NIV). This reflects the pattern of God who is the defender of widows and father to the fatherless.

Joseph was the patriarchal prototype of one who provided for the widows and fatherless. He administered the gathering of grain in good times and the storing of it through uncertain times. Ephrem the Syrian pointed to the prudent and generous character of Joseph: "Then at the end of the good years, when those of famine came, Joseph took special care of the orphans, widows and every needy person in Egypt so that there was no anxiety in Egypt" (Ephrem, Commentary on Genesis 36.1; Gen. 41:55).[68] Joseph had a long-range plan to help the defenseless in times of urgent need.

## 3. The Prophets' Call to Defend the Widow

A prophetic warning: Those who take advantage of the widow will learn that the widow's cry will come before the Lord and the Lord will hear her and his anger be aroused (Exod. 22:23-24). Yahweh will judge oppressors.

67. PG 56:880; ACCS NT 1b:172*.
68. FC 91:188; ACCS OT 2:272.

He offers the oppressed his special care and favor (Mal. 3:5; Isa. 1:17; Ps. 94:6).

Prophets frequently protested the bad treatment of widows. Isaiah warned against viewing widows as prey, robbing the fatherless, depriving the poor of their rights, or withholding justice from the oppressed (Isa. 10:2). He castigated those who loved bribes more than the defense of the widow and the fatherless (1:23). The wisdom literature continues the same theme. Job answered his accusers: "If I have . . . let the eyes of the widow grow weary" or "if I have seen anyone perishing for lack of clothing," or "if I have raised my hand against the fatherless," then "let my arm fall from the shoulder, let it be broken off at the joint" (Job 31:16-22, NIV). Job's great generosity caused the widow's heart to sing (29:13).

### 4. The Widow in the New Testament Church

This plea for the cause of widows is sustained throughout the New Testament. In 1 Timothy 5:9 we learn of a list of widows who were being supported by gifts of believers. The godly widow was "well attested for her good deeds, as one who has brought up children, shown hospitality, washed the feet of the saints, relieved the afflicted, and devoted herself to doing good in every way" (5:10, RSV).

The church herself is something like a widow, vulnerable to worldly vicissitudes, yet specially cared for by God. "The church is called Christ's widow, because she is stripped of all worldly help and places her hope solely in the Lord. Like a widow, she suffers the shameful actions of evil men, the most cruel plundering of the wicked. Like a woman deprived of a husband's aid, she always grieves and is always worn out, yet she enjoys the unchanging steadfastness of a most chaste mind. . . . She is called a widow because she is bereft of worldly protection and has placed her hope in her heavenly Bridegroom, who has transformed her darkness into beauty, her error into uprightness, her abrasiveness into devotion, and her frailty into total constancy" (Cassiodorus, Explanation of the Psalms 131.15; 1 Tim. 5:5).[69]

The church became a surrogate family for the worthy widow without family (1 Tim. 5:16). She was not to be overlooked in the daily distribution of food (Acts 6:1). Jerome wrote: "A widow who has ceased to have a hus-

---

69. ACWCa 53:329; ACCS NT 9:198*.

band to please, and who in the apostle's language is a 'widow indeed,' needs nothing more than perseverance. Remembering past enjoyments, she knows what gave her pleasure and what she has now lost" (Jerome, Letters 54.7; 1 Tim. 5:5).[70]

## 5. The Family's Duty in Protecting the Widow

The family of the widow has first responsibility to care for their own kin: "It is the children and grandchildren who should learn their religious duties, namely, to care for widowed forebears" (Theodore of Mopsuestia, Commentary on 1 Timothy; 1 Tim. 5:4).[71]

This is a clear test of family cohesion and accountability: "If while instructing others, someone neglects his own family, though he has greater capacities and a higher obligation to benefit those nearby, will it not be said: 'Aha! These so-called Christians show some kind of affection! They neglect their own relatives! He is worse than an infidel.' Thus one who has no will to benefit those far away has even less will to benefit those nearer. What is meant is this: The law of God and of nature is violated by him who does not provide for his own family" (Chrysostom, Homilies on 1 Timothy 14; 1 Tim. 5:8).[72]

## I. The Gifts and Hospitality of True Widowhood

Women proved themselves to be exceptionally courageous in early Christianity: "The title of true widow is not a title of calamity but of honor, even of the greatest honor," wrote Chrysostom. "'Heavens,' cried a sophist teacher, 'what women there are among the Christians!' Great is the admiration and praise enjoyed by widowhood not only among ourselves but also among those who are alien to the church" (Chrysostom, Letter to a Young Widow 2; 1 Tim. 5:10c).[73]

70. NPNF 2 6:104-5; ACCS NT 9:197*.
71. TEM 2:155-56; ACCS NT 9:197.
72. NPNF 1 13:453*; ACCS NT 9:199*.
73. NPNF 1 9:122*; ACCS NT 9:201*.

## 1. The True Widow

In writing to Timothy, Paul makes a distinction between three categories of widows: Those who have children and grandchildren who can provide for them; younger widows who may remarry; and what he calls "real widows" (1 Tim. 5:5, RSV). By "real widows" (or those who are "widows indeed," KJV) he means those living a responsible life without a family to support them, without protection, unable to help their children. Provided they have a proven character of caregiving, these "true widows" are especially noted on the list of widows for whom the church takes major responsibilities as needed (5:3-16).

Chrysostom described the "true widow" in this way: "She is most truly a widow who has lost not only the consolation of a husband, but that arising from children, yet she has God in the place of all this human emptiness" (Chrysostom, Homilies on 1 Timothy 13; 1 Tim. 5:5).[74] The true widow has set her heart on God (1 Tim. 5:5). "The loss of a husband does not constitute a true widow, but rather patience, with chastity and distance from all temptations. Such widows Paul justly bids us honor, and indeed support. For they need support, being left desolate and having no husband to stand up for them" (Chrysostom, Homilies on 1 Timothy 13; 1 Tim. 5:3).[75] The Bible holds the widow in high esteem as a model of faith for others: "Being aware of all this, the blessed Paul said, 'Let not widows be enrolled under threescore years of age.' And even after this great qualification of age he does not permit her to be ranked in this sacred society but mentions some additional requisites. She must be 'well reported of for good works, if she has brought up children, if she has lodged strangers, if she has washed the saints' feet, if she has relieved the afflicted, if she has diligently followed every good work.' Heavens! What testing and scrutiny! How much virtue does he demand from the widow! How precisely does he define it! He would not have done this had he not intended to entrust to her a position of honor and dignity" (Chrysostom, Letter to a Young Widow 2; 1 Tim. 5:10c).[76]

Ambrose described the "true widow" as one who is "distinguished by virtue. It is not I who give this command but the apostle. I am not the only

---

74. NPNF 1 13:450-51*; ACCS NT 9:197*.
75. NPNF 1 13:450*; ACCS NT 9:196*.
76. NPNF 1 9:122*; ACCS NT 9:201*.

person to do them honor, but the teacher of the Gentiles did so first when he said, 'Honor widows that are widows indeed. But if any widow has children or nephews, let her first learn to govern her own house and to take care of her parents.' Thus we encourage every inclination of affection in a widow to love her children and fulfill her duty to her family" (Ambrose, Concerning Widows 2.7; 1 Tim. 5:3).[77]

Women must be braced against potentially deceptive communications with those who would take advantage of them: "Paul speaks of idle persons and busybodies who go from house to house calling on married women. They display an unblushing effrontery greater than that of an actor on a stage. Cast them away from you as you would the plague. For 'evil communications corrupt good manners' [1 Cor. 15:33]. Do not encourage the lowest level of appetites. Such deceivers may tempt them, saying, 'My dear creature, make the best of your advantages, and live while life is yours,' and, 'Surely you are not laying up money for your children.' Do not give slack to wine and wantonness" (Jerome, Letters 22.29; 1 Tim. 5:13).[78]

### 2. The Widow's Prayer for Others

Widows have a special calling to intercessory prayer. All laity are called to a ministry of intercession, but the godly widow is in a position to demonstrate this ministry most powerfully, according to Augustine: "When the Lord exhorted us to pray always and not to faint [cf. Luke 18:1-5], he told of the widow whose continuous appeal brought a wicked and impious judge, who scorned both God and man, to hear her cause. From this it can be easily understood how widows, beyond all others, have the duty of applying themselves to prayer, since an example was taken from widows to encourage us all to develop a love of prayer. But in a practice of such importance, what characteristic of widows is singled out? Their very poverty and desolation. Therefore, insofar as every soul understands that it is poor and desolate in this world, as long as it is absent from the Lord [cf. 2 Cor. 5:6], it surely commends its widowhood, so to speak, to God its defender, with continual and most earnest prayer" (Augustine, Letters 130.15.29-30; 1 Tim. 5:5).[79] So we see

---

77. NPNF 2 10:392; ACCS NT 9:196*.
78. NPNF 2 6:35*; ACCS NT 9:202-3*.
79. FC 18:400; ACCS NT 9:197-98.

that scripture and tradition do not bemoan the widow's plight, but view it as a special gift and vocation from God.

In speaking of "real widows" Paul was also thinking of those women who now "have a greater opportunity of pleasing God, because all their chains are now loosened. There is no one to hold them fast, no one to compel them to drag their chains after them. They are separated from their husband but are united to God. They do not have a husband for a companion, but they have their Lord" (Chrysostom, Homilies on 1 Thessalonians 6; 1 Tim. 5:5).[80] Real widows have special opportunities, fewer family responsibilities, and are given special gifts of intercession and service.

### 3. The Widow's Hospitality

The widow is also called to a quiet, yet active, ministry of hospitality: "Observe, the hospitality here spoken of is not merely a friendly reception but one given with zeal and alacrity, with readiness, and going about it as if one were receiving Christ himself" (Chrysostom, Homilies on 1 Timothy 14; 1 Tim. 5:10a).[81]

Theodoret commented: "In emphasizing hospitality and the care of the saints as important qualifications for the widow, Paul's goal is not to focus on a certain quantity of virtuous activity for her, but rather on her quality of mind" (Theodoret, Interpretation of the First Letter to Timothy; 1 Tim. 5:10b).[82]

The special gifts of the widow set an example for the serving ministry of the whole church. All the faithful share in the same ministry of washing the feet of the saints, for example, but she shows the others how, according to Origen: "It is possible that even one who is a saint needs the washing of feet, since even the widow who is enrolled in the list of widows is examined, along with her other good works, especially about this, 'If she has washed the feet of saints.' . . . Consequently, all the faithful are obliged to do this in whatever station of life they happen to be, whether bishops and presbyters, whom one might think to be in ecclesiastical prominence, or even those in other positions of honor in the world — they too, like the

---

80. NPNF 1 13:351*; ACCS NT 9:197*.
81. NPNF 1 13:454; ACCS NT 9:201.
82. PG 82:819A-20A; ACCS NT 9:201*.

master, come to wash the feet of the believing servant, and parents the feet of their son" (Origen, Commentary on John 32.131-33; 1 Tim. 5:10b).[83]

## 4. The Disposition of Giving Seen in the Widow's Gift

It was a widow who became, for Jesus, a prototype of the fullest measure of generosity. It is written that Jesus "sat down opposite the treasury, and watched the multitude putting money into the treasury. Many rich people put in large sums. And a poor widow came, and put in two copper coins, which make a penny. And he called his disciples to him, and said to them, 'Truly, I say to you, this poor widow has put in more than all those who are contributing to the treasury. For they all contributed out of their abundance; but she out of her poverty has put in everything she had, her whole living'" (Mark 12:41-44, RSV; cf. Luke 21:1-4).

The widow's gift was here measured not by quantity or weight or monetary value, but by the unfeigned goodwill by which it was offered. The Lord paid little attention to the paucity of her money, but only to the abundance of her motive and her generosity. The quantity of possessions does not count in the kingdom's audits. She gave all she had, as Jerome commented: "The poor widow cast only two pennies into the treasury; yet because she gave all she had it is said of her that she surpassed all the rich in offering gifts to God. Such gifts are valued not by their weight but by the good will with which they are offered" (Jerome, Letter 118.5 "To Julian"; Mark 12:41-44).[84]

It is not the quantity but the intention. "Which one is more worthy of the kingdom of heaven — Zacchaeus who gave half his goods to the poor, or the widow who gave two pennies?" asked Augustine. "Each will possess an equal share there. What is greater than that the same kingdom should be worth treasures to the rich man, and a cup of cold water to the poor?" (cf. Matt. 10:42) (Augustine, On the Psalms 112.3; Mark 12:43).[85]

All the faithful are similarly called to respond generously from the heart to the full extent of their means. "One cannot buy heavenly things with money," wrote John Chrysostom.

---

83. FC 89:367; ACCS NT 9:201*.
84. NPNF 2 6:223*; ACCS NT 2:177*.
85. Cetedoc 0283, 40.111.3.5; NPNF 1 8:547; ACCS NT 2:178*.

If money could purchase such things, then the woman who deposited the two small copper coins would have received nothing very large. But since it was not money but rather her intention that prevailed, that woman received everything because she displayed unfeigned faith. Therefore, let us not say that the kingdom may be bought with money. It is not bought with money, but rather with an unsullied intention that may manifest itself by means of money. So someone asks, is there no need for money? There is no need for money as such, but for a Christian disposition. If you have this, you will even be able to be received into the kingdom by freely offering two small copper coins. Without this disposition, one will not be able to do with ten thousand talents of gold the very thing that the two coins would do with pure intent. If you should have much and give less, you may have given alms in a certain sense, but not the same kind of alms that the widow gave. For you were not depositing it with the same kind of eagerness that characterized the widow. (Chrysostom, Homilies on Philippians; Mark 12:42)[86]

### 5. Giving Freely, Offering All

The widow in Jesus' parable shows that the intention of charity sanctifies the gift. Like everything else in the Gospel, the usual perspective is reversed, wrote Cyprian: "Look in the Gospel at the widow mindful of the heavenly commandments, doing good in the very middle of the pressures and hardships of poverty. She throws two mites that were her only possessions into the treasury. . . . She was a greatly blessed and glorious woman, who even before the judgment day merited to be praised by the voice of the Judge. Let the rich be ashamed of their sterility and their misfortunes. A poor widow is found with a great offering. Much that is given is offered to orphans and widows. But here we have as giver the very one who might justly be receiving" (Cyprian, Works and Almsgiving 15; Luke 21:1-4).[87] The pattern of offering oneself without reservation is the cross.

It may be vexing to the rich that the widow offered so little. But she possessed nothing more than what she offered. "This may perhaps irritate some among the rich. We will therefore address a few remarks to them.

86. TLG 2062.160, 62.290.40; cf. NPNF 1 5:251; ACCS NT 2:177*.
87. FC 36:241*; ACCS NT 3:316*.

You delight, O rich person, in the abundance of your possessions," wrote Cyril of Alexandria. "You do not offer in proportion to your means. What you give, you will never miss. So out of a great abundance, you give little. The woman offered two farthings, but she possessed nothing more than what she offered. She had nothing left. With empty hand but a hand bountiful of the little she possessed, she went away from the treasury" (Cyril of Alexandria, Commentary on Luke, Homily 138; Luke 21:1-4).[88]

Jerome joked: "There is an old saying that a tightwad lacks as much what he has as what he has not. One may have a whole world of wealth, another not a single scrap. Let each one live 'as having nothing and yet possessing all' [2 Cor. 6:10]" (Jerome, Letter 53.11 "To Paulinus"; Mark 12:44a).[89]

## 6. The Disposition of Good Will in Giving

Giving is a matter of the heart. If you give all of your possessions to the poor, even surrender your body to the flames, but do it without love, you gain nothing (1 Cor. 13:3). "When alms are given, we attend to nothing else except the disposition required. And if you say that money is needed, and houses and clothes and shoes, read those words of Christ, which he spoke concerning the widow, and stop being anxious. For even if you are extremely poor, and among those that beg, if you cast in your two small coins, you have done all in your power. Though you offer only a barley cake, having only this, you will have arrived at the heart of the matter" (Chrysostom, The Gospel of Matthew 52.5; Mark 12:43).[90] The pattern of God's own giving is to give all out of love.

A good will alone is sufficient for readiness for the kingdom (Mark 12:43). According to Caesarius of Arles, "Those who possess good will have everything. This alone can be sufficient even if there are no other resources. But if it is lacking, whatever they possess will profit nothing. If this will is present, it alone suffices, but everything else avails nothing if charity alone is lacking" (cf. 1 Cor. 13:3) (Caesarius of Arles, Sermons 182.3; Mark 12:43).[91]

88. CGSL 552**; ACCS NT 3:316*.
89. Cetedoc 0620, 53.54.11.464.17; NPNF 2 6:102**; ACCS NT 2:178.
90. TLG 2062.152, 58.523.19; NPNF 1 10:324*; ACCS NT 2:178.
91. Cetedoc 1008, 104.182.3.42; FC 47:470*; ACCS NT 2:178*.

Temporal acts have eternal consequences. Unnoticed deeds may embody noteworthy motives. Bede succinctly grasped the psychology of true giving: "The treasure in one's heart is the intention of the thought, from which the searcher of hearts judges the outcome. Hence it quite frequently occurs that some persons perform good deeds of minor importance with a greater reward of heavenly grace. This is because it is the intention in their hearts to accomplish a greater good if they could. Others, though they display greater works of virtue, are allotted smaller favors from the Lord on account of the indifference in their lukewarm hearts. The deed of the widow who contributed two copper coins to the temple was preferred to the large contributions of those who were rich by the One who weighs what is within our hearts" (Bede the Venerable, Homilies on the Gospels, Homily 2.25; Mark 12:43).[92] Begin even the smallest work of mercy with the same motive that shaped God's own self-giving on the cross.

### 7. Having Nothing, Possessing All

One having nothing may possess all. One having much may lack the condition of truly possessing anything. The poor widow was incomparably rich. "That precious poverty of hers was rich in the mystery of faith. So are the two coins that the Samaritan of the Gospels left at the inn to care for the wounds of the man who had fallen among robbers [Luke 10:35]. Mystically representing the church, the widow thought it right to put into the sacred treasury the gift with which the wounds of the poor are healed and the hunger of wayfarers is satisfied" (Ambrose, Letters to Laymen 84 "To Irenaeus"; Luke 21:1-4).[93] With what remedy are the wounds of the poor relieved? Finally, God's own incomparable self-giving love, as seen on the cross.

Whatever we have in this life is given us only for a short time. All can learn from the widow who freely gave all. Anyone can invest with the Lord all that one possesses. The only inhibition is in the will. Paulinus called for such an investment:

We have been entrusted with the administration and use of temporal wealth for the common good, not with the everlasting ownership of

92. Cetedoc 1367, 2.25.121; CSBH 2:259*; ACCS NT 2:178*.
93. FC 26:469-70**; ACCS NT 3:316.

private property. If you accept the fact that ownership on earth is only fleeting and for a time, then you may be ready for eternal possessions in heaven. Call to mind the widow who forgot herself in her concern for the poor and, thinking only of the life to come, gave away all her means of subsistence. To this the final judge himself bears witness. Others, he says, have given of their superfluous wealth. But she, possessed of only two small coins and more needy perhaps than many of the poor — though in spiritual riches she surpassed all the wealthy — she thought only of the world to come, and had such a longing for heavenly treasure that she gave away, all at once, whatever she had that was derived from the earth and was destined to return there. Let us then invest with the Lord what he has given us, for we have nothing that does not come from him. We are dependent upon him for our very existence. (Paulinus of Nola, Letters 34, 2-4; Mark 12:44b)[94]

The widow understood this. "She had but a grain of mustard seed, but she put her leaven in the measures of flour" (Jerome, Letter 54.17 "To Furia"; Mark 12:42).[95]

### J. Overview of Good Works: Feeding, Quenching, Welcoming, Clothing, Relieving, and Visiting

The parable of the last judgment serves as the bridge into Part Two, where we will examine the particular good works especially cited by Jesus as exemplary.

This is why we focus on the most concise overview in scripture of faith's characteristic good works. It is set forth by Jesus in Matthew 25 — the parable of the sheep and the goats at the last judgment. It is from this key text that the Fathers derived a common, familiar, and integrated way of ordering the many-sided subject of good works.

Thesis: Our final judgment *at the end of time* is defined in relation to the way we treated those *in time* who came to us with real needs.

---

94. JF B 132-33; CSEL 29:305-6; ACCS NT 2:179*.
95. LCLJ 263*; Cetedoc 0620, 54.54.17.484.18; cf. NPNF 2 6:108; ACCS NT 2:177.

## 1. The Revelation of the Last Day

The scene is the last day. God knew from the outset what would happen on the last day, because God's relation with time is radically different from ours, seeing all moments in eternal simultaneity. We are creatures of time. God is the creator of time. God knows all time now. God's relation with time is characterized by full knowledge of every moment of time — past, present, and future. Each moment is, from God's point of view, now. God has no difficulty foreseeing the end, because for God it is already viewed as now, although for us it is yet in the future.

On the last day we will see clearly what we now see through a glass darkly. It is only then that we will know "how great is the Lord's bond of love for humanity, and has been from the beginning." In God's foreknowledge of our choices, he has already prepared a place for us. "He did not say 'take' but 'inherit' as one's own. What is the Father's is yours, as if set aside for you from the first. 'For before you were,' he says, 'these things had been prepared and made ready for you, because I knew you would be such as you are'" (Chrysostom, The Gospel of Matthew, Homily 79.2; Matt. 25:34).[96] Time is viewed in the kingdom from the end to the beginning, with the cross at the center.

We will not know our eternal destiny until judgment day, and even then we are likely to be quite surprised. For within time, "between the righteous and the wicked there is no apparent difference. Even as in wintertime you cannot tell the healthy trees apart from the withered trees but in the beautiful springtime you can easily tell the difference, so too each person, according to the workings of his faith, will be exposed. The wicked will not have any leaves or show any fruit, but the righteous will be clothed with the leaves of eternal life and adorned with the fruit of glory" (Opus Imperfectum in Matthaeum, Homily 54; Matt. 25:32-33).[97] Only on the last day will we know our destiny, and it will hinge mightily upon our treatment of "the least" as an expression of our faith.

---

96. PG 58:719; NPNF 1 10:476; ACCS NT 1b:232*.
97. PG 56:942; ACCS NT 1b:231*.

## 2. Our Own Choices Affect Our Eternal Destiny

To those who are not responsive to the neediest, the Lord "does not say they are cursed by the Father, for the Father had not laid a curse upon *them*, but only their own *works*. He does not say that the eternal fire is prepared only for you but 'for the devil and his angels.' 'I prepared the kingdom for you,' he says, 'but the fire I did not prepare for you but for the devil and his angels. But you have cast yourselves in it. You have imputed it to yourselves'" (Chrysostom, The Gospel of Matthew, Homily 79.2, italics added; Matt. 25:41-44).[98]

The sharp eye of John Chrysostom carefully noted this detail in the parable: "Note that the judgment is in effect made indirectly by their fellow servants. This has happened before, when the virgins are judged by the virgins [Matt. 25:1-13] and in the case of the drunken and gluttonous servant who was judged by the faithful servant. It happened once again in the case of the man who buried his talent, who was judged by the actions of those who produced more [25:14-30]. . . . This is said to bring them to the point of answering, 'When did we see you hungry?'" (Chrysostom, The Gospel of Matthew, Homily 79.2; Matt. 25:35-40).[99]

## 3. The Left and Right Hand of God

Each one has chosen his own destiny, exercising his own freedom. "He will justly place the righteous at his right hand, because they never knew the left side; he will justly place the wicked at the left, because they never wanted to know the right side" (Opus Imperfectum in Matthaeum, Homily 54; Matt. 25:32-33).[100] This means: Since the righteous have nothing to do with evil, they hardly know the left side (the proud and ungodly and self-centered), so it is just that they be placed on the right hand of God. The wicked voluntarily did not even want to know the good, the right side, so it is just that they be placed under judgment, at the left hand of God.

Both the unrighteous and the righteous are surprised at being judged by this criterion. The righteous do not keep a log or an account of

98. PG 58:719; NPNF 1 10:476; ACCS NT 1b:234.
99. PG 58:718-19; NPNF 1 10:476; ACCS NT 1b:232-33*.
100. PG 56:943; ACCS NT 1b:232.

their good works, or even remember them as good. Origen was prone to note details in the text, and here he pointed out that

> He could have said to the *unrighteous,* "I was sick, and you did not visit me; I was in prison, and you did not come to me." Instead he abbreviated his discourse and compressed both phrases into one, saying, "I was sick and in prison, and you did not visit me," for it was proper for a merciful judge to be attentive to their good deeds, but to skim over their evil deeds. The *righteous,* however, *dwell on each word,* saying, "When did we see you hungry, and feed you; or thirsty, and give you drink?" And "when did we see you a stranger, and take you in; or naked, and clothe you?" Or "when did we see you sick or in prison, and come to you?" It is characteristic of the righteous, out of humility, to make light of each of their good deeds as they are held up to them. It is as though to the Lord's words, "This, that and the other good thing you did to me," they disavowingly reply, "Neither this, that nor the other thing did we do to you." But the *unrighteous* do not treat each opportunity singularly. They are quick to say, "When did we see you hungry, or thirsty, or a stranger, or naked, or sick or in prison, and did not minister to you, for we ministered the word to you," lumping all acts together, as if to give a clue that it might appear worse for them if they had enumerated them one by one. For it is characteristic of the ungodly to mention their faults, by way of excuse, as being either non-existent or few and far between. (Origen, Commentary on Matthew 73, italics added; Matt. 25:41-44)[101]

God's leniency is seen in the fact that he first addresses those on his right hand — but why the right hand first? Again every tiny detail in the parable is noticed by the Fathers, for all things in scripture have the purpose of edification: "Why will he not address first those at his left? Because God is always more willing to praise than to denounce. For he gives good things to those who are good because he is good, in line with his original intention. But to those who are bad, because he is a judge, he reluctantly gives bad things, even contrary to his original intention for creatures. . . . Indeed, the kingdom of heaven has not been created according to what human righteousness deserves but according to what God's power prepares.

101. GCSO 10.2:173; ACCS NT 1b:234-35*.

'I was hungry, and you gave me food'" (Opus Imperfectum in Matthaeum, Homily 54; Matt. 25:34).[102]

Ponder this: The final judgment of sin is against God's original will, because his original will is that all not fall. God's reluctance to judge is due to his original will to create and redeem. But God's righteous willing *in consequence of the history* of sin calls for judgment of those whose hearts are hardened, and mercy toward those whose hearts are turned toward the good. This turning is seen in works of love — feeding, clothing, visiting.

Sheep and goats refer to whom? "The sheep signify righteous people by reason of their gentleness, because they harm no one, and by reason of their patience, because when they are harmed by others, they bear it without resistance. He refers to sinners as goats, however, because these vices characterize goats: capriciousness toward other animals, pride and belligerence" (Opus Imperfectum in Matthaeum, Homily 54; Matt. 25:32-33).[103]

### 4. Without Excuse

The unrighteous have no excuse, Chrysostom taught, for they have seen the Lord hungry yet neglected to offer food. "'For I was hungry, and you gave me no food.' When you meet your enemy, should not his very suffering be enough to overcome your resistance to being merciful? And what about his hunger, cold, chains, nakedness, and sickness? What about his homelessness? Are not these sufferings sufficient to overcome even your alienation? But you did not do these things even for a friend, much less a foe. You could have at once befriended and done good. Even when you see a dog hungry you feel sympathy. But when you see the Lord hungry, you ignore it. You are left without excuse" (Chrysostom, The Gospel of Matthew, Homily 79.2; Matt. 25:41-44).[104]

They were judged more for what they omitted than for what they did, more for sins of omission than commission. "Neither were they condemned because of the active wrong they *did*, nor did the Lord say to them, 'Depart from me, you wicked, because you committed murder or adultery or theft.' But instead: because I was hungry and thirsty in my ser-

---

102. PG 56:943; ACCS NT 1b:232*.
103. PG 56:942; ACCS NT 231-32.
104. PG 58:719-20; NPNF 1 10:476; ACCS NT 1b:234*.

vants, and *you did not* minister to me" (Epiphanius the Latin, Interpretation of the Gospels 38, italics added; Matt. 25:45-46).[105] Omission and negligence turn into a witness against the will.

They are rejected, according to the Opus Imperfectum, "who did not
clothe the naked either by teaching justice or by baptizing in Christ; who
did not welcome strangers in the world through the Word or introduce
them into the household of faith; who did not heal the sick; who did not
lead out, through penance, those who were sitting in the prison of ungodliness. If it is ungodly not to offer material things to bodies that cannot live
forever, can you imagine how ungodly it is not to administer spiritual gifts
to souls in danger but who could live eternally with God if only these gifts
were made available to them?" (Opus Imperfectum in Matthaeum, Homily
54; Matt. 25:41-44).[106]

### 5. The Hungering, Thirsting, Shivering, Homelessness, Infirmity, and Imprisonment of God the Son

Who will be our judge on the last day? God? Yes, but more specifically the
incarnate Lord who has become man — one who has fully engaged in our
human condition as Son of Man. He will be our judge in the last judgment.
But: "How can he be the Son of man when he is God and will come to
judge all nations?" asked Epiphanius.

> He is the Son of man because he appeared on earth as a man and was
> persecuted as a man. Therefore this person who they said was a man
> will raise all nations from the dead and judge every person according
> to his works. Every race on earth will see him, even those who rejected
> him, and those who despised him as a man. They will see him then, but
> not everyone in the same way. Some will see him in punishment and
> others in heavenly blessedness [Dan. 12:2]. All nations will be gathered
> together by the angels. The plan has been working itself out from the
> foundation of the world, beginning first with Adam and Eve down to
> the last person on earth — among any who have experienced birth.
> "And he will separate them one from another as a shepherd separates

105. PL *Suppl.* 3:902; ACCS NT 1b:235.
106. PG 56:946; ACCS NT 1b:235*.

the sheep from the goats." He, our Lord, who knows our thoughts, who foresees all human works and knows how to judge righteously, will separate them according to the merits of each person, as a shepherd separates the sheep from the goats. (Epiphanius the Latin, Interpretation of the Gospels 38; Matt. 25:32-33)[107]

God the Son is said to "hunger" in the form of human hunger and "thirst" in the form of human thirst. At this point Epiphanius wondered:

> How does our Lord hunger and thirst? Is he who made everything in heaven and on earth, who oversees the angels in heaven and every nation and race on earth, who needs nothing that belongs to the earth since he is unfailing in his own nature — is this one naked? It is incredible to believe such a thing. Yet what must be confessed is easy to believe. For *the Lord hungers not in his own nature but in his saints;* the Lord thirsts not in his own nature but in his poor. The Lord who clothes everyone is not naked in his own nature but in his servants. The Lord who is able to heal all sicknesses and has already destroyed death itself is not diseased in his own nature but in his servants. Our Lord, the one who can liberate every person, is not in prison in his own nature, but in his saints. Therefore, you see, my most beloved, that the saints are not alone. They suffer all these things because of the Lord. In the same way, because of the saints the Lord suffers all these things with them. (Epiphanius the Latin, Interpretation of the Gospels 38, italics added; Matt. 25:35-40)[108]

God does not hunger as the Godhead but as the embodied, incarnate Lord. It is the Son who hungers and thirsts, and has no place to lay his head.

Not only is the Son hungry, but thirsty and in need of a place to stay: "This can also be said of teachers who gave the food of learning to those *hungry* for righteousness, so they might be fed and grow healthy in good actions; who administered the drink of truth to those *thirsty* for the knowledge of God. Teaching in the Word, they certainly fed them and also gave to drink, baptizing in the Holy Spirit those who are strangers in the world. For all souls are truly *strangers* on this earth who can say, 'For I am your passing

---

107. PL *Suppl.* 3:899; ACCS NT 1b:231*.
108. PL *Suppl.* 3:900-901; ACCS NT 1b:234*.

guest, a sojourner, like all my fathers' [Ps. 39:12 (38:13 LXX)]. Preaching the word of faith, they welcome souls from the spreading of error and make them fellow citizens and family members of the saints" (Opus Imperfectum in Matthaeum, Homily 54, italics added; Matt. 25:35-40).[109]

## 6. Summing Up the Poverty Motif

On the road toward his own martyrdom, Polycarp summarized the good works of faith in his letter to the church at Philippi: "Be compassionate and merciful toward everyone, turning back the sheep that have gone astray, visiting the sick, not neglecting a widow or an orphan or a poor man, but providing always for that which is honorable in the sight of God and of men" (Polycarp, Epistle to the Philippians 6; 2 Cor. 8:21).[110]

In the next section we will explore each of these discrete and characteristic good works. Having now discussed the overarching need to serve the poor, the widow, and fatherless, we now turn to specific good works of saving faith cited in Jesus' parable: feeding the hungry, assuaging thirst, welcoming the stranger, clothing the naked, offering shelter for refugees, displaced persons, and the homeless, and visiting the sick.

109. PG 56:944; ACCS NT 1b:233.
110. AF 97; ACCS NT 7:276*

## PART TWO

# FOOD AND HOSPITALITY

*The Good Works of Saving Faith: "You Relieved My Suffering"*

The traditional sequence for considering the order of good works is embedded textually in Jesus' parable of the sheep and the goats. We will consider faith's typical acts in this familiar scriptural sequence:

Feeding the Hungry: "You Gave Me Food"
Giving Drink to the Thirsty: "You Gave Me Drink"
Welcoming the Stranger: "You Welcomed Me"
Clothing the Naked: "You Clothed Me"
Visiting the Sick: "You Visited Me"
Visiting Those in Prison: "You Remembered Me"

First on this agenda: food and hospitality.
Everyone is interested in food. It is a daily need. It is a daily joy.

## A. Feeding the Hungry: "You Gave Me Food"

The churches in classical Christianity were actively engaged in organized food relief long before modern relief efforts. As modern observers, we do not expect the ancient Christian teachers to be all that engaged in such mundane matters as food. They are expected to be focused only on "spiritual matters," not bread for children. They would be surprised that we are surprised that they were steadily concerned with reliable provisions of food for the hungry.

## 1. Feeding as the First Good Work

The first good work is feeding the hungry. For who can live a life of any sort without food? And whose responsibility is it to feed those who have no food under conditions of scarcity?

Jesus said: "I was hungry, and you fed me" (Matt. 25:31-46, TEV). Listen closely to the Fathers and you will discover how classic Christianity understood food relief. The pattern for feeding the hungry in the Christian life is Jesus' own feeding them, as seen in the miracle stories of the New Testament.

Everyone knows how it feels to be hungry. We will first consider how and why God made our bodies to hunger, and only then the calling to feed the hungry as the precondition of any other bodily good.

## 2. God Made Our Bodies to Hunger

It is not an embarrassment to God that our bodies get hungry. This is how we are made as embodied souls. To be a body is to face potential hunger. So it has been from the days of Eden when Adam was given a task of gardening.

There is a telling moment of the Gospel narrative where the Lord was "unwilling to send them away hungry" (Matt. 15:32, RSV). On this little phrase Theodore of Heraclea reasoned: "Christ understood the weakness of our nature and that we require food for the health of our bodies. He makes preparation even for this, that it might be evident that *he is concerned not only to care for our souls but for our bodies as well.* For he himself is the Creator of both soul and body" (Theodore of Heraclea, Fragment 97; Matt. 15:32).[1] The Giver of the body-soul interface understands what the body needs. The incarnate Lord himself understood hunger, being himself a body.

Physical food is needed for physical nurture. Spiritual food is needed for spiritual nurture. Gregory of Nyssa explored their relationship: "The

---

1. MKGK 83; ACCS NT 1b:34*.

divine apostle also, in calling the Lord 'spiritual food and drink,' suggests that he knows that human nature is not simple, but that there is an intelligible part mixed with a sensual part and that a particular type of nurture is needed for each of the elements in us — *sensible food* to strengthen our bodies and *spiritual food* for the well-being of our souls" (Gregory of Nyssa, On Perfection, italics added; 1 Cor. 10:3).[2] Lacking either of the two kinds of food, body-soul health cannot prosper.

Jesus spoke frequently of food. His messianic mission sharply reinterpreted the food laws of ancient Israel. Eating is viewed in relation to the new law of love. John Chrysostom reflected on the narrative when the disciples plucked grain on the Sabbath: "At that time Jesus went through the grain fields on the Sabbath; his disciples were hungry, and they began to pluck heads of grain and to eat" (Matt. 12:1, RSV). Jesus "never broke the law without adequate cause, and always by giving a reasonable justification. His purpose in doing so was to bring the old law to an end, yet not in a defiant manner," wrote Chrysostom. "His appeal is to the necessity of nature in this case, since his disciples were hungry" (Chrysostom, The Gospel of Matthew, Homily 39.1; Matt. 12:1).[3] To live, we must eat, according to the necessities of our bodily nature.

### 3. Christ Fed the Hungry — The Gospel Was Proclaimed through Food Offered

Repeatedly in scripture we see the picture of the servant Messiah feeding the hungry: "Lest the multitude weaken in the course of their worldly passage, in their workaday world, he wants now to feed them with his food and fortify them with his bread. In this way they can complete the formidable task of the entire journey, for the disciples were complaining that there was no bread in the desert. Indeed, they had previously imbibed the lesson that nothing is impossible with God. But what is signified by the events to come exceeds the measure of our understanding" (Hilary of Poitiers, On Matthew 15.7-9; Matt. 15:33).[4] The messianic feeding miracles transcend human explanations, while pointing to the ordinary necessity of food.

2. FC 58:107*; ACCS NT 7:92.
3. PG 57:433-34; NPNF 1 10:255**; ACCS NT 1a:234.
4. SCH 258:42-44; ACCS NT 1b:34-35*.

Jesus wanted to offer the crowds food in the desert, rather than send them back to buy food. Hilary commented: "When the disciples advised that the crowds be sent away into the neighboring villages to buy food, he answered, 'They do not need to go away.' This signaled that these people whom he healed with the food of teaching, teaching that was not for sale, had no need to go back to Judea and buy food. He ordered the apostles to give them something to eat. But was Jesus unaware there was nothing to give? Did he not know the disciples possessed a limited amount of food? He had the power of knowing their minds, so he knew" (Hilary of Poitiers, On Matthew 14.10; Matt. 14:17).[5] He knew in advance what they needed — not only food for the soul but for the body as well.

John Chrysostom often noticed minuscule details in biblical narratives. He explored the easily neglected fact that it had been three days since the people had come into the desert. It is not incidental that the miracle of the feeding of the multitude occurred *in* the desert, which is, like a tomb, far away from any usual provisions, and *on* the third day:

> Lest someone might say that they came having provisions for the way, Jesus noted, "They have been with me now *three days* and have nothing to eat." So even if some had come with provision, they had by now been consumed. Therefore he did not do this on the first or second day but only when everything had been entirely consumed, in order that having first been in need, they might more eagerly receive the miracle of food. When he then offered them compassion, saying, "I will not send them away hungry, lest they faint on the way," he implied that both the distance to food was great and that they had nothing at all left. The disciples asked: If you are not willing to send them away hungry, then, "where are we to get bread enough in the desert to feed so great a crowd?" Jesus answered: "Are your hearts so hardened? Having eyes, do you not see? Having ears, do you not hear?" (Chrysostom, The Gospel of Matthew, Homily 53.1; Matt. 15:34)[6]

Timing is of the essence of a good work. This is especially so in the case of hunger. Untimely food does not cause the heart to sing.

In the narrative, by three days everyone was hungry. This magnified

---

5. SCH 258:20-22; ACCS NT 1b:9-10*.
6. PG 58:525; NPNF 1 10:326-27; ACCS NT 1b:35*.

the contrast between the urgency of human need and the abundance of God's gifts. Here we learn that the hungry know far better how to enjoy food and drink than do those already satisfied. The hearts of the poor are comforted even with a morsel of bread (Judg. 19:5). The Fathers marveled at how frequently food and eating and feasting appeared as a crucial metaphor in scripture. They remembered the proverb that it is better to have a dinner of simple herbs where there is love, than a huge feast where there is no love (Prov. 15:17).

### 4. God Feeds All Humanity

The scene is "a lonely place," far away from provisions. It is just here, in the desert, that he is "ready to feed the world." Just when "the day is now over," and the night is drawing nigh, there is a miracle of the multiplications of loaves and fishes (Chrysostom, The Gospel of Matthew, Homily 49.1; Matt. 14:18).[7]

This miracle is not for feeding alone, but for teaching: "In this miracle Jesus was teaching them humility, temperance, charity, to be of like mind toward one another and to share all things in common. He did so in his choice of location, by providing nothing more than loaves and fishes, by setting the same food before all and having them share it in common and by affording no one more than another" (Chrysostom, The Gospel of Matthew, Homily 49.3; Matt. 14:19).[8] Simply to come into Jesus' presence is already to share in his generosity.

In feeding the multitude, the seven baskets were understood by the Fathers as a reflection on the sevenfold gifts of the Spirit noted by Isaiah. These gifts were now being offered to the Gentiles, to all humanity. We have transcended the old dispensation in which these gifts were being given primarily to a particular people, Israel. Now, according to Hilary of Poitiers: "They brought forward *seven* loaves of bread. . . . because of the grace of the Spirit whose sevenfold light is, as Isaiah said, a gift [Isa. 30:26, LXX]. . . . The fact that seven baskets are filled indicates the overflowing and multiplied abundance of the Spirit of sevenfold light. What he generously gives, abounds. Having been satisfied, the gift becomes ever more

7. PG 58:497; NPNF 1 10:304; ACCS NT 1b:8*.
8. PG 58:499; NPNF 1 10:306; ACCS NT 1b:8.

richly endowed and full. The fact that *four* thousand gather together refers symbolically to a multitude of countless people from the four corners of the earth. In terms of the future, a certain number of people are satisfied in as many thousands of places as there are thousands of believers who hasten to receive the gift of heavenly food" (Hilary of Poitiers, On Matthew 15.10, italics added; Matt. 15:37).[9]

In this way the *numbers* (seven and four) combined with the metaphor of a thousand provided the Fathers with what they thought was an obvious clue to their hidden meaning — the Gentiles in the four corners of the earth in all their multitudes were to be fed in the coming kingdom. Numbers were never accidental and always important in rabbinic interpretations of the sacred text in the first century, and so also in Christian interpretations. Those who treat numbers as purely fanciful or superstitious have not taken seriously the rabbinic ways of reading scripture, out of which the Fathers were reflecting on Jesus' ministry.

The Word of God is our food, rightly understood. "Having taken the bread and the fish, the Lord looked up to heaven, then blessed and broke them. He gave thanks to the Father that, after the time of the law and the prophets, he himself was soon to be changed into evangelical food" (Hilary of Poitiers, On Matthew 4.11; Matt. 14:19).[10] The Lord himself was to become living Bread for the hungry world, the Gentiles.

## B. The Bread of Life

### 1. God Offered Manna in the Desert

The miracle of God's feeding his people in the desert is typified by *manna*. The rain of manna in the desert underscores the simple point that food is always God's free gift. The manna "took away all the toil of human labor and by its pleasant dew [Exod. 16:13-14], offered and spread out heavenly produce for the hungry" (Peter Chrysologus, Sermon 166; Exod. 16:4).[11] The people did not have to work for manna. It was a gift. It required no sweat, as did the labors of the fallen Adam.

9. SCH 258:44-46; ACCS NT 1b:36*.
10. SCH 258:22; ACCS NT 1b:8.
11. FC 17:273; ACCS OT 3:86.

In the wilderness "quails rained down like the heaviest shower, and the Jews received manna to get their fill," explained Cassiodorus. This was "a prefiguration" that the Incarnate Lord's coming "could be visualized in this blessing, for he is 'the living bread which came down from heaven' [John 6:51]. . . . He filled them with the bread of heaven [Ps. 105:40]" (Cassiodorus, Exposition of the Psalms 104.40; Exod. 16:4).[12] What happened in the desert was a taste of what was to come in the coming kingdom. All this was symbolized by freely offered food. In the history of salvation, food is of pivotal importance, a central feature of the narrative.

Origen views the manna within the context of the exodus event: The people have "come out of Egypt. They are following the pillar of fire and cloud. They are entering the wilderness. Then the Lord comes down from heaven to them and offers them a small, thin food, like to the food of angels; so that 'man eats the bread of angels' [Ps. 78:25]" (Origen, Commentary on the Song of Songs 1.4; Exod. 16:14).[13] Angelic beings have spirit but no embodiment. To receive manna for the long, dangerous wilderness trek is like being sustained in the way that angels are sustained. They ate angels' food and were sent away full (Ps. 78:23-25).

For the Fathers the crucial point of the manna narrative was that it pointed beyond itself to Christ feeding the hungry in the way that only the incarnate Lord finally accomplishes. In the exodus, "the manna from heaven fell and, with a prefiguring of the future, showed the nourishment of heavenly bread and the food of the coming Christ" (Cyprian, Letter 69.14; Exod. 16:16).[14]


## 2. God's Word as Manna

The fineness of this food gave Caesarius of Arles the opportunity to reflect on the root meaning of manna: "*Manna* means 'What is this?' See whether the very power of the name does not provoke you to learn more of it, so that when you hear the law of God read in church you may always ask and say to the teachers: What is this? Thus it is that toward which the manna points. Therefore if you want to eat the manna, that is, if you desire to re-

---

12. ACWCa 53:62-63; ACCS OT 3:86.
13. ACWOs 26:78; ACCS OT 3:87.
14. FC 51:255; ACCS OT 3:87.

ceive the word of God, know that it is small and very fine like the seed of the coriander" (Caesarius of Arles, Sermon 102.3; Exod. 16:15).[15] The bread we receive in the Eucharist prompts us to ask: "What is this?" This in turn prompts the eucharistic response: "It is the bread your Lord has given you" (Exod. 16:15, NIV).

Food becomes the visible means by which God's invisible grace is conveyed, according to Origen: "So the manna itself is a word. This is made clear from the reply Moses made to the question of the children of Israel, when they said 'to one another: What is that?' What then did Moses say? 'This is the bread which the Lord has given you to eat; this is the word which the Lord has commanded' [Exod. 16:15]" (Origen, Fragment 63; Matt. 4:4).[16] God is speaking through the bread. Bread is a way of speaking, analogous to a word.

We are given the written Word for nourishment, just as bread nourishes. Ambrose wrote: "'This is the bread that God gave' to you 'to eat.' Hear who this bread is: 'The word which God has ordained,' scripture says. This then is the ordination of God. This food nourishes the soul of the wise. It illuminates and it sweetens, resplendent with the gleam of truth and soothing, as if with a honeycomb [Prov. 16:24], by the sweetness of different virtues and the word of wisdom" (Ambrose, Letter 54[64].2; Exod. 16:15).[17] The taste of God's word is sweet: "By this bread the souls of the prudent are fed and delighted, since it is fair and sweet, illuminating the souls of the hearers with the splendor of truth and drawing them on with the sweetness of the virtues" (Ambrose, Letter 55[8].7; Exod. 16:15).[18]

We are asking how the Fathers understood the food they offered to the poor. The answer is found in their explicit exegesis of scripture texts on bread, manna, being hungry, and being satisfied.

### 3. True Bread

The metaphor of bread runs constantly through the scripture narratives: Bethlehem is the House of Bread. Jesus himself is the Bread of Life.

---

15. FC 47:105; ACCS OT 3:87.
16. GCSO 1241.1:41; ACCS NT 1a:59*.
17. CSEL 82 2:73; ACCS OT 3:87*.
18. CSEL 82 2:79; ACCS OT 3:87.

Jesus made a distinction between the manna that the patriarchs ate in the desert (John 6:31) and the bread he would freely offer. For he was giving his "own flesh." It was being given "for the life of the world" (John 6:51, KJV). He himself *is* the Living Bread that comes down from heaven. He himself *is* what hungry humanity needs for eternal sustenance. He distinguished between the meat that perishes and the meat that endures to everlasting life (John 6:27). He gives true bread (John 6:27-32). He himself is the true bread. In the end there will be no more hungering or thirsting (Rev. 7:16).

The Lord prepares a table before us (Ps. 23:5). In his last meal with his disciples, Jesus took bread, blessed it, broke it, and gave it to his disciples (Luke 22:19). After the Resurrection, he was made known to them "in the breaking of bread" (Luke 24:35). "My Father gives you the true bread from heaven," which "gives life to the world" (John 6:32-33, NKJV). One who eats of this bread shall live eternally (John 6:38).

### 4. Bread Not for Acquisition

In the narrative of the feeding of the multitude, the bread is perishable and cannot be hoarded. Like the manna in the desert, "The bread that they had before they crossed the lake was no longer of any use to them when they reached the other side," observed Origen. This is why Jesus admonished them "after the crossing, to be careful and be on your guard. The Pharisees and Sadducees offered a different dough of teaching, a truly ancient yeast restricted to the bare letter [cf. Rom. 2:29; 7:6; 2 Cor. 3:6] and therefore not free from corruption. Jesus does not want his disciples to eat of it any longer. Instead, he mixed a new spiritual dough when he himself offered to any who are ready to abandon the duplicitous yeast of the Pharisees and Sadducees and come to him, the living bread which came down from heaven and gives life to the world" [John 6:51] (Origen, Commentary on Matthew 12.5; Matt. 16:5).[19]

"The 'living bread that came down from heaven,' furnishes the energy for eternal life. Whoever eats this bread 'will not die ever,' for it is the body of Christ [John 6:49-58]. . . . The manna was subject to corruption if kept only for a second day. The bread of life, however, is foreign to every

---

19. GCSO 1140:75-76; ANF 9:452; ACCS NT 1b:39-40**.

corruption. Whoever tastes it in a holy manner shall not be able to feel corruption. For Israel, water flowed from the rock. For you, blood flows from Christ. Water satisfied them for the hour. Blood satisfies you for eternity" (Ambrose, The Mysteries 8.48; 1 Cor. 10:3).[20] Manna and the eucharistic bread are both alike and unlike, hence analogous. An analogy can only be drawn between two things that are different. The water flowing from the rock of Moses anticipates the flowing of Christ's blood on the cross.


## 5. According to Need

The ephemeral nature of the daily manna prevented hoarding. "Note that they partook *according to their need*. They did not receive food in order to take it away with them. Fragments were left, as a symbol for measuring use according to need, rather than introducing acquisitiveness that goes beyond what is needful" (Theodore of Mopsuestia, Fragments 86, 87, quoted in Reuss, italics added; Matt. 15:36).[21]

Need determines priority. "The manna was once received in the wilderness for those of Israel. Now, behold, again in the desert he has provided ungrudgingly for those in want of food, as though bringing it down from heaven. For to multiply what is little and to feed such a multitude as though out of nothing would not be out of keeping with the former miracle. At that time Israel was to partake *according to need;* they had not received food in order to take it away with them" (Cyril of Alexandria, Fragment 178, quoted in Reuss, italics added; Matt. 14:20).[22] The hungriest are not to be stuck at the end of the line. Nor are they to hoard.

God is offering to each needy person whatever is fitting to that particular person's need, whether milk or meat. We are not to give meat to those who are not yet strong enough to digest it (cf. 1 Cor. 3:21). "Not immediately at first do we feast on all foods, nor do we drink all drinks. 'First drink this,' he says. Thus there is a first, then a second thing that you drink. There is also a first thing that you eat, then a second, and then a third. At first there are five loaves, then there are seven [Matt. 14:17; 15:34]. . . . The Lord consents to bestow on us nourishment according to the strength of

20. FC 44:22-23*; ACCS NT 7:92*.
21. MKGK 127-28; ACCS NT 1b:36.
22. MKGK 211; ACCS NT 1b:9*.

each, *lest either too strong a food oppress the weak or too meager a nourishment not satisfy the strong*" (Ambrose, Exposition of the Gospel of Luke, 6.71-72, italics added; Luke 9:16).[23]

These themes echo throughout scripture: The hungry are more ready to hear the good news, because to the hungry soul, every bitter thing is sweet (Prov. 27:7). The fool eats and still does not have enough (Hos. 4:10). Jesus, in the sermon on the plain (Luke 6:21), pronounces as blessed those who are hungry, for they shall be filled. And he pronounces woe upon those who are full, for they shall be hungry (Luke 6:25). Hunger and gluttony in this world are turned upside down in relationship to the coming kingdom. "Many that are first shall be last, and the last shall be first" (Matt. 19:30, KJV). In relation to the coming rule of God, Paul learned to be content under all circumstances (Phil. 4:11).

## 6. Why Divine Creation Permits Famine and Drought

Famine can result from inexorable natural causes, such as blight (Amos 4:9), insects (Joel 1:4-20), or drought (Hag. 1:10-11). Or it may come as a result of human decisions, such as invading armies that deliberately cause famine in order to take a city under siege (Lam. 4:8-10). How does scripture reason about why the incomparably good God allows famine and drought?

The risk of the shortage of food and water belong inherently to living in this world. God gives intelligence to human creatures to find ways to conserve water, build dams, channel irrigation, travel the desert, raise crops, build storage, and live through winter on the previous year's food. In the mystery of his providence, God allows conditions of deprivation that call human creatures to greater awareness of their dependence upon the Giver, and to elicit a humble and contrite heart. Under the original conditions of Eden, there was plenty of water and food. Under the conditions of the fallenness of Adam and Eve and Cain, there came to be unfruitfulness in the earth (Gen. 3:17-18; 4:12). Abraham (Gen. 12:10), Isaac (Gen. 26:1), and Jacob (Gen. 46:1–47:12) were all forced to immigrate in order to find food. The prophets frequently interpreted famine and drought as divine judgment on the recalcitrant sins of humanity (Amos 4:6).

23. EHG 218**; ACCS NT 3:152*.

Not all disasters are the result of divine punishment (see Ruth 1:1; Gen. 12:10; 26:1; Luke 3:14; Acts 11:28). Whenever God does allow drought or famine, it is viewed on a larger scale as permitting the people to come to a needed repentance (Hos. 2:8-23; Amos 4:6-8). By this rigorous pedagogy, God draws his people into greater awareness of his justice and love (Mark 13:8).

### 7. How Misdeeds Cause Hunger

The Fathers were aware that hunger would often be caused by bad decisions, as was the case with the prodigal son. "Nothing is enough for prodigal enjoyment. He who does not know how to be filled with eternal nourishment always suffers starvation" (Ambrose, Exposition of the Gospel of Luke, 7.215; Luke 15:11-24).[24]

The hunger of the prodigal came as a result of proud self-assertion. It was more a famine of good works than of food, said Ambrose: "'A mighty famine came there in that country' [Luke 15:14]. It was not a famine of fasts but of good works and virtues. What hunger is more wretched? Certainly whoever departs from the Word of God hungers, because 'man lives not by bread alone but by every word of God' [Luke 4:4]. Whoever leaves treasure lacks. Whoever departs from wisdom is stupefied. Whoever departs from virtue is destroyed" (Ambrose, Exposition of the Gospel of Luke, 7.215; Luke 15:11-24).[25]

### 8. The Discipline of Fasting

Fasting is a spiritual discipline cautiously commended in scripture (Joel 1:14). Why fast? To pray intentionally for grace amid temptation; to gather strength for mission; to put the body under control. But when it becomes a public or conspicuous act, it tempts toward self-righteousness. The Pharisees fasted often and with public display. The disciples of Jesus were instructed to fast only under special conditions of temptation and challenge, and always without any public display (Matt. 6:16-18).

24. EHG 319*; ACCS NT 3:249.
25. EHG 318*; ACCS NT 3:249.

Jesus fasted forty days and nights (Mark 1:12-13; Luke 4:1-2). The disciples fasted for the consecration of Barnabas and Saul (Acts 13:2-3). Paul fasted at the time of conversion (Acts 9:9). Daniel fasted under conditions of captivity and persecution (Dan. 9:3). Isaiah correlated fasting closely with active good works, in relation to seeking justice. To fast rightly is to loose the chains of injustice, undo heavy burdens, free the oppressed, break yokes that are heavy burdens, give bread to the hungry, and welcome the homeless (Isa. 58:6-7).

### 9. Daily We Pray for Bread for That Day

Food is necessary for every other step God calls us to take. The faithful pray daily: "Give us this day our daily bread" (Matt. 6:11, KJV). The prayer is for life-sustaining bread, not exotic foods. Each day we ask God to supply us with food for that day, not all future days. "What is 'daily bread'?" asked John Chrysostom. "Just enough for one day. Here he is speaking to people who have natural needs of the flesh, who are subject to the necessities of nature. He does not pretend that we are angels. He condescends to the infirmity of our nature in giving us his commands. The severity of nature does not permit you to go without food. So for the maturing of your life, he says, you require necessary food. You do not have any complete freedom from natural necessities. But note how even in things that are bodily, there are spiritual correlations that abound. It is not for riches or frills that we pray. It is not for wastefulness or indulgent finery, but only for bread. And only for bread on a daily basis, so as not to 'worry about tomorrow' [Matt. 6:34]" (Chrysostom, The Gospel of Matthew, Homily 19.8; Matt. 6:11).[26]

The Fathers pondered why such a small request (daily bread) would be so crucial to the way of life enabled by almighty God: "How could it be that he who enjoined upon us to ask for great and heavenly favors, should command us to intercede with the Father for what is small and of the earth?" Origen wondered.

It is as if he had forgotten — so some would have it — what he had taught. For the bread that is given to our flesh is neither heavenly, nor

26. PG 57:280; NPNF 1 10:135**; ACCS NT 1a:135-36*.

is the request for it a great windfall. We, on our part, following the Master himself who teaches us about the bread, shall treat of the matter explicitly. In the Gospel according to John he says to those who had come to Capernaum seeking for him: "Amen, amen, I say to you, you seek me, not because you have seen miracles, but because you did eat of the loaves and were filled" [John 6:26]. He who has eaten of the bread blessed by Jesus and is filled with it, tries all the more to understand the Son of God more perfectly, and hastens toward him. Hence his admirable command: "Labor not for the meat which perishes, but for that which endures to life everlasting, which the Son of man will give you" [John 6:27]. . . . The "true bread" is that which nourishes the true humanity — the person created after the image of God. (Origen, On Prayer 27.2; Matt. 6:11)[27]

Those whom he fed physically, he sought to feed spiritually. Ultimately the bread we most pray for is the clarity and truthfulness of our own purpose and destiny.

### 10. Daily Bread and the Eucharist

Why do we pray for daily bread every day, not once a month? Because our need for bread is daily. It is hard for the body to go more than one day without food. By praying daily, we learn each day anew of our dependence upon God.

The modest prayer for daily bread, thought Cyprian, is best understood in relation to the Eucharist. This is a highly personal petition, spoken by each of us to "our Father," concerning "our daily bread." "'Daily bread' may be understood both spiritually and simply, because both meanings are of divine efficacy in terms of salvation. For Christ is the bread of life. This bread is not the bread of all generally, but it is *our* bread. We say 'Our Father,' because he is the father of those who understand and believe. So too we say 'our bread,' because Christ is the bread of those who receive his body. Now we ask that this bread be given to us today, lest we who are in Christ and receive his Eucharist daily as the food of salvation should be separated from Christ's body through some grave offense that prohibits us from re-

27. GCSO 32:363-64; ACWOp 19:92-93; ACCS NT 1a:135*.

ceiving the heavenly bread. For according to his words: 'I am the living bread which came down from heaven; if anyone eats of this bread, he will live forever; and the bread which I shall give for the life of the world is my flesh' [John 6:51]" (Cyprian, Treatises, On the Lord's Prayer 18; Matt. 6:11).[28]

New birth, as typified in baptism, is a single, unrepeatable event. Unlike baptism, the Lord's Prayer is prayed daily. The Eucharist is repeated. Why? To provide ongoing sustenance for the ongoing life of faith that begins with the new birth manifested in baptism. The Supper offers food. Without the visible bread and wine, the Eucharist is incomplete.

Summing up, we are freely to offer what food we have to those in need, even as God has offered us the food we need. John Chrysostom drew the point together deftly: "Paul reminds us that the Master gave up everything, including himself, for us, whereas we are reluctant even to share a little food with our fellow believers. But if you come for a sacrifice of thanksgiving, do not do anything unworthy of that sacrifice. Do not dishonor your brothers or neglect them in their hunger. . . . Give thanks for what you have enjoyed. Do not cut yourselves off from your neighbors" (Chrysostom, Homilies on the Epistles of Paul to the Corinthians I.27.5; 1 Cor. 11:24).[29] If we who come to his table fail to offer our table to others, we have not rightly received his food and drink.

## C. Not by Bread Alone

### 1. Feeding upon the Word

It was in the desert, tempted by the Adversary, that Jesus said: "It is written, 'Man shall not live by bread alone, but by every word that proceeds from the mouth of God'" (Matt. 4:4, NKJV). Jesus was quoting Deuteronomy: "And you shall remember all the way the Lord your God has led you through the wilderness, that he might humble you, testing you to know what was in your heart, whether you would keep his commandments or not. And he humbled you and let you hunger and fed you with manna, which you did not know, nor did your fathers know; that he might make you know that man does not live by bread alone" (Deut. 8:2-3, RSV).

---

28. CCL 3a:101; ANF 5:452*; ACCS NT 1a:135*.
29. NPNF 1:12:161; ACCS NT 7:113.

A person lives by bread, but "not by bread alone" (Deut. 8:3, NAB). The Word of God supplies all that is needed for our bodies and souls. "Some may object and insist that they have often seen the just man hungry and in need of food. This is rare and happens only where no one else is just. Let him then read the beautiful sentence, 'It is not by bread alone that the just man lives, but by the Word of the Lord,' who is the true bread, the bread of heaven (John 6:33, 41). The good man is never really in want as long as he adheres to faith in God. For he can ask for and receive whatever he needs from the Father of all. He can enjoy whatever belongs to him, if only he obey his Son" (Clement of Alexandria, Christ the Educator 3.7.39-40; Deut. 8:3).[30]

## 2. How the Oneness of the Loaf of Bread Signifies the Oneness of the People

The making and sharing of bread teaches the faithful of their unity. It must be gathered, crushed, moistened, and fired. Augustine refined this analogy: "So by bread you are instructed as to how you ought to cherish *unity*. Was that bread made of one grain of wheat? Were there not, rather, *many* grains? However, before they became bread, these grains were separate. They were joined together in water after a certain amount of *crushing*. For unless the grain is ground and moistened with water, it cannot arrive at that form which is called bread. So, too, you were previously ground, as it were, by the humiliation of your fasting and by the binding up of demonic powers. Then came the baptism of *water*. You were moistened, as it were, so as to arrive at the form of bread. But without *fire*, bread does not yet exist" (Augustine, Easter Sunday 227, italics added; 1 Cor. 10:17).[31] Unity of the body of Christ is created by its being gathered, separated, crushed, baptized, and purified by fire.

John Chrysostom commented on how we all partake of one bread: "Just as the bread, which consists of many grains, is made one to the point that the separate grains are no longer visible, even though they are still there, so we are joined to each other and to Christ. But if we are all nourished by the same source and become one with him, why do we not also

---

30. FC 23:232; ACCS OT 3:287-88*.
31. FC 38:197; ACCS NT 7:98*.

show forth the same love and become one in this respect too? This was what it was like in ancient times, as we see in Acts 4:32: 'For the multitude of those who believed were of one heart and one soul'" (Chrysostom, Homilies on the Epistles of Paul to the Corinthians I.24.4; 1 Cor. 10:17).[32] God is feeding all humanity in the living bread of the Eucharist. We recognize our oneness as believers as we receive God's nourishment that dwells within us. This unity points beyond itself to the hidden unity of all humanity in God: "Every soul who receives the bread that comes down from heaven becomes himself a house of bread, the bread of Christ, being nourished and having his heart strengthened by the support of the heavenly bread which dwells within. Hence Paul says, 'We are all one bread.' Every faithful soul is Bethlehem, just as what is called Jerusalem is that which has the peace and tranquility of the Jerusalem on high which is in heaven. That is the true bread, which, after it was broken into bits, has fed all humanity" (Ambrose, Letters to Priests 45 "To Horontianus"; 1 Cor. 10:17).[33]

### 3. The Bread Must Be Broken

This one loaf, the heavenly bread, is broken for us, not left intact, but fragmented into broken pieces. This is an indication of God the Son's own brokenness for us on the cross. Jerome wrote: "He looked up to heaven that he might teach them to keep their eyes focused there. He then took in hand five loaves of bread and two fish; he broke the loaves and gave the food to the disciples. By the breaking of the bread, he makes it into a seed-bed of food — for if the bread had been left intact and not pulled apart and broken into pieces, they would have been unable to feed the great crowds of men, women and children. The law with the prophets are therefore pulled apart and broken into pieces. Mysteries are made manifest, so that what did not feed the multitude of people in its original whole and unbroken state now feeds them in its divided state" (Jerome, Commentary on Matthew 2; Matt. 14:19).[34] When we partake of the broken bread of life, its nourishment is reduplicated and redistributed.

It is a paradox, wrote Ambrose, that "the bread in an incomprehensi-

---

32. NPNF 1 12:140; ACCS NT 7:97.
33. FC 26:236; ACCS NT 7:97-98*.
34. CCL 77:122; ACCS NT 1b:8.

ble fashion is visibly increased when it is broken, when it is distributed, and when it is eaten even without our grasp of how it is provided" (Ambrose, Exposition of the Gospel of Luke, 6.86; Luke 9:16).[35]

Ephrem burst into song: "Grant, Lord, that I and those dear to me may together there find the very last remnants of your gift!" (Ephrem the Syrian, Hymns on Paradise 9.27, 29; Mark 8:8a).[36] Similarly, the fourth-century Latin poet Prudentius wrote joyfully of the loaves and fishes:

> You, our bread, our true refection,
> Never failing sweetness are.
> He can never more know hunger,
> Who is at your banquet fed.
>
> (Prudentius, Hymns for Every Day
> 9.61-62; Luke 9:17; cf. John 6:35, 56)[37]

### 4. Christ Known in the Breaking of Bread

In providing food relief for the hungry, Christians remember that the risen Lord revealed himself in the breaking of bread. "Remember, though, dearly beloved, how the Lord Jesus desired to be recognized in the breaking of bread, by those whose eyes had been kept till then from recognizing him. The faithful know what I'm talking about. They know Christ in the breaking of bread" (Augustine, Sermon 234.2; Luke 24:28-30).[38]

Jesus was belatedly recognized by the Emmaus travelers but only upon the breaking of bread. This is precisely where the risen Lord intended to be recognized, according to Augustine:

> "We," they said, "had hoped that he was the one to redeem Israel." O my dear disciples, you had hoped! So now you no longer hope? Look, Christ is alive! Is hope dead in you? Certainly, certainly, Christ is alive! Christ, being alive, found the hearts of his disciples dead, as he appeared yet did not appear to their eyes. . . . Where did the Lord wish to

---

35. EHG 225*; ACCS NT 3:151*.
36. HOP 146*; ACCS NT 2:106.
37. FC 43:64; ACCS NT 3:152.
38. WSA 3 7:37*; ACCS NT 3:382.

be recognized? *In the breaking of bread.* We're all right, nothing to worry about — we break bread, and we recognize the Lord. It was for our sake that he didn't want to be recognized anywhere but there, because we weren't going to see him in the flesh, and yet we were going to eat his flesh. So if you're a believer, any of you, if you're not called a Christian for nothing, if you don't come to church pointlessly, if you listen to the Word of God in fear and hope, you may take comfort in the breaking of bread. The Lord's absence is not an absence. Have faith. The one you cannot see is with you. Those two [on the road to Emmaus], even when the Lord was talking to them, did not have faith, because they didn't believe he had risen. Nor did they have any hope that he could rise again. They had lost faith, lost hope. They were walking along, dead, with Christ alive. They were walking along, dead, with life itself. Life was walking along with them, but in their hearts life had not yet been restored. (Augustine, Sermon 235.2-3, italics added; Luke 24:13-16)[39]

## 5. The Bread of the Word Is to Be Eaten

No one learns to savor a food simply by *hearing* its flavor described with words. Similarly we must *taste* the bread of life, according to Basil the Great: "Just as it is impossible for someone to know what honey is like simply by being told about it, because he must taste it in order to find out, so too the goodness of the heavenly bread is not properly communicated by teaching alone. We must taste the goodness of the Lord by our own experience" (Basil the Great, quoted in Cramer, Catena in Epistolas Catholicas; 1 Pet. 2:3).[40]

The bread of the Eucharist is offered to strengthen faith for good works. The preached Word looks toward behavioral change awakening mercy and justice, as Augustine observed: "In expounding holy Scriptures, I am, so to speak, now breaking bread for you. If you hunger to receive it, your heart will sing out with the fullness of praise (Ps. 138:1). And if you are thus made rich in your banquet, why would you then be niggardly in good works and deeds of mercy? What I am distributing to you is not my own.

39. WSA 3 7:41*; ACCS NT 3:378-79*.
40. CEC 51; ACCS NT 11:84.

What you feast upon, I also feast upon" (Augustine, Sermons on New Testament Lessons 45.1; Mark 8:6).[41] Eucharistic bread wants to be transformed into deeds of mercy.

## D. Quenching Thirst: "You Gave Me to Drink"

Even more demanding than hunger is thirst. Water is necessary for life. This necessity calls for the next good work mentioned in Jesus' parable: offer the thirsty a cup of cold water in the name of Christ.

In satisfying thirst, timing is crucial. We are called to provide what the thirsty most need at the time they most need it. To delay a day will only make thirst all the more desperate. Tomorrow may be too late. The need is now.

The refreshing fountain of grace is forever being freely offered. The ancient Christian writers pondered its mystery and depth.

### 1. The Pattern

Jesus himself said: "I was thirsty and you gave me drink" (Matt. 25:35, NKJV). The "I" refers both to the Lord himself and to "the least of these," the thirsty neighbor.

What good works flow from Christian love? Simple acts that respond to the here-and-now needs of "the least" — in this case those with least water, the thirstiest.

In what vessel are good works conveyed? By such modest means as a cup.

How does this good work refract God's own good news? The pattern for assuaging the thirst of humanity in the Christian life is Jesus' own offering of refreshment to humanity as the water of life. The Lord is not only "the bread that comes down from heaven" (John 6:50, NIV), as we have seen above, but also the "living water" (John 4:10, NIV).

Small acts of mercy are large in the Lord's eyes. Jesus said: "And whoever gives to one of these little ones even a cup of cold water because he is a

---

41. Cetedoc 0284, 95.38.581.15; NPNF 1 6:406**; cf. WSA 3 4:24* (Sermon 95.1); ACCS NT 2:105.

disciple, truly, I say to you, he shall not lose his reward." The requirement may be something quite light, but not useless. This is epitomized by simple cold water. Wrote Hilary: "No deed of a good conscience is useless" (Hilary of Poitiers, On Matthew 10.29; Matt. 10:42).[42]

## 2. Giving the Thirsty a Cup of Cold Water

Why not hot water? It is not accidental, Jerome reasoned, that Jesus selected such a common offering as "cold water." "But suppose someone objects, saying, 'Due to my poverty I cannot give anything. I cannot serve as a host.' Jesus undercut this excuse too by the easily fulfilled command that we should offer a cup of cold water with our whole heart. He said 'cold water' rather than 'hot water' so that we could not even object because of our lack of resources, such as fuel for hot water" (Jerome, Commentary on Matthew 1; Matt. 10:42).[43] What is needed is the simplest relief — nothing we could pretend is too costly for us. There is no room in this commandment for self-deceit.

No one can plead poverty as an excuse to evade this command, argued Gregory of Nyssa: "God never asks his servants to do what is impossible. The love and goodness of his Godhead is revealed as richly available. It is poured out like water upon all. God furnishes to each person according to his will the ability to do something good" (Gregory of Nyssa, On the Christian Mode of Life; Mark 9:41).[44]

Thirst is common to everyone and understood by all. This is why the metaphor of thirst occurs so frequently in the Bible. If anyone is thirsty, said Jesus, let him come to me and drink (John 7:37). The peace to come is compared to a river to the thirsty (Isa. 66:12). Even in the wilderness, God provides streams to slake our thirst (Isa. 35:6). When their tongue is too dry to speak, the Lord hears them (Isa. 41:17). There is a river, the streams whereof shall make glad the city of God (Ps. 46:4).

---

42. SCH 1254:250-52; ACCS NT 1a:214*.
43. CCL 77:75-76; ACCS NT 1a:214-15*.
44. FC 58:157*; ACCS NT 2:130.

### 3. The Icon of Rebekah: Offering Water

A daily habit of attentiveness is the best preparation for that extraordinary moment when it is possible to do a simple act of mercy. This is seen in the story of Rebekah. In early Christian art, Rebekah is often pictured offering water.

None of the details of the Rebekah narrative were incidental as Origen saw it: "Rebekah came to the wells daily; she drew water daily. And because she spent time at the wells daily, therefore, she could be found by Abraham's servant and be united in marriage with Isaac. Do you think these are tales and that the Holy Spirit tells stories in the scripture? This is instruction for souls and spiritual teaching which instructs and teaches you to come daily to the wells of the scripture, to the waters of the Holy Spirit, and always to draw water and carry home a full vessel just as also holy Rebekah used to do." He continues, "Unless, therefore, you come daily to the wells, unless you daily draw water, not only will you not be able to give a drink to others, but you yourself also will suffer 'thirst for the word of God' [cf. Amos 8:11]" (Origen, Homilies on Genesis 10.2-3; Gen. 24:15).[45]

It was at that well of hospitality that Rebekah was found by the servant of her future husband Isaac. "Rebekah is found 'at a well.' Rebekah in turn finds Isaac 'at a well' [Gen. 24:62, the well Beer Lahai Roi]. There she gazed upon his countenance for the first time. There 'she dismounted from the camels' [Gen. 24:64]. There she sees Isaac who was pointed out to her by the servant. Do you think these are the only words related about wells?" (Origen, Homilies on Genesis 10.5; Gen. 24:20).[46]

In ancient Christian frescos, Rebekah was a holy image or icon to show forth the offering of life. She was not viewed either as a simply mythic or simply historic figure. She became a type pointing beyond herself, anticipating the readiness of the faithful community to serve. Rebekah is especially a prototype of the quenching of thirst, particularly in her willingness to respond immediately to need, and indeed to a stranger: "How important it was that a tender maiden while drawing water not only did not decline the request, but also took down the water jar from her shoulders and gave the petitioner his fill, stranger though he was

45. FC 71:159-61; part also ACCS OT 2:126.
46. FC 71:165; ACCS OT 2:128.

and quite unknown to her" (Chrysostom, Homilies on Genesis 48.15; Gen. 24:12).[47]

It was over a thousand years later, in the fourth century A.D., that a traveler's account was written of her visit to Rebekah's well. There Rebekah offered a cup of cold water. There Rebekah met Isaac. Egeria of Spain was among the earliest Christian visitors to write of it: "A Psalm was sung, another prayer was said, and, after the bishop had blessed us, we went outside. Then he graciously agreed to guide us to the well from which the holy woman Rebekah had drawn water. And the holy bishop said to us: 'Here is the well from which the holy woman Rebekah watered the camels of Abraham's servant Eliezer" (Egeria, Diary of a Pilgrimage 20).[48] The place is still being remembered.

## 4. The Water of Life

In scripture, water is a pervasive symbol not only of relieving thirst, but also of cleansing (Lev. 11:32-28), of service (Jesus washing the feet of the disciples), and of renewal (Ezek. 47:1-12). When guests arrive in the house, their sandals are removed and their feet are washed (John 13:3-11). To assuage the thirst of others is to experience our own lives as refreshed. "One who waters will himself be watered" (Prov. 11:25, RSV).

The water of baptism is a sign of God's refreshing gift to humanity, so much so that "except a man be born of water and the Spirit, he cannot enter the kingdom of God" (John 3:5, KJV*). Those who are coming to God with parched throats are invited to come to this water (Isa. 55:1). The Shepherd leads the faithful to living fountains of water (Rev. 7:17).

## 5. Thirsting after Righteousness

Thirst is an overpowering desire that can be applied by analogy to our urgent need for God. "'Blessed are those who hunger and thirst after righteousness,' not on the surface, but with the entirety of their desire. By contrast, the most characteristic feature of covetousness is a strong desire,

47. FC 87:33*; ACCS OT 2:125.
48. EDP 82.

where we are not so hungry for food and drink, as for more and more things. Jesus urged us to *transfer this desire to a new object, freedom from covetousness*" (Chrysostom, The Gospel of Matthew, Homily 15, italics added; Matt. 5:6).[49]

Chromatius of Aquileia saw in human thirst a metaphor for passionate longing for a holy life: "He taught that we must seek after righteousness with earnest desire, not with fainthearted lethargy. He calls those blessed whose search for righteousness virtually burns with passionate longing in their hunger and thirst" (Chromatius, Tractate on Matthew 17.5.1; Matt. 5:6).[50] Those who thirst in this way will be filled, according to Apollinaris of Laodicea: "Whoever thirsts for the righteousness of God has already found what is truly desirable. The yearning for righteousness is not satisfied by analogy to the appetite alone. Justice is not desired in the same way as food or water. That is only half the total picture. Jesus represented this yearning for righteousness as the heat and burning of an intense longing. He says that such a person 'will be filled'" (Apollinaris, Fragments on Matthew; Matt. 5:6).[51] To thirst for righteousness is to recognize how dry is one's soul, and how happy to be filled.

To thirst for righteousness is to desire to live righteously, acting in a way that is fitting to God's own righteousness. "The Lord, in John's Gospel, does not simply call everyone to drink, but only those who are thirsty, saying: 'If anyone thirst, let him come to me and drink' [John 7:37b]. Similarly it was not for nothing that he spoke of those who 'hunger and thirst for righteousness.' Whoever hungers for righteousness wants to live actively according to God's righteousness. This is fitting to the person with a good heart. One who thirsts for righteousness wants to acquire that knowledge of God. This can only be acquired by the study of scripture. This is fitting to the person with an obedient heart. 'For they shall be satisfied.' They are filled with the abundance of God's reward, for greater are the rewards of God than even the most avid desires of the saints" (Opus Imperfectum in Matthaeum, fifth century, Homily 9; Matt. 5:6a).[52] Those who come to scripture thirsty will be satisfied. For here is found the river whose streams bless the city of God (Ps. 46:4).

---

49. PG 57:227; NPNF 1 10:94**; ACCS NT 1a:84*.
50. CCL 9a:273; ACCS NT 1a:84*.
51. MKGK 4; ACCS NT 1a:84**.
52. PG 56:682; ACCS NT 1a:84*.

To those who seek righteousness first, the rest will be added. John Chrysostom commented on this irony: "It is commonly thought that the rich are made wealthy through their own greed. But Jesus says in effect: No, it is just the opposite. For it is righteousness that produces true wealth. Thus so long as you act righteously, you do not fear poverty or tremble at hunger" (Chrysostom, The Gospel of Matthew, Homily 15; Matt. 5:6).[53] God uses even the discomfort of our thirst to bring us to living waters. The soul that naturally thirsts for water also naturally thirsts for God, and most of all in a dry and thirsty land where there is no water (Ps. 63:1).

## E. At Table with the Lord

### 1. The Pattern

The way in which Christians offer food for the hungry and drink for the thirsty is modeled by Jesus who offers his very body and blood as food and drink in the Eucharist. Listen carefully to the Fathers, and you will discover the richness of classic Christian reflection on sitting at table with the incarnate Lord. Food and drink are central to Christian worship.

### 2. Jesus Offered Himself as Food and Drink

Jesus chose food and drink to convey the truth of his presence. Through bread and wine, he comes to us again and again, as Jerome observed: "Even as Melchizedek, the priest of the most high God, had prefigured Christ by offering bread and wine (Gen. 14:18), so Jesus would exemplify this with his real body and blood" (Jerome, Commentary on Matthew 4; Matt. 26:26-27).[54]

To sit at the Lord's table is to eat and drink to our comfort, health, and good cheer. If you wish to learn what it means to eat and drink, go with Jesus to the "upper room." Origen doubtless had visited the precise location in third-century Jerusalem where this room was remembered as having been located. He described the scene vividly:

53. PG 57:227; NPNF 1 10:94**; ACCS NT 1a:85*.
54. CCL 77:251; ACCS NT 1b:248.

If therefore we wish to receive the bread of blessing from Jesus, who is eager to give it, we should enter the city and go into the house, prepared beforehand, where Jesus kept the Passover with his disciples. We ascend to the "large, furnished upper room" [Luke 22:12] where he "took the cup" from the Father and, "when he had given thanks, he gave it to them" who had gone up there with him and said, "Drink this, for this is my blood of the new covenant." The cup was both consumed and poured out. It was consumed by the disciples. It was "poured out for the remission of sins" committed by those who drink it. If you want to know in what sense it was poured out, compare this saying with what was written [by Paul]: "God's love has been poured into our hearts" [Rom. 5:5]. If the blood of the covenant was poured into our hearts for the remission of our sins, then by the pouring of that cleansing blood into our hearts, all the sins we have committed in the past will be remitted and wiped clean. The Lord who took the cup and said "drink this all of you" will not depart from us. He will drink it with us, since he himself is in each of us. For we are unable alone or without him either to eat of the bread or to drink of the fruit of the true vine. You should not marvel that he who is himself the bread also eats the bread with us. So *he who is himself the cup of the fruit of the vine also drinks it with us.* This is possible because the Word of God is omnipotent and is at once the bearer of many different names, for the multitude of his virtues are innumerable, since he is himself every virtue. (Origen, Commentary on Matthew 86, italics added; Matt. 26:26-27)[55]

To visit with the Lord is to sit at his table, to eat and drink with him, and to take him into our very bodies, in remembrance of his atoning work. Christians come to worship for this very purpose.

Food and drink are viewed by the worshiping community from the vantage point of the cross. The gathered community receives refreshment and nurture. There at his table they remember his self-giving until he comes again.

The food and drink Christians offer in turn to those who are suffering is finally best understood as the Word of the incarnate Lord himself. The drink they offer the thirsty is his cup poured out for us. Origen commented:

55. GCSO 1038.2:199-200; ACCS NT 248-49*.

That bread which God the Word confesses to be his own body, is the Word that nourishes souls, the Word proceeding from God, the very bread that comes from the living bread which is set out upon our table of which was written: "You prepare a table before me in the presence of my enemies" [Ps. 23:5]. That drink which God the Word confesses to be his blood is the Word that gives refreshment and exhilarates the heart. . . . This drink is the fruit of the true vine [cf. Mark 14:25; John 15:1] — the blood of the grape cast in the winepress of the Lord's passion. So also the bread is the word of Christ made from that corn which, falling onto good ground, brought forth much fruit [Matt. 13:8; Mark 4:8; Luke 8:8]. He was not speaking only of the visible bread alone which he was holding in his hands. He was also speaking of his body. His body bears the Word. The bread to be broken was the mystery of himself. Nor did he call that visible drink as such his blood, but the word in the mystery of which that drink was to be poured out. For to what else could the body and blood of the Lord refer other than the atoning Word that nourishes and gladdens the heart? (Origen, Commentary on Matthew 85; Mark 14:22b)[56]

To offer food and drink to the needy is to point beyond these toward the living Word, and the bread of life. Those famished amid the history of sin are here refreshed and filled.

### 3. The Incarnate Lord Understood Hunger and Thirst

The Lord of glory shared our human condition. He "was hungry" (Mark 11:12b, KJV). On the cross he said, "I thirst" (John 19:28, KJV). He felt the welling up of tears. Hilary of Poitiers pondered the paradox of the vulnerability of the Incarnate Lord to hunger and thirst: "As we behold the mystery of his tears (cf. John 11:35), hunger, and thirst [cf. John 19:28], let us remember that the one who wept also raised the dead to life, rejoicing for Lazarus. From the very One who thirsted flowed rivers of living water [cf. John 4:10]. . . . This was the mystery of his hunger, grief, and thirst — the Word was assuming flesh. His humanity was entirely exposed to our weaknesses, yet even then his glory was not wholly put away as he suffered these

56. AEG 5:263-64**; cf. TLG 2042.030, ad loc.; PG 898; ACCS NT 2:206*.

indignities. . . . In his incarnate humbling he was demonstrating the reality of his own human body by hungering, by doing what ordinary human bodies do. And when he ate and drank, it was not a concession to some necessity external to himself, but to show his full participation in the human condition" (Hilary of Poitiers, On the Trinity 10.24; Mark 11:12b).[57] There is no understanding of the Eucharist or the cross without the premise of his true humanity.

God offers our hungering and thirsting souls living bread for eternal sustenance and living water for eternal life. This living water is the incarnate Lord, truly human, truly God. According to Origen, the Lord Jesus himself "admits that he hungers when he says: 'I was hungry and you gave me to eat' [Matt. 25:35]. Again, on the one hand although he himself is 'the living water' [John 7:38] and gives drink to all who thirst, on the other hand, he himself says to the Samaritan woman, 'Give me to drink' [John 4:7]. . . . A soul such as this, then, which does all things patiently, which is so eager and is undergirded with so much attentiveness, and which has been accustomed to draw streams of knowledge from the depths, can itself be united with Christ as if in marriage" (Origen, Homilies on Genesis 10.3; Gen. 24:15).[58] Jesus teaches us to give water to the thirsty. In doing so, we are united with him as closely as two souls can be, like marriage partners.

To offer this gift of water rightly, Origen says, you must keep the wellsprings of your own soul free from pollution: "Since our Isaac has come, let us receive his advent and dig our wells. Let us remove the mud from them. Let us purge them from all filth and from all muddy and earthly thoughts and let us discover in them that 'living water' which the Lord mentions: 'He who believes in me, as the scripture has said, 'Out of his heart shall flow rivers of living water' [John 7:38]. Note how great is the Lord's generosity: the Philistines filled our wells and hindered our small and trifling veins of water, but in place of these, springs and rivers are restored to us" (Origen, Homilies on Genesis 13.3; Gen. 26:22).[59] Now that our Isaac (prefiguring Christ) has come, even though the Philistines pollute, we receive ever new wellsprings of fresh water for eternal life.

---

57. Cetedoc 0433, 62a.10.24.3; NPNF 2 9:188**; ACCS NT 2:157-58*.
58. FC 71:161; ACCS OT 2:127.
59. FC 71:192; ACCS OT 2:163*.

## F. Offering Hospitality to the Stranger: "You Welcomed Me"

### 1. The Pattern

Hospitality appears in a distinct sequence of characteristic good works cited by Jesus himself: having fed the hungry ("you gave me food") and offered water to the thirsty ("you gave me to drink"), we now come to the next most crucial act of service to needy neighbors: offering a bed and comfort to the stranger: "you welcomed me" (Matt. 25:35, RSV). "I was a stranger and you took me in" (Matt. 25:35, Douay-Rheims).

The "I" refers to Jesus himself and "you" to the least of these, the sojourner in need of shelter. The pattern of hospitality for the Christian life is Jesus himself, who in his incarnation reached out for those in hazardous transit, not yet at home.

Jesus himself was no stranger to travel. He and his disciples were often on the road. Walking long distances, he depended upon the kindness of strangers. He openly spoke with all sorts and conditions of men and women in their actual situations of living. He knew the importance of welcoming strangers. He knew well the sting of rejection, for when "he came unto his own, his own received him not" (John 1:11, KJV*). Listen carefully to the Fathers, and you will glimpse the importance of hospitality in early Christianity.

It is within the range of every believer to practice this uncomplicated good work. It does not require special education or abilities. It requires a good will, however, to do this good work. That good will is prepared, enabled, and brought to fulfillment by grace.

### 2. The Godly Work of Welcoming Strangers

Genuine hospitality is freely offered, without grousing or bellyaching. Theophylact wrote: "Note that when Peter mentions love he immediately goes on to commend hospitality 'without grumbling.' That is a sure sign of what love is" (Theophylact, Commentary on 1 Peter; 1 Pet. 4:9).[60] Those whose lives are transformed by grace practice hospitality easily, inconspicuously. They receive the stranger as if he were the Lord himself.

60. PG 125:1241; ACCS NT 11:117*.

Chrysostom held a high standard of hospitality: "If you receive your neighbor as though he were Christ, you will not complain or feel embarrassed but rather rejoice in your opportunity to serve. But if you do not receive him as if he were Christ, you will not receive Christ either, because he said: 'Whoever receives you, receives me' [Matt. 10:40]. If you do not show hospitality in this way, you will not finally receive it" (Chrysostom, quoted in Cramer, Catena in Epistolas Catholicas; 1 Pet. 4:9).[61] The clue to Christian hospitality is to grasp who the neighbor is — the incarnate Lord himself visiting you inconspicuously.

### 3. You Welcomed Me: Receive the Lord in Your Meeting with the Stranger

Hear the unique triune logic of Christian hospitality, not found in any other religion: To receive the stranger is to receive God's own Son, and to receive the Son is to receive the Father. Jesus said: ". . . whoever receives Me, receives not Me but Him who sent Me" (Mark 9:37, NKJV). In offering hospitality, according to Origen, we "welcome the Son of God who became a stranger and the members of his body who are strangers in the world" (Origen, Commentary on Matthew 72; Matt. 25:35-40).[62]

It is characteristic of patristic scripture interpretation to focus on the analogy between human hospitality now and God's hospitality for the faithful on the last day, and indeed in the whole of history. Our hospitality to the neighbor is most powerfully understood and fully offered in response to God's own hospitality toward fallen humanity. Paul stated the hospitality analogy with precision: "Welcome one another, therefore, as Christ has welcomed you, for the glory of God" (Rom. 15:7, RSV).

Receive the stranger with a heart of thankfulness. "Do not receive without prayer one who enters your house, especially if that one is a stranger, lest he turn out to be an angelic messenger [cf. Heb. 13:12]. Do not offer your earthly refreshments as if apart from receiving this heavenly refreshment" (Tertullian, On Prayer 26; Mark 9:37).[63]

61. CEC 77; ACCS NT 11:117*.
62. GCSO 1038.2.169; ACCS NT 1b:233.
63. Cetedoc 0007, 26.1; ANF 3:690**; ACCS NT 2:127*.

## 4. The Incarnate Lord Willingly Depended
on the Hospitality of Others

Jesus' ministry modeled both receiving hospitality from others and offering hospitality to others. Jesus himself was willing to be a traveler in a far country. He himself was often a stranger. He comes to us in the least of these. They have nowhere else to go. They bear grace to us inconspicuously (Matt. 25:35). Those who have risked their lives to spread his Gospel abroad understand what it means gratefully to receive the hospitality of others.

To receive the Son who is sent is to receive the Father who sent him. To receive the apostle is to receive the One who sent the apostle. If you receive a little child in the Lord's name, you are receiving the Lord. "Those who dedicate themselves to good works ought to be received by their brothers and be held in honor by being provided with whatever they might need" (Origen, Commentary on the Epistle to the Romans; Rom. 16:2).[64]

Throughout his earthly ministry the incarnate Lord and his disciples were often dependent on the hospitality of others. Cyril of Alexandria noted that when Jesus sent out the seventy, he commanded them to be content "to stay in one house, and from the same house to take their departure. For it was right that those who had once received them should not be deprived of the gift" (Cyril of Alexandria, Commentary on Luke, Homily 47; Luke 9:3-5).[65] The gift of his coming and presence was to be specially given to those who were most ready to receive it.

## 5. Jesus Invited the Most Neglected

The narratives of Jesus often focus on the scandal of his pattern of welcoming the lame, the blind, and "the least of these" to his table. For this he was criticized by the Pharisees.

Jesus taught his disciples not to seek for some honor or compensation as a reward for acts of hospitality. It is evidence of "a greedy disposition" if you seek to be "rewarded for hospitality" (Ambrose, Exposition of the Gospel of Luke 7.195; Luke 14:1-6).[66]

---

64. CER 5:244; ACCS NT 6:369.
65. CGSL 211**; ACCS NT 2:148*.
66. EHG 312*; ACCS NT 3:235.

The Son of Man himself comes to us as the stranger, "like a man going on a journey" (Mark 13:34, RSV). So also the apostles journeyed often and far in their attempt to tell his story, and themselves embodied and re-enacted the journey of the Son of Man.

In Christ, there is neither Jew nor Greek, there is neither bond nor free, neither male nor female, for all are one in Jesus Christ (Gal. 3:28). So in this community, all are called to be hospitable and welcoming to all the nations, all the classes, all sorts and conditions of persons, all viewed in relationship to their hidden oneness in Christ.

The Lord indeed reminds his hearers that he has "other sheep which are not of this fold" (John 10:16, NAS). His embrace is larger than ours with our economic interests and blind spots and barriers that keep us from recognizing his other sheep. But he has made of one blood all the nations (Acts 17:24-26). We all drink of one Spirit, from the water that flows from the rock (1 Cor. 12:13; 10:4).

## 6. Aliens, Strangers, and Pilgrims

The early believers understood themselves to be strangers and pilgrims on earth (Heb. 11:13). In writing to the Christians of Pontus, Galatia, Cappadocia, Asia, and Bithynia, Peter says that he was writing to the alien residents scattered throughout these distant areas (1 Pet. 1:1), the vast peninsula we now call Turkey. These are the Gentile outsiders to whom the apostle was writing, whom he addresses as strangers and pilgrims (1 Pet. 2:11).

There are times when the pilgrims will be like pelicans in the wilderness (Ps. 102:6), or like animals fending for themselves (Hos. 8:8-9). They may seem to wander as blind men in the street (Hos. 8:8-9). They may so acquire the habit of defensiveness that they flee even when no one is pursuing (Lev. 26:17). Moses himself knew what it meant to be a fugitive (Exod. 2:15). Israel had been a people without a land, so they understood alienation. The apostles were compelled to go "about in sheepskins and goatskins . . . ; they wandered in the deserts, the mountains, in dens, and in the caves of the earth" (Heb. 11:37-38, KJV*).

Origen knew from experience what it meant to be exiled from his own country. In commenting on Romans 12:13, he wrote: "We must not look on [strangers] as beggars but see them as people who have needs like our own. The practice of hospitality does not simply mean that we should entertain those who come to us. It means also that we should go out and invite others to come in [cf. Luke 14:12-14]" (Origen, Commentary on the Epistle to the Romans; Rom. 12:13).[67]


## 7. Whether Hospitality Depends upon the Worthiness of the Visitor's Motives

We are warned against hinging our acts of hospitality on a presumptive inquiry into the worthiness of the visitor's motives. "He who meddles in a quarrel not his own is like one who takes a passing dog by the ears" (Prov. 26:17, RSV). Similarly, when you yourself are a guest passing by, do not intrude into strife which does not belong to you. It is like taking the dog by the ears. We are to be neither busybodies in others' matters (1 Pet. 4:15) nor contentious (Prov. 17:14).

The criterion is need, not worthiness of motive. We are not to search out only those we consider worthy, Augustine argued: "Let in the unworthy, in case the worthy might be excluded. You cannot be a judge and sifter of hearts" (Augustine, Sermon 359a.11; Luke 16:9-13).[68]

"There are poor people here," Augustine said in one of his sermons preached in the port city of Hippo, "who have no dwellings where they themselves can welcome you" (Augustine, Sermon 41.6; Luke 16:19-22).[69] Homelessness was not a theoretical question in Hippo. The homeless do not need an investigation, but a place of shelter.

There is no simple rule of thumb as to how long guests may stay. Erring toward the side of generosity, Diodore wrote: "The point here is that we should honor the saints and take care of their needs until they no longer have them" (Diodore, quoted in Staab, Pauline Commentary from the Greek Church; Rom. 12:13).[70]

---

67. CER 5:72; 74 ACCS NT 6:316*.
68. WSA 3 10:216*; ACCS NT 3:255.
69. WSA 3 2:230-31*; ACCS NT 3:263.
70. NTA 15:106; ACCS NT 6:316.

## 8. The Ministry of Hospitality

Church leaders in early Christianity were to be persons ready to offer hospitality, whose lives were characterized by generosity (1 Tim. 5:10; 3:2). From high to low offices of service, but especially in the office of *episkopos*, a welcoming spirit fits the office. A haughty attitude is never called for. The leader is called always to be hospitable, to "love what is good. . . be self-controlled, upright, holy, and disciplined" (Tit. 1:8, TEV/Good News). One who would serve among the list of true widows was notably called to an ongoing ministry of hospitality — one who has "washed the feet of the saints, relieved the afflicted, and devoted herself to doing good in every way" (1 Tim. 5:10, RSV).

Hospitality is the duty of all Christians (Rom. 12:13, 1 Pet. 4:5). It expresses how the life of faith is lived out in active love toward those in need of shelter or other necessities (Heb. 13:1-2; 1 Pet. 4:8-9). When we welcome the stranger we may be entertaining angels unawares (Heb. 13:2; cf. Matt. 25:31-46). Share food with the hungry. Provide the wanderer with shelter. Clothe the ill-clad. "Beloved, it is a loyal thing you do when you render any service to the brethren, especially strangers, who have testified to your love before the church. You will do well to send them on their journey as befits God's service" (3 John 5, RSV).

Paul requested the church at Rome to welcome Phoebe, who herself had a notable ministry of hospitality: "I ask you to receive her in the Lord in a way worthy of the saints and to give her any help that she may need from you, for she has been a great help to many people, including me" (Rom. 16:2, NIV). The hospitality offered by Phoebe was rewarded many fold, according to Theodoret: "It is probable that Phoebe helped Paul by offering him hospitality in her house at Corinth during his time there (Acts 18:18). In return Paul opened the whole world up to her" (Theodoret, Interpretation of the Letter to the Romans; Rom. 16:2).[71] Ambrosiaster commented: "Paul praises Phoebe as highly as he does because she is a person whose life shows her high excellence. The more her good deeds became visible, the more she is sought out to help, and the more she will in due time receive the help due to her in love" (Ambrosiaster, On Paul's Epistle to the Romans; Rom. 16:2).[72] The body of Christ is characterized by

71. PG 82:220; ACCS NT 6:370*.
72. CSEL 81:477; ACCS NT 6:370**.

mutuality, reciprocal relationships, and cooperation that manifests God's love in the world.

## G. Biblical Models of Hospitality

### 1. The Sojourner

A sojourner is one who is on the road, traveling from place to place, and is temporarily without a home, a place. The sojourner is by definition a stranger, an alien, not a recognized member of the community. Old Testament law protected the sojourner and defined the justice due him. The sojourner must be given a fair trial. He was given the right of gleaning from the fields, of attending sacrifices, of rest on the Sabbath. One simple way to help the sojourner is to leave in your vineyard grapes that have fallen (Lev. 19:10). Do not pick them all up. Leave them for the traveler, the stranger, the poor.

The people of Israel know what it means to be a stranger in a strange land (Exod. 2:22). Israel in its early history was, and in many ways still remains, a sojourner nation. The people of Israel had themselves been mistreated as foreigners in Egypt. Their experience as sojourners was to be regularly recalled and taught to children. The mercy that God showed to his people should also be shown to every other sojourner (Exod. 23:9; Lev. 19:34; Deut. 23:7).

### 2. The Sojourner People

The land of the Canaanites was the place through which the patriarchs sojourned when they became the inheritors of God's promise (Gen. 17:8; Exod. 6:4). Israel was invited to receive the land as a trust, on condition of full accountability to God (Rev. 25:3; 1 Chron. 29:15; Heb. 11:8-16). This history required them to provide hospitality to strangers, invite them freely in, not grudgingly, but as honored guests, providing whatever was needed (Deut. 10:17-18). When Isaiah pictured the city of the righteous, it was open: "Your gates shall be open continually; day and night they shall not be shut" (Isa. 60:11, RSV).

Just as Israel was a sojourner people, so was the Christian community in relation to the temporal world (1 Pet. 1:1; 1:17; 2:11; Heb. 13:14). Paul writes in 1 Corinthians 4:11 that even to this present hour, we have no certain dwelling places. Remember that "the Son of Man [had] no place to lay his head" (Matt. 8:20b, NIV).

David held up this recollection before God in prayer: "For we are strangers before thee, and sojourners, as all our fathers were; our days on the earth are like a shadow, and there is no abiding" (1 Chron. 29:15, RSV). When viewed from the perspective of the coming kingdom and the eternal hospitality of God, however, the faithful "are no more strangers and foreigners, but fellow citizens with the saints in the household of God" (Eph. 2:19).

### 3. Icons of Hospitality

Biblical motifs of hospitality were frequent in the earliest expressions of Christian art in the first millennium. Sarcophagi, frescos, mosaics, and early paintings portrayed hospitality to the stranger, as seen in the familiar Old Testament narratives of Melchizedek in Canaan (Gen. 14:18), Jethro's hospitality toward Moses (Exod. 2:20), and the widow of Zarephath caring for Elijah (1 Kings 17:10-24). Rahab's act of hospitality to the spies in Jericho (Josh. 6:17-25) is remembered as a special case in Hebrews 11:31 and James 2:25. She typified the unworthy woman who was ready to trust God's promise by caring for sojourners.

Early Christian icons often portrayed the hospitality of Abraham, Lot, and others. While the Church Fathers were teaching hospitality, the artisans and visual artists of early Christianity were portraying these icons of hospitality. They were visual aids showing the welcoming of strangers. Iconography accompanied exegesis in portraying them, bringing them to visual expression. The icons served Christian teaching with vital, recognizable images. They gave visual palpability to the Fathers' teaching. They were crucial in Christian education for those preparing for baptism.

### 4. Patriarchal Prototype of Eagerness to Receive the Stranger: Abraham

Look, for example, at ancient Christian portrayals of Abraham's reception of visitors at Mamre (Gen. 18:1-7). You can see them in fifth-century mosaics in Rome at Santa Maria Maggiore, or earlier in the hypogeum of Via

Della Compagnia in Rome (c. 320-360), or later in Ravenna and Constantinople. Abraham is portrayed in scripture as eager to receive guests, and even "on the outlook" to greet them. Origen notes how Abraham "ran out" to meet the strangers at his door! "Notice that Abraham immediately is energetic and eager in his duties. He *runs* to meet them and when he had met them, 'he hastens back to the tent,' the text says, and then says immediately to his wife: 'Hasten to the tent.' All this hastening! It shows his eagerness to receive" (Origen, Homilies on Genesis 4.1, italics added; Gen. 18:2).[73] Faith hurries to welcome the stranger, without delaying or debating or hesitating.

Abraham served the strangers his best food, noted Caesarius of Arles, in his description of this scene, where the text says: "'Abraham ran to the herd and picked out a calf.' What kind of a calf? Perhaps the first one he could find? Not at all, but particularly a 'good, tender' calf. Therefore, he took the calf, 'and gave it to the servant who hastened to prepare it' [Gen. 18:7]. See, brothers, and notice how you should receive strangers with a warm spirit. Behold Abraham himself runs, his wife hastens, and the servant hurries. No one is lazy in the home of the wise man"[74] (Caesarius of Arles, Sermon 83.3).[75] The icons taught the worshipers to follow the pattern of Abraham's hospitality.

Abraham washed the feet of his guests, in anticipation of the servant messiah who would wash the feet of his disciples. Where the text described this scene, Origen commented that "Abraham, the father and teacher of nations, is, indeed, teaching you by these things how you ought to receive guests and why you should wash the feet of guests. Nevertheless, even this is said mysteriously. For he knew that the mysteries of the Lord were not to be completed except in the washing of feet [cf. John 13:6]" (Origen, Homilies on Genesis 4.2; Gen. 18:4).[76]

### 5. The Plight of the Traveler

Abraham was a long-distance traveler himself. He traveled the entire length of the fertile crescent from Ur to Egypt. As remembered in scripture, Abraham knew how important it was to welcome strangers.

73. FC 71:104; ACCS OT 2:63*.
74. Cf. Philo, De Abrahamo 109; cf. Origen, Homilies on Genesis 4.1, FC 71:104.
75. FC 47:12*.
76. FC 71:105; ACCS OT 2:64.

Ambrose described the predicament of the traveler: "While we are in this body, there often arises the necessity of traveling. Therefore that which you will have denied to others, you will have decided against yourself and you will show yourself worthy of that which you will have offered to others. If everyone decided not to receive guests, where would those who are traveling find rest? Then we would have to abandon human habitations and seek out the dens of the wild beasts" (Ambrose, On Abraham 1.5.34; Gen. 18:2).[77] The norm of assisting travelers is intuitively grounded in the golden rule of empathy, that everyone knows how they would wish to be treated in a similar situation, so do to others as you would have them do to yourselves.

Abraham moved frequently from here to there, with great amenability and a spirit of flexibility. John Chrysostom commented:

The patriarch "struck camp and moved on until settling at the oak of Mamre which is at Hebron." After accepting the promise, and following Lot's parting, he changed his campsite to the vicinity of the oak of Mamre. Notice his sensible attitude, his high sense of responsibility in effecting the transfer with ease and making no difficulty of changing from place to place. I mean, you will not find him shackled and hidebound by any custom, something that frequently affects a great number of people, even those considered wise and those generally free from worrying. If the occasion should require us to change and move in a different direction, even in many cases for a matter of spiritual importance, you would find many of us troubled, almost beside ourselves, regretting the change on account of our being prisoners of habit. The righteous man, on the other hand, wasn't like that. He showed good sense from the very outset. Like a stranger or pilgrim he moved from here to there and from there to the next place, and in all cases his concern was to give evidence of his God-fearing attitude in his actions. (Chrysostom, Homilies on Genesis 34.12; Gen. 13:18)[78]

Abraham knew how to empathize with the foreigner, never forgetting who he was in God's presence.

Abraham did not give the stranger a reason to shake off the dust

77. CSEL 32 1:528; ACCS OT 2:64*.
78. FC 82:297*; ACCS OT 2 20*.

from his feet and leave, so as to risk bringing upon himself judgment on the last day. Abraham immediately took in the stranger as if he were welcoming an angel of God. Caesarius of Arles reflected on how Abraham was blessed through these acts of hospitality, as if they were offered to God himself:

> Learn from blessed Abraham, brothers, to receive strangers gladly, and to wash their feet with humility and piety. Wash, I repeat, the feet of godly strangers, lest there remain in them some dust that they will be able to shake off of their feet to your judgment. For in the Gospel we read: "Whoever does not receive you — go forth and shake off the dust from your feet. Amen. I say to you, it will be more tolerable for the land of Sodom and Gomorrah in the day of judgment than for that town" [Matt. 10:14-15]. Abraham foresaw this, and for this reason wanted to have the opportunity to wash their feet, lest perchance any dust remain which might be kept and shaken off on judgment day as an evidence of unbelief. Therefore, the wise Abraham says: "I will bring water, that you may wash your feet." Carefully listen to this, brothers, if you are unwilling to exercise hospitality and to receive even your enemy as a guest. Behold while blessed Abraham welcomed those men warmly, he prepared himself to receive God as a dimension of his hospitality. Christ further confirmed this in the Gospel when he said: "I was a stranger and you took me in" [Matt. 25:35]. Therefore, do not despise strangers, lest perhaps he himself be the one you have rejected. (Caesarius of Arles, Sermon 83.4; Gen. 18:4)[79]

Abraham received strangers with personal warmth: "Abraham received passers-by and travelers just as they were. He did not leave them to his servants. On the contrary, he asked his wife to bring flour, even though they must have had domestic help. But both he and his wife wanted to enjoy the blessing, not only of hospitality, but of service also. This is how we are to show hospitality, by doing all the work ourselves, so that we may be set apart for God's final welcome" (Chrysostom, quoted in Cramer, Catena in Epistolas Catholicas; 1 Pet. 4:9).[80] "The imitator and lover of the saints will practice hospitality following the examples of Abraham and Lot as

---

79. FC 47:13-14; ACCS OT 2:64-65*.
80. CEC 77; ACCS NT 11:117*.

righteous men [cf. Gen. 18:1-5; 19:1-3]" (Ambrosiaster, On Paul's Epistle to the Romans; Rom. 12:13).[81] Our next figure is Lot.

### 6. Lot's Hospitality

Lot welcomed strangers, even on the outskirts of an evil city. He washed their feet. He made them a feast and baked unleavened bread (Gen. 19:2-3). The wanderers were invited to "lodge here this night" (Num. 22:8, KJV).

The case of Lot in Sodom is complicated, since it portrays an act of sincere hospitality that had entirely unexpected consequences. Lot was living near the Sodomites. Lot was ready to invite tired travelers despite their impiety and immorality. Origen cautiously noted that "Lot was not inside Sodom, but 'at the gate.' I might have said, just as Abraham was sitting outside his tent, due to his hospitality, even at an inconvenient time (for it was the middle of the day) on the lookout for travelers. So his relative and the imitator of his morality 'was sitting at the gate' ready to invite those passing through the land, even though evening had now come. For he surely knew the impiety of the Sodomites, and that there was no rest for the stranger in that place" (Origen, Catena on Genesis 1114; Gen. 19:1).[82]

Lot was honored to entertain strangers, as Chrysostom notes: "'Now, on seeing them,' the text goes on, 'Lot rose to meet them.' Let this be heeded by those who are given to repulsing people who call on them with requests to make and causes to plead, and who make themselves annoying. I mean, see how this good man did not wait till the visitors reached him. Rather, like the patriarch, without knowing who the visitors were but presuming that they were travelers of some kind, he well nigh jumped for joy on seeing them, as though falling upon his prey and not missing the object of his desire" (Chrysostom, Homilies on Genesis 43.9; Gen. 19:1).[83]

On seeing the visitors at Sodom's gate, Lot "'rose to meet them and prostrated himself on the ground.' He gave thanks to God for being found worthy to welcome the visitors. Notice this virtue of his soul: he considered it a great kindness on God's part to encounter these men and by welcoming them to fulfill his own need to be with others. Now, don't tell me they were

81. CSEL 81:407; ACCS NT 6:316.
82. PG 12:116; ACCS OT 2:74*.
83. FC 82:440; ACCS OT 2:74*.

angels; remember, rather, that this good man did not realize that yet, but behaved as though receiving unknown travelers. He said, 'Please, sirs, break off your journey at your servant's house; rest and bathe your feet; then rise early and resume your journey.' These words are sufficient to reveal the virtue residing in the good man's soul" (Chrysostom, Homilies on Genesis 43.10; Gen. 19:2).[84] Chrysostom continued: "This man of good name and reputation, enjoying great prosperity, a householder, addresses as master these travelers, these strangers, unknown, anonymous wayfarers, no connections of his. . . . Evening has fallen, he says. Grant my wish. Assuage the day's hardship by resting in the home of your servant. I mean, surely I'm not offering you anything wonderful? 'Bathe your feet' wearied with traveling, 'and rise early and resume your journey.' So do me this favor and don't refuse my entreaty" (Chrysostom, Homilies on Genesis 43.10; Gen. 19:2).[85]

It is always tempting to find excuses for not offering hospitality. But Lot persisted. "'They replied,' the text goes on, 'No, instead, we shall rest in the street.' Seeing that despite his entreaty they declined, he did not lose heart. He did not give up what he was intent on. He did not have the kinds of feelings we often do. If at any time we want to win someone over and then we see him somewhat reluctant, we immediately back off. This is due to our taking mild initiatives, without truly desiring to, and giving ourselves the rationalization that we have excuse enough to be able to say that at any rate we did our best. What do you mean, you have done your best? You have let slip the goal. You have missed the treasure. Is this your best? You would have done your best if you had not let the treasure slip through your fingers, if you had not bypassed the objective, if your display of hospitality was not limited to a perfunctory remark" (Chrysostom, Homilies on Genesis 43.11; Gen. 19:2).[86] This is typical of the tenacity we find in early Christian hospitality.

### 7. Entertaining Angels Unawares

Caesarius of Arles commented on Genesis 19:1-3, where we learn that "Even Lot *deserved to receive the angels, because he did not reject strangers.*

84. FC 82:440-41; ACCS OT 2:74*.
85. FC 82:441; ACCS OT 2:74*.
86. FC 82:441; ACCS OT 2:74-75*.

Note how the angels entered a hospitable home, but those houses that were closed to strangers were soon to be burned with flames of sulphur" (Caesarius of Arles, Sermon 83.3, italics added; Gen. 18:7).[87]

Chrysostom was fascinated by the persistence of Lot's welcome:

> When he saw them resisting and bent on resting in the street (the angels did this out of a wish to reveal more clearly the just man's virtue and to teach us all the extent of his hospitality), then he in turn did not stop at inviting them in, not only by his words but by his forceful actions. It was in this sense that Christ would also say, "Men of violence seize the kingdom of heaven" [Matt. 11:12]. In other words, where spiritual advantage is involved, active initiative is in order and forcefulness is commendable. "He compelled them," the text says. It seems to me he drew them in almost against their will. Then when they saw the just man applying this effort and not desisting until he should achieve the object of his desire, "they turned aside to him and entered his house. He prepared a meal for them, cooking flat bread for them. They ate before lying down." Do you see here how hospitality is manifested? It is not in richness of fare but in generosity of attitude. I mean, when he succeeded in bringing them into his house, at once he gave evidence of other signs of hospitality. He occupied himself in attending on them, providing something to eat and giving evidence of respect and attention to the visitors in his belief that they were only human beings, travelers of some kind. (Chrysostom, Homilies on Genesis 43.12; Gen. 19:3)[88]

What Lot did not realize was that these were God's own angels who came to visit him. "This, you see, is what a fervent and vigilant soul is like: far from being impeded by any obstacles from giving evidence of its virtue, it is spurred on to greater heights by the very impediments in particular and burns with a brighter flame of desire" (Chrysostom, Homilies on Genesis 43.9; Gen. 19:1).[89]

Hospitality of this sort brings unexpected gifts and benefits, according to Ambrose: "Hospitality is a good thing and it has its recompense.

---

87. FC 47:12*; ACCS OT 2:66*.
88. FC 82:441-42*; cf. ACCS OT 2:75*.
89. FC 82:440; ACCS OT 2:74.

First of all it has the recompense of human gratitude; then, more importantly, the divine reward. In this earthly abode we are all guests; here we have only a temporary dwelling place. We depart from it in haste. Let us be careful not to be discourteous or neglectful in receiving guests, lest we be denied entrance into the dwelling place of the saints at the end of our life" (Ambrose, On Abraham 1.5.34; Gen. 18:2).[90]

## 8. Rebekah as an Icon of Hospitality

The Fathers paid special attention to Rebekah, as noted earlier. She is seen in the icons of the Vienna Genesis (sixth century) and in the Mausoleum of the Exodus at El-Bagawat in Egypt (early fifth century). "'She hastened' the text goes on, remember, 'to empty the water jar into the trough, and ran to draw more at the well, and watered all the camels.' See her heightened enthusiasm," notes Chrysostom. She "neither neglected him as an utter stranger nor declined his request on the pretext of prudence, but rather saying with great restraint, 'Drink, sir.' I ask you to consider how very proper, despite her tender years, was her modesty, her surpassing humility, and the extent of her hospitality" (Chrysostom, Homilies on Genesis 48.16; Gen. 24:20).[91]

Rebekah *ran* to announce to her family the stranger in their presence. "When he saw the child's candor and learned everything from her clearly, then he, in turn, made known to her who he was. Through his thanksgiving to God, he made clear to her the fact that he had not come from some alien house, but that the man who had sent him was brother to Nahor. On learning this 'the girl ran off,' the text says, with great joy. See how *in everything done by her she shows her enthusiasm for hospitality — by running, by her words, by her restraint*" (Chrysostom, Homilies on Genesis 48.19, italics added; Gen. 24:28).[92] Icons served the purpose of teaching hospitality.

90. CSEL 32 1:528; ACCS OT 2:64*.
91. FC 87:33-34*; ACCS OT 2:128*.
92. FC 87:35*; ACCS OT 2:131.

9. *So?*

The ancient Christian writers viewed acts of hospitality in the light of God's hospitality to us, as seen finally in the welcoming acts of the incarnate Lord. They were active humanitarians long before modern humanitarianism. We do well now to unlearn much of what we have presupposed about them. We expect them to be hardened ideologues without a heart. We are surprised when they turn out to be kind, gentle, and caring.

## H. Clothing the Naked: "You Clothed Me"

### 1. *The Pattern*

We proceed with the same order for considering good works that the Fathers found embedded textually in Jesus' parable of the sheep and the goats.

The next good work: clothe the naked. Listen carefully to the ancient Christian exegetes and you will discover the Christological richness of classic Christian reflection on clothing for the needy. It is about more than fabrics.

### 2. *You Clothed Me*

The pattern in the Christian life for clothing the naked is Jesus' own clothing of our nakedness of sin and guilt. Not only did Jesus *cover our nakedness,* but we are called to *cover his,* viewed from the perspective of the "least of these." This is the surprising reversal in his statement: "I was naked and *you clothed me*" (Matt. 25:36, RSV). Jesus himself indeed had his raiment taken from him on the cross: "For his vesture, they did cast lots" (John 19:24, KJV*).

Patristic comment was not satisfied with simply commending the physical clothing of the naked, although indeed that is an absolutely crucial task. Rather it was concerned with a much wider reflection on the body, its clothing, and the relation of the body and clothing to God's larger purpose. Much of the patristic comment on clothing focuses on God's provision for the human condition, of which clothing is a prevailing symbol. Acts of mercy for the naked are best understood in the context of the larger arena of human destiny — the unclothed state of Paradise and the end of human destiny in the resurrection where the faithful are clothed in Christ's righteousness. Failure to understand this context results in a failure to understand the clothing of the naked.

Rightly to understand the clothing of the naked requires some further reflection on a subject some might view as surprising: the glory of nakedness in Eden. Clothing is viewed in relation to the shamelessness of the body in the original state. The need for clothing the naked belongs to the fallen state of the human history of sin. Only in that frame, the Fathers argued, will we understand the importance of clothing the naked in the fallen world.

### 3. The Glory of Nakedness in the Original State, Now Fallen

The nakedness of baptism is a reminder of the blessed nakedness of Adam and Eve in the Garden. Chrysostom speaks of baptism as a reconstitution of our original human condition: "After stripping you of your robe, the priest himself leads you down into the flowing waters. But why naked? He reminds you of your former nakedness, *when you were in paradise and you were not ashamed.* For Holy Writ says, 'Adam and Eve were naked and were not ashamed,' until they took up the garment of sin, a garment heavy with abundant shame" (Chrysostom, Baptismal Instruction 11.28, italics added; Gen. 2:25).[93]

There is nothing shocking about nakedness from God's point of view. God made us that way. Clothing was not necessary in the original state. It was only when Adam hid himself from God that he even became aware of his own nakedness. Let Augustine explain: "When Adam heard God's voice, he answered that he hid because he was naked. His answer was wretchedly in error, as if a man naked, as God had made him, could be displeasing to him. *It is a distinguishing mark of error that whatever anyone finds personally displeasing he imagines is displeasing to God as well.* We should understand the loftier meaning of these words of the Lord, 'Who told you that you were naked, unless because you have eaten from that tree about which I told you that from it alone you should not eat?' Previously he was naked of any dissimulation, clothed with divine light. But from this

---

93. ACWCh 31: 170; ACCS OT 1:72.

light he turned away and turned toward himself. This is the meaning of his having eaten from that tree. He saw his nakedness, and it was displeasing to himself because he now did not even have his own body properly ordered" (Augustine, Two Books on Genesis Against the Manichaeans 2.16.24, italics added; Gen. 3:10-12).[94]

Adam's denial of his nakedness was pivotal in the fall. He was dishonest with himself and with God. Listen to Symeon the New Theologian develop this important passage (Gen. 3:10-13), which stands at the head of all passages of scripture dealing with nakedness and clothing:

> Do you see, dear friend, how patient God is? For when he said, "Adam, where are you?" and when Adam did not at once confess his sin but said, "I heard your voice, O Lord, and realized that I am naked and hid myself," God was not angered, nor did he immediately turn away. Rather, he gave him the opportunity of a second reply and said, "Who told you that you are naked, unless you ate of the tree of which I commanded you not to eat." Consider how profound are the words of God's wisdom. He says, "Why do you say that you are naked but hide your sin? Do you really think that I see only your body but do not see your heart and your thoughts?" *Since Adam was deceived, he hoped that God would not recognize his sin.* He said something like this to himself, "If I say that I am naked, God in his ignorance will say, 'Why are you naked?' Then I shall have to deny and say, 'I do not know,' and so I shall not be caught by him and he will give me back the garment that I had at first. If not, as long as he does not cast me out, he will not exile me!" While he was thinking these thoughts . . . God says, "How did you realize that you are naked, unless you ate of the tree of which I commanded you not to eat?" It is as though he said, "Do you really think that you can hide from me? Do you imagine that I do not know what you have done? Will you not say, 'I have sinned'? You scoundrel! Say rather: 'Yes, it is true, Master, I have transgressed your command. . . . Have mercy on me!'" But he does not humble himself. He does not bend. The neck of his heart is like a sinew of iron [cf. Isa. 48:4]! For had he said this he might have stayed in paradise. (Symeon the New Theologian, Discourses 5.5, italics added; Gen. 3:10-12)[95]

94. FC 84:120-21; ACCS OT 1:85*.
95. CWSS 95-96; ACCS OT 1:85-86*.

## 4. While the Fallen Adam Needed Clothing, the Ascended Lord Did Not

Another surprising wrinkle in the patristic view of clothing is this: The risen Lord did not take clothes along with him in the resurrection or ascension. What happened to his clothes? Ephrem the Syrian deliberately explores the resurrection narrative on this point: "If he left his clothes behind in the tomb, it was so that Adam could enter into paradise without clothing, just as he had been before he had sinned [cf. Gen. 2:25]. In place of having to leave paradise clothed, he now had to strip himself before entering there again. He abandoned clothing to symbolize the mystery of the resurrection of the dead. *Just as the Lord rose into glory without clothes, so we also will rise with our works and not with our clothes*" (Ephrem the Syrian, Commentary on Tatian's Diatessaron 21.23, italics added; Luke 24:12).[96] That is the world-historical frame of reference for viewing the need for clothing, in the patristic view.

That Christ ascended without clothes is only shocking from the viewpoint of human fallenness. Why would clothing be needed in the resurrection? "Adam, who desired clothing, was conquered (cf. Gen. 3:7). He who laid down his clothes conquered. He ascended in the same way that nature formed us with God as Creator" (Ambrose, Exposition of the Gospel of Luke, 10.110; Luke 23:34).[97]

## 5. God's Provision of Covering That Does Not Wear Out

The forty years of wilderness wandering in Sinai provided the prevailing metaphor for God's provision of clothing, analogous to the food provided in the desert. But clothing differed from food in one decisive way: The manna God gave the wandering people of Israel to eat was given every day. It was *perishable*, not hoardable, not storable. Unlike the perishable food, the clothing God gave them to wear in the desert *did not wear out*. "God granted to the garments of the Israelites their proper state without any damage for forty years. If so, how much more does he grant a very happy temperament to the bodies of those who obey his command until they

---

96. ECTD 328; ACCS NT 3:376*.
97. EHG 424*; ACCS NT 3:362.

may be turned into something better?" (Augustine, On the Good of Marriage 2.2; Deut. 8:4).[98]

Rightly viewed, the clothing we are being given by God does not wear out, as does our ordinary clothing. God's provision of durable clothing for the people of Israel stands in strict contrast with the ephemeral nature of manna. God continued both to clothe and feed Israel even when they were unfaithful. "If God nourished Israel for forty years in the desert while they were murmuring and disbelieving, and effortlessly preserved their sandals and clothing, how much more so in the case of believers?" (Ephrem the Syrian, Commentary on Tatian's Diatessaron 6.18a; Deut. 8:4).[99]

Our temporal clothing stands in counterpoint to the resurrection, in which nothing wears out, neither our resurrected bodies nor the righteousness we have "put on." According to Ambrose: "Is he not good, who in the wilderness fed with bread from heaven such countless thousands lest any famine should assail them, without need of toil, and in the enjoyment of rest? For the space of forty years, their raiment did not grow old, nor were their shoes worn out. This is a figure by which to the faithful point toward the resurrection to come" (Ambrose, On the Christian Faith 2.2.23; Deut. 8:4).[100] John's Revelation (Rev. 3:5; 7:9) looks toward the final day when all who come into God's eternal presence will be clothed in a way fitting to the resurrected state. The faithful "put on" Christ's compassion as their garment for the celestial city. Having "put on" Christ in baptism, they are not without the garment of Christ's righteousness that is fitting for the end-time wedding. "They welcome Christ himself and, by teaching righteousness, clothe those who are naked and lacking any garment of righteousness. As is written: 'Put on, then, compassion, faith, peace and kindness' [Col. 3:12]. That is to say, they clothe Christ and baptize them in Christ, as is written: 'For as many of you as were baptized into Christ have put on Christ' [Gal. 3:27]" (Opus Imperfectum in Matthaeum, Homily 54; Matt. 25:35-40).[101]

Putting on clothing is seen under the analogy of putting on Christ. Origen wove the fabric analogy beautifully: "We have received the fabric of

---

98. FC 27:11*; ACCS OT 3:288.
99. ECTD 121; ACCS OT 3:288.
100. NPNF 2 10:226; ACCS OT 3:288*.
101. PG 56:944; ACCS NT 1b:233*.

wisdom from God that we may impart knowledge to some and clothe them with 'compassion, chastity, kindness, lowliness' and the other excellent behaviors. All these are the spiritual garments of those who have listened to the words of those who teach these virtues, according to him who says, 'Put on, then, compassion, kindness, lowliness, gentleness' and so forth. They are characteristic of life in Christ, who is all these things to the faithful, according to him who said, 'Put on the Lord Jesus' [Rom. 13:14]. Therefore, *when we have clothed with garments of this sort 'one of the least' who believe in Christ, we have apparently clothed the Lord himself,* so that the word of God in the world will not go naked" (Origen, Commentary on Matthew 72, italics added; Matt. 25:35-40).[102] Thus patristic reflection on the good work of clothing the naked goes much deeper than the physical and temporal act of providing clothing that wears out. Rather it is an act viewed in relation to the eternal destiny of humanity in the life to come.

Do we therefore, as we are clothing the naked, tell them these stories of Adam, Moses, and the resurrection? It is better first to help them get warm under the conditions of actually fallen human history. Then when the fitting moment occurs, the opportunity will come to speak of the One in whose name the warm clothing has been offered.

### 6. Caring for the Body in Proper Balance without Anxiety

The body is good, and yet its goodness, because good, is subjected by our choices to fallenness and corruption. Our bodies are not incorruptibly good, otherwise they would seem to take an equal place with God's own incomparable goodness. How our bodies become corrupted is the story of our fallen lives, each of them different, yet the basic story line remains for all the same. As the body God gives is good, so is the clothing to protect the body proximately good under the alienated conditions of the history of sin.

The faithful are not embarrassed over having bodies, but over bringing corruptions to the temple of God, the body that God provides for us to live in. "*We do not want to be delivered from the body, but only from the corruption which is in it,*" wrote Chrysostom. "Our body is a burden to us, not because it is a body, but because it is corruptible and liable to suffering. But

102. GCSO 1038.2:169; ACCS NT 1b:233*.

when the new life comes it will take away this corruption, yet the corruption, I say, is not the body itself" (Chrysostom, Homilies on the Epistles of Paul to the Corinthians 10.3, italics added; 2 Cor. 5:4).[103]

Are we thus given license by the Gospel to neglect either our bodies or our clothing? Caesarius of Arles deliberately explored this question: "Perhaps someone says, 'Who can always be thinking of God and eternal bliss, since all must be concerned about food, clothing and the management of their household?' God does not ask us to be free from all anxiety over the present life, for he instructs us through his apostle, 'If any man will not work, neither let him eat.' The same apostle repeats the idea with reference to himself when he says, 'We worked night and day so that we might not burden any of you' [1 Thess. 2:9; 2 Thess. 3:8]. God advises *reasonable concern for food and clothing*, so long as avarice and ambition are not predominant" (Caesarius of Arles, Sermons 45.1, italics added; 2 Thess. 3:10).[104]

## 7. Anxiety about Clothing: Consider the Lilies

The faithful are aware of the vulnerability of everything humans pretend to possess. This is especially poignant in the case of clothing, which is so petty and pitiable when seen in relation to Eden and final judgment.

Jesus raised the fundamental question quite personally: "Why are you anxious about clothing? Consider the lilies of the field, how they grow; they neither toil nor spin; yet I tell you, even Solomon in all his glory was not arrayed like one of these. But if God so clothes the grass of the field, which today is alive and tomorrow is thrown into the oven, will he not much more clothe you?" (Matt. 6:28-30, RSV).

Chrysostom noted "the acceleration of images: Just when the lilies are decked out, he no longer calls them lilies, but 'grass of the field.' He then points further to their condition of vulnerability, by saying 'which today is.' Then he does not merely say, 'and tomorrow is not,' but rather more harshly 'cast into the oven.' These creatures are not merely clothed, but 'so clothed' in this way, as to be later brought to nothing. Do you see how he everywhere abounds in amplifications and intensifications? And this he

103. NPNF 1 12:327; ACCS NT 7:240*.
104. FC 31:226-27*; ACCS NT 9:124*.

does in order to press them home. So then he adds: *'Will he not much more clothe you?'* The force of the emphasis is upon you yourself, to indicate quietly how great is the value God sets upon your personal existence, and the concern God shows for you alone. It is as though he were saying: 'It is you, to whom he gave a soul, for whom he fashioned a body, for whose sake he made everything in creation, for whose sake he sent prophets, and gave the law, and wrought those innumerable good works, and for whose sake he gave up his only begotten Son'" (Chrysostom, The Gospel of Matthew, Homily 22.1, italics added; Matt. 6:27-30).[105]

The faithful need not be anxious about what they put on. Excess does not increase benefit, according to Cyril, nor does deficiency reduce it. Jesus called his disciples to "abandon unnecessary anxiety. He does not allow a careworn and frenetic diligence that would make you wish to gather what exceeds your necessities. In these matters excess adds nothing to your benefit. 'Do not be anxious,' therefore, he says, 'about your life, what you shall eat, nor about your body, what you shall put on. For life is more than food, and the body more than clothing' [Matt. 6:25]. He did not simply say, 'Do not be anxious,' but added 'about your life,' that is, do not give too much attention to food and clothing as such, but devote your earnestness to that which is of far greater importance. For *life indeed is of more importance than food, and the body is more important than clothing.* Since, therefore, we are at risk concerning both life and body, and pain and punishment are justly decreed against those who are determined not to live uprightly, let all anxiety be laid aside with regard to clothing and food" (Cyril of Alexandria, Commentary on Luke, Homily 90, italics added; Luke 12:22-28).[106] This does not make clothing the naked unimportant, but its importance is seen in relation to the Source and End of all that is.

Still we are prone to ask anxiously about who will provide what we need. According to Cyril: "Understandably you may reply: 'Who then will give us the necessities of life?' Our answer to this is as follows: The Lord is worthy to be trusted, and he clearly promises to you and through little things gives you full assurance that he will be true also in great things. 'Consider,' he says, 'the ravens: they neither sow nor reap, they have neither storehouse nor barn, and yet God feeds them.' . . . Through the birds and the flowers of the field, he invites you to a firm and unwavering faith. He

---

105. PG 57:299; NPNF 1 10:150**; ACCS NT 1a:145*.
106. CGSL 363**; ACCS NT 3:209-10*.

does not give us any room to conjure up doubt, but rather gives us the certainty that he will grant us his mercy and stretch out his comforting hand, that we may have sufficiency in all things" (Cyril of Alexandria, Commentary on Luke, Homily 90; Luke 12:22-28).[107]

God who gives us a capacity for reason invites us to trust his provision after the pattern of the flowers who lack speech, reason, and a wide range of self-determination. "Even the non-rational things are so clothed by God's providence that they do not lack in their use of grace or for ornament. One can never lack who believes, and by believing places all his usefulness in God's hand. He does not dishonor the faith or waver in any way" (Ambrose, Exposition of the Gospel of Luke, 7.125; Luke 12:22-28).[108]

### 8. Toward Modesty

Ambrose puts clothing in proper perspective in commending modesty: "A noble thing, then, is modesty, which, though giving up its rights, seizing on nothing for itself, laying claim to nothing and in some ways somewhat retiring within the sphere of its own powers, yet is rich in the sight of God, in relation to whom no temporal creature is rich. Richness is modesty, for it is the portion of God. Paul asked that prayer be offered up with modesty and sobriety" (Ambrose, Duties of the Clergy 1.18.70; 1 Tim. 2:9a).[109]

Modesty enhances attractiveness. This seemliness is pleasing to God, Ambrose thought: "Let us then hold fast modesty and that moderation which adds to the beauty of the whole of life. For it is no light thing in every matter to preserve due measure and to bring about order. In this what we call decorum, or seemliness, is made more conspicuous. This is so closely connected with what is virtuous that one cannot separate the two" (Ambrose, Duties of the Clergy 1.45.228; 1 Tim. 2:9a).[110] This point brings us to the texts and icons portraying John the Baptist.

107. CGSL 364**; ACCS NT 3:210*.
108. EHG 282**; ACCS NT 3:210**.
109. NPNF 2 10:13*; ACCS NT 9:164*.
110. NPNF 2:10:36-37; ACCS NT 9:164*.

## 9. The Icon of John the Baptist

You cannot separate the kind of faith you have from the kind of life you live. This includes clothing. When asked by his hearers, "What shall we do?" to evidence sincere repentance, John the Baptist answered: "He who has two coats, let him share with him who has none" (Luke 3:11b, RSV). No patristic account of clothing the naked would neglect discussing the distinctive clothing of John the Baptist. It runs directly counter to modern narcissism.

John's own clothing typified the Nazirite life — ascetic, set apart for the desert, spare to the extreme. But Maximus of Turin noticed something else about the Baptist's clothing — highly symbolic — he was clothed with the skins of an "unclean" animal (a camel)! "Indeed, when Christ's forerunner wore a coarse camel-hair garment, what else does it signify but that the coming Christ would be vested in the garb of a human body, thick with the coarseness of sinners, and that, girded with the skins of a most unclean animal, the Gentile people, he bore their very own deformity?" (Maximus of Turin, Sermons 88.3; Matt. 3:4).[111] So Christ was humbled in the incarnation to assume a human body, in some ways analogous to John who wore a coarse garment. Christ identified with the Gentiles, just as John became clothed in the skins of an unclean animal. These are details that fascinated the Fathers.

Does the modest clothing of the faithful point to their seriousness about repentance? Peter Chrysologus struck this analogy concerning the clothing of John the Baptist: "He wore a garment of camel's hair with nothing refined about it, nothing graceful, nothing comely. By nature it was intended for hard work and heavy burdens, and suggested simple obedience. The teacher of repentance ought to be vested with such a garment, so that those who had turned away from virtue in their education and given themselves shamelessly over to sin might be subdued by the great burden of penance, consigned to the rigors of restitution, and experience the heavy sighs of contrition. Thus refashioned and slimmed down into the form of a needle, they might obtain ample remission through the narrow opening of penance, and the Lord's words would then be fulfilled concerning a camel passing through the eye of a needle" (Peter Chrysologus, Sermon 167.8; Matt. 3:4).[112]

---

111. CCL 23:360; ACCS NT 1a:40-41.
112. CCL 24b:1028-29; ACCS NT 1a:41*.

John the Baptist's garb spoke as loudly as the repentance he preached in the royal court. John Chrysostom, the preacher to the imperial court of Constantinople, did not hesitate to attest this, even though it would later cost him his life:

> It was fitting that the forerunner of the One who was to put away all the ancient ills, the labor, the curse, the sorrow, the sweat, bear tokens of the situation prior to the fall of Adam. This is why he neither tilled the land, nor ploughed furrows, nor ate bread by the sweat of his brow. Rather his table was hastily supplied, and his clothing more easily furnished than his table, and his lodging even less troublesome than his clothing. For he needed neither roof, nor bed, nor table, nor any other earthly comfort. He lived a kind of angelic life in this our flesh. For this reason his very garment was of hair, that by his very dress he might instruct persons to separate themselves from all worldly things, to have nothing in common with the earth, but to hasten back to their original undefiled nobility — the condition in which Adam lived before he required garments or robe. Thus *John's very garb bore tokens of nothing less than the marks of the coming kingdom,* and of repentance. (Chrysostom, The Gospel of Matthew, Homily 10.4, italics added; Matt. 3:4)[113]

John's clothing was like his food — modest to the extreme. "The heavenly life and glorious humility of John are demonstrated in his manner of living and in his clothing. He who held the world in modest regard did not seek costly attire. He who had no use for worldly delights did not have any desire for succulent foods. What need was there of fancy worldly attire for one who was vested with the cloak of justice? What dainty food of the earth could he desire who fed on divine discourses and whose true food was the law of Christ?" (Chromatius of Aquileia, Tractate on Matthew 9.1; Matt. 3:4).[114]

Most Byzantine places of worship featured a *deesis,* an invocation or invitation, in which the figures of John the Baptist and the Virgin Mary accompanied the Lord. The iconic portrayal of John typically emphasizes his rugged clothing. John the Baptist remains the patristic model for a modest

---

113. PG 57:188; NPNF 1 10:64**; ACCS NT 1a:40*.
114. CCL 9a:231; ACCS NT 1a:40*.

and constrained way of life. Byzantine iconography made this unmistakable to the worshiping community who saw John portrayed in every Eucharist.

When penitents went out to see John the Baptist, they did not see one clothed in soft finery. "'What did you go out into the wilderness to behold? A man clothed in soft raiment?' A lover of present pleasure who gladly made use of the earthly goods of the present? Didn't you see that his garment was of camel's hair, and he wore a leather girdle around his waist? And his food was locusts and wild honey. By the testimony of his own way of life, Jesus sentenced the world and its goods, and yet he remained steadfastly in the world" (Opus Imperfectum in Matthaeum, Homily 27; Matt. 11:8).[115]

As was typical of Origen, he found spiritual significance in even the locusts and honey on which John the Baptist survived: "John ate locusts, suggesting that the people of God were being nourished by a word which traveled high aloft in the air, and had not yet passed over the earth. In the second place John ate honey, which is not obtained by men by their own efforts" (Origen, Fragments, Commentaries on the Gospel of Matthew 41; Matt. 3:4).[116]

## 10. So, What Does This All Mean?

Returning to our theme, does this ascetic emphasis mean that the actual offering of actual clothing to needy people was unimportant, and that their spiritual clothing only was important to the Fathers? The opposite is true. The physical clothing of the naked remains a good work for which we will be accountable on the last day. Someone is cold. Help make them warm. The vast import of the actual clothing of the naked is best seen in the light of human creation, the fall, redemption, and final human destiny. By clothing the naked, wrote Origen, "we have woven a garment for the cold and shivering Christ" (Origen, Commentary on Matthew 72; Matt. 25:35-40).[117]

Where brothers and sisters are shivering, we are called to cover them with warm clothing, just as we would the body of Christ. Those who live in luxury while neglecting the naked will face a hard time on judgment day. Those who deprive the poor of their basic needs while attending only to

115. PG 56:773-74; ACCS NT 1a:221*.
116. GCSO 4112.1:32; ACCS NT 1a:41*.
117. GCSO 3810.2:169; ACCS NT 1b:233.

their own comfort and ostentation will have little defense, according to John Chrysostom: "For what reason will you be able to state your defense when the Lord lays these pearls to your charge and brings the poor who have perished with hunger into your midst? For this reason, Paul said, 'not with braided hair, or gold, or pearls or costly raiment.' For these would be a snare. . . . *Take off all ornament and place it in the hands of Christ through the poor*" (Chrysostom, Instructions to Catechumens 2.4, italics added; 1 Tim. 2:9b).[118]

One of the specific trials reported by Paul in his demanding ministry was nakedness. Paul went through a wide range of experiences, including hunger, thirst, weariness, and pain, but also, he says, nakedness (2 Cor. 11:27). Paul may have been referring to those times when he had "shivered with cold, without enough clothing to keep me warm" (1 Cor. 11:27, Tay). "I have been through toil and hardship. I have passed many a sleepless night; I have endured hunger and thirst; I have often been without food; I have known cold and nakedness" (1 Cor. 11:27, TCNT). Everyone knows how uncomfortable that can feel. Yet he pursues the analogy in the light of his participation in Christ, teaching that however exposed we may be, our nakedness is not "able to separate us from the love of God" (Rom. 8:39, KJV).

## I. Sheltering Refugees and Displaced Persons: "You Took Me In"

### 1. The Pattern

The pattern for understanding and caring for the refugee begins with Jesus' own human experience of refugee status. Classic Christianity begins reflection on refugee relief by remembering Jesus' own deportation, expatriation, expulsion, exile, and émigré position. He became a refugee himself on our behalf.

Listen carefully to the Fathers, and you will discover the richness of classic Christian reflection on *good works among displaced persons*. It is about more than migration or population shifts. It is about human displacement, God's own identification with the exiled, and the displaced neighbor in Christ.

118. NPNF 1 9:169-70*; ACCS NT 9:164-65*.

He had no place to lay his head. Even the first episode of his child-hood narrative stresses that he and his family fled their native country as displaced persons, escaping persecution to a safe haven — Egypt.

## 2. Doing Good for the Refugee

What good can we do for the refugee, who is expelled from his people and in desperate flight? First we learn to empathize, as did Israel through the experience of being an "outcast" people (Jer. 30:17, KJV). As refugees, the faithful in foreign slavery and captivity learned to "sing the Lord's song in a strange land" (Ps. 137:4, KJV). This is where empathy for refugees is most deeply learned — by the experience of displacement. We grasp it by having been placed in refugee status ourselves, just as happened to Israel, when "by the rivers of Babylon, there we sat down and we wept when we remem-bered Zion" (Ps. 137:1, KJV*).

God is "a refuge" for the faithful in time of trouble (Ps. 62:8, KJV). Christianity has poignant memories of early Christians who were them-selves persecuted and forced to flee for refuge: we "have fled for refuge to lay hold upon the hope set before us" (Heb. 6:18, KJV). The refugee takes refuge in "the shadow of God's wings" (Ps. 36:7). There they discover that the Lord is their "rock" of protection (Ps. 71:3, RSV).

Out of the experience of being a refugee, the people of Israel learned not to vex strangers or oppress them, since they themselves once "were strangers in the land of Egypt" (Exod. 22:21, RSV). The covenant people themselves have been in the position of the "poor of the earth who hide themselves together" (Job 24:4, KJV*). The people of God know what it means to be huddled in a "hiding place from the wind and a covert from the tempest, as rivers of waters in a dry place, as the shadow of a great rock in a weary land" (Isa. 32:2, KJV). From the saints and prophets we learn how special is the sense in which they are "blessed who take refuge in God" (Ps. 2:12, NIV*).

## 3. Interceding for the Refugee

What can the covenant people do for the refugee? Even if they are power-less, they can at least intercede for them, pray that God will guard them

(Ps. 91:11), that the peace of God will be with their hearts and minds (Phil. 4:7), that they be kept from the evil one (John 17:15), that their lives would be protected (Ps. 64:1), that they might dwell in safety (Ps. 4:8). Such prayers are offered up in virtually every Christian service of worship.

Whatever refugees need, they should be treated by the faithful as the needy in the most urgent sense, that is, subject to the special emergency conditions that prevail in refugee status. There one is in the most absolute sense a stranger, standing in dire need to be cared for, without protection of the government, family, or friends. This is why it is not incidental for Christian good works that the holy family itself is portrayed as a refugee family. This ironic fact fascinated the Fathers.

### 4. The Holy Family Themselves Were Displaced Persons: The Flight to Egypt

The holy family was a fugitive family in a foreign country. From the outset, even as a child, Jesus was a displaced person. This is evident from the narrative of the flight to Egypt.

Early Christian iconography repeatedly portrayed this picture: the holy family in flight. You can see this portrayed in Ravenna, Rome, and most powerfully in the Chora church of Constantinople. John Chrysostom observed that Jesus lacked a home "even when he came in swaddling clothes. Thus you see even at his birth a tyrant raging, a flight ensuing, and a departure beyond the border. For it was because of no crime that his family was exiled into the land of Egypt. Similarly, you yourself need not be troubled if you are suffering countless dangers. Do not expect to be celebrated or crowned promptly for your troubles. Instead you may keep in mind the longsuffering example of the mother of the Child, bearing all things nobly, knowing that such *a fugitive life is not inconsistent with the hidden ordering of spiritual things.* You are sharing the kind of travail Mary herself shared. So did the Magi. All of them were willing to retire secretly in the humiliating role of fugitive" (Chrysostom, The Gospel of Matthew, Homily 8.3, italics added; Matt. 2:13).[119] Under the conditions of the history of sin, Christians are not surprised at (or overcome by) the horrible conditions of displacement.

---

119. PG 57:83-84; NPNF 1 10:51-52**; ACCS NT 1a:31*.

## 5. What Does Jesus' Flight from Death Teach about Ministry to Refugees?

The Fathers understood that the flight to Egypt was not motivated by any personal fear, but by the requirements of salvation history. "His flight then was not occasioned by fear but by what had come through the mystery of prophecy" (Peter Chrysologus, Sermons 150.11).[120] "It was not out of fear that he withdrew. By doing the things he did, he taught us to escape from persecutors" (Cyril of Alexandria, Fragments on Matthew 34, quoted in Reuss; Matt. 4:12).[121]

The faithful are not to seek persecution. If, however, it becomes the only available recourse, they face with equanimity its limitations and consequences. "When you flee Egypt, you come to these steep ascents of faith and action. You face a tower, a sea and waves. The way of life is not pursued without the waves of temptation" (Origen, Homilies on Exodus 5.3; 2 Tim. 3:12).[122]

The holy family had to flee in order to allow Jesus to grow up, and to grow up in order to take on his messianic vocation, and to live in order to die for us: "Christ fled for us, not for himself," wrote Peter Chrysologus. "Christ fled that by granting absolution he might take away the source of abuses to come, and that he might give proof of faith to those who would believe. Christ fled in time that he might bestow on us hope of escape. In the face of persecution, it is better to flee than to refuse. For Peter, because he was unwilling to flee, foreswore; John, lest he foreswear, fled" (Peter Chrysologus, Sermon 150.11; Matt. 2:13).[123]

The death Jesus escaped as a refugee infant he would not flee as an adult: "Christ promised that he would come in the flesh, that he would go through the phases of life, that he would announce the glory of the kingdom of heaven, that he would proclaim the way of faith, and that by the power of his word alone he would put to flight demons. He promised that he would give sight to the blind, gait to the lame, speech to the mute, hearing to the deaf, remission for sinners, and life to the dead. All these things were promised through the law and the prophets. Thus it was that Christ,

---

120. CCL 24b:938, ACCS NT 1a:31.
121. MKGK 163; ACCS NT 1a:66.
122. FC 71:280; ACCS NT 9:265*.
123. CCL 24b:938-39; ACCS NT 1a:31-32*.

when he was to become a man, was not to flee the death he escaped as an infant" (Peter Chrysologus, Sermon 150.10; Matt. 2:14).[124]

Obviously the presence of the Christ child was unwelcome to the civil authorities. The flight was covert. Joseph "rose and took the child and his mother *by night,* and departed to Egypt" (Matt. 2:14, RSV, italics added). John Chrysostom commented: "Mary had never even passed over the threshold of her own house" after the birth of Jesus, "yet she was commanded to undergo this long ordeal of adversity for the sake of this wonderful birth, and for her own spiritual travail. Isn't this remarkable: *While Palestine plots, it is Egypt that receives* and preserves the One for whom the plots are designed! This is reminiscent of the patriarch Jacob who also sought succor in Egypt [Gen. 45:25–46:7], anticipating the coming of our Lord" (Chrysostom, The Gospel of Matthew, Homily 8.3, italics added; Matt. 2:14).[125] The mother of Jesus was willing to undergo hardship and flight from dangerous civil authorities for her child.

It was necessary, within salvation history, for the holy family to become displaced persons under threat from the civil authorities. The narrative in Matthew is filled with this irony, according to John Chrysostom: "Nothing restrained Herod. This is how wickedness works — it stumbles over its own greed, always attempting vain objectives. What utter folly. So on any premise his craftiness was bizarre. It was also folly for him to think that the wise men would take him more seriously than the Child whom they had come so far to see, whose identity had been confirmed by prophecy. How could Herod hope to persuade the wise men to betray this Child to him, even before they had seen the One for whom they had so long hoped? Nevertheless, as many as were the good reasons to hold him back, Herod persisted with his evil attempt, having 'summoned the wise men secretly and ascertained from them' [Matt. 2:7]" (Chrysostom, The Gospel of Matthew, Homily 7.3; Matt. 2:8).[126] "With all these miscalculations, [Herod] called in the wise men privately and sought to discern the timing of the star. The object of his pursuit was far more than a star. For the star, I think, must have appeared and been visible a long time before, because it took a long time for the wise men to come on their journey to find him in swaddling clothes. If the star appeared at the moment of his birth in Pales-

---

124. CCL 24b:938; ACCS NT 1a:32-33*.
125. PG 57:85; NPNF 1 10:52**; ACCS NT 1a:32*.
126. NPNF 1 10:45-46**; ACCS NT 1a:24*.

tine, it would have already been seen by many in the distant East. It would have consumed a lot of time to get there. As to his slaying all children 'who were two years old and under,' this shows the extent of his irrational wrath and dread in trying to prevent even one from escaping" (Chrysostom, The Gospel of Matthew, Homily 7.3; Matt. 2:8).[127]

Meanwhile the faithful are still called to remain subject to rulers and authorities (Rom. 13:1; 13:5; Tit. 3:1; 1 Pet. 2:13). "But our commonwealth is in heaven, and from it we await a Savior, the Lord Jesus Christ, who will change our lowly body to be like his glorious body, by the power which enables him even to subject all things to himself" (Phil. 3:20-21, RSV).

## J. The Homeless: "He Had No Place to Lay His Head"

The pattern in the Christian life for sheltering the homeless presupposes Jesus' own lack of shelter, and his provision of shelter for the faithful. Not only did Jesus provide us shelter, but we are called to provide him shelter, viewed from the perspective of the "least of these."

Jesus responded to a scribe who wanted to follow him wherever he might go: "Foxes have holes, and birds of the air have nests; but the Son of man has nowhere to lay his head" (Matt. 8:20, RSV). The incarnate Lord was himself homeless, having no place to lay his head. Our pattern for caring for the homeless remains Jesus' own participation in their homelessness by himself becoming homeless on behalf of fallen humanity. Listen carefully to the Fathers, and you will discover the richness of classic Christian reflection on the care of the homeless.

### 1. The Good Work of Offering Shelter

Patristic reflection on the good work of offering shelter goes much deeper than the physical and temporal act of providing a roof. Rather, simple acts of mercy for the homeless are best understood in relation to the eternal destiny of humanity in its origins and in the life to come.

Patristic comment was not satisfied with simply commending the physical provision of shelter, although indeed that is what is most immedi-

---

127. NPNF 1 10:46**; ACCS NT 1a:24*.

ately required. In addition, it was concerned with a much wider understanding of the home of the human spirit, the shelter of God's grace, and assured identity within the inheritance and family of God. Failure to understand this context results in a failure to understand the vitality underlying the Christian's concern for sheltering others.

It is within the range of every believer to practice this simple good work — offering shelter. It does not require special education or abilities. It only requires a good will transformed by grace to do this good work.

The churches in classical Christianity were engaged in organized and regular ministries to the homeless long before the appearance of modern urban homelessness. Most modern readers will not bring an expectation to the Fathers that they could have sympathized with the tragic proportions of modern homelessness. We expect them to be focused more on intact families, not on the alienated who have no viable families, on upright citizens living in houses, not the homeless. We are surprised when the Fathers turn out to be very actively engaged in ministries offering shelter to the homeless, and in interpreting those ministries.

We are asking how the ancient Fathers understood the shelter they actually offered to the homeless. The answer is found in their homilies on scripture texts on the homelessness of the people of Israel, the manger, and the house not made with hands.

## 2. Manger Born

Jesus identified decisively with the homeless by himself living without shelter. The fact that the incarnate Lord was born in a manger without a place to lay his head was a preliminary indication of how far God is willing to go to identify with the homeless.

We are prone to demean the homeless today who live in miserable conditions. But we forget that Jesus himself was born in a stable reeking of animal feces. Jerome, who lived for decades in Bethlehem on the traditional site of that very stable, reflected in this way on God's own homelessness: "He is not born in the midst of gold and riches, but in the midst of dung, in a stable where our sins were filthier than the dung. He is born on a dunghill in order to lift up those who come from it: 'From the dunghill he lifts up the poor' [Ps. 113:7 (LXX 112:7)]" (Jerome, On the Nativity of the Lord; Luke 2:6-7).[128]

This irony was also noted by Ambrose: "He had no other place in the inn, so that you may have many mansions in the heavens [cf. John 14:2; Eph. 2:6]. 'He, being rich, became poor for your sakes, that through his poverty you might be rich' [2 Cor. 8:9]. Therefore his poverty is our inheritance, and the Lord's weakness is our strength. He chose to lack for himself, that he might abound for all" (Ambrose, Exposition of the Gospel of Luke, 2.41; Luke 2:6-7).[129]

But his lack of shelter did not diminish his glory: "He who sits at the right hand of the Father goes without shelter from the inn, that he may prepare for us many mansions [John 14:2] in the house of his heavenly Father. . . . He was born not in the house of his parents but at the inn, by the wayside" (Bede the Venerable, Exposition of the Gospel of Luke 2; Luke 2:6-7).[130]

### 3. Swaddling Clothes

We first meet the Christ child in the most modest raiment — what Luke called "swaddling clothes" (Luke 2:7, KJV). Bede reflected upon this paradox: "It should be noted that the sign given of the Savior's birth is not a child enfolded in the purple of Tyre, but one wrapped with rough pieces of cloth. He is not to be found in an ornate golden bed, but in a manger. He took upon himself our lowly mortality. Also for our sakes he took upon himself the clothing of the poor. Though he was rich, yet for our sake he became poor, so that by his poverty we might become rich [2 Cor. 8:9]. Though he was Lord of heaven, he became a poor man on earth, to teach those who lived on earth that by poverty of spirit they might win the kingdom of heaven" (Bede the Venerable, Exposition of the Gospel of Luke, 1; Luke 2:6-7).[131]

128. FC 57:221**; ACCS NT 3:39.
129. EHG 52-53**; ACCS NT 3:38*.
130. SSGF 1:103-4; ACCS NT 3:40*.
131. CCL 120:51-52; ACCS NT 3:38-39*.

### 4. So, What Does This All Mean?

Returning to our theme, does this tolerance for ascetic deprivation mean that the actual offering of shelter to homeless people was unimportant? The opposite is true. The practical offering of actual shelter remains a good work for which we will be accountable on the last day. If someone is out in the weather, provide them a roof.

Jerome portrayed the irony of the unwelcome presence of Jesus in this world in this way: "There was no room for him in the inn. The entire human race had a place, and the Lord about to be born on earth had none. He found no room among men. He found no room in Plato, none in Aristotle, but in a manger, among beasts of burden and brute animals, and among the simple, too, and the innocent. For that reason the Lord says in the Gospel: 'The foxes have dens, and the birds of the air have nests, but the Son of Man has nowhere to lay his head' [Luke 9:58]" (Jerome, Homilies on the Psalms 44; Luke 2:6-7).[132] When we reach out for "the least of these," the homeless, we are reaching out for the One who became homeless on our behalf.

As one who himself faced the perils of North African persecution, Tertullian knew that many of the faithful, like their Lord, would have no place to lay their heads: "You act after the Lord's pattern. He walked in humility and obscurity. He had no definite home. 'The Son of man has nowhere to lay his head.' He is unadorned as to dress. He exercised no right of power even over his own followers. Though knowing his own kingdom, he shrank back from being made a king" (Tertullian, On Idolatry 18; Matt. 8:20).[133]

## K. Nursing the Sick: "You Visited Me"

The right ordering of good works is embedded textually in Jesus' parable of the last judgment. It includes not only visiting the sick, but nursing them back to health, staying with them amid their limitations.

Not only did Jesus visit us in our sickness, he also called us to visit him in his sickness. He meets us in the form of the "least of these." Not

132. FC 48:331-32*; ACCS NT 3:39-40.
133. CCL 2:1119; ANF 3:72-73*; ACCS NT 1a:166*.

only did the Anointed One come to visit us in our predicament; he came to take on our infirmities and bear our sickness (Matt. 8:17). This is an astonishing claim, not found in other world religions that lack the premises of incarnation and trinity.

We will let the Fathers speak for themselves on how Christ meets us in those who are sick, and how we are to be attentive to the sick as the here-and-now situation demands. We can read their homilies, essays, and letters on how to pray for the sick, and why good people suffer illness. We learn from them how sickness affects the whole person — body and soul, how pain may accompany good treatment, and how Jesus' ministry to the sick was passed on to the worshiping community in history.

## 1. The Good Work of Visiting the Sick

Patristic reflection on the good work of caring for the sick goes much deeper than the dutiful act of a hospital visit. Rather, simple acts of mercy for the sick are best understood in relation to God's own compassionate care for all humanity amid our chronic dysfunctions. Patristic comment was not satisfied with simply commending sick visitation, although indeed that is what must be done now, and done well. In addition it was concerned with a much wider reflection on the health of the human spirit, viewed in the light of human history and destiny. Failure to understand this context results in a failure to understand the vitality underlying the Christian's perennial concern for visiting the sick.

The modern mentality rather expects the ancient Christians to be more focused on a judgmental stance and superstitious treatments, than on nursing, helping, and healing. Listen carefully, however, to the Fathers, and you will discover the richness of classic Christian reflection on the care of the sick. It is about more than a cheerful greeting.

The first deliberately established hospital in western history was started by St. Basil of Caesarea in fourth-century Cappadocia. Following this, the churches in classical Christianity were actively engaged in organized and regular ministries for the sick long before modernity.

## 2. The Pattern

We are asking how the ancient church understood (theologically, biblically, and ethically) the nursing, treatment, and caregiving they were actually offering. The answer is found in their detailed exegesis of scripture texts on sickness and health, the body, and God's healing work amid the human condition.

The pattern in the Christian life for healing the sick is Jesus' own healing of human sickness in his messianic ministry. Finally on the last day all will realize that it is in meeting the least of these, the sick and diseased, that we meet the final judge himself.

The care for the sick remains a good work for which we will be accountable on the last day. The vast import of caregiving is best seen in the light of human creation, the fall, redemption, and final human destiny.

## 3. Care for the Sick Is a Work of Love

To visit the sick is to engage in a crucial work of love. Many varied acts of caring for the sick and responding to their ever-changing needs are implied in the simple phrase: "I was sick and you visited me" (Matt. 25:36, RSV).

Faith expresses itself concretely in minute daily works of love. This is what scripture means by "good works." Our faith is tested in our responses to the sick who are unable to care for themselves.

It is within the range of every believer's capacity to practice this simple good work — visiting the sick. It does not require special education or abilities. It requires a good will transformed by grace, however, to do this good work.

## 4. Attentiveness as the Situation Demands

The kind of balm or medicine offered depends entirely upon the particular need of the person at that time. Care is closely related to timing. The principle of timing is this: There is no way for the caregiver or physician to anticipate what a sick person is going to need specifically until the moment that sickness is treated. One remedy may call for salve for the eyes (Rev. 3:18), another for rest (Mark 6:31), another for wine for the stomach's sake (1 Tim. 5:23); another may find that merely having a cheerful heart is a good medicine (Prov. 17:22). Timing is of the essence in medicine and nursing.

Jesus offered care of the sick according to the needs of their circumstances. He "traveled throughout Galilee; like a devoted doctor he attended the seriously ill, dispensing suitable 'medicines' for each and every ailment, because all those weak and suffering people could not come to the doctor" (Opus Imperfectum in Matthaeum, Homily 8; Matt. 4:23).[134] Following the pattern of the servant Messiah, the faithful seek to comfort and cure the sick, with both palliative and curative care. This duty does not displace medical science, but places medical science in a larger salvation history context.

### 5. Simply Being Present Where Suffering Exists

The visitor of the sick must be willing to be physically and emotively present with those who are sick. You are not visiting if you are not there.

Gregory of Nazianzus proposed this analogy: "To blame Jesus for mingling with sinners would be like *blaming a physician for stooping down over suffering and putting up with vile smells in order to heal the sick*" (Gregory Nazianzus, The Second Oration on Easter, italics added; Mark 2:16).[135]

The Opus Imperfectum stated the core of the analogy: "One who visits the sick and those languishing with the disease of earthly vices, who heals them with the medicine of good doctrine, heals the suffering Christ in them" (Opus Imperfectum in Matthaeum, Homily 54; Matt. 25:35-40).[136] As Christ was present to the suffering of the sick, so are the faithful called to be.

### 6. Pain May Accompany the Treatment Itself

As in surgery or cauterization, some pain may be temporarily necessary for the remedy itself. This unintended pain is seen in relation to its purpose.

---

134. PG 56:677; ACCS NT 1a:74.
135. NPNF 2 7:433**; ACCS NT 2:30-31.
136. PG 56:944; ACCS NT 1b:233*.

The sufferer can be helped to understand why treatment itself may require discomfort.

Gregory of Nyssa refined this analogy: "They who use the knife or heat to remove certain unnatural growths in the body, such as cysts or warts, do not bring to the person they are serving a method of healing that is painless, though certainly they apply the knife without any intention of injuring the patient. Similarly whatever material excrescences are hardening on our souls, which have been made carnal by collusion with inordinate passions, will be, in the day of the judgment, cut and scraped away by the ineffable wisdom and power of him who, as the Gospel says, 'healed those that were sick.' For as he says, 'they who are well have no need of the physician, but they that are sick.' Just as the excision of the wart gives a sharp pain to the skin of the body, so then must there be some anguish in the recovering soul which has had a strong bent to evil" (Gregory of Nyssa, The Great Catechism 8; Mark 2:17a).[137] The anguish of the soul may bring one closer to salvation.

The caregiver does not set out to cause pain, but to elicit healing. Augustine commented on the irony of the text: "I will strike and I will heal" (Deut. 32:39, Douay-Rheims). "The surgeon isn't being heartless when he lances the tumor, when he cuts or burns out the suppurating sore. He is causing pain — he certainly is, but in order to restore health. It's a horrid business; but if it wasn't, it wouldn't be any use" (Augustine, Sermon 77.3; Deut. 32:39).[138]

### 7. The Doctor-Patient Relationship

The wise comforter or nurse or physician does not cater simply to fleeting emotive desires of the patient, but does what is best for the patient, even if it is a difficult or lengthy or hazardous remedy. "What competent doctor, when asked to cure a sick person, would simply follow the desires of the patient, and not act in accordance with the requirements of good medicine?" asked Irenaeus. "Ignorance, the mother of intractability, is driven out by knowing the truth. Therefore the Lord imparted to his disciples knowledge of the truth, by which he cured those who were suffering, and restrained

137. TLG 2017.046; NPNF 2 5:483-84**; ACCS NT 2:31.
138. WSA 3 3:318; ACCS OT 3:335-36.

sinners from sin. So he did not speak to them in accordance with their previous assumptions, nor answer according to the presumptions of inquirers,
but according to sound teaching, without any pretense or pandering"
(Irenaeus, Against Heresies; Mark 2:17a).[139] Emotive empathy is not the
whole of medicine, though it indeed is the proper beginning for it.

Like a caring physician, God offers what the patient needs, not wants.
"Note in this regard, my brothers, that God does not inquire into the wants
of those who are deliriously ill. He does not wait to see the faith of the ignorant or probe the distraught wishes of the sick. Yet, he does not refuse to
help the faith of another, so that by grace he confers whatever is proper of
the divine will. In fact, my brethren, when does a doctor ever inquire into
or examine the wishes of those who are ailing, for a patient is always of a
contrary mind in his wishes and demands?" (Peter Chrysologus, Sermons
50.4; Matt. 9:2).[140]

Reliable care hinges on what is needed, not what the patient in his
troubled state would temporarily prefer. "Let the sick man, then, not presume on his own strength. They are not made well by their own strength
alone [Ps. 33:16]. Their illness may elicit a kind of delirium that deceives.
They are like those out of their minds, who imagine themselves in such
good health that they do not consult a physician, and even fall upon him
with blows as if he were an intruder!" (Augustine, Letter 157 "To Hilarius";
Mark 2:17a).[141] The good physician views the delirium as a symptom to be
listened to, not a message to be avoided.

### 8. How the Prayer of the Righteous Is Made Effective

Those who pray for the healing of sickness are called to act in ways fitting to
the holy God who is petitioned, according to Maximus the Confessor:
"There are two ways in which the prayer of a righteous man is made effective. The first is when the one praying does so by offering to God his works
done according to his commands. Then the prayer is not just a matter of
words blurted out with the empty echo of the tongue, but powerful and living and inspired with the spirit of the Lord's commandments. For the true

---

139. LCC 1:377*; ACCS NT 2:31.
140. CCL 24:279-80; ACCS NT 1a:174*.
141. Cetedoc 0262, 157.44.2.453.15; FC 20:323**; ACCS NT 2:31**.

basis of prayer and supplication is the fulfillment of the commandments through works of love. This makes the prayer of a righteous person strong and full of power. The second way is when the person who asks for the prayers of a righteous man fulfills the works of the prayer itself by putting his own life aright. Then he makes the prayer of the righteous man strong, because it is reinforced by his own wonderful conversion" (Maximus the Confessor, quoted in Cramer, Catena in Epistolas Catholicas; Jas. 5:16b).[142]

"God loves to be asked," wrote Bede, "so he can give" (Bede the Venerable, Homilies on the Gospels 2.14; Jas. 5:16b).[143] Intercessory prayer for the sick is commanded in scripture. It has been a component of public worship since the beginnings of Christianity. The key text is James 5:16 (NIV): "The prayer of a righteous man is powerful and effective."

Bede explained the context of this passage:

James has already advised the person who has been injured or is "in trouble" [Jas. 5:13]. Now he offers counsel to one who is ill [Jas. 5:14-16]. In order to prevent foolish sufferers from excessive complaining, he counseled them to pray and sing. Now he tells the person who is ill, either in body or in faith, to call the elders in for prayer. This is assessed in proportion to the gravity of the illness he is enduring. James does not advise the sick to call in neophytes in counsel. They are less experienced in such matters, and may run the risk of saying or doing something that will only make matters worse. We read in the New Testament that the apostles prayed in this way, and their custom was retained in the church: the elders would anoint a person who is ill and pray for his healing. This is not the exclusive prerogative of elders, for in cases of necessity any Christian may do this (though it is hoped that he would use the holy oil consecrated by the bishop). And of course anyone who anoints a sick person in this way must invoke the name of God over him while doing so. (Bede the Venerable, Concerning the Epistle of St. James; Jas. 5:14)[144]

The apostolic practice of anointing did not await slow historical development, but was in effect from the beginning: "The apostles did this

---

142. CEC 37; ACCS NT 11:61*.
143. CSBH 1:126; ACCS NT 11:61-62.
144. PL 93:39; ACCS NT 11:60**.

even during the time when our Lord was still on earth. They anointed the sick with oil and healed them [Mark 6:13]" (Oecumenius, Commentary on James; Jas. 5:14).[145] According to Caesarius of Arles, "Whenever some illness comes upon a man, he should hurry back to the church. Let him receive the body and blood of Christ, be anointed by the presbyters with consecrated oil and ask them and the deacons to pray over him in Christ's name. If he does this, he will receive not only bodily health but also the forgiveness of his sins" (Caesarius of Arles, Sermons 19.5; Jas. 5:15).[146] "The prayer of faith shall save the sick" (Jas. 5:15, Douay-Rheims). Hilary of Arles wisely noted that the prayer of faith is not an individual act, but an act of the community of faith: "The prayer of faith is the consensus of the whole church, as it is said in the Gospel, 'whatever you ask in my name shall be done for you' [John 16:23]" (Hilary of Arles, Introductory Tractate on the Letter of James; Jas. 5:15).[147]

### 9. The Righteous Suffer — But Why?

Paul's own ministry was troubled by some serious unidentified ailment, which he called a thorn in his flesh. "You know how handicapped I was by illness when I first preached the gospel to you" (Gal. 4:13, Phillips). It was of such importance that it might have threatened his ministry in Galatia, according to Ambrosiaster: "The ailment of the apostle was a trial to the Galatians. But they were found constant, not doubting as to his faith. For they could have stumbled and said, 'What virtue or hope is there in this faith when its minister is so humiliated?'" (Ambrosiaster, On Paul's Epistle to the Galatians 4.14.1-2; Gal. 4:14b).[148]

The strength of active faith does not necessarily prevent the faithful from catching diseases or experiencing bodily harm. Timothy apparently had frequent ailments (1 Tim. 5:23). Epaphroditus was sick, even near death (Phil. 2:26-27). Paul left Trophimus ill at Miletus (2 Tim. 4:20). Each of these passages intrigued the Fathers, and they sought out the divine purpose in these mysteries.

145. PG 119:508; ACCS NT 11:60.
146. FC 31:101; ACCS NT 11:60.
147. PL Suppl. 3:81; ACCS NT 11:60*.
148. CSEL 81.3:47; ACCS NT 8:62*.

Sickness is not to be condemned as absurd or meaningless, though its meaning may be unrecognized. "Of course, even good men can be sick. They too continue to suffer from that disobedience which is the penalty of a primal disobedience which, therefore, is a wound or weakness in a created nature that is good in itself. It is because of this wound that the good who are growing in grace and living by faith during their pilgrimage on earth are given these counsels: 'Bear one another's burdens, and so you will fulfill the law of Christ' [Gal. 6:2], and elsewhere, 'We exhort you, brothers, reprove the irregular, comfort the fainthearted, support the weak, be patient toward all men. See that no one renders evil for evil'" (Augustine, The City of God 15.6; 1 Thess. 5:14).[149] A good counsel is offered within a larger conception of flowing time, and finally toward time's end. Our passing sicknesses are viewed by classic Christian teaching in the context of the whole history of sin from Adam on to its final resolution.

Medications for the body best work with spiritual care for the soul. "It is in this way that citizens of the City of God are given medicine during their pilgrimage on earth while praying for the peace of their heavenly fatherland. And, of course, the Holy Spirit operates within to offer healing power through the medicine which is applied externally. Without the Spirit no remedy is of any avail. Even though God makes use of one of his obedient creatures, as when he speaks in human guise to our ears — whether to the ears of the body or to the kind of ears we have in sleep — it is only by his interior grace that he moves and governs our minds" (Augustine, The City of God 15.6; 1 Thess. 5:14).[150] The Spirit works inwardly along with outward remedies and medications.

### 10. In Sickness the Whole Person Is Sick

In caring for the sick, we care for the whole person, body, soul, and spirit. Any personal experience occurs to the whole person, and is felt within the whole arena of his personhood. As persons we prefer to be treated not as a bundle of parts or objects, but as a whole, as a living, cohesive, interconnected organism. "The whole head is sick and the whole heart faint" (Isa. 1:5, KJV).

149. FC 14:422; ACCS NT 9:96*.
150. FC 14:423; ACCS NT 9:96*.

Sickness is not merely a sickness of the body, but of the heart. Soul and body are always interfacing intimately. To detach one from the other is not really to "visit the sick," since the sick are actually persons living out crises in the complex interface between body and spirit. To visit the sick is to visit them as they are, in their common infirmities, and in their actual human condition.

The psalmist wrote: "My heart is wounded within me" (Ps. 109:22, KJV). When my heart is wounded, I feel the whole impact from the center to the circumference of my being. It is then that I need a companion, a visitor, someone to come and be present to me in my suffering. Those who visit the hurt neighbor come gently bearing God's good news and God's own love. They visit the wounded with God's own mercy, hope, and love.

God heals the broken-hearted (Ps. 147:3). God comes to us "with healing in his wings" (Mal. 4:2, KJV). We may, like the woman of Mark 5:26, have "suffered much under many physicians" (Mark 5:26, RSV; cf. Luke 8:43). We may have tried every available avenue of therapy and medicine, and having suffered from all of them, still look for the deeper remedy of the whole person. It is this remedy that Christianity hopes to bring to those willing to hear. And it is this remedial action that we, in visiting the sick, share with those willing to receive.

To treat the troubled body without treating the troubled soul is shortsighted, according to John Chrysostom: "If we have any bodily ailment, we contrive everything possible to be rid of what pains us. Yet when our soul is ailing, we delay, and draw back. For this reason we are not delivered from bodily ailments. The indispensable corrective has become for us secondary, while the dispensable secondary matters seem indispensable. While we leave unattended the fountain of our ills, we still hope to have the streams unpolluted" (Chrysostom, The Gospel of Matthew, Homily 14.5; Matt. 4:24).[151]

## 11. Every Disease?

When he spoke of "disease," this pertains to bodily ailments. But when he said *"every disease,"* this pertains more broadly to the spiritual ailments of the soul. The ailments of the soul are not fewer than those of

---

151. PG 57:221; NPNF 1 10:89**; ACCS NT 1a:74-75.

the body. . . . Now when he says "every disease," he includes every kind of either serious or minor ailment. We can understand both clauses as pertaining to both ailments: that is, "every disease" whether bodily or spiritual; and "every sickness" whether bodily or spiritual. We understand "disease" as being some disorder, infirmity or infidelity affecting the whole person. A person who is subject to the disorder of avarice or lust or vainglory suffers a disease of the soul. The person who ignores the mystery of God's calling is sick in faith. For many are those who would be quite able to do good works and please God, but who do not actually do them, for they ignore the mystery of God's calling. . . . Jesus cured bodily ailments by the power of divinity and spiritual ailments by the word of compassion. Even as medicine benefits an ailing body, a word may benefit an ailing soul. . . . It was not believed that Christ was able to do mighty works simply because he preached the truth, but rather it was believed that he preached the truth because he was doing mighty works. "They brought to him all who were ill and who were possessed . . . and he cured them" [Mark 1:34]. (Opus Imperfectum in Matthaeum, Homily 8, italics added; Matt. 4:24)[152]

God's redemptive purpose is to bring fallen humanity into the fulfillment of complete health, healing human sicknesses of every sort, both body and soul. This is why Jesus went about "healing every disease and every infirmity among the people" (Matt. 4:23, RSV). Chromatius commented: "To this end the teacher of life and heavenly physician Christ the Lord had come that by his direction he might draw people toward life and with his heavenly medicine cure the sickness of both body and soul. He came that he might free bodies beset by the Devil and restore the afflicted to true and complete health. By the word of divine power he cured the weaknesses of the body, but by the medicine of heavenly teaching he healed the wounds of the soul" (Chromatius of Aquileia, Tractate on Matthew 16.4; Matt. 4:23).[153]

The whole Gospel to the whole world seeks to enable in every person a new wholeness. We are complete in him (Col. 2:10). We are called to let patience have her perfect work that we may be perfect and entire, wanting nothing (Jas. 1:4).

152. PG 56:678-79; ACCS NT 1a:75-76**.
153. CCL 9a:266; ACCS NT 1a:74*.

## 12. They Brought Him All Who Were Sick

In his healing ministry Jesus dealt with a wide range of illnesses, including leprosy (Matt. 8:2; 26:6; Mark 1:40; 14:3), withered hands (Mark 3:1-3), fever (Mark 1:30; Matt. 8:14; Luke 4:38), deafness, speech impediments, blindness, lameness, hemorrhaging (Mark 5:25), paralysis (Matt. 8:6; 9:2; Mark 2:3; Luke 5:18), epilepsy (Matt. 17:15), dropsy (Luke 14:2), and even a flesh-wound injury to a slave's ear (Luke 22:50-51). This Gospel portrait shows Jesus as providing the most complete pattern of caring for the sick, pointing to the wide embrace of God's grace.

In Jesus' ministry the sick were laid in the street as he drew near, and they sought him out in order that they might touch him, even if it were but the border of his garment (Mark 6:56). Even to come close to the servant Messiah was experienced by some as having healing power. So it is with the faithful. They bring themselves and their families as close as possible to him personally.

Healing of the whole person looks toward basic behavioral change. "The Lord himself testified that he came as the physician of the sick, saying, 'Those who are well have no need of a physician, but those who are sick; I came not to call the righteous, but sinners.' How, then, are the sick to be made strong? How are sinners to repent? Is it by merely holding fast to what they are presently doing? Or, on the contrary, by undergoing a great change and reversal of their previous behavior?" (Irenaeus, Against Heresies; Mark 2:17a).[154]

The Lord gives his people the task of healing and binding up wounds (Hos. 6:1). God's primordial will prior to the fall is the good of all he creates. God's consequent will, consequent to the fall, is to give humanity a remedy, even amid sin, and to cure by the most fitting means available (Jer. 33:6). Nonetheless there are times when there seems to be no cure, no balm in Gilead, no physician there (Jer. 8:22). God's long-range purpose must be viewed in God's own time. It may be revealed through some circuitous route, but its purpose is complete wholeness (Jer. 33:6). "As many as he touched were made perfectly whole" (Matt. 14:36, KJV*).

The incarnate Lord has "borne our griefs and carried our sorrows" (Isa. 53:4, RSV; cf. Matt. 8:17). He bore our human sickness on the cross, that God may be glorified, and that the works of God might be shown even

---

154. LCC 1:377**; ACCS NT 2:31.

through our sicknesses. Anticipating the resurrection, we realize that our "sickness is not unto death, but for the glory of God that the Son of God might be glorified by it" (John 11:4, KJV*).

### 13. Continuing an Apostolic Ministry

The ministry of healing passed from the Son to the Spirit to the apostles to the whole church. Hilary of Poitiers commented on this succession: "The time of the law was over, and five thousand were brought into the church from Israel (Acts 4:4). The believing people now were being saved through faith, not by their fulfillment of the law as such. They offered to God the persons among them who were feeble and ill. These persons wanted to touch the hem of his garment to be made whole through faith. From the hem of the garment, the whole power of the Holy Spirit came forth from our Lord Jesus Christ. This power was then given to the apostles, who were also going out as it were from the same body, and it afforded healing to those who wished to touch the garment" (Hilary of Poitiers, On Matthew 14.19; Matt. 14:36).[155]

Jesus passed on to his apostles the ministry of healing, visitation, intercession, and comfort. Jesus gave authority to the apostles to heal diseases (Matt. 10:1; Luke 9:1) by laying on of hands (Mark 16:18) and anointing the sick with oil (Mark 6:13, Jas. 5:14). Even handkerchiefs and aprons were viewed as instruments symbolic of God's willingness to heal the sick through various means (Acts 19:12).

The body of Christ is his continuing incarnation in history after the resurrection. Jesus commissioned his disciples to continue his ministry (Matt. 10:5-10; Mark 6:7-13; Luke 9:1-6). In the book of Acts, we find that healing ministries continued. James 5:14 advised that if anyone is ill, they should call upon the elders. The faithful participate in God's own acts of healing, comfort, and care, that restore the fortunes of Israel (Hos. 6:11; 7:1). This healing activity restores the soul (Ps. 19:7).

155. SCH 258:32; ACCS NT 1b:16*.

## 14. *Summing Up the Enabling Motif*

We have considered faith's typical acts as specifically set forth in this sequence: feeding, refreshing, welcoming, sheltering, clothing, and visiting. This way of ordering the consideration of good works emerges directly out of Jesus' parable of the last judgment.

Not only did Jesus come to humanity to care for us in our suffering, but we are called to care for him in his suffering, as presented to us concretely in the "least of these."

We have listened to the Fathers speaking for themselves on how Christ meets us in those who are hungry, thirsty, strangers, naked, and sick. The Fathers go much deeper than commending the perfunctory performance of these duties. Simple acts of mercy are best understood in relation to God's own compassionate care for humanity in its predicament. The vast import of caregiving is best seen in the light of human creation, the fall, redemption, and final human destiny.

The pattern in the Christian life for these works of love is Jesus' own work of love on our behalf in his messianic ministry, as seen ultimately on the cross. On the last day we will realize all too plainly that it is in "the least of these" that we have been meeting Christ himself. For these good and evil works we will be called to accountability on the last day.

This is why the churches in classical Christianity were actively engaged in organized and regular ministries for the hungry, thirsty, ill-clad, and sick long before modern transformations of these concerns into state functions. Within the narrow frame of reference of our modern conceits and historical ignorance, we are usually surprised when these ministries are seen to have been their active concern for two thousand years.

It is within the range of every believer to practice these simple good works: shelter, water, food, and comfort. They do not require special education or abilities. They do require a good will, however, transformed by grace, rightly to do these good works in a way that is glorifying to God.

## PART THREE

# REACHING OUT
# FOR THE OUTCAST

The faithful have a good reason to reach out for the outcast, the marginalized, the leper, the handicapped, the blind, the deaf, those who cannot speak for themselves, the disabled, the paralyzed, and the addicted. The reason? They themselves have been in various ways cast out, blind, dysfunctional, and marginalized.

## 1. *The Next One I Meet*

The outreach is not limited to selected clientele, but to the neighbor. "Neighbor" means, in biblical language, *the next one I meet*. The neighbor, or next one, is not a physical location, but an existential meeting. Whomever I meet next is my neighbor.

The overarching theme of this Part is *inclusion* — with special reference to those most often *excluded* — the outcasts. Why is inclusion such a central motif for good works? Not only because the good news of God's good work is for the whole world, for all classes, for all races, for all generations, for all societies — that is so; but more specifically I am to include in my attentiveness every particular person I meet, with a special concern to recognize those in need and those others have neglected. To do good works is to be awake to the outcasts.

We all know how we would wish to be treated if we were hungry, thirsty, a stranger, naked, a refugee, or sick. Hence there is no way to hide behind the appeal to ignorance, claiming that we do not know how to treat others as we would have them treat us. We know.

## 2. The Inclusion Motif: To the Ends of the Earth

It is a historical fact that the apostolic witnesses went to the ends of the known earth, beginning from Judea and Samaria, toward Antioch, Ephesus, and Rome. It meant going north past the Taurus Mountains, east toward China through the silk route, south to Ethiopia and Nubia, and west to African Numidia and the Celts in Wales. It meant going from Jerusalem to all the nations, the Gentiles, the world that had never heard about God's covenant with Israel.

For Paul this meant heading for Spain with many stops along the way. For Mark it meant dying in Africa. For Athanasius it meant being exiled repeatedly. For Peter it meant reaching out for the edges of the known world in Pontus on the Black Sea. For Gregory the Wonderworker it meant going to Armenia to spend thirteen years in a cave prison. For Thomas it meant (according to a weighty tradition) heading for India. For Sister Egeria it meant traveling from Spain to the Egyptian desert to Bethlehem. For Mother Theodora it meant the desert of Scetis. For Patrick it meant an untamed Ireland. For Irenaeus it meant the primitive territory of the Rhône Valley. All this happened with astonishing rapidity, as Eusebius reported.

Everywhere they went after Pentecost, the churches of ancient Christianity were engaged in worldwide inclusive ministries to the outcast and marginalized: hospitals, food relief, the poor, the ransom of prisoners. This is what good works is all about. This occurred long before modern "inclusion ideologies" sought to transform them into state functions and bureaucracies. We will set forth the evidence of these inclusive ministries. Modern biases have reinforced in our minds the premise that early Christianity was more prone toward exclusiveness than inclusiveness, more ethnically biased than catholic in their sympathies, more class bound than class transcending. We will present some of the contrary evidence.

We are now asking how the ancient church understood its ministries to the marginalized. The answer is found not only in their letters, prayers, poetry, and hymnody, but also in their homilies on scripture texts on lepers, the addicted, those cast away because they were thought to be under demonic compulsions, the lame, the deaf, and the blind.

*3. The Pattern*

The central pattern in the Christian life for these outreaching works of love is Jesus' own work of outreaching love on our behalf, all the way to the cross. Jesus came into our deteriorated human condition to redeem it and give it new life. We are called to do likewise, following through wherever possible to redeem the suffering of our fellow humans.

Simple acts of mercy are best viewed in relation to God's own compassionate care for all humanity, including those most neglected. The mission to the alienated is best seen in the light of the larger story of God's mission to our human alienation, from within the larger frame of reference of human creation, the fall, redemption, and final human destiny.

Patristic comment was not satisfied with simply commending these good works as generous moral acts. It did this, but in addition it sought to show how these works are to be rightly grasped within the larger scheme of things, set in the frame of reference of the whole of history, gratefully understood in relation to God's boundless love for broken humanity. Putting good works in theological and historical perspective does not detract from but deepens their meaning. The Fathers sought to show how these discrete acts are seen in the light of human destiny from creation to consummation. Failure to understand this salvation-history context results in a failure to understand the vitality underlying the biblical mandate for good works toward the outcasts.

## A. Touching the Untouchables: Reaching Out to the Leper

The pattern in the Christian life for embracing the outcast is first seen in the way in which Jesus himself reached out for those who were at the farthest range of human exclusion — *lepers.*

From the vantage point of the coming kingdom, nothing God created is lacking in goodness and in the potentiality of glorifying God. This affirmation is most rigorously tested in the hard case of lepers, whose untouchability seemed to be so clearly justified in ancient cultures. Leprosy was considered to be a dangerous and unclean disease, yet Jesus did not hesitate to move among and touch and heal lepers. He healed ten of them on a single occasion, one of whom was a Samaritan (Luke 17:12; cf. Matt. 8:2 and Luke 5:12), a people most despised by many Jews.

### 1. Touching the Untouchable

Origen had early recognized a most amazing detail of Matthew's story of the healing of the leper — Jesus *touched him* (Matt. 8:3)! "Why did he touch him, since *the law forbade the touching of a leper?*" asked Origen. "He touched him to show that 'all things are clean to the clean' [Tit. 1:15]. He touched him because the filth that is in one person does not adhere to others. External uncleanness does not defile the clean of heart. So he touched him in his unclean state, that he might instruct each of us in humility. He touched him that he might teach us *that we should despise no one,* or abhor them, or regard them as pitiable, because of some wound of their body or some blemish. . . . So, stretching forth his hand to touch him, the leprosy immediately departs. The hand of the Lord is found to have touched not a polluted person, but a body already made clean! Think about this, beloved. Is there anyone here who has the taint of leprosy in his soul? Or the contamination of guilt in his heart? If he has, instantly adoring God, let him say with the leper: 'Lord, if you will, you can make me clean'" (Origen, The Healing of the Leper, italics added; Mark 1:41).[1] The miracle is that by the time the clean touched the unclean, the unclean was already made clean. What the Lord did in touching the leper, he does in touching us in our uncleanness.

When John Chrysostom searched the same scripture, he noted: "He did not simply say, 'I will, be cleansed,' but he also 'extended his hand, and touched him'! This is an act we do well to examine. If he cleansed him merely by willing it and by speaking it, why did he also add that 'he touched him'? For no other reason, it seems to me, than that he might signify by this that he is not under the hand of the law, but the law is in his hands. Hence to the pure in heart, from now on, nothing is impure [cf. Tit. 1:15]. He touched the leper to signify that he heals not as physician but as Lord. For the leprosy did not defile his hand, but his holy hand cleansed the leprous body" (Chrysostom, The Gospel of Matthew, Homily 25.2; Mark 1:41).[2]

---

1. SSGF 1:301-2*; ACCS NT 2:25-26*.
2. TLG 2062.152, 25; NPNF 1 10:173**; ACCS NT 2:26*.

In the final week of his earthly ministry, Jesus visited the house of another leper, Simon. "About to suffer for the whole world and to redeem all nations by his blood, Jesus tarried in Bethany, 'the house of obedience.' He stayed in the house of Simon the leper — but he was no longer a leper. Nonetheless, even after he had been cured by the Savior, he was still known by his earlier name, Simon the leper, that the power of the healer might be made manifest" (Jerome, Commentary on Matthew 4; Matt. 26:6-7).[3] Even amid the crisis of this critical hour, Jesus took time to visit the leper he had healed.

## 2. Including the Outcast

Lepers were those most cast out from all social interactions and companionship. They were made to feel utterly alone and worthless. Jesus was reaching out for those whom society had most systematically isolated and marginalized. Ambrose takes us through this crucial narrative in Luke 5, where the leper, having fallen on his face in humility, showed his wounds and begged for a remedy. "It is a mark of humility and modesty that each feel shame for the sins of his life. But however deep his humility, it did not diminish the strength of his confession. He showed the sores of his body. He begged for a remedy. His confession is full of trusting faith. '*If you will*,' he said, 'you can make me clean.' He thereby conceded all power to the Lord's will" (Ambrose, Exposition of the Gospel of Luke, 5.2-3, italics added; Luke 5:14-15).[4] As the Son was about to submit his will to the Father in his final act, so the leper was submitting his will unreservedly to the Son.

The leper's faith was condensed in the phrase: If you will, you can. The Lord confirmed the leper's complete readiness to receive the kingdom he was bringing into being: "Jesus did not say: 'Be clean,' but rather responded to the leper's faith by saying: '*I will.* Be clean.'" This left no doubt as to whether the leper's assumption was correct. Jesus simply confirmed it, wrote Chrysostom. "Many and great were the signs he would offer, but only here did he utter a unique word about his own authority" (Chrysostom, The Gospel of Matthew, Homily 25.2, italics added; Matt. 8:3).[5] "The leper

---

3. CCL 77:246; ACCS NT 1b:239-40*.
4. EHG 147**; ACCS NT 3:90*.
5. PG 57:328; NPNF 1 10:172**; ACCS NT 1a:159*.

did not pray, 'Lord, cleanse me.' Rather he left everything to the Lord. He made his own recovery depend entirely on him. In this way he testified truly that all authority belongs to him" (Chrysostom, The Gospel of Matthew, Homily 25.2; Matt. 8:2).[6]

The despised leper who recognized his authority had already, by his words, placed himself under that authority. "Here we learn that there is no obstacle in between God's command and his work. He commands and the deed is done. Thus he spoke, and his work immediately came into being [Ps. 33:9 (LXX 32:9)]. You see that it cannot be doubted that the will of God is power. If, therefore, his will is power, those who understand that the Triune God is One will know that the power manifested here is God's own power. Thus the leprosy departed immediately. By this we can see that when he brought healing to the leper's body, he brought the light of truth to him as well" (Ambrose, Exposition of the Gospel of Luke, 5.3; Luke 5:14-15).[7]

Lepers were throwaway persons in ancient society — without social value, wholly shunned by proper society. In this episode, Jesus teaches us how we are to treat those who have been cast aside in society, the most marginalized, even the most untouchable: Actively reach out for them. The faithful are called to touch the despised with the same love and gentleness that Jesus himself showed to the leper.

## B. Care for the Handicapped: Enabling the Deaf to Hear

Some might imagine that a serious ethic of care for the handicapped is a recent moral interest and achievement. But both scripture and the Fathers had much to say about "the least of these" who are unable fully to function in some ways.

The ancient Christian writers were actively engaged in ministries to the handicapped long before modern political efforts to make correctives through legislation. We are prone to assume that the classic Christian teachers could not have been sophisticated enough to have these empathic concerns. We are surprised when they turn out to be especially attentive to the lame, halt, and blind.

6. PG 57:328; NPNF 1 10:172**; ACCS NT 1a:159*.
7. EHG 148**; ACCS NT 3:90-91*.

## 1. Embracing the Dysfunctional

Our theme is inclusion, and especially how human outcasts are included in the embrace of God's love. We are now asking how the ancient church understood its own ministries to the handicapped.

Simple acts of mercy toward the lame and blind are best viewed in relation to God's own compassionate care for our human lameness and blindness. The mission to the handicapped is best seen in the light of the larger story of God's mission to our human handicap after the fall. Now it is possible to look at it from within the larger frame of reference of human creation, redemption, and final human destiny. Failure to understand this salvation-history context results in a failure to understand the vitality underlying faith's biblically mandated concern for good works.

The pattern in the Christian life for these works of love is Jesus' own work of love on our behalf in his messianic ministry and on the cross. Jesus came into our condition of human dysfunction to restore it to fullness. We are called to follow him by seeking to help and remedy the dysfunctions of our fellow humans when they cannot speak, walk, or hear well.

## 2. Caring for the Handicapped

Job is the biblical type of one who became "eyes to the blind and feet to the lame" (Job 29:15, RSV). This is what the faithful still seek to do — offer the handicapped whatever they lack in function. They offer this freely, as an expression of gratitude for God's becoming feet for our lameness.

Caring for the handicapped is viewed in scripture under the analogy of God's ongoing care for our human infirmities. This analogy, already present in Israel, was transformed by messianic expectations. Isaiah had prophesied that in the messianic future the lame would leap like a deer and the tongue of the dumb sing for joy (Isa. 35:6).

Many persons with handicapping conditions came to Jesus. He received and healed them (Matt. 11:5; 15:30-31). This was central to his messianic ministry. The lame were invited to the Lord's table (Luke 14:13, 21). He healed the man with the withered hand (Mark 3:1). The blind came to him and tried to touch him (Mark 8:22). The impotent man waited for him beside the pool (John 5:7). When Jesus healed a man who "could hardly talk"

(Mark 7:32, NIV), the multitudes recognized that he was fulfilling ancient messianic promises.

Jesus carried our sicknesses. He himself bore our scars and hurts. His hands and feet were nailed to the cross. He was wounded for our transgressions (Isa. 53:5). It is his heel that was bruised, according to the Bible's first prophetic reference (Gen. 3:15). His side was pierced. Through the incalculable empathy of the Incarnation, Jesus himself actively reached out for those who were least able to hear, see, and walk.

### 3. Do Not Add Even More Woes
### to Those Who Cannot Hear

Hearing is crucial to normal human functioning. Those who cannot hear are put at a serious disadvantage. The law of Moses stated: "You shall not revile the deaf or put a stumbling block before the blind; you shall fear your God: I am the Lord" (Lev. 19:14, NRSV). Those who share in the covenant community do not lay heavy burdens on others (Matt. 23:4). The people of Israel knew what it meant to be put under an absurd handicap when the Pharaoh said, "You shall no longer give the people straw to make bricks" (Exod. 5:7, RSV), but the number of bricks was not lessened. By hard experience Israel learned to empathize with the slaves, the heavily burdened, the oppressed.

Gregory the Great noted that "to speak evil of the deaf is to disparage one who is absent and does not hear. To put a stumbling block before the blind is to do a thing that might seem innocuous of itself, but which affords an occasion of scandal to one who fails to understand its injustice" (Gregory the Great, Pastoral Care 3.35; Lev. 19:14).[8] Do not jest lightly about deafness.

Listen to what the Fathers say about relating to the deaf and you will get a glimpse of the richness of classic Christian reflection on reaching out for those who have disabilities.

---

8. ACWG 11: 226; ACCS OT 3:189*.

## 4. Opening the Ears

In the healing of the deaf and mute man, Jesus "put his fingers into his ears, and he spat and touched his tongue. He looked up to heaven, and with a deep sigh said to him, 'Ephphatha!' (which means, 'Be opened!'). At this the man's ears were opened, and his tongue loosened, and he began to speak plainly" (Mark 7:33-35, NIV*).

In commenting on this incident, the poet Ephrem the Syrian stood in awe in the presence of the One who gives the capacity for hearing, and restores it when lost. Who is this One? Without a classic Christology it is hopeless to explain the way in which the One who is beyond touching touches our human condition. "That power which may not be handled came down and clothed itself in members that may be touched, that the desperate may draw near to him, that in touching his humanity they may discern his divinity. *For that speechless man the Lord healed with the fingers of his body.* He put his fingers into the man's ears and touched his tongue. At that moment with fingers that may be touched, he touched the one [incarnate Lord] that may not be touched [the Godhead]. Immediately this loosed the string of his tongue [Mark 7:32-37], and opened the clogged doors of his ears. For the very architect of the body itself and artificer of all flesh had come personally to him, and with his gentle voice tenderly opened up his obstructed ears" (Ephrem the Syrian, Homily on Our Lord 10, italics added; Mark 7:33).[9] From this narrative we learn that speech was given to Adam in order to be heard; that ears are for hearing, that the architect of hearing wishes to enable hearing, and that the One who created hearing with his own fingers, so to speak, was bodily present in the incarnate Lord to touch deaf and mute humanity.

In the early tradition of baptismal chrismation (anointing), the *presbuteros* (elder, priest) anoints with oil the ears and nostrils of those newly born. Such an opening of the ears occurs upon encountering the living Word, argued Ambrose. There are powerful liturgical echoes that sound from this miracle of the opening of the ears of the deaf: "Every Sabbath we witness the 'opening up' of a mystery. It is in outline form the type of that liturgical opening when the minister once touched your ears and nostrils. What does this mean? Remember in the Gospel, our Lord Jesus Christ, when the deaf and dumb man was presented to him, touched his

9. NPNF 2 13:309**; ACCS NT 2:103*.

ears and his mouth: the ears, because he was deaf; the mouth, because he was without speech. And he said: 'Ephphatha,' a Hebrew word, which in Latin means *adaperire* [be opened]. In this way the minister is now touching your ears, that your ears may be opened to this sermon and exhortation" (Ambrose, Concerning the Mysteries 1.4; Mark 7:34).[10] The metaphor of deafness describes our own resistance to the Word. The rite of baptismal chrismation points toward the grace that overcomes our inveterate spiritual deafness.

### 5. The Word Is for Hearing

When the deaf man's ears were opened, his tongue was released, according to Lactantius: "He thereby declared that it would shortly come to pass, that those who were destitute of the revealed truth would both hear and understand the majestic words of God. Accordingly you may truly call those deaf who do not hear the heavenly things that are true, and worthy of being performed. He loosed the tongues of the dumb. They spoke plainly. This is a power worthy of admiration [Matt. 9:33; Mark 7:37] even in its ordinary operation. There was also contained in this display of power another level of meaning. It would shortly come to pass that those who were previously ignorant of heavenly things, having received the instruction of wisdom, might soon be speaking God's own truth" (Lactantius, Divine Institutes 4.26; Mark 7:35).[11] Speaking and hearing are crucial to the Gospel, which is news to be spoken and heard. This is why Jesus opens ears and loosens tongues.

Prudentius sets forth the same point poetically:

> Deafened ears, of sound unconscious,
> Every passage blocked and closed,
> At the word of Christ responding,
> All the portals open wide,
> Hear with joy friendly voices and
> The softly whispered speech.
> Every sickness now surrenders,

10. Cetedoc 0155, 1.4.90.17; FC 44:269**; NPNF 2 10:317; ACCS NT 2:103-4*.
11. ANF 7:127**; ACCS NT 2:104*.

Every listlessness departs,
Tongues long bound by chains of silence
Are unloosed and speak aright,
While the joyful paralytic
Bears his pallet through the streets.

(Prudentius, Hymns 9; Mark 7:36;
cf. Matt. 9:6-7; Mark 7:34-35; Luke 6:18-19; John 5:9)[12]


## C. Enabling the Disabled

The pattern in the Christian life for enabling the disabled is the way in which Jesus himself freed and empowered those who were least mobile, least able to get themselves around. He enabled what was lacking in their abilities. These events were signs of the coming kingdom. We, too, are called to continue his ministry by helping those who have lost limbs and cannot now function with a full and healthy body. As Job became eyes to the blind, we are to become arms and legs for those lacking them.


### 1. The Man with the Withered Hand

The disabled have been a central concern for the Christian community from its very beginnings. The narrative of the man with the withered hand is typical and illustrative. Walk with John Chrysostom through the narrative of the way Jesus healed a disabled person on the Sabbath: "Jesus said to the man with the withered hand, 'Come here.' Then he challenged the Pharisees as to whether it would be lawful to do good on the Sabbath. Note the tender compassion of the Lord when he deliberately brought the man with the withered hand right into their presence" (Luke 6:8). Jesus took the issue directly to the abusers. "He hoped that the mere sight of the misfortune might soften them. He hoped that they might become a little less spiteful by seeing the affliction. Perhaps out of sorrow they would mend their own ways. But they remained callous and unfeeling. They preferred to do harm to the name of Christ than to see this poor man made whole. They betrayed their wickedness not only by their hostility to Christ, but

12. Cetedoc 1438, 9.64; FC 43:64-65**; ACCS NT 2:104.

also by their doing so with such contentiousness that they treated with disdain his mercies to others" (Chrysostom, The Gospel of Matthew, Homily 40.1; Mark 3:4).[13]

Jesus taught empathy by empathizing, by directly confronting abusers, by bringing the disabled into his company, and by attending to their needs. Jesus showed the way toward recognizing needs quickly and identifying with human disabilities deeply. In doing so he had to struggle against the religious establishment's tendency to put rules above service to the needy neighbor.

The disciples brought to him the lame, the halt, and the blind (Luke 14:21; cf. John 5:3). They came to him powerless, dysfunctional, and unable. In his presence they found their possibilities restored, their hopes renewed. The repair of the human body so as to restore it in some measure to its original function is a key theme of the apostles' ministry, as seen in the healing of the lame and the crippled (Acts 3:1-10; 14:8-10). The theme of restored bodily function is intrinsic to the early Christian understanding of the Gospel.

With a simple word, Jesus healed the disabled man. His withered hand was restored to useful service: "The use of the disabled man's hand had atrophied. That function of his body had withered, by which he was able to do or share in certain tasks. So the Lord ordered him to stretch out his hand, which was restored to him as fully as the other one. His whole cure rested on the word of the healer alone. The hand was restored to the same condition as the functioning hand. It was thereby made a partner in the service of the apostles in their duty of offering salvation" (Hilary of Poitiers, On Matthew, 12.7; Matt. 12:13).[14]

John Chrysostom exposed those who fail to help the disabled: "'Is it allowed to heal on the Sabbath?' Allowed?" asked Chrysostom. "Jesus was amazed at their insensitivity. While in other cases he healed by touch, by the laying on of his hands, in this case he only speaks and gazes. But nothing would make gentle his detractors. Their condition was getting worse even as the disabled man was being healed. Jesus sought also to heal their bitterness even as he healed the withered hand" (Chrysostom, The Gospel of Matthew, Homily 40.1; Matt. 12:10).[15] When the religious establishment

---

13. NPNF 1 10:259*; ACCS NT 2:38*.
14. SCH 1 254:274; ACCS NT 1a:239*.
15. PG 57:440; NPNF 1 10:259-60**; ACCS NT 1a:238**.

ignored the lame and crippled, and focused only on religious rules that turned aside from the neighbor in need, Jesus challenged them.

## 2. Withered Minds

In a homily attributed to Athanasius, the withered limb of the handicapped man was compared with the withered minds of the beholders: "In the synagogue of the Jews was a man who had a withered hand. If he was withered in his hand, the ones who stood by were withered in their minds. And they were not looking at the crippled man nor were they expecting the miraculous deed of the one who was about to work. But before doing this good work, the Savior plowed up their minds with words. For knowing the evil of the mind and its bitter depth, he first softened them up in advance with words so as to tame the wildness of their understanding, asking: 'Is it permitted to do good on the Sabbath or to do evil; to save a life or to destroy one?'" (Athanasius, Homilies 28; Mark 3:4).[16] Withered minds must be tilled and overturned in order to recognize withered hands.

The law, rightly viewed, does not prohibit a good work on the Sabbath. This was the issue under debate in the healing of the disabled man. Jesus "affirmed Sabbath law, but added: 'except this: regarding that which will be done for the sake of a life.' Again if a person falls into a hole on a Sabbath, Jews are permitted to pull the person out [Matt. 12:11]. This not only applies to a person, but also an ox or a donkey. In this way the law agrees that things relating to preservation may be done, hence Jews prepare meals on the Sabbath. Then he asked them about a point on which they could hardly disagree: 'Is it permitted to do good?' [Mark 3:4; Luke 6:9]. But they did not even so much as say, 'Yes,' because by then they were not in a good temper" (Athanasius, Homilies 28; Mark 3:4).[17] Life trumps law.

The homily contrasted debating with healing: "While the withered hand was restored, the withered minds of the onlookers were not. For they went out and immediately, according to the reading [Mark 3:6], were debating what they would do to Jesus. Are you debating what you will do? Worship him as God. Worship the wonder worker. Worship one who

16. TLG 2035.069, 28.165.6-39; cf. PG 28:144-68; ACCS NT 2:37.
17. TLG 2035.069, 28.165.6-39; cf. PG 28:144-68; ACCS NT 2:37*.

worked good things on behalf of others" (Athanasius, Homilies 28; Mark 3:5d).[18] Rather than debating, Jesus acted.

### 3. Faultfinding Does Not Help the Disabled

The resistance was violent. In response to this incident, "the Pharisees went out and took counsel against him, how to destroy him" (Matt. 12:14, RSV). Jerome commented: "Envy is responsible for the fact that they set a trap for our Lord. What had he done to incite the Pharisees to kill him? Certainly it was because the man had stretched out his hand. Who of the Pharisees did not stretch out his hand on the Sabbath day when he was carrying food, when he was offering a drinking cup and performing the other actions that are necessary for nourishment?" (Jerome, Commentary on Matthew 2.12.14; Matt. 12:14).[19]

Chrysostom commented: "By this Jesus makes it clear that some deluded souls are not even persuaded by miracles. . . . When they see someone delivered either from disease or iniquity, then that immediately cues them off further to find fault. They become like wild beasts" (Chrysostom, The Gospel of Matthew, Homily 40.2; Matt. 12:14).[20] Jesus would ultimately face their fury.

Jesus healed on the Sabbath to offer new life to the limbs of the disabled, but the beholders responded with envy. "A miracle sometimes converts to faith those who had disbelieved the word," wrote Cyril of Alexandria, "but the Pharisees watched him in this case merely to see if he would heal on the Sabbath. The nature of an envious person is such that he makes the praises of others food for his own disease. He is maddened by their good reputation. But once again Jesus revealed the 'deep and mysterious things; he knows what is in the darkness, and the light dwells with him' [Dan. 2:22]. And why did Jesus reveal this? Perhaps it might be to move the cruel and unpitying Pharisee to compassion. The man's malady [his withered hand] perhaps might have shamed them and persuaded them to quench the flames of their envy. Jesus' response is most wise indeed and a most suitable statement to meet their folly. If it is lawful to do good on the

---

18. TLG 2035.069, 28.165.39-168.26; cf. PG 28:144-68; ACCS NT 2:39*.
19. CCL 77:90-91; ACCS NT 1a:239*.
20. PG 57:440; NPNF 1 10:260**; ACCS NT 1a:239*.

Sabbath and nothing prevents the sick being pitied by God, cease picking up opportunities for fault-finding" (Cyril of Alexandria, Commentary on Luke, Homily 23; Luke 6:6-11).[21] Those who are envious make health the food for their own disease.

### 4. The Imperative: Use Your Restored Limb to Help Restore Others' Limbs

Those whose disabilities have been remedied are called to help others in similar conditions. If your hand is in working order, stretch it out to help the neighbor. Ambrose warned: "You who think that you have a healthy hand beware lest it is withered by greed or by sacrilege. Hold it out often. Hold it out to the poor person who begs you. Hold it out to help your neighbor, to give protection to a widow, to snatch from harm one whom you see subjected to unjust insult. Hold it out to God for your sins [cf. Isa. 1:15, 17]. The hand is stretched forth; then it is healed. Jeroboam's hand withered when he sacrificed to idols; then it stretched out when he entreated God [1 Kings 13:4-6]" (Ambrose, Exposition of the Gospel of Luke, 5.40; Luke 6:6-11).[22] Hands are made to use.

It is wasteful of grace to receive God's renewing strength in our muscles and then do nothing to exercise those muscles. Rather, according to John Chrysostom: "I exhort you that you not carelessly slumber so as to leave everything to God. Nor, when diligent in your endeavors, imagine that by your own exertions the whole work is achieved. God does not will that we should be indolent. For God does not do the whole work by himself by fiat. Nor is it his will that we should be entirely self-sufficient. For God does not commit the whole work to us alone [cf. Ps. 146:5; Isa. 41:10; 50:7; Acts 26:22]" (Chrysostom, The Gospel of Matthew 82; Mark 3:5c).[23]

Those who have struggled with lameness are called to use their own circumstances, however limited, as a means of bestowing wholeness upon others: "'Let your right hand become full and tender' [cf. Matt. 13:15]. . . . In effect Jesus was saying: 'Do not continue to beg because of having a withered hand, but after you finally have received it healthy and whole and

---

21. CGSL 122*; ACCS NT 3:99*.
22. EHG 162*; ACCS NT 3:100.
23. GMI 59*; ACCS NT 2:38-39.

have begun to work, stretch out your own hand to the poor. Rise up and stand in their midst. Become a marvel to those who see. In you the struggle concerning the Sabbath is finally being contested. Stand in their midst, so that the ones who are lame in their legs might stand'" (Athanasius, Homilies 28; Mark 3:5d).[24]

### 5. Carry the Mat That Carried You

Jesus challenged the paralytic: "Rise, take up your bed and go home" (Matt. 9:6, RSV). Peter Chrysologus grasped the irony of this phrase: "Take up your bed. Carry the very mat that once carried you. Change places, so that what was the proof of your sickness may now give testimony to your soundness. Your bed of pain becomes the sign of healing, its very weight the measure of the strength that has been restored to you" (Peter Chrysologus, On the Healing of the Paralytic; Mark 2:11).[25] If you have been given strength to carry your own mat, use that strength for others.

This compounded the irony. The paralyzed man was instantly required to perform an act that presupposed that he had already been healed. Ambrose noticed this detail in the text: "He charged the man to perform an action of which health was the necessary condition, even while the patient was still praying for a remedy for his disease. . . . It was our Lord's custom to require of those whom he healed some response or duty to be done [John 5:8; 8:11]" (Ambrose, Of the Christian Faith 4.8.54-55; Mark 2:11).[26] A walking response was fitting to a miracle that enabled walking.

### 6. Paralysis as Descriptive of the General Human Condition

Augustine pointed to our inveterate tendencies to becoming paralyzed in other ways than physical: "You have been a paralytic inwardly. You did not take charge of your bed. Your bed took charge of you" (Augustine, On the Psalms 41.4; Mark 2:11).[27] One who becomes captive to the very

24. TLG 2035.069, 28.165.39-168.26; cf. PG 28:144-68; ACCS NT 2:39.
25. SSGF 4:191**; PL 52:339; ACCS NT 2:29.
26. Cetedoc 0150, 4.5.37; GMI 48*; ACCS NT 2:29.
27. Cetedoc 0283, 38.40.5.10; NPNF 1 8:129; ACCS NT 2:29.

bed that is supposed to comfort, has become paralyzed not only out-
wardly but inwardly.

The healing of the paralytic pointed back to the original condition of
humanity before the fall. According to Hilary of Poitiers, the incarnate Lord
wanted it "understood that he himself was in a body and that he could forgive sins and restore health to others' bodies. . . . Then he said to the paralytic, 'Arise, take up your pallet.' He could have simply said: 'Arise,' but since
the reason for doing this cried out for explanation, he added: 'Take up your
pallet and go home.' First, he granted remission of sins. Then he showed his
ability to restore health. Then, with the taking up of the pallet, he made it
clear his body would be freed from infirmity and suffering. In all this, he
was showing believers the way back to the original condition that Adam
and his progeny had lost" (Hilary of Poitiers, On Matthew 8.7; Matt. 9:6).[28]
We participate in God's love for paralytics by doing all we can to relieve
their paralysis. Only then can they be challenged to use their limbs to their
utmost ability even within remaining limitations.


## 7. The Healing Community

Origen noticed the factor of proximity in the healing miracles: the closer
they came to the incarnate Lord, the more they felt the power of his messianic ministry. Even now those who come within hearing distance of the
community of faith may begin to feel God's healing power. "Even those
who come only to the edges, just the extremities of the body of Christ, who
feel themselves unworthy to obtain such things, are being healed. So now
you come into the congregation of what is more commonly called the
church. See the catechumens? They are by custom cast in the far side or
back of those who are in the body. It is as if they were at the extreme end of
the body, as if coming merely to the feet of the body of Jesus — the church.
They are coming to it with their own deafness and blindness and lameness
and crookedness. In time they will be cured according to the Word. You
would not be wrong in saying that these people have gone up with the
multitudes into the church, up to the mountain where Jesus sits, and have
been cast at his feet and are being healed. And so the multitudes are aston-
ished at beholding the transformations that are taking place" (Origen,

28. SCH 1 254:200-202; ACCS NT 1a:175*.

Commentary on Matthew 11.18; Matt. 15:30).[29] To enter the church, even at its very last row, is already to come into the presence of God's power to transform life.

The crowds that came to Jesus brought their lame and put them at his feet (Matt. 15:30). Origen thought this metaphor anticipated the church today that sits as if on a hill amid vast crowds of broken people, some of whom come within the range of hearing of the Word in the church. "Not only people who were healthy but also those suffering from various disorders went up on the mountain where Jesus was sitting. Think of this mountain to which Jesus went up and sat as the church. It has been set up through the word of God to speak to the rest of the world. All sorts of people come to it. To this assembly have come not only the disciples, as if they were leaving behind the multitudes, as they did in the case of the Beatitudes. Rather, there are great crowds here, many of whom are deaf or suffer from many afflictions" (Origen, Commentary on Matthew 11.18; Matt. 15:30).[30] The church is like a lofty mountain that draws the paralyzed world toward itself.

So to this mountain come the maimed, lame, deaf, blind, and suffering. "Look at the crowds who come to this mountain where the Son of God sits. Some of them have become deaf to the things that have been promised. Others have become blind in soul, not looking toward the true light.[31] Others are lame and not able to walk according to reason. Others are maimed and unable to work profitably. Each of these who are suffering in soul from such things go up along with the multitudes into the mountain where Jesus sits. Some who do not draw near to the feet of Jesus are not healed. But those who are brought by the multitude and cast at his feet are being healed" (Origen, Commentary on Matthew 11.18; Matt. 15:30).[32] The church is still a place where those excluded are included, where those disabled are enabled, and where dead limbs are given new life.

29. GCSO 11:65; ANF 9:447; ACCS NT 1b:33*.
30. GCSO 11:65; ANF 9:447; ACCS NT 1b:33*.
31. Origen interprets the physical as symbolic of the spiritual. The various diseases of the body suggest various diseases of the soul.
32. GCSO 11:65; ANF 9:447; ACCS NT 1b:33.

## D. Becoming as Eyes to the Blind:
## "You Were as My Eyes"

### 1. You Became as Sight to Me

As Jesus came into our condition of human blindness to offer sight, we are called to continue his ministry by seeking to remedy the dysfunctions of our fellow humans when they cannot see. We are called to become "eyes to the blind" (Job 29:15, KJV), offering to them what they cannot do — see for them, while seeking remedies for their blindness.

Simple acts of mercy toward the blind are best viewed in relation to God's own compassionate care for our human blindness. Christianity views blindness from within the larger frame of reference of human creation, the fall, redemption, and final human destiny. To ignore the salvation-history context results in a failure to understand the unique motivating power of faith's good works.

Irenaeus called for empathic compassion toward the blind. Hardness or lack of sympathy, he said, "is not the behavior of those who heal and give life. Rather it tends to aggravate disease and increase ignorance. The law shows itself much truer than the lawyer when it says whoever leads a blind man astray from the way is accursed. The apostles were sent to find those who were lost and to bring sight to those who did not see. They brought healing to the sick. They did not approach the blind under the frame of reference of the law, but by the new revelation of the truth. For no one would be acting rightly if one told the blind who were already beginning to fall over the precipice to continue in their dangerous way as if it were a sound one and as if they would come through it all right" (Irenaeus, Against Heresies 3.5.2; Deut. 27:18).[33] Who would lead a blind man astray but one unconscionably cruel?

### 2. The Blind Saw Hope in the Messianic Lord

The blind found hope merely by coming into the presence of Jesus. "When he entered the house, the blind men came to him; and Jesus said to them, 'Do you believe that I am able to do this?' They said to him, 'Yes, Lord.'

33. LCC 1:376-77; ACCS OT 3:321*.

Then he touched their eyes, saying, 'According to your faith be it done to you' [Matt. 9:28-29, RSV]" (Chromatius, Tractate on Matthew, 48.20.2; Matt. 9:27).[34]

With good humor, Hilary, the ever-alert examiner of the text, asked the question of how the blind men could recognize Jesus' passing by if they were blind. His curiosity led him to a pensive reflection on the narrative of Matthew 9:27: "*If they could not see, how could the blind men know of the Lord's departure* as well as his name?" Hilary concluded that "they saw because they believed, not believed because they saw." "The Lord showed them that *faith should not be expected as a result of health, but rather that health can come from faith*" (Hilary of Poitiers, On Matthew 9.9, italics added; Matt. 9:27).[35]

### 3. His Touch Gave Sight

In another passage two blind men sitting by the roadside, hearing that Jesus was passing by, addressed him by the messianic title of "Son of David." When they asked for mercy, Jesus stopped and asked: "'What do you want me to do for you?' They said to him, 'Lord, let our eyes be opened.' And Jesus in pity touched their eyes, and immediately they received their sight and followed him" (Matt. 20:32-34, RSV). Their readiness to "receive is seen both in what they cried out and that they followed. They were persevering before the gift and after the gift. For it says that they then followed him" (Chrysostom, The Gospel of Matthew, Homily 66.1; Matt. 20:33-34).[36]

The touch of Jesus was a mystery to the Fathers because it was the touch of the incarnate Lord. When Jesus touched the eyes of the blind with compassion (Matt. 20:34), he did so as one who is truly human, truly God, prompting this reflection: "Jesus actually touched the eyes of the blind. As *truly human*, he touched them with the hands of his flesh. As *truly God* he healed them by the word. He touched them because they called him the Son of David. He healed them because they believed in his power. Thus in one and the same person, God and man, his work of healing both re-

---

34. CCL 9a:437; ACCS NT 1a:187.
35. SCH 1254:212-14; ACCS NT 1a:186*.
36. PG 58:626; NPNF 1 10:404-5; ACCS NT 1b:121*.

warded their faith and admonished their faithlessness" (Opus Imperfectum in Matthaeum, Homily 36, italics added; Matt. 20:33-34).[37]

One act of healing blindness pointed beyond itself to the whole story of humanity with God. "In touching their *eyes,* the Lord Jesus also touched the eyes of the *mind* of the nations. He was giving to them the grace of the Holy Spirit. For Christ's touch gives with it the grace of the Holy Spirit. Those nations, when they were enlightened, followed him with good works, and did not abandon him afterward" (Opus Imperfectum in Matthaeum, Homily 36, italics added; Matt. 20:33-34).[38]

He healed both physical blindness and soul blindness, according to Eusebius: "To the blind he gave sight, offering the power of seeing to those whose bodily vision was destroyed. He showered those in ancient times who were blind in their minds to the truth with the vision of the light of true religion" (Eusebius, The Proof of the Gospel 3.1.88; Luke 4:16-21).[39]

Mark reported that Jesus took the blind man of Bethsaida "by the hand, and led him out of the village; and when he had spit on his eyes and laid his hands upon him, he asked him, 'Do you see anything?'" (Mark 8:23, RSV). At first he could see men vaguely, like trees walking, but with a second laying on of hands, he could see everything clearly. This called forth a baptismal reflection from Ambrose on the several layers of analogy between the mud and the lowly way, between the washing and baptism, and between conversion and the opening of the eyes of the blind. "So too he placed mud upon you. This symbolizes modesty, prudence, and consideration of your frailty," wrote Ambrose. "You went, you washed, you came to the altar, you began to see what you had not seen before. Through the washing of the font of the Lord and the preaching of the Lord's passion, your eyes were opened. You who seemed before to have been blind in heart began to see the light of the sacraments" (Ambrose, The Sacraments 3.15; Mark 8:23).[40] Nothing opens eyes more surely than Word and Sacrament. The church is a place where people come to see more clearly.

---

37. PG 58:834; ACCS NT 1b:121*.
38. PG 58:834; ACCS NT 1b:122*.
39. POG 1:102*; ACCS NT 3:80*.
40. FC 44:295*; ACCS NT 2:109*.

## E. Loosening the Tongues of the Speechless:
## The Demoniac Set Free

In speaking to humanity, God wills to be heard. Speaking and hearing are crucial and defining aspects of human existence. Yet after the fall, the free flowing speech that God wills for humanity has become marred and tainted by a history of sin.

The pattern in the Christian life for enabling speech for those who cannot speak is the way in which Jesus himself loosened the tongues of the speechless.

### 1. Slow of Tongue

The Old Testament prototype of the speechless one is the young Moses. The New Testament prototype of the speech enabler is seen in the miracle narratives of Jesus. The patristic writers examined the phenomena of speech and speechlessness by inquiring into those texts that deal with these biblical prototypes.

As God gave Moses, who was once speechless, the power of speech, so does he wish to give the faithful an analogous power of speech, according to Origen: "In Exodus we have written in the codices of the church's scripture that Moses responded to the Lord and saying, 'Provide, Lord, another whom you will send. For I am feeble in voice and slow in tongue.' You have in the Hebrew copies, 'But I am uncircumcised in lips'" (Origen, Homilies on Genesis 3.5; Exod. 4:10),[41] to which the Lord replied: "I will help you to speak" (Exod. 4:12, NIV).

Being mute and being given speech are both typified by Moses. "When the people of Israel were in Egypt, before they had received the law, they too were without words and reason and thus in a sense mute. Then they received the Word. Moses was the type of it" (Origen, Homilies on the Gospel of Luke 5.3; Exod. 4:10).[42] Moses personified the new gift of speech that God was giving in the law.

God the Spirit desires to take our faltering tongues and loosen them for language: "Moses shows that it could happen that one who was not elo-

41. FC 71:96; ACCS OT 3:27*.
42. FC 94:21; ACCS OT 3:27*.

quent the day before, or the day before that, could suddenly become eloquent, from the time when the Lord began to speak to him" (Augustine, Questions on Exodus 7; Exod. 4:10).[43]


## 2. The Grace of Speech

The same grace of speech that poured out to Moses is poured out once again upon the church. The Holy Spirit at the right time enables speech to the faithful, according to Ambrose: "The Lord himself also opened his mouth and said to the apostles, 'Receive the Holy Spirit' [John 20:22]. By these words he declared that he was the one who said to Moses, 'I will open your mouth and will teach you what you are to say.' Therefore this wisdom, divine, 'indescribable' [Wis. 17:1], 'unmixed and uncorrupted,' pours its grace into the souls of the saints and reveals knowledge, so that they may look upon his glory" (Ambrose, Letter 2(65).4; Exod. 4:12).[44] Enabling speech and hearing is central to God's purpose in salvation history.

Since God's grace transforms human willing, it reshapes human speaking, according to Augustine. Grace opens the way for a new will to speak the truth: "It is clear that not only the instruction that comes from his mouth but also its being opened pertains to the will and grace of God. For God does not say, 'You open your mouth, and I will instruct you,' but promised both: 'I shall open, and I shall instruct.' Elsewhere he says in a psalm, 'Open your mouth, and I shall fill it' [Ps. 81:10]. This signifies the will in man to receive what God gives to one who is willing. Thus 'open your mouth' pertains to the responsibility of the will. 'I shall fill it' pertains to the grace of God" (Augustine, Questions on Exodus 9; Exod. 4:12).[45] God fills the prophet with speech. The prophet must then be willing to open his mouth.

The gift of speech was first given to Adam. Truthful speech then became confused in Eden, and became disastrous at Babel, due to human pride. It was again enabled by God with Moses through the law. But when lost and distorted, speech was restored by the messianic Servant. The Fathers put in the context of the history of salvation these Gospel stories of the healing of speech and hearing.

---

43. CCL 33:71; ACCS OT 3:27.
44. CSEL 82 1:16; ACCS OT 3:28.
45. CCL 33:72; ACCS OT 3:28*.

### 3. The Isolated World of the Blind and Dumb Demoniac

In the wretched sufferer whom the scriptures called "the blind and dumb demoniac," the whole world of disability was typified. According to the Opus Imperfectum, that disabled world was "presented to Jesus as if in a single person. He was a blind, mute man who neither saw nor spoke, nor was he capable of even recognizing his Maker or giving thanks to him. What was visibly done in the case of this one single person therefore could be understood to have spiritual significance for all" (Opus Imperfectum in Matthaeum, Homily 29; Matt. 12:22).[46] He could not see. He could not speak. All the paralysis and dysfunction of the fallen world was brought at once to Jesus in Galilee.

When the Pharisees responded that "It is only by Beelzebub, the prince of demons, that this fellow drives out demons" (Matt. 12:24, NIV), Jesus asked, "how can anyone enter a strong man's house and carry off his possessions unless he first ties up the strong man?" (Matt. 12:29, NIV). The "strong man" is the demonic power that blocked speaking, seeing, and hearing.

In meeting the incarnate Word, the speechless man became the vessel of speech: "A blind, mute man who was the dwelling place of a demon was being prepared as one fit for God, that he might behold God in Christ and might praise the works of Christ by his acknowledgment of God" (Hilary of Poitiers, On Matthew, 12.11; Matt. 12:22).[47]

### 4. Enabling Speech

In another episode, after touching the eyes and healing the two blind men in Galilee (Matt. 9:27-31), as the news of Jesus' miracles was spread, "a dumb demoniac was brought to him. And when the demon had been cast out, the dumb man spoke; and the crowds marveled" (Matt. 9:32-33, RSV). With his eye for textual detail, Chrysostom noted a man who "needed others to lead him to Jesus. He could not even make a request by himself, because he was quite unable to speak. . . . And as his tongue was fettered, so was his soul. This is why Jesus did not require any confession of faith from

46. PG 56:781; ACCS NT 1a:244*.
47. SCH 1:276-78; ACCS NT 1a:244.

him. He immediately healed the disease" (Chrysostom, The Gospel of Matthew, Homily 32.1; Matt. 9:32).[48]

Jerome commented: "What is called in Greek *kophos* is more commonly known as deaf rather than dumb, but the Scriptures indiscriminately use *kophos* to mean dumb or deaf. Spiritually, just as the blind men receive light, so too the dumb man's tongue is loosened that he may speak and give glory to him whom he once rejected" (Jerome, Commentary on Matthew 1; Matt. 9:32).[49]

Speech-enabling thus became a sign of the coming kingdom. "The crowds were amazed, saying, 'Never was anything like this seen in Israel'" (Matt. 9:33, RSV*). "He healed easily; he healed quickly; he healed a multitude of cases of disease; he healed diseases that were incurable. Hence the people reacted with wonder" (Chrysostom, The Gospel of Matthew, Homily 32.1; Matt. 9:32).[50] Let Ephrem sing it: "Then his mouth which had been so closed up that it could not give birth to a word, gave birth to praise him who made its barrenness fruitful. The One who immediately had given to Adam speech without teaching, gave speech to him so that he could speak easily a language that is learned only with difficulty [cf. Gen. 1:27-28; 2:20]" (Ephrem the Syrian, Homily on Our Lord 10; Mark 7:33).[51]

### 5. With Demons Cast Out, Tongues Were Loosed

These miracles of speech anticipated the coming miracle of the conversion of the Gentile believers who in turn would speak to all nations. The Fathers taught that these episodes pertained especially to the opening of the eyes and loosening of the tongues of the Gentiles. Already in the Galilean ministry of Jesus, the Gentiles were being prepared for the coming kingdom.

Epiphanius Scholasticus wrote: "The entire population of Gentiles was blind, sitting in darkness and in the shadow of death. They could not see Christ with the eyes of their hearts blinded. This was because they did not know the law and could not praise God. They were possessed by de-

---

48. PG 57:378; NPNF 1 10:211; ACCS NT 1a:188**.
49. CCL 77:61-62; ACCS NT 1a:188.
50. PG 57:378; NPNF 1 10:211; ACCS NT 1a:188*.
51. NPNF 2 13:309**; ACCS NT 2:103.

monic powers, because after such great idolatry and collusion with demons they were led captive as it were by an unclean spirit." It was in this context that "'a blind and dumb demoniac was brought to him.' . . . Jesus cured him in their presence, 'in such a way that he might speak and see.' He *spoke* because he praised God through his faith. He *saw* Christ because the light had shined on the eyes of his heart" (Epiphanius Scholasticus, Interpretation of the Gospels 24; italics added; Matt. 12:22).[52]

This healing miracle occurred in a meaningful sequence, according to Hilary. The demonic powers were first cast out, and only then the tongue was loosened: "In the deaf and dumb demoniac appear the need of the Gentiles for a complete healing. Beleaguered on all sides by misfortune, demonic influence was suspected in many types of infirmities of the body. And in this regard a proper order of things is observed. For the devil is first cast out. Only then do other bodily benefits follow suit. With the folly of all superstitions put to flight by the knowledge of God, sight and hearing and words of healing are introduced. . . . Indeed, he who was unable to be helped by the law was made well by the power of the Word" (Hilary of Poitiers, On Matthew 9.10; Matt. 9:33).[53]

Hilary thought that these Messianic miracles intentionally prefigured the mission of the apostles first to Israel and then to the Gentiles: "It was not without reason that, although he had said that all the multitudes were healed together, now a blind, mute man possessed by a demon was offered to him so that the same order of understanding might follow without any ambiguity. The Pharisees accused the apostles of plucking ears of corn, that is, of prematurely gathering the men of their age. But in his presence mercy was praised over sacrifice. A man with a withered hand was then offered up in a synagogue and was cured. Yet these deeds appeared to be not useful in converting *Israel.* Meanwhile the Pharisees even entered into a plot to murder. So it was necessary that *the salvation of the Gentiles* happen after these events in the dramatic definitive form of a single person — a blind, mute demoniac" (Hilary of Poitiers, On Matthew 12.11; Matt. 12:22).[54]

The point is not that believers today are required to do such miracles, but they are called and invited to participate in God's own signs and won-

52. PL *Suppl.* 3:861; ACCS NT 1a:245*.
53. SCH 1:214; ACCS NT 1a:188*.
54. SCH 1:276-78; ACCS NT 1a:244*.

ders, not the least of which is giving speech and hearing to those without them. Each small step toward helping out those with speech impediments is one way of participating in the coming kingdom.

## F. Binding Up Demonic Powers

Works of love for those caught in demonic syndromes are best viewed in relation to God's own determination to overcome all demonic powers in human history, and to reclaim fallen humanity to its original purpose. Christianity views demon possession from within the larger frame of reference of human creation, the fall, redemption, and final human destiny. Without this salvation-history context, it is impossible to understand the unique vitality underlying faith's biblically mandated concern for those today regarded as mentally ill or viewed according to similar metaphors.

What is the Christian pattern of good works for those caught in baffling, mysterious, veiled, and obscure syndromes of demonic bondage? It is seen in the way in which Jesus himself dealt with these demons. The incarnate Lord himself entered directly into the arena of battle with the demonic, and in his messianic ministry decisively bound up the demonic powers. These miracles were signs of the coming kingdom. We, too, are called to continue his ministry by seeking remedies for the demons that plague and stultify our lives.

### 1. Freeing the Demon-Possessed

The Gerasene demoniac was a pitiable figure. He "lived among the tombs" (Mark 5:3, RSV). "Just look how far human life has fallen!" Peter Chrysologus exclaimed: "This is the very man who was promised all the glories of this world. He is now found to dwell — where? In the tombs! [Cf. Luke 8:27.] Surrounded by the putrid rottenness of dead bodies" (Peter Chrysologus, Sermons 17; Mark 5:3).[55] These are the very ones the servant Messiah came to free and make whole.

One hymn by Prudentius sketches the rough picture of this desperate Gerasene demoniac to whom Christ reached out:

55. GMI 97; ACCS NT 2:67*.

Then a man bereft of reason,
Dwelling in sepulchral caves,
Bound with cruel and grinding fetters
And with raging frenzy torn,
Rushes forth and kneels in worship,
As the saving Christ draws near.

(Prudentius, Hymn 9; Mark 5:3; cf. Luke 8:28)[56]

### 2. Why the Demons Were First to Recognize the Messiah

The Gerasene demoniac "lived among the tombs; and no one could bind him any more, even with a chain; for he had often been bound with fetters and chains, but the chains he wrenched apart, and the fetters he broke in pieces, and no one had the strength to subdue him. Night and day among the tombs and on the mountains he was always crying out, and bruising himself with stones. And when he saw Jesus from afar, he ran and worshiped him; and crying out with a loud voice, he said, 'What have you to do with me, Jesus, Son of the Most High God? I adjure you by God, do not torment me'" (Mark 5:3-7, RSV).

Athanasius commented on the first recognition of the Lord, not initially by the crowd, but by the demons! "The spirits especially see through what is unseen by human eyes. . . . What human disbelief doubts, the evil spirits see clearly: he is God. For that reason they flee from him and fall at his feet, still crying out: . . . We know who you are, the holy one of God [Mark 1:24; Luke 4:34; cf. Mark 5:7; Luke 8:28]" (Athanasius, Incarnation of the Word 32; Mark 5:7).[57]

This was a frightening case. Jesus is seen as ready to heal the most imprisoned of human souls. Lactantius marveled at the transformation the text reports: "'Neither could anyone tame him.' Give me a reprobate who is impetuous, foul-mouthed and overbearing. With few words the Lord will render him as gentle as a lamb. Give me one who is covetous, avaricious, grasping. The Lord will restore him to liberality, and he will dispose of his resources bountifully of his own hand. Show me one who trembles at the idea of pain and of death, and soon I will show you one who has learned to

---

56. Cetedoc 1438, 9.52; FC 43:63; ACCS NT 2:67-68.
57. TLG 2035.002, 32.4.1; NPNF 2 4:53; LCC 3:86; ACCS NT 2:68.

disdain crosses, flames and the bull of Phalaris" (Lactantius, Divine Institutes 3.26; Mark 5:4).[58] Lactantius doubtless witnessed persons in early
North African Christian communities who were undergoing just such personal transformations.

Of the Gerasene demoniac the text in Luke says that "For a long time
this man had not worn clothes or lived in a house, but lived in the tombs"
(Luke 8:27, NIV). Cyril of Alexandria poignantly commented: "In great
misery and nakedness, he wandered among the graves of the dead. He was
in utter wretchedness, leading a disgraceful life. He was a proof of the cruelty of the demons and a plain demonstration of their impurity." Their ef-
fects were devastating. "Whoever they possess and subject to their power,
at once they make him an example of great misery, deprived of every blessing, destitute of all sobriety, and entirely deprived even of reason. Some
say, 'Why do they possess people?' I answer those who wish to have this explained that the reason of these things is very deep. Somewhere one of his
saints addressed God by saying, 'Your judgments are a vast abyss' [Ps. 36:6
(LXX 35:7)]. As long as we bear this in mind, we will not miss the mark.
The God of all purposely permits some to fall into their power. *He does not
do this in order to cause them directly to suffer, but that we may learn by their
example how the demons treat us* and may avoid the desire of being subject
to them. The suffering of one edifies many" (Cyril of Alexandria, Commentary on Luke, Homily 44, italics added; Luke 8:26-27).[59] Through
providence, the faithful are made more aware of their freedom by seeing
the horrible consequences of freedom abused and bound.

### 3. Exorcising the Demons of Compulsive Behavior

The Messiah came to heal "demoniacs, epileptics, and paralytics" (Matt.
4:24c, RSV). Demonic forces are especially active in psychosomatic illness,
according to Origen: "You will see the variety of evils in prodigality or avarice, boorishness or licentiousness, in silliness, knavery, insolence, cowardice, and every opposing vice. The soul's trials circle around money, fame,

58. GMI 98**; ANF 7:128; ACCS NT 2:68. Phalaris, the tyrant of Acragas (c. 560 B.C.),
was famous for his "ingenious cruelty, especially for the hollow brazen bull in which his victims were roasted alive" (*Oxford Dictionary of the Christian Church*, 2nd ed. [London, 1974],
p. 809).

59. CGSL 191**; ACCS NT 3:139*.

poverty, and obscurity. The demons dishonor bodies by causing willing souls to become active in sinning and madness. . . . Irrationally angry responses indicate a paralysis of souls, such that when they succumb to it their vigor is slackened both for action and for living. 'Weakness' of the soul is a term used by the Greeks, in a general sense, for any sickness arising from vice. More specifically it refers to that which is opposed to endurance, a kind of giving up in the face of patience and sufferings and anguish" (Origen, Fragment 77; Matt. 4:24c).[60] This is not simply direct supernatural predetermination without any willing human cooperation. The demonic powers tempt the weakness of the free soul itself to cooperate with sin and madness.

Why do the demonic powers have a morbid interest in tripping up human wills? In the case of the boy who foamed and ground his teeth and became rigid, Minucius Felix wrote: "These demonic spirits therefore, having lost the simplicity of their created being and the primitive integrity of their nature, are now clogged and laden with evil. Utterly *undone themselves, they make it their whole business to undo others, for companions in misery.* Being depraved themselves they would infuse the same depravity into others. . . . When we command them by the one true God, the wretches, bitterly against their will, fall into horrible shiverings, and either spring straightaway from the bodies they possess or vanish by degrees, according to the faith of the patient or the grace of the physician" (Minucius Felix, Octavius 24-27, italics added; Mark 9:18).[61] It is likely that Minucius Felix himself had witnessed such exorcisms.

It was Festus, the procurator of Judea in the reign of Nero, who accused Paul of madness: "'Paul, you are mad; your great learning is turning you mad.' But Paul said, 'I am not mad, most excellent Festus, but I am speaking the sober truth'" (Acts 26:24-25, RSV). Jesus himself was at one point thought by some to be "beside himself" (Mark 3:21, KJV), so much so that his family came to seize him. His very presence elicited a debate about madness: "There was again a division among the Jews because of these words. Many of them said, 'He has a demon, and he is mad; why listen to him?' Others said, 'These are not the sayings of one who has a demon. Can a demon open the eyes of the blind?'" (John 10:19-21, RSV).

Christ drove out the demonic powers: "He is recognized by demons

60. GCSO 1241.1:46; ACCS NT 1a:75*.
61. GMI 204**; ANF 4:190; ACCS NT 2:123*.

[cf. Luke 4:33-34; Mark 1:23-24], drives out demons [cf. Matt. 8:16; Mark 1:34], drowns deep a legion of spirits [cf. Matt. 8:32; Mark 5:9; Luke 8:30, 33] and sees the prince of demons falling like lightning [cf. Luke 10:18]" (Gregory of Nazianzus, Oration 29.20, "On the Son"; Mark 5:7).[62] The incarnate Lord threw out demons from ruling our bodies, just as he threw the moneychangers out of the temple.

With deep pathos Jesus told his disciples that they could not cast out this demon "because of your little faith" (Matt. 17:20, RSV). Soberly, Origen wrote: "Let us examine this statement: 'This kind is not cast out except through prayer and fasting' [Mark 9:29, KJV]. If at any time it is necessary that we should be engaged in the healing of one suffering from such a demonic disorder, we are not to solemnly urge or put questions or speak to impure spirits, as if we could command them by our speech. But by devoting ourselves to prayer and fasting, we may be effective as we pray for the sufferer, and by our own fasting the unclean spirit may be thrust out" (Origen, Commentary on Matthew 13.7; Matt. 17:20).[63]

The Greek word translated in the King James Version as "feeble-minded" (oligopsuchos) can refer to the timid, despondent, fainthearted. We are instructed in scripture to comfort them: "Let us then bravely bear the ills that befall us. It is in war that heroes are discerned; in conflicts that athletes are crowned; in the surge of the sea that the art of the helmsman is shown; in the fire that the gold is tried. And let us not, I ask you, have concern for only ourselves, but let us rather look out for the rest, indeed more for the sick than for the healthy. It is an apostolic command to 'comfort the feeble-minded, support the weak.' Let us, then, stretch out our hands to them that lie low, let us tend their wounds" (Theodoret of Cyr, Letters 78; 1 Thess. 5:14).[64] The One who gives freedom and life calls us not to be fainthearted.

When the demonic powers find an opening weakness in the human will, they are portrayed as moving into the vacuum to take over. It then may seem like moving a mountain to set them free. Origen commented on the intimidating appearance of these perceived mountains:

The mountains here spoken of, in my opinion, are the hostile powers that have their being in a flood of great wickedness, such as are settled

62. GNF 259; TLG 2022.009, 20.9; ACCS NT 2:68.
63. GCSO 1140:198; ANF 9:479; ACCS NT 1b:61*.
64. NPNF 2 3:274; ACCS NT 9:97*.

down, so to speak, in some souls. But when someone has complete faith, such that he no longer disbelieves in anything found in the written Word, and has faith like that of Abraham, who so believed in God to such a degree that his faith was reckoned to him as righteousness [Gen. 15:6], then he has all faith like a grain of mustard seed. Then such a man will say to this mountain — I mean in this case the deaf and dumb spirit in him who is said to be epileptic — "Move from here to another place." And it will move. This means it will move from the suffering person to the abyss of nothingness. Remember what the apostle, taking this as his starting point, said with apostolic authority, "If I have all faith, so as to remove mountains" [1 Cor. 13:2]. He who has all faith — which is like a grain of mustard seed — moves not just one mountain but also more just like it. And nothing will be impossible for the person who has so much faith. (Origen, Commentary on Matthew 13.7; Matt. 17:20)[65]

Demonic powers can be dislodged no matter how long seated.

Our modest purpose here is to set forth the Fathers' view of good works enacted toward those with what today is called mental illness. The sacred texts that the Fathers found to address these good works were those narrating the healing of demoniacs. The messianic miracles of restoring reason and purpose to human life reveal the larger pattern of what God is doing in history.

We are not being indiscriminately commissioned to exorcise demons, but rather we are called and invited to participate in God's own mighty works of binding up the demonic powers. Any small step of kindness toward those who are demonically trapped in compulsive syndromes may be our way of participating in the coming kingdom. These texts on demonic possession help us understand those who are caught in deep inexplicable syndromes of bondage — economically, politically, and psychologically. For us, it is impossible to break through these syndromes, but for God nothing is impossible.

---

65. GCSO 11:197; ANF 9:479; ACCS NT 1b:61*.

## G. Uprooting Addictions

People with persistent addictive behaviors present special obstacles to those who want to help them and who will to do them good. However complex the dependency patterns may be in addictions, it is clear that these patterns have puzzled and intrigued classic Christian teaching from its earliest centuries.

We are now asking about good works as they pertain to those who have become trapped in addictions of all sorts — addicts, alcoholics, compulsive liars, sexual abusers, and their co-dependents. These are creatures of God who have fallen, deeply and often it seems irretrievably, into persistent behavioral spirals.

We must not bypass those lying in the gutter, pleaded Caesarius of Arles: "You are commanded to pull out the ass or the ox which is lying in the mud. Do you then see a Christian like yourself, who was redeemed by the blood of Christ, lying in the sewer of drunkenness and wallowing in the mud of dissipation and remain silent? Do you pass by and not stretch forth the hand of mercy?" (Caesarius of Arles, Sermon 225.4; Exod. 23:5).[66]

Are addictions like other human weaknesses and troubles? Can they be helped? Can any good works be done for them? As with our other demons, this task goes beyond our human strength. The attempt to do some good work on their behalf often only proves our inadequacies. The very freedom of the person has itself become bound.

The Church Fathers looked for ways of relearning and displacing addictive behaviors. They found the major clues in the way in which Jesus and his apostles met and dealt with the addicted — confronting them candidly with their addiction, and by requiring decision, calling them out of it, as if from death to life.

According to the Fathers, this confrontation has occurred and still occurs within a particular understanding of history — within the urgent expectation of the coming kingdom that demands decision. Works of love for those with addictions are best viewed in relation to God's own saving work of forgiving and transforming human bondage into freedom through love. To miss this placement of the question within salvation-history is to lose touch with the unique vitality underlying Christian concern for the addicted.

66. FC 66:154; ACCS OT 3:118.

### 1. The Dilemma of Addictive Behaviors

Compulsive behaviors are not limited to alcohol and habit-forming drugs. Instances of addiction in the Bible range from the Pharisees' addiction to judgmental legal correctness, to Matthew and Zacchaeus in their addiction to money; from Solomon's addiction to sex to Ananias and Sapphira's addiction to deceptive behaviors; from the Sodomites' addiction to homosexuality to the sluggard of Proverbs who is addicted to strong drink; from Cain's violent temper to the rich young ruler who had many possessions but went away sorrowfully when he learned that he had to give up his idolatry of possessions, for he had many.

Addiction is dependency behavior in which the source of addiction (drugs, alcohol, smoking, excessive eating, and sexual addictions) has taken control of the will. The very citadel of human self-determination has been seized and taken over. This take-over is always a complex story with many personal, social, physical, and psychological entanglements and reverberations. An addiction may at first appear to the tempted as a solution rather than a problem, since it may seem to diminish guilt feelings and inhibitions. The person returns to the addiction to relieve perceived symptoms. But the presumed satisfaction thought to be gained by addictive dependency is illusory (Prov. 20:1; 21:17).

Those burdened with addictions are often trapped between helpless dependence upon and hopeless hatred of the addiction. The families are the victims, with children most often taking the full brunt. Evasion, rationalization, and deception are common. Addictions tend to corrupt relationships, and lead toward cynical acts of contempt of persons in ways unthinkable apart from the addiction (Joel 3:3).

### 2. Admonitions against Self-Destructive Habit Formation

Our bodies are not our own to use or abuse as we please, to damage and destroy (Prov. 23:19-21; 1 Cor. 6:19-20). Rather our bodies are God's temples. When we throw our bodies away to addictions, we throw away the most valuable gift God has given us in our creation.

The most familiar addiction in the ancient world was to strong drink. Even among righteous men, beginning with Noah, there were times when drinking got out of hand (Gen. 9:21). In ancient Israel, rulers, priests, and prophets were instructed to avoid habit-forming intoxicants, and Nazirites were pledged to total abstention (Judg. 13:4, 7, 14; 1 Sam. 1:15-16; Luke 21:34).

The Fathers commented extensively on warnings in scripture about all forms of intemperate excess. These are deeds of the flesh (Gal. 5:21). Addictions can ruin a person's career, family, health, and self-respect (Prov. 23:20-21). They finally catch up with us and become tyrants of our willing. Jesus warned: "Take heed to yourselves lest your hearts be weighed down with dissipation and drunkenness and cares of this life, and that day come upon you suddenly like a snare" (Luke 21:34, RSV). These will not be among those who "inherit the kingdom of God" (1 Cor. 6:10, RSV). Those who are firmly habituated to starting early in the day to "run after strong drink" (Isa. 5:11, RSV*) find themselves easily trapped in a vicious syndrome of self-destruction. The longer they wait, the more difficult they will find it to put their wine away from them (1 Sam. 1:14). Each of these texts has a long history of interpretation in early Christian teaching.

We are not to become self-sold "slaves to drink" (Tit. 2:3b, RSV). Origen commented: "Therefore, he wants those for whom 'the Lord is their portion' [Num. 18:20; cf. Ps. 119:57] to be sober, to fast, to be vigilant at all times, but especially when they are present at the altar to pray to the Lord and to offer sacrifices in his presence. . . . In the same way, setting up the rules of life for the priests or the chief priests to this, he tells them that they ought not to be enslaved 'to much wine' but to be 'sober' [Tit. 1:7-8; 2:2-3]. Sobriety is the mother of virtues, drunkenness the mother of vices" (Origen, Homilies on Leviticus 7.3-4; Tit. 2:3b).[67]

This is not to say that wine as such is evil. Paul urged Timothy to take a little wine for his stomach (1 Tim. 5:23). Jesus himself blessed wine at the marriage in Cana (John 2:3-10). Psalm 104:15 recognizes that wine may make a man's heart glad. In due proportion, "wine gladdens life" (Eccles. 10:19, RSV). In emergency cases, the Proverbs call for giving "wine to those in bitter distress" (Prov. 31:6-7, RSV).

But wisdom lies in even temper and proper balance. "Immoderate indulgence makes one rash, passionate, prone to stumbling, anger and severity. Wine was given to gladden us, not for intoxication" (Chrysostom, Homily on Ephesians 19; Eph. 5:18a).[68] There is a great deal of suffering

---

67. FC 83:130*; ACCS NT 9:295.
68. IOEP 4:288; ACCS NT 8:191.

that comes out of addictive behaviors. Avoid those who drink too much, we are warned (Prov. 23:20). Do not accompany "those who are heroes at drinking wine" (Isa. 5:22, RSV).

### 3. Confronting Addiction

But warnings and maxims are of little value to one who is already hooked on abusable substances. So what wisdom can be derived from scripture and the Fathers concerning good works toward those who have become entrapped in addictive behaviors?

First we are called to be humble in the presence of others' demons. Augustine wrote: "If a man prays so that he may throw out someone else's demon, how much more important it is that he may cast out his own? That he may cast out his own drunkenness, his own dissipation. How much more important is it that he may cast out his own impure motives. How great are the sins in human beings! If they persist in them, they do not allow them to enter the kingdom of heaven!" (Augustine, Sermon 80.3; Matt. 17:19).[69] Put away self-righteousness before correcting another.

Pastors and teachers and parents, who have the task of caring for the souls of others, would do well to model sobriety in their own behavior. Ambrosiaster urges the bibulous caregiver first to sober up: "It is good conduct that strikes awe in the wrongdoer. Only one who is sober is prepared to guide another realistically and with confidence. One feels less resentment when one knows how reliably good is the actual conduct of the one who admonishes him. But where there is intoxication there is also debauchery, and debauchery causes base deeds. Therefore it is our duty to be sober, so that the requirements of good conduct may be observed" (Ambrosiaster, On Paul's Epistle to the Ephesians; Eph. 5:18a).[70] If you stand already in a relation of responsibility toward the addict (as parent, counselor, pastor, or friend), do not pretend to be holy just because you do not have his addiction.

---

69. PL 38:495; NPNF 1 6:350 (Sermon 30); ACCS NT 1b:61*.
70. CSEL 81.3:116-17; ACCS NT 8:191*.

## 4. Self-Constraint over the God of the Belly

The Fathers were aware that, according to scripture, food can become addictive. Basil notes that it was through gluttony that Adam fell, "through it Noah was mocked, Canaan was cursed (Gen. 9:21-25). Through it Esau was deprived of his birthright" (Basil, On Renunciation of the World; Gen. 25:31-32).[71] Clement of Alexandria wrote: "Surely we have been commanded to be the master and lord, not the slave, of food" (Clement of Alexandria, Christ the Educator 2.9; 1 Cor. 8:10).[72] "We must restrain the belly and keep it under the control of heaven. God will finally bring to nothing all that is made for the belly, as the apostle says" (Clement of Alexandria, Christ the Educator 2.5; 1 Cor. 6:13).[73]

Chrysostom asked what the belly is for. "Your belly is given to you so that you may nourish it, not so that it may burst. Your body is given you that you may rule it, not so that you may have it as a mistress. It is given that it may serve you for the nourishment of the other members, not so that you may be in bondage to it. Do not exceed these bounds. The sea at flood tide does not do as much harm to its boundaries as our bellies do to our bodies and our souls. The flood overwhelms only part of the land. The god of the belly overwhelms the whole body. Set self-constraint as a bound to this idolatry, as God sets the sand to the sea" (Chrysostom, Homily on Philippians 14; Phil. 3:19).[74]

The Gospel calls the faithful to pray for grace *beyond* human willing in order to break the bonds of behavioral addiction *within* human willing. It calls forgiven sinners to lend a hand to those who are fallen. Christianity has learned that the redirective power of a higher affection can displace addiction. A lower love can be reshaped by a higher love. Faith's good works respond to that love which is the source of all our loving.

## 5. Summing Up the Including Motif

Jesus was counter-cultural in his treatment of the outcasts. He physically touched the leper, against all expectations, to show in his healing ministry

---

71. FC 9:25; ACCS OT 2:152*.
72. FC 23:101; ACCS NT 7:78.
73. FC 23:96*; ACCS NT 7:56.
74. IOEP 5:144; ACCS NT 8:277*.

that nothing God created is lacking in goodness and potentiality. Jesus brought life and movement to paralyzed limbs. He commanded the paralytic to take up his bed and walk. In the Gospel narratives, paralysis becomes as a metaphor for the larger bondage of human freedom within the whole range of fallen history. As Jesus enabled hearing among the deaf, so we are to do what we can to give ears to the deaf, as Job did, and eyes to the blind. Jesus cast out demons. Tongues were loosed. The lame were able to walk. In healing the man with the withered hand, Jesus taught empathy for the disabled. He confronted addictive behaviors with the call to decision in the light of God's coming kingdom. As Jesus brought speech to the speechless and new abilities to the disabled, so are we called to share in these ministries, not in the form of messianic healing as such, but sharing his ministry of healing mission as the occasion presents.

Our central motif in this Part has been *inclusion* — especially of outcasts. Inclusion is a persistent theme of good works. Why? Because we ourselves have been included as Gentiles in the plan of God for salvation, for the redemption of all that has fallen. Israel who was "not my people," by God's grace became "my people" (Rom. 9:25-26, RSV; cf. Hos. 2:23). The Gentiles by grace are being brought into the covenant apart from merit under the law.

The churches of ancient Christianity were practically engaged in organized and regular ministries to the alienated, disabled, and addicted long before modern transformations of these concerns. These ministries to lepers, outcasts, pariahs, and rejects had been proceeding for two millennia prior to the advent of modern inclusion ideologies that claimed to humanize them. We are surprised when these ministries are found to have persisted for two millennia. It is a fantasy of the modern imagination that the ancient sources had no clear understanding of the importance of inclusion of the outcasts.

The good news has always been inclusive. It speaks of God's whole good work for the whole world, for all classes, for all races, for all generations, for all societies, for all languages. The outreach of Christian love extended to those most excluded.

The idea of inclusiveness has been reduced in our time to an oversimplified statist political ideology. It is political because it sees inclusion largely in terms of legal restraints, administrative law, equal representation, quotas and the like, and not a matter of the heart. It is oversimplified because it remains naïve about the variable requirements of equity. It has not adequately learned from the western moral tradition that equity requires making weighted decisions that hinge variably upon ever-new circumstances.

The central pattern in the Christian life for these active outreaching works of love is Jesus' own work of outreaching love on our behalf, all the way to the cross. All who have been included are called to reach out to include others.

The Fathers go much deeper than commending the perfunctory performance of these good works. These simple acts of mercy are best understood in relation to God's own compassionate care for humanity amid the history of sin, even among the most demeaning, desperate, and devolved. Failure to understand this salvation-history context results in a failure to understand the vitality underlying faith's biblically mandated concern for good works.

It is not beyond our powers to practice these simple good works. Just do it: Show mercy to the outcast, the alienated, and the lost. This does not require special education or abilities. It simply requires a will transformed by grace.

## PART FOUR

# THE IMPRISONED
# AND THE PERSECUTED

The ancient Christian leaders were engaged in ministries to the imprisoned long before the advent of modern institutional prison ministries.

To place prison ministries in context, we return to the order of characteristic good works found in the parable of the sheep and goats. We have now come full circle to the last of those listed: the imprisoned. Let us review the order:

| The Needy | The Good Work |
|---|---|
| The Hungry | Feeding |
| The Thirsty | Assuaging |
| The Stranger | Welcoming |
| The Naked | Clothing |
| The Sick | Nursing |
| The Imprisoned | Visiting |

This is not to be considered an exhaustive list, but representative of works of love indicated by Jesus himself. Survey the sequence: The first good work is to feed the hungry, to preserve the body, a basic need for survival. The last good work is equally important: visiting those in prison where survival itself is so harsh.

## A. Visiting Those in Prison: "You Came to Me"

To visit is not merely to come to see, but actively to attend and care for. Being completely helpless and isolated, the imprisoned are especially in need of trusted relationships, links with the outside, care, comfort, and above all hope.

Here the theological power of patristic reflection deepens. The pattern in the Christian life for responsibility to the imprisoned is the way in which Jesus himself *ransomed humanity from bondage to sin, guilt, and death.*

### 1. Christ Gave His Life as a Ransom for Captives

To be redeemed is to be bought from slavery. Origen explained redemption in this way: "'Redemption' is the word used for what is given to enemies in order to ransom captives and restore them to full liberty. Human beings were held in captivity by the Adversary until the coming of the Son of God, who became for us not only the wisdom of God, and righteousness and sanctification [cf. 1 Cor. 1:30], but also redemption. He gave himself as our ransom, that is, he surrendered himself to our enemies and poured out his blood on those who were thirsting for it. In this way redemption was obtained for believers" (Origen, Commentary on the Epistle to the Romans; Rom. 3:24).[1]

Those who visit the imprisoned are themselves bought with a price. "If the price of our life is the blood of the Lord, see to it that it is not an ephemeral earthly field which has been purchased, but rather the eternal salvation of the whole world" (Maximus of Turin, Sermons 59.2; 1 Pet. 1:18a).[2]

Jesus took upon himself the yoke of slavery intended for others (Matt. 11:29). In doing so, he provides a pattern for our taking responsibility for those who are enslaved. Only divine grace enables the yoke to be borne. With grace the yoke is light. We are promised that God will not test us more than we can endure without providing a way out. For the soul who is freed inwardly, there is no outward prison that can conquer this hope, this freedom, which is fully and finally received at the end of history.

1. CER 2:110; ACCS NT 6:101*.
2. ACWM 50:142; ACCS NT 11:79.

Those who trust God's mercy in the cross are no longer under the power of the jailer, the Adversary. "They are justified freely because they have not done anything nor given anything in return, but by faith alone they have been made holy by the gift of God. Paul testifies that the grace of God is in Christ, because we have been redeemed by Christ according to the will of God so that once set free we may be justified, as he says to the Galatians: 'Christ redeemed us by offering himself for us' [Gal. 3:13]. For he overcame the fierce attacks of the devil, who was outwitted. For the devil received Christ in the nether world, thinking that he could hold him there, but because he could not withstand his power he lost not only Christ but all those whom he held at the same time" (Ambrosiaster, On Paul's Epistle to the Romans; Rom. 3:24).[3]

## 2. As If in Prison with Them

The faithful come to *visit* those in prison. They do not ignore. They are present. They show up. They reach out. In doing so they become like epistles from the Lord himself. The single metaphor of visiting draws together all manner of good works to prisoners. The faithful remember that they have all been captives in a sense, as children of the exodus. We all came out of Egypt (Exod. 13:3).

This empathic analogy is embedded in a sacred text in Hebrews — the faithful *"remember those who are in prison, as though in prison with them"* (Heb. 13:3, RSV, italics added). They come bodily to the prison to minister to the prisoner. Those who come to attend the imprisoned participate in the outreach of Christ after his death to the spirits in prison, the souls in the nether world. He preached to them (1 Pet. 3:19), and when he ascended, he led a host of former captives to eternal life (Eph. 4:8).

Jesus said: "I was in prison and you visited me" (Matt. 25:36, NRSV). You came in that rotten place to be with me. You listened to my voice. You attended to my needs. You will find yourself unexpectedly blessed by me in being there.

Human bondage, which is brief in relation to eternity, is a passing hour: "But now for a brief moment favor has been shown by the Lord our God, to leave us a remnant, and to give us a secure hold within his holy

3. CSEL 81; ACCS NT 6:101*.

place, that our God may brighten our eyes and grant us a little reviving in our bondage. For we are bondmen; yet our God has not forsaken us in our bondage, but has extended to us his steadfast love before the kings of Persia" (Ezra 9:8-9a, RSV).

### 3. Bought with a Price

To visit those in prison is to convey that we share with them in Christ's mission of redeeming captives. Redemption is viewed not in a short time frame, but in the largest time frame — all history unto eternity.

Christ voluntarily became a curse that we might be free, as Ambrose explained: "It is profitable to me to know that for my sake Christ bore my infirmities, submitted to the human limitations and affections of my body, that for me and for all humanity, he was made sin and a curse. Thus for me and in my human frame he was humbled and made subject [Phil. 2:8]. For me he is the lamb [cf. John 1:29, 36], the vine [cf. John 15:1-5], the rock [cf. 1 Cor. 10:4], the servant [cf. Isa. 53:11; Matt. 12:18; Phil. 2:7], the Son of a handmaid [cf. Luke 1:38]" (Ambrose, Of the Christian Faith 2.92; Mark 10:45).[4]

Gregory Nazianzus summed it up in this poetic way:

He is our sanctification,
As himself being purity,
That the pure may be encompassed by his purity.
He is our redemption, because he sets us free
Who were held captive under sin,
Giving himself as a ransom for us,
The sacrifice to make expiation for the world.

(Gregory Nazianzus, Theological Orations 4.20,
spaces added; Mark 10:45; cf. Tit. 2:14;
2 Tim. 2:26; Matt. 20:28; Mark 10:45;
Heb. 7:26-27; 9:24-26; 10:10-12)[5]

---

4. Cetedoc 0150, 2.11.32; NPNF 2 10:236; ACCS NT 2:151*.
5. LCC 3:192*; TLG 2022.010, 20.32; ACCS NT 2:151.

## 4. Paul Wrote from Prison

Saul of Tarsus had a bad previous record of imprisoning and persecuting Christians. He severely attacked the church with threats and death (Acts 8:3; 22:4; 26:10). The blood of Christians was on his hands.

The reversal in Paul's conversion changed him from being persecutor to one willing to suffer persecution. He suffered repeated imprisonments for his Lord. Paul cataloged his extensive afflictions in 2 Corinthians 6:4-5 and 11:23-29. By the time of his second letter to the Corinthians, he had already been confined in prisons in Jerusalem, Caesarea, and Rome.

Many of Paul's letters were written from a prison cell. John Chrysostom ponders the significance of this: "All of Paul's letters are holy, but those he writes behind bars are especially advantageous for the reader. Those include, for instance, the letters to the Ephesians and Philemon, that to Timothy, that to the Philippians and the one before us. For Colossians was written while Paul was imprisoned, since he writes in it: 'for which I am also in bonds: that I may make it manifest as I ought to speak'" (Chrysostom, Homilies on Colossians 1; Col. 4:9).[6] Paul spoke from behind prison bars to attest freedom in Christ. He asked that the churches "'not be discouraged by my tribulations for you, which are your glory' [Eph. 3:13]" (Chrysostom, Homilies on Ephesians 7; 1 Thess. 3:3).[7]

## 5. Remembering the Saints in Prison

The apostles experienced the silent connection of the saints with each other and with Christ, the fellowship of suffering. Chrysostom noted Paul's constant recollection of godly persons in his ministry as he sat alone in prison: "Within the very walls of his prison cell he affectionately remembers the Philippians. This is no small form of praise. . . . It is wonderful that he has them in his heart in his imprisonment. Even *in my defense* before the judgment seat, he says, you did not slip from my memory" (Chrysostom, Homily on Philippians 2, italics added; Phil. 1:7b).[8] During his trial he was keenly aware of those who were praying for him.

6. NPNF 1 13:257*; ACCS NT 9:56-57.
7. NPNF 1 13:81*; ACCS NT 9:74*.
8. IOEP 5:12; ACCS NT 8:220.

Those willing to suffer for the ones they love are prone to think of their suffering as a small thing when viewed within the context of eternal love. Those who suffer as the body of Christ are made all the more aware of each other's prayers when apart than when together.

Compared with martyrdom, would vast armies or extensive learning make witness to the Gospel more persuasive than one's free willingness to suffer? Chrysostom drew this analogy: "Suppose there had been some great number of us, not merely twelve! Suppose we had been instead of 'unlearned and ignorant,' those wise and skilled in rhetoric and mighty in speech. What would have come of our proclamation? Suppose we had been kings in possession of armies and an abundance of wealth? Would we have been thereby more persuasive in proclaiming this kingdom of peace? When we despise our own safety, why do they pay all the more heed to us?" (Chrysostom, The Gospel of Matthew, Homily 33.4; Matt. 10:18).[9] We do not need to seek protection from being misunderstood and misinterpreted. God will right these wrongs in God's own time.

### 6. The Ambassador in Chains

It is not just imprisonment as a symbol or metaphor, but the actual reality of imprisonment that we are talking about. Paul repeatedly spoke of his chains, referring to them personally as "my chains" (Phil. 1:7, 13, 14, 16, NKJV). He described himself as an "ambassador in chains" (Eph. 6:20, RSV). His imprisonment is not incidental to his apostolic activity, but intrinsic to it. It refracts Christ's own meekness. So when in Colossians 4:1 he asks the church to "remember my bonds," it is not simply asking them to be aware of his discomforts, but of the meaning of his suffering within salvation history, and of the suffering saints everywhere.

Paul's chains confirmed his testimony and apostolic authority, according to John Chrysostom: "His chains are without doubt a confirmation of the Gospel. How? Because if he had refused the bonds, he would have obviously been viewed as a deceiver. But take note of the one who endures everything, including persecution and imprisonment. He shows unmistakably that he does not suffer them for any human reason but on account of God's goodness, who rights the balance. . . . See how this

9. PG 57:391; NPNF 1 10:221-22*; ACCS NT 1a:200*.

absolutely turns everything on its head!" (Chrysostom, Homily on Philippians 2; Phil. 1:7c).[10] To suffer with joy for God's kingdom is already to bear the most plausible witness to the truth for which one suffers.

When the faithful bear adversity with joy in prison, they inspire the faith of others, even those far away. "'My chains,' he says in effect, 'have themselves become the source of courage to others. They can easily see that I bear adversity with joy. In this way others will come to preach the divine Gospel fearlessly" (Theodoret, Epistle to the Philippians; Phil. 1:14a).[11] In his commentary on Ephesians, Theodoret wrote: "When Paul recalls his chains his intent is to encourage his hearers to rise above their own infirmities to moral excellence. It is as if he were saying: 'Remember that it is in relation to you that I am in prison" (Theodoret, Epistle to the Ephesians; Eph. 4:1a).[12] His chains attested his faithfulness.

It was through Paul's imprisonment that Onesimus became a believer. Paul shows his affection for Onesimus, reminding Philemon of his service to Christ. "'I have begotten him in my bonds,' he says, so that also on this account Onesimus was worthy to obtain much honor, because he was begotten in Paul's very conflicts, in his trials in the cause of Christ" (Chrysostom, Homilies on Philemon 2; Philem. 10).[13]

### 7. Listening to Paul's Chains

How do Paul's chains speak? Chrysostom writes, "Listen to Paul's chains. You will then understand that to be in affliction is no indication of our being forsaken. Would you like to wear silken robes? Better to remember Paul's chains. These fine clothes will then appear to you as worthless as rags. Would you array yourself with gold trinkets? Listen in your mind to Paul's chains, and trinkets will seem to you no better than a withered bulrush" (Chrysostom, Homilies on Colossians 12; Col. 4:18).[14] The sound of trinkets does not inspire faithfulness, but chains do.

The authority of witnessing by chains is likened to the authority of an ambassador from heaven. Ambrosiaster commented on Paul's confi-

10. IOEP 5:12-13; ACCS NT 8:220*.
11. TCPE 2:47; ACCS NT 8:223*.
12. TCPE 2:22; ACCS NT 8:158.
13. NPNF 1 13:551*; ACCS NT 9:313.
14. NPNF 1 13:315*; ACCS NT 9:57*.

dence as "an ambassador in chains" (Eph. 6:20a, RSV). "Custom and law forbid the infliction of harm on human ambassadors. So would it not be presumptuous and rash to bring harm to the ambassadors of God, and not only harm but death?" (Ambrosiaster, On Paul's Epistle to the Ephesians 6.20.3; Eph. 6:20a).[15] The confidence of the ambassador hinges on who he is representing.

Faith cannot be bound. "It is not possible to bind a sunbeam or to shut it up within the house. So neither can the preaching of the word be bound. And what is much more, when the teacher is bound, the word flies abroad. Paul inhabited the prison, and yet his teaching winged its way everywhere throughout the world!" (Chrysostom, Homilies Concerning the Statutes 16.5; 2 Tim. 2:9a).[16] The credibility of a witness to Christ increases through unjust imprisonment.

God's Word is not bound. "Our hands are bound but not our tongue, since nothing can bind the tongue but cowardice and unbelief. Where these are not, though you fasten chains upon us, the preaching of the Gospel is not bound" (Chrysostom, Homilies on 2 Timothy 4; 2 Tim. 2:9b).[17]


## 8. Confident Witness amid Imprisonment

A surprising note of joy emerges out of these prison letters, not tarnished by any hint of self-pity. This imprisonment was for the Lord (Phil. 1:13). It was ordered by a divine providence that gave Paul, even in incarceration, more confidence and determination. He viewed his own imprisonment as a veritable embodied living act of defense of the Gospel and participation in the living Christ (Phil. 1:16). Paul is saying in effect, according to Chrysostom: "'It is confidence *in the Lord,* not in me as such, that is elicited by my chains. As others take courage from my bonds, so do I. As I become the cause of confidence to others, much more does this have an effect within myself'" (Chrysostom, Homily on Philippians 3; Phil. 1:14a).[18]

It was by means of his imprisonment that the Gospel became known to the Praetorian Guard (Phil. 1:13). Ambrosiaster commented: "His impris-

15. CSEL 81.3:125; ACCS NT 8:215*.
16. NPNF 1 9:450*; ACCS NT 9:244*.
17. NPNF 1 13:489; ACCS NT 9:244.
18. IOEP 5:20; ACCS NT 8:223.

onment for Christ's sake is becoming known. This is his distinctive honor. Now others who love him may rejoice with him" (Ambrosiaster, On Paul's Epistle to the Philippians 1.17.1; Phil. 1:13a).[19] Chrysostom concluded: "Paul preached the Gospel even when bound and scourged. O those blessed chains, with what great effort did they labor that night, and what children did they birth! Yes, of them, too, may he say, 'Whom I have begotten in my bonds'" (Chrysostom, Homilies on Ephesians 8; Philem. 10).[20]

### 9. Faithful Women, Too, Suffered Imprisonment

Paul spoke of a courageous woman as a fellow-prisoner. Her name was Junia. She may have been a relative of Paul's. She was deemed worthy by Paul to be called an apostle. She and Andronicus "were in Christ before I was" (Rom. 16:7, NRSV). "It was the greatest of honors to be counted a fellow prisoner of Paul's," wrote Chrysostom. "Think what great praise it was to be considered one among the apostles. These two were of note because of their works and triumphs. Think how great the devotion of this woman Junia must have been, that she should be worthy to be called an apostle! But even here Paul does not stop his praise, for they were Christians before he was" (Chrysostom, Homilies on Romans 31; Rom. 16:7).[21]

Theodoret wrote of the women cited in the last chapter of Romans that they "were companions of Paul in his sufferings and even shared imprisonment with him. . . . They are not to be regarded as his pupils but as his teachers, and not among the ordinary teachers but among the apostles. He even praises them for having been Christians before him" (Theodoret, Interpretation of the Letter to the Romans; Rom. 16:7).[22] These women, along with Aristarchus (Col. 4:10) and Epaphras (Philem. 23), would be remembered as bearing the special honor of attesting the Gospel with Paul in prison, even and precisely through their chains, where every thought was taken captive for Christ (2 Cor. 10:5). Priscilla and Aquila risked their lives for Paul, he writes in Romans 16:4, as did Epaphroditus (Phil. 2:30). Paul, Peter, and Barnabas repeatedly risked their lives for their witness

---

19. CSEL 81.3:133; ACCS NT 8:223.
20. NPNF 1 13:89*; ACCS NT 9:313*.
21. NPNF 1 11:554-55; ACCS NT 6:372*.
22. PG 82:220; ACCS NT 6:372*.

(Acts 15:26). We, like they, are called to embody that witness. These witnesses point to the determination of the Christian community to identify with the least of these, among whom are the prisoners, whom the faithful are called to visit, for in doing so, they meet Christ himself incognito.

## B. Witnessing in Prison

It is not a matter of shame to be imprisoned for the sake of righteousness. The list of the faithful in prison includes many heroes of faith: Joseph (Gen. 39:20), Micaiah (1 Kings 22:27), Jeremiah (Jer. 32:2; 33:1), John the Baptist (Matt. 4:12; 14:3; Mark 1:14; 6:17; Luke 3:20). The pattern weaving through all of these narratives was that God was using their weakness to reveal his strength, their humiliation to bring his purpose to fuller glory. Their imprisonment was testifying to God's faithfulness.

### 1. The Icon of Joseph as Prototype of Faithful Witness in Prison

The key Old Testament text on witnessing in prison is the narrative of Joseph, who was imprisoned first by the deceit of his own brothers, then by false charges.

Ancient Christian visual arts portray Joseph in prison, as can be seen, for example, in the Vienna Genesis, a fourth-century Vatican sarcophagus, and a fifth-century martyrium of Seleucia. The ironies of Joseph's imprisonment amazed the Fathers, as seen in the account written by the hymnist Ephrem the Syrian: "With no mercy they cast him into a pit in the desert, but they wept over Joseph with tears in the house. They sold him naked to the Arabs but wept over him and wailed in the presence of the Canaanites. They put irons on his hands and feet and sent him on his way but composed lamentations over him in the village. Joseph went down to Egypt and was sold; within a few days he had changed owners twice" (Ephrem the Syrian, Commentary on Genesis 33.2; Gen. 37:36).[23]

Ambrose meditated on the instruction and consolation that Joseph provided for those imprisoned:

23. FC 91:182; ACCS OT 2:241.

Even in the lowliest status, people should learn that their character can be superior and that no state of life is devoid of virtue if the soul of the individual knows itself. The flesh may be subject to slavery, while the spirit remains free. Many humble servants are freer than their masters, if in their condition of slavery they consider that they should abstain from acting like a slave. Each little sin in fact is slavish. Meanwhile blamelessness is free. On this account the Lord also says, "Everyone who commits sin is a slave of sin" [John 8:34]. Indeed, how is each greedy person not a slave, seeing that he auctions himself off for a very tiny sum of money? The person who has piled up what he is not going to use is afraid that he may lose all that he has piled up. The more numerous his acquisitions, the greater the risk he will run in keeping them. (Ambrose, On Joseph 4.20; Gen. 37:36)[24]

To know oneself is to know to whom one's soul belongs. One who knows his own soul is not intimidated by being imprisoned in body. Those who allow themselves to be defined as slaves will tend to become slaves to external circumstances.

It is precisely when virtue is most under attack that it reveals its character. This we see in early Christian visual portrayals of Joseph's imprisonment: "Do you see how things proceed gradually, and how in every circumstance Joseph shows his characteristic virtue and endurance? It is like the athlete who nobly contends for the kingdom's garland. He will be crowned," wrote Chrysostom. "Joseph taught those who sold him that no advantage accrued to them from their awful ruse. Virtue, you see, has such power that *even when under attack it emerges more conspicuous*. Nothing, after all, is stronger than virtue, nothing more powerful . . . not because it has such power of itself but because the one who acquires it also enjoys grace from on high" (Chrysostom, Homilies on Genesis 61.20, italics added; Gen. 37:36).[25] The growing power of virtue under challenge derives its vitality not from itself but from the grace by which it is empowered.

Imprisonment deepened Joseph's capacity to reflect God's holiness: "Just as a pearl reveals its peculiar beauty even if someone buries it in the mire, so too virtue, wherever you cast it, reveals its characteristic power,

24. FC 65:201-2*; ACCS OT 2:241-42*.
25. FC 87:197*; ACCS OT 2:242*.

whether it is found in servitude, in prison, in distress or in prosperity" (Chrysostom, Homilies on Genesis 63.2; Gen. 39:21).[26] The beauty of a holy life is not marred by imprisonment.

God accompanied holy Joseph in his lonely cell: "That woman [Potiphar's wife] did what she threatened. She lied to her husband and was believed. Still God was patient. Holy Joseph was thrown into prison. He was held captive like a guilty man, although he had done no offense. . . . God did not fail him. The Lord was with holy Joseph. Because he loved what was holy, he was not overcome by the love of a woman" (Caesarius of Arles, Sermon 90.3; Gen. 39:19).[27]

### 2. Joseph Was Happier Being Righteously in Prison Than Free Lacking Righteousness

Due to his modesty, Joseph was happier in prison than if he were freely colluding with sin. "Therefore I might say Joseph was happier when he was put into prison, because he was giving witness on behalf of chastity. Modesty is a good gift, but one of lesser value when it involves no risk. Where it is maintained at the risk of one's safety, however, there it wins a more abundant crown. With his case unheard, his truthfulness unexamined, Joseph is sent into prison as if guilty of a crime [Gen. 39:19-20]. But the Lord did not abandon him even in prison. The innocent should not be troubled when they are attacked on false charges, when justice is overcome and they are shoved into prison. God visits his own even in prison, and so there is more help for them there, even where there appears to be more danger" (Ambrose, On Joseph 5.26; Gen. 39:20).[28]

As risks increase, so may the potential fruits of virtue. "Joseph was more blessed when he was cast into prison, for he endured martyrdom in defense of chastity. The gift of purity is a great thing, even when it is preserved without danger, but when it is defended at the risk of personal safety, then it is crowned still more fully" (Caesarius of Arles, Sermon 92.4; Gen. 39:20).[29] This is why "the holy man considered that prison to

26. FC 82:212; ACCS OT 2:258*.
27. FC 47:45; ACCS OT 2:256-57*.
28. FC 65:207; ACCS OT 2:257*.
29. FC 47:56; ACCS OT 2:258.

be a palace. Joseph himself was a palace in his prison, because where faith, chastity and modesty are, there the palace of Christ is, the temple of God, the dwelling of the Holy Spirit" (Chromatius, Sermon 24.2; Gen. 39:20).[30]

"Nothing is so characteristic of slavery as constant fear," said Ambrose. "But whatever one's servile status, he will always be more free when not seduced by [false] love. One who is held by the chains of greed or bound by fear of reproach is in worse bondage than one who is unafraid of the future. Doesn't it seem to you that a person of the latter kind is the master even in slavery, while one of the former kind is a slave even when supposedly free? Joseph was a slave, and Pharaoh a ruler. The slavery of the one was much happier than the sovereignty of the other. Indeed, all Egypt would have collapsed from famine unless Pharaoh had made his sovereignty subject to the counsel of a mere servant [Gen. 41:55-56]" (Ambrose, On Joseph 4.20; Gen. 37:36).[31] Even the slave is free when he lives virtuously. Even the king is slave when trapped in illusions.

It is precisely in unjust imprisonment that the righteous most profoundly rediscover the justice of God, as we learn from Joseph: "The Lord visits his own even in prison. Where the danger is greater, the help is greater" (Caesarius of Arles, Sermon 92.4; Gen. 39:21).[32]

## 3. Joseph as a Type of Christ

The African church father Quodvultdeus viewed Joseph's imprisonment as a type, a picture of the future, an anticipation of Christ's death. "Joseph was imprisoned. Our Joseph, that is, Christ, as Isaiah says, 'was numbered with the transgressors' [Isa. 53:12]. The innocent man is led among the guilty by the wisdom of God, who 'went down with him' — as was written — 'into the pit, and did not leave him in bonds' [Wis. 10:13-14]. This Joseph of ours, Christ, claims, 'became as a man without help, free among the dead' [Ps. 88:4-5 (87:5-6 LXX)]. What followed had to happen, that is, the fact that Joseph found in the commander of the prison the grace of which he was full and that all the keys and the entire surveillance were

---

30. SCC 2:70; ACCS OT 2:257.
31. FC 65:202*; ACCS OT 2:242*.
32. FC 47:56*; ACCS OT 2:258*. Cf. Ambrose, FC 65:207; ACCS OT 2:257.

given to him [Gen. 39:21-23]" (Quodvultdeus, Book of Promises and Predictions of God 1.28.40; Gen. 39:20).[33]

Christ himself meets us in prison, since present in the "least of these," according to Ambrose: "But what wonder if Christ visits those who lie in prison? He reminds us that he himself was shut up in prison in his followers, as you find it written, 'I was in prison, and you did not come to me' [Matt. 25:43]. Where does God's mercy fail to enter in? Joseph found favor of this sort. He who had been shut up in the prison kept the locks of the prison, while the jailer withdrew from his post and entrusted all the prisoners to his power [Gen. 39:21-23]. Consequently Joseph did not suffer from prison but even gave relief to others as well from the calamity of imprisonment" (Ambrose, On Joseph 5.27; Gen. 39:21).[34]

The Fathers found endless variations in the analogies between Joseph and Christ: "Joseph was rejected by his own brothers but received by the Ishmaelites [Gen. 37:25-27]. In the same manner our Lord and Savior was rejected by the Jews and received by the pagans. Remember the Ishmaelites who received Joseph carried along with them all kinds of perfumes. This curious fact showed that the pagans, by embracing the faith, would in due time spread the different perfumes of justice all over the world" (Chromatius, Sermon 24.3; Gen. 37:25).[35]

### 4. The Imprisonment of John the Baptist

Herod imprisoned John the Baptist to prevent his teaching, but his teaching was thereby only made more powerful. According to Origen: "Notice that even while in prison [John] is teaching. He also had his disciples in that place. Why did they stay there, unless John exercised the office of teacher even in prison and taught them with divine words?" (Origen, Homilies on the Gospel of Luke 27.4; Luke 3:19-20).[36]

John's freedom in prison would transcend Herod's madness in court. He "died confidently and was beheaded without resistance, strengthened by the words of the Lord himself and believing that he in

33. SCQ 1:238; ACCS OT 2:257.
34. FC 65:207-8; ACCS OT 2:258*.
35. SCC 2:74; ACCS OT 2:238*.
36. FC 94:113*; ACCS NT 3:64-65.

whom he believed was truly the Son of God. This is what we have to say about John's freedom and Herod's madness: To his many other crimes Herod also added this one: he first shut John in prison and afterward beheaded him" (Origen, Homilies on the Gospel of Luke 27.4; Luke 3:19-20).[37] Herod is remembered for his sins and madness; John for his righteousness and integrity.

### 5. Jesus in Dying Preached to the Imprisoned Souls

The Fathers were intrigued by the thought that Jesus himself entered prison and ransomed captives. The key text here is 1 Peter 3:18-20a (RSV): "For Christ also died for sins once for all, the righteous for the unrighteous, that he might bring us to God, being put to death in the flesh but made alive in the spirit; in which he went and preached to the spirits in prison, who formerly did not obey." This text gave the ancient Christian writers much to ponder, not only regarding Christology, but also the good work of visiting the imprisoned.

Cyril portrayed the crucified Lord as entering hell, breaking its gates, and leading the prisoners out. "Going in his soul, he preached to those who were in hell, appearing to them as one soul to other souls. When the gatekeepers of hell saw him, they fled; the bronze gates were broken open, and the iron chains were undone. And the only-begotten Son shouted with authority to the suffering souls, according to the word of the new covenant, saying to those in chains: 'Come out!' and to those in darkness: 'Be enlightened.' In other words, he preached to those who were in hell also, so that he might save all those who would believe in him" (Cyril of Alexandria, quoted in Cramer, Catena in Epistolas Catholicas; 1 Pet. 3:19).[38]

The "spirits in prison" to whom the crucified Lord preached, according to Clement of Alexandria, did not visibly "see his form, but they heard the sound of his voice" (Clement of Alexandria, Fragments 1.1, quoted in Cassiodorus, Adumbrations 1; 1 Pet. 3:19).[39]

Thinking out of Psalm 16, Origen pondered another approach to the puzzling issue of Jesus' visit to the souls in prison: "If the text possesses a hid-

37. FC 94:113*; ACCS NT 3:65.
38. CEC 66; ACCS NT 11:107.
39. FGNK 3:81; ANF 2:572*; ACCS NT 11:107.

den meaning, we ought not to pass over it. . . . It is said in Psalm 16: 'You will not leave my soul in hell.' And Peter, in his general epistle, mentions Jesus' descent into hell. Therefore the one who can show the meaning of both sojourns in a worthy manner is able to unloose Jesus' shoes" (Origen, Commentary on John 6.174-76; 1 Pet. 3:19).[40] Here is an instance where several texts of scripture must coalesce before any of them are properly understood.

In the nether world Christ was recognized by those whose faith had become active in works of love while they were yet alive, according to Severus of Antioch: "Forgiveness was not granted to everyone in hell, but only to those who believed and acknowledged Christ. Those who cleansed themselves from evil by doing good works while they were alive recognized him. For until he appeared in the lower regions everyone, including those who had been educated in righteousness, was bound by the chains of death and was awaiting his arrival there, for the way to paradise was closed to them because of Adam's sin" (Severus of Antioch, quoted in Cramer, Catena in Epistolas Catholicas; 1 Pet. 3:19).[41]

After his death, Jesus preached, according to Ammonius: "When the king of all is present, it is not possible for the tyrant and his servant, I mean death, to retain their captives any longer. So what did the Lord do? He died. He preached the way which leads to eternal salvation on earth, and to all who were in hell, so that they might believe in the Father and in him who became man and died for us and who went down into hell by the power of the Holy Spirit. And those who believed he brought back with him, but those who did not believe, he cast back again into their previous state" (Ammonius, quoted in Cramer, Catena in Epistolas Catholicas; 1 Pet. 3:19).[42]

So goes the speculation, but what is unmistakable about these descent into hell passages is Jesus' willingness to identify with sinners, with those in prison, with those cast away. The Latin poet Prudentius celebrated Jesus' act of identification with those imprisoned in the nether world, focusing on the metaphor of smashing the gates of hell, in this hymn:

> Into hell with love he entered;
> to him yield the broken gates

40. FC 80:218; ACCS NT 11:107*.
41. CEC 67-68; ACCS NT 11:108.
42. CEC 68; ACCS NT 11:108.

As the bolts and massive hinges
fall asunder at his word.
Now the door of ready entrance,
but forbidding all return
Outward swings as bars are loosened
and sends forth the prisoned souls
By reversal of the mandate,
treading its threshold once more.

(Prudentius, Hymns 9.71-75; 1 Pet. 3:19)[43]

The law is being transformed by the Gospel. The threshold is hell.
The Gospel offers new life to the dead.

### 6. Ransom from Bondage

We are called, where possible, to break the yoke off the neck of the one who
is yoked, and to burst the bonds of the one tied up (Jer. 30:8). The faithful
are called to accompany Jesus, insofar as possible, in ransoming those unjustly bound. The prophecy in Isaiah 61:1b (RSV) was fulfilled in Jesus: He
was sent to "bind up the broken-hearted, proclaim liberty to the captives,
and to open the prison of those who are bound." Those who sit in darkness
are brought out of their alienation (Isa. 42:7).

The angel of the Lord opened prison doors for the apostles and
brought them out by night, so that by daybreak they were teaching in the
Jerusalem temple (Acts 5:19). Luke's account reads like a novel: "An angel
of the Lord suddenly appeared and a light shone in the cell; and he struck
Peter's side and woke him up, saying 'Get up quickly.' And his chains fell
off his hands." The angel said: "'Wrap your cloak around you and follow
me.' And he went out and continued to follow, and he did not know that
what was being done by the angel was real, but thought he was seeing a vision. When they had passed the first and second guard, they came to the
iron gate that leads into the city, which opened for them by itself" (Acts
12:7-10a, NAS).

Later, in the prison of Philippi, when "Paul and Silas were praying
and singing, . . . suddenly there came a great earthquake, so that the foun-

43. FC 43:65; ACCS NT 11:108.

dations of the prison house were shaken; and immediately all the doors were opened and everyone's chains were unfastened" (Acts 16:25-26, NAS). The yoke is shattered (Isa. 9:4). Captives are set free (Zech. 9:11). God delivers Israel from the snare of the fowler (Ps. 91:3). The godly are rescued from fire and trial (2 Pet. 2:9).

Each of these passages has a history of patristic interpretation that is too detailed to examine within these pages. But for those who wish to do so, the specific passages may be found in the Ancient Christian Commentary on Scripture.

The life of charitable good works is a life that is devoted intentionally to freeing the slave. Where the Spirit of the Lord is, there is freedom (2 Cor. 3:17). It is for this freedom that Christ has set us free (Gal. 5:1). This is what good works do for captives. They seek to free them.

## C. Care for the Persecuted: The Martyrs' Gift

All that the scripture says about ministering to the imprisoned takes on special tenderness and poignancy when applied to those being unjustly persecuted. They are engaged in a special work of love on behalf of the whole body of the faithful. They are silently witnessing to the truth by means of their very lives.

The martyrs are those who have died for the faith. The confessors are those who have been willing to die for their faith. The saints are those who have lived the holy life. The martyrs and confessors and saints are honored in classic Christian liturgy, iconography, and teaching, for their life witness.

### 1. The Pattern

The pattern in the Christian life for understanding care of those suffering persecution is Jesus himself, who suffered persecution, and by his death redeemed those in bondage.

It is with awe that we come to this subject. *It is a unique good work to be willing to be persecuted for righteousness' sake.* Those facing martyrdom in attesting Christ find in Jesus' last days the pattern for patient endurance for the sake of witness. He faced his own death for others, and thereby ransomed humanity from the demonic powers.

Listen carefully to the Fathers, and you will discover the richness of how classic Christianity has reflected on unjust persecution. Those who resort to contorted psychological explanations of martyrdom (such as masochism or sexual dysfunction) demean the saints.

Those facing harassment, persecution, and unfair treatment are held up constantly in the baptismal and eucharistic prayers by the church around the world. In these prayers, the Spirit is petitioned to give special grace for our participation in Christ's death and resurrection. The most complete expression of faith's good work is the willingness to put one's very life at risk, if need be, for the truth. *The martyr by his or her embodied witness participates decisively by grace through faith in God's own good work for us.* There is no more holy or efficacious act enabled by grace than that of martyrdom. By giving one's all, the wholeness of self-giving divine love is demonstrated and embodied.

### 2. The Icons of the Persecuted

Shadrach, Meshach, and Abednego knew what it meant to be persecuted when they refused to worship the image of the king (Dan. 3). Christian iconography is full of images of persecution and martyrdom.

The prophets were persecuted because they all too clearly declared the Word of God (Amos 7:10-12; Jer. 15:37-38; 26:20-23). God has a history of taking special care of those who boldly attest his revelation in history. This history remembers Israel's experience in Egypt (Deut. 6:7), Israel's bondage in the exile (Ps. 137), Christ's death, and the holy history of Christian martyrs.

When the risen Christ met Paul on the road to Damascus, he announced himself straightforwardly: "I am Jesus, whom you persecute" (Acts 9:5b, TEV/Good News). Whom did Paul persecute? The defenseless church. The saints. Those who attested the truth. This moment is made visual in the art and icons of early Christianity.

### 3. How Jesus Related to His Persecutors

Jesus, who himself was subject to persecution and torture, pronounced his blessing upon all who are persecuted for righteousness' sake (Matt. 5:10).

He was subject to constant harassment by judges, priests, lawyers, and religious authorities (Matt. 5:21-48; Mark 3:6), and finally by the civil powers.

A vivid picture of torture is portrayed in Psalm 129:3 (KJV*): "The plowers plowed upon my back and made long their furrows." This is a moving image of torment. Even the most faithful are not spared being oppressed and persecuted. For his sake they also "have borne reproach" (Ps. 69:7, KJV).

Jesus realistically warned his disciples that they would be persecuted for righteousness' sake (Matt. 10:16-23), just as were the prophets before them (Matt. 5:12, 23, 31). They were. "If they have persecuted me, they will also persecute you" (John 15:20b, KJV). They did. Jesus warned the faithful that they themselves would be offered up as a sacrifice. "For they will deliver you up to councils and scourge you in their synagogues" (Matt. 10:17, NKJV). The Fathers meditated on this irony: "As though they were doing it for the greater glory of God, they will whip you in their synagogues. Where there are prayers and praises and readings or sacrifices, there they will punish the apostles as though offering to God a sacrifice" (Opus Imperfectum in Matthaeum, Homily 24; Matt. 10:19).[44]

Following the Lord, the faithful go "outside the camp," beyond the city wall, bearing his reproach (Heb. 13:13, RSV). "Therefore I take pleasure in infirmities, in reproaches, in necessities, in persecutions, in distresses for Christ's sake: for when I am weak, then am I strong" (2 Cor. 12:10, KJV). All who share life in Christ are called to bear his cross (1 Pet. 3:13-18; 4:12-19; 5:6-14), no exceptions.


## 4. The Wicked Serve the Good without Being Aware of It

We are taught in the sacred text that the wicked inadvertently serve the good even when they seem to be victors. Caesarius of Arles offered a series of analogies to develop this theme: "How, then, do the wicked serve the good? As persecutors serve the martyrs; as a file or hammer, gold; as a mill, wheat; as ovens, the baking of bread: those are consumed, so that these may be baked. How, I say, do the wicked serve the good? As chaff in the furnace of the goldsmith serves gold." The gold cannot be tested without a furnace. The witness to Christ is not consumed with anger, but love:

44. PG 56:758; ACCS NT 1a:200*.

"Hence if in an evil spirit someone who is inflamed with the fury of wrath tries to stir up a good man, it is still doubtful whether the good man can be consumed with rage, but there is no doubt that the evil man is already glowing with anger. Perhaps that good man who is full of spiritual vigor and the refreshment of the Holy Ghost will not get excited, even if the fire of persecution is inflicted; but without any doubt the one who tried to arouse him cannot fail to burn with passion" (Caesarius of Arles, Sermon 86.4; Gen. 25:23).[45] God turns evil into good. For this reason the faithful do not despair that evil is powerful in the passing world. God can always find a way of working through it toward some greater good, now unseen and unknown, but certain.

Even when evil seems to be triumphing across every horizon, it is always serving some hidden good. This is how providence works. This we see from the narrative of Joseph, whose imprisonment was intended for evil, but God found a way of making it work for good. Joseph tells his brothers: "You meant evil against me, but God meant it for the good" (Gen. 50:20a, RSV*). On this premise, the faithful are given grace to bless those who curse them (Luke 6:28; cf. Rom. 12:14). In this way Joseph's imprisonment itself became a unique good work that flowed as a consequence of his faith in God's promise.

### 5. A Larger Justice Hidden in Injustice

Unjust suffering may work by grace toward a much greater hidden justice, even if the just outcome is obscured temporarily from view, according to Oecumenius: "There are two benefits to be gained from unjust suffering. First, the righteous person who suffers may grow in righteousness as a result of his patience. Second, the sinner who is spared in this way may find his own life turned around by seeing someone else suffer on his behalf" (Oecumenius, Commentary on 1 Peter; 1 Pet. 3:17).[46] Those locked up unjustly with the keys thrown away are precious to the community of faith.

It surely should not be surprising to the faithful that the church faces the perplexing ambiguities of wheat and tares within the body itself. For the ecclesia is composed of actual people living in real history. Caesarius

45. FC 47:27-28; ACCS OT 2:148-49*.
46. PG 119:553; ACCS NT 11:105*.

saw this realistically: "The number of the wicked is always greater than that of the good. So just like those two children in the womb of Rebekah, so these two will struggle in the womb of the church until judgment day, as we said above, while the proud resist the humble, while adulterers persecute the chaste, while drunkards whose number is infinite rail at the sober, while the envious rival the good, while robbers desire to destroy those who give alms" (Caesarius of Arles, Sermon 86.4; Gen. 25:23).[47] The struggle within a mixed church will continue until the end, only to be resolved in eternity.

Although the metaphor of imprisonment refers first of all to those physically locked up by corrupt authorities, it also echoes through psychological and spiritual bondage among those who experience captivity in their inward life, vocations, families, and social relationships.

### 6. You Are Blessed When Falsely Reviled for Christ's Sake

When persecution for Christ's sake becomes unavoidable, the faithful are promised grace to receive its blessing calmly and gratefully. Jesus' beatitude announced: "Blessed are you when men revile you and persecute you and utter all kinds of evil against you falsely on my account" (Matt. 5:11, RSV). This does not mean that anyone who is suffering is by that bare fact blessed. They are blessed who suffer unjustly for righteousness' sake. John Chrysostom made this distinction: "To keep you from supposing that being bad-talked of itself makes people blessed, he has added two qualifications: first that it happen for Christ's sake, and second, that what is said be false. Do not expect to be blessed if you are being reviled for something evil, and what is being said is true" (Chrysostom, The Gospel of Matthew, Homily 15.4; Matt. 5:11).[48] If these two conditions prevail, you will be blessed.

They are especially blessed who suffer unfairly for the truth. This is Jesus' own promise:

> He has just been speaking about enduring persecution. Now it is as if someone were asking God: "God, what if we are not enduring persecu-

47. FC 47:28; ACCS OT 2:149*.
48. PG 57:228; NPNF 1 10:95; ACCS NT 1a:90*.

tion for your sake, or for the sake of justice? What if we are facing the reproach and the evil talk of wicked people?" You will be blessed, Jesus says, not only if you endure persecution, but also if others "utter all kinds of evil against you falsely on my account." Many people because of God become our enemies, but they do not persecute us openly. Maybe they do not have the power to do so. Nevertheless, they go all about and demean us and say about us deplorable things. The scripture says: "You will be blessed when men revile you and persecute you and utter all kinds of evil against you falsely on my account." So your reward does not end the moment you have given a glass of water compassionately. If somebody does us a wrong of even a single slight word, your soul will not be lacking a reward. (Opus Imperfectum in Matthaeum, Homily 9; Matt. 5:11)[49]

So put harsh words in perspective. Let them become for you a blessing through grace.

## 7. The Spirit Will Help You Speak the Truth

You need not be practiced in rhetoric. You must be practiced in holy living. Focus therefore on the Spirit's witness amid imprisonment and persecution. The Lord commanded: "Settle it therefore in your minds, not to meditate beforehand how to answer; for I will give you a mouth and wisdom, which none of your adversaries will be able to withstand or contradict" (Luke 21:14-15, RSV).

Do not become fixated on what you cannot do, but on what God can do. This we hear from Cyprian of Carthage who himself suffered exile, persecution, and death:

Just as in Exodus God speaks to Moses, when he delays and fears to go to the people, saying, "Who gave a mouth to man and who made the dumb and the deaf, the seeing and the blind? Did not I the Lord God? Go now, and I shall open your mouth, and I will teach you what you shall speak" [Exod. 4:11-12]. It is not difficult for God to open the mouth of a man devoted to him and to inspire constancy and confi-

49. PG 56:683-84; ACCS NT 1a:90*.

dence in speaking in one who confesses him, who in the book of Numbers made even an ass speak against Balaam the prophet [Num. 22:28-30]. Therefore *let no one consider amid persecution what danger the Adversary brings, but rather let him bear in mind what assistance God brings.* Let not the disturbances of men weaken the mind, but let divine protection strengthen the faith. Each one according to the Lord's promises and the merits of his faith receives so much of God's help as he is ready to receive. There is nothing that the Almighty cannot grant, excepting when the frail faith of the recipient is unready to receive it. (Cyprian, Exhortation to Martyrdom 10, italics added; Exod. 4:11)[50]

Grace will be supplied as needed in times of persecution. "It is as though Jesus said to them: 'You see me hungry and you believe that I am the heavenly bread. You see me thirsty and you believe that I am the spring of water welling up to eternal life [John 4:14]. You believe in me and declare that I speak the truth. How are we to understand this human faculty that sees one thing and believes another and then professes that belief? So, if now at a time when there is no danger, my grace is at work in you, how much more will it be in you when persecution comes? For he who sustains you in peace will help you all the more in active combat'" (Opus Imperfectum in Matthaeum, Homily 24; Matt. 10:20).[51] Even when enmeshed in the powers of evil, the faithful do not cease to have confidence in God's saving power.

## 8. Endurance

Those who suffer persecution are enabled by grace to "rejoice and be glad, for your reward is great in heaven, for so men persecuted the prophets who were before you" (Matt. 5:12, RSV). "Not only should we patiently endure all the horrible treacheries of the persecutors that can be contrived in a time of persecution for Christ's name against the just, or the various reproaches that can be heaped upon us, or the punishments that can be applied to the body. Rather we are freed even to welcome them with exultation's joy because of the coming glory. For he says, 'Rejoice in that day and

50. FC 36:330-31; ACCS OT 3:27*.
51. PG 56:759; ACCS NT 1a:201*.

exult; I tell you this, because your reward is great in heaven.' How glorious is the endurance of this persecution, the reward for which the Lord says is in heaven! And so, taking into account the reward of the proposed glory, we should be ready with devout faith for every endurance of suffering, so that we may be made ready to be partners in the prophets' glory" (Chromatius, Tractate on Matthew 17.9.2-3; Matt. 5:12).[52] Those who respond rightly to persecution share in the prophets' glory.

Each blessing of those suffering persecution is seen in the light of the coming kingdom. "Look then at the reward again: 'For your reward is great in heaven,'" wrote John Chrysostom. "Do not suppose that the reward of the kingdom of heaven belongs only to the poor in spirit. It also belongs to those who hunger for justice, and to the meek, and to all these blessed others without exception. For he set his blessing upon all these excellent behaviors to keep you from expecting something belonging only to this material world. For if one wore a prize or garland for things that are to be dissolved together with the present life, things that flit away faster than a shadow, would he be blessed?" (Chrysostom, The Gospel of Matthew, Homily 15; Matt. 5:12).[53] God is weaning the faithful away from unworthy goals.

When persecuted for righteousness' sake, keep in focus only the end-time judgment and heavenly promise, advised Origen, who himself faced exile, imprisonment, and torture: "I beg you to remember in your entire present contest the great reward laid up in heaven for those who are persecuted and reviled for righteousness' sake. Be glad and leap for joy on account of the Son of man [cf. Matt. 5:10-12], just as the apostles once rejoiced when they were counted worthy to suffer dishonor for his name [Acts 5:41]" (Origen, Exhortation to Martyrdom 4; Luke 6:20-26).[54]

The calamities of our times are viewed by the faithful in relation to God's own timing, not according to short-term calculations. Bede argued: "Peter says that we must still suffer for a little while, because it is only through the sadness of the present age and its afflictions that it is possible to reach the joys of eternity. He stresses the fact that this is only 'for a little while,' because once we have entered our eternal reward, the years we spent suffering here below will seem like no time at all" (Bede the Venerable, On

---

52. CCL 9a:277; ACCS NT 1a:90*.
53. PG 57:228, NPNF 1 10:95; ACCS NT 1a:90*.
54. CWSO 43*; ACCS NT 3:106.

1 Peter; 1 Pet. 1:6).[55] The "little while" is historical time, the whole of which is seen now in relation to eternity.

### 9. Do Not Seek Persecution

Jesus did not commend foolhardiness or daredevil risk-taking. "When they persecute you in one town, flee to the next" (Matt. 10:23a, RSV). Cyril of Alexandria took this realistic view: "In saying this he is not telling his disciples to be cowardly. He is telling them not to cast themselves into dangers and die at once, for that would be a loss to those who otherwise will benefit from their teaching" (Cyril of Alexandria, Fragments on Matthew, Fragment 120, quoted in Reuss; Matt. 10:23).[56]

There is no reason for those who are facing persecution to seek it or tempt others to do so. Jacob was the patriarchal prototype of this: "Just as Jacob overcomes evil men by fleeing and not resisting, so also do his children. For just as Jacob's mother then approached him and said, 'Son, listen to me and flee to Mesopotamia until the anger of your brother subsides' [Gen. 27:43-44], so also does the church teach its children daily. Whenever they suffer persecution, it advises: 'If you have been persecuted in one city, flee to another' [Matt. 10:23] and never avenge yourselves [Rom. 12:19]" (Opus Imperfectum in Matthaeum, Homily 1; Matt. 1:2).[57] Flight does not necessarily imply a lack of courage.

Do not be inordinately ready to be persecuted, but when necessary respond to persecution with an equanimity grounded in hope. When reproached, the faithful view that reproach in the light of the end time, and therefore receive it joyfully.

Bede commented on 1 Peter 3:9: "Peter forbids us to return evil for evil and even commands us to bless those who harm us, but he also reminds us by quoting Psalm 34:12-16 that God keeps an eye on both the good and the bad and will reward us in eternity for the kindness that we show when we choose to do good to those who persecute us. Furthermore, he will also punish our persecutors if they do not repent, but if they do turn their lives around, we will also receive a crown of thanksgiving, be-

---

55. PL 93:43: ACCS NT 11:71.
56. MKGK 192; ACCS NT 1a:203*.
57. PG 56:614; ACCS NT 1a:5-6.

cause we have prayed to the Lord for their salvation" (Bede the Venerable, On 1 Peter; 1 Pet. 3:9).[58] This is why it is less important that we escape our persecutors than that we pray for their salvation.

What are we to do today for persecuted Christians? Advocate for them. Pray for them. Give them relief. Acknowledge the connectedness we have with them in Jesus Christ. Moreover, we are called to give them that which they often ask for even more avidly: access to the written word of God. Even today those who witness to the living Lord are, like the prophets, "stoned, sawn asunder, tempted, and slain with the sword" (Heb. 11:37a, KJV*). Priscilla and Aquila risked their lives for Paul, he writes in Romans 16:4, as did Epaphroditus (Phil. 2:30). Paul, Peter, and Barnabas repeatedly risked their lives for their witness (Acts 15:26). We, like they, are called to embody that witness.

## D. Blessing Persecutors

The excellent moral behaviors that persecution may engender were of special interest to the ancient Christian teachers. Among these virtues are intercession, tolerance, patience, endurance, and hope.

### 1. The Persecuted Pray That through Their Persecution Grace Will Transform the Persecutors

The persecuted are called upon to pray for their persecutors, to bless precisely those who do them harm. Cassiodorus observed that the persecutors themselves may be transformed into believers by the steady witness, confession, and courage of the confessors and martyrs: "Sinners undergo a contrary experience. Even when the persecutor most fatally stiffens his neck against the Lord, he may discover that the believer views the yoke as sweet, attesting the humility that brings salvation. We recall that this often befell persecutors, so that having earlier maintained their idols by the most sacrilegious compulsions, they themselves became proclaimers of our most holy religion" (Cassiodorus, Exposition of the Psalms 128.4; Exod. 32:9).[59] The

---

58. PL 93:56; ACCS NT 11:102*.
59. ACWCa 3:309; ACCS OT 3:141*.

writings of Paul, Justin Martyr, Cyprian, and other early saints give evidence that many hardened persecutors were touched by the Holy Spirit precisely during their own acts of persecution, and brought to faith.

This same converting power of persecution was assessed by Bede the Venerable: "It often happens that pagans who once reviled the faith of Christians, because they had abandoned their gods, stop doing so after they see what a holy and pure life these believers lead in Christ. They begin instead to glorify and praise God, who is shown by acts of goodness and righteousness to be good and righteous himself" (Bede the Venerable, On 1 Peter; 1 Pet. 2:12a).[60]

Jesus himself warned that "Brother will deliver up brother to death, and the father his child, and children will rise against parents" (Matt. 10:21, RSV). Hilary commented: "We will be offered up to earthly judges and kings, who attempt to secure either our silence or our collusion. Amid this, we are to bear testimony of the truth to these men and to the Gentiles. After that testimony has been borne, our persecutors will be deprived of the excuse that they are ignorant of religion. When Christ has been prophesied by the words of the martyrs amid the tortures of savage persecutors, the way will be open for the Gentiles to believe in him, though they remain stubborn" (Hilary of Poitiers, On Matthew 10; Matt. 10:21).[61] God the Spirit works with great power among those willing to suffer for the truth.

What can protect the faithful from being misunderstood by enemies as demonic? Can they ever guarantee their reputation in the eyes of the fallen world? John Chrysostom, who himself died in exile from being tortured and abused, pressed the same point further: "Some may object, saying, 'How, then, will others come to faith, when they see on our account children being slain by their fathers, and brothers killing brothers, and all things filled with abominations?' How could this sort of warfare work out? Will not we be treated as though we ourselves were destructive demons? Will we be seen as though we ourselves were a plague, and pests to be driven out from every corner? Won't they see that the earth is filled with the blood of kinsmen fighting kinsmen? Even so our sole purpose is to bring peace into their houses, even amid so much conflict. And this peace is beautiful" (Chrysostom, The Gospel of Matthew, Homily 33.4; Matt.

---

60. PL 93:52; ACCS NT 11:91*.
61. SCH 1:230; ACCS NT 11:201*.

10:18).[62] The angry world thirsts for that tiny oasis of peace quietly brought into being by faith active in love.

## 2. Bless Your Persecutors

The most difficult good work amid persecution is learning to bless the persecutor. Paul called upon the persecuted to bless their persecutors (Rom. 12:14). Origen explained: "Paul does not want those who believe in Christ to curse their persecutors, but rather to speak and to pray for good things for them, so that they may come to be servants of a good Lord and disciples of a good Master. . . . We may be provoked by our enemies or afflicted by harm. Paul warns us not to repay curses with curses but to do what he says he himself did, as he wrote: 'When reviled, we bless' [1 Cor. 4:12]" (Origen, Commentary on the Epistle to the Romans; Rom. 12:14).[63] Provocation becomes opportunity to witness.

"Your enemy will let you get a reward for persecution, but you will earn a further blessing by praying for him. By doing so you will be demonstrating an exceedingly great sign of love for Christ. Just as the man who curses his persecutor shows that he is not pleased to be suffering this for Christ's sake, he who blesses his persecutor shows the greatness of his love [cf. 1 Thess. 5:15]" (Chrysostom, Homilies on Romans 22; Rom. 12:14).[64] To curse is to confirm non-acceptance of the way of faith.

When maltreated, we are called to forgive not just seven times, but seventy times seven (Matt. 18:22). Patience, endurance, and steadfastness are commended at all times, but especially amid persecution (Rom. 12:12; 1 Thess. 2:14-16). Persevere amid afflictions: "And let us not grow weary in well-doing, for in due season we shall reap, if we do not lose heart" (Gal. 6:9, RSV).

## 3. The Power of Deeds

Let your deeds speak for you when reviled, not your words, Bede advised: "Act in such a way that those who revile you because they cannot see your

---

62. PG 57:391; NPNF 1 10:221*; ACCS NT 1a:200*.
63. CER 5:74, 76; ACCS NT 6:317*.
64. NPNF 1 11:506; ACCS NT 6:317*.

faith and your hope for a heavenly reward may see your good works and be put to shame by them, because they cannot deny that what you are doing is good" (Bede the Venerable, On 1 Peter; 1 Pet. 3:16).[65] Truth shines through all deceptions.

These deeds take away the excuses of the persecutors, as Gennadius of Constantinople observed: "Paul wants them to exhibit such brotherly love that those who want to persecute them will have no excuse for doing so [cf. Prov. 25:21-22]" (Gennadius of Constantinople, quoted in Staab, Pauline Commentary from the Greek Church; Rom. 12:14).[66]

Let conscience guide your behavior amid frustrations. "Your conscience is the part of your consciousness which embraces what is good and which rejects evil. It is like the doorkeeper of a house which is open to friends and closed to enemies" (Hilary of Arles, Introductory Commentary on 1 Peter; 1 Pet. 3:16).[67] Conscience seeks to protect from temptation.

## 4. Sheep among Wolves

Jesus was intentional in preparing his followers for persecution, according to Cyril of Alexandria: "He would have them prepared for all that can cause people grief. He wants them ready to endure patiently so that approved they may enter the kingdom of God. He warns them that before his coming from heaven at the consummation of the world, tribulation and persecution will precede him" (Cyril of Alexandria, Commentary on Luke, Homily 117; Luke 17:22-25).[68]

In this way, Jesus taught believers "a new sort of warfare: He sends them out exposed, with only one coat, barefooted, and without a staff, without clothing or provisions. The manner of their battle array is entirely unimpressive. He calls them to allow themselves to be totally supported by the generosity of such as receive them. All this is to accentuate God's unspeakable power. Then, to press this reverse strategy to its limits, he tells them to exhibit the gentleness of sheep, even though they are going out among wolves, and not simply toward the wolves, but trustfully moving

65. PL 93:57; ACCS NT 11:105.
66. NTA 15:405; ACCS NT 6:317.
67. PL *Suppl.* 3:96-97; ACCS NT 11:105*.
68. CGSL 468**; ACCS NT 3:271.

right into the midst of the wolves" (Chrysostom, The Gospel of Matthew, Homily 33.1; Matt. 10:19).[69]

The faithful will be treated "as lambs in the midst of wolves" (Luke 10:3b, RSV). Jesus sent out "the seventy disciples whom he appointed and sent out in pairs. . . . He sends lambs among wolves in order that the saying may be fulfilled, 'Then wolves and lambs shall feed together' [Isa. 65:25]" (Ambrose, Exposition of the Gospel of Luke 7.44, 46; Luke 10:3).[70]

How could God be so callous as to set up the faithful for destruction? Cyril of Alexandria asked: "Why then does the Lord command the holy apostles, who are innocent men and 'sheep,' to seek the company of wolves, and go to them of their own will? Is not the danger apparent? Are they not set up as ready prey for their attacks? How can a sheep prevail over a wolf? How can one so peaceful conquer the savageness of beasts of prey? 'Yes,' he says, 'for they all have me as their Shepherd: small and great, people and princes, teachers and students. I will be with you, help you, and deliver you from all evil. I will tame the savage beasts. I will change wolves into sheep, and I will make the persecutors become the helpers of the persecuted. I will make those who wrong my ministers to be sharers in their devout designs. I make and unmake all things, and nothing can resist my will'" (Cyril of Alexandria, Commentary on Luke, Homily 61; Luke 10:3).[71] The Shepherd promises the sheep protection, viewed not through the lens of time alone, but through eternity.

## 5. The Evil Depths of Human Freedom

Jesus called the faithful to "beware of men" (Matt. 10:17a, KJV). For the worst evils come out of the human heart. Human beings can cause much more devastation than any other creatures. The fifth-century Latin commentary, Opus Imperfectum, says:

> He therefore told them to be wary of men as though of the most dangerous of evils. Now if he had not said this it might have been sufficient for him to say: "Beware, for they will betray you." But now he

69. PG 57:389; NPNF 1 10:219-20; ACCS NT 1a:200*.
70. EHG 252*; ACCS NT 3:171.
71. CGSL 263-64**; ACCS NT 3:171-72*.

adds: "Beware of men," for he intends to show that of all evils that is worst which comes out of the human heart. In fact, if you compare human beings to the wild animals, you will find that the human heart is much the more dangerous. For though an animal may show cruelty, its cruelty falls short of man's cruelty. For an animal lacks proportionality. But when a man, who is rational, attacks, it is no small task to escape his cruelty. . . . The moment a snake is threatened, it becomes deadly; but if it is not threatened, it slithers away. Man, on the other hand, even when not threatened, may fly into a rage. He may rage even more against those who have not even threatened him. In short, every wild animal has a peculiar evil of its own, whereas man has every evil potentially embedded within himself. (Opus Imperfectum in Matthaeum, Homily 24; Matt. 10:21)[72]

Amid persecution, the faithful learn to become most realistic about the awful depths of human fallenness.

When the ocean of troubled waters is stirred up, those who are rootless are liable to being washed away. This Athanasius well understood from his own exilic experience:

Let us, therefore, following the faith of the apostles, hold frequent communion with our Lord. For the world is like the sea to us, beloved, of which it is written, "There go the ships, and Leviathan that You formed to sport in it" [Ps. 104:26]. We float upon this sea, like wind, with everyone directing his own course with his own free will. Under the pilotage of the Word, however, one may safely approach the port. But, if possessed by wayward inclinations, one is in peril by storm and may suffer shipwreck. For as in the ocean there are storms and waves, so in the world there are many afflictions and trials. The unbelieving "have no root in themselves, but endure for a while. Then, when tribulation or persecution arises on account of the word, immediately they fall away" [Mark 4:17]. So the Lord said that they are not likely to endure the complications which arise from afflictions if they are fixed upon the temporal and not confirmed in the faith. (Athanasius, Letter 19.7, Easter, 347; Mark 4:17)[73]

72. PG 56:758; ACCS NT 1a:201-2*.
73. NPNF 2 4:547**; ACCS NT 2:56*.

## E. Absorbing Hatred

The persecuted are hated. How do the faithful handle the temptations to resentment and despair?

### 1. Absorbing Hatred

God "wants to take away from us the habits of anger which are common to fallen humanity, so that instead of cursing others in anger, which we once did so easily, we might rather overcome our anger and bless them [see Matt. 5:43-45; Luke 6:35]" (Ambrosiaster, Commentary on Paul's Epistles; Rom. 12:14).[74]

The faithful are forewarned to expect the worst when evil is on its ascendancy. The New Testament was shockingly clear: "You will be hated by all for my name's sake" (Matt. 10:22a, RSV). On this Chrysostom soberly reflected: "The courts of justice will go against you. Kings will assail you, and so will governors. So will the synagogues of the Jews. So will the magistrates of the Gentiles. Both rulers and those who are ruled will fight you. Jesus was preparing his disciples not only for what was to befall them in Palestine, but throughout the world. For they were soon to be sent to the Gentiles with this same proclamation. In doing so they would find that the whole world would oppose them. In this spiritual warfare all that dwell upon the earth, all peoples, tyrants, and kings, will be arrayed against them" (Chrysostom, The Gospel of Matthew, Homily 33.4; Matt. 10:22).[75] Those who most love must be prepared to be most hated.

Every insult offers an opportunity to the faithful to draw closer to God, according to Gregory of Nyssa. The surest discipline comes when we are "hated because of Christ, being driven, and enduring every insult and shame in behalf of his faith in God. For such a person, whose entire life centers on the resurrection and future blessings, all insults and scourging and persecution and the other sufferings leading up to the cross are all pleasure and refreshment and surety of heavenly treasures. For Jesus says, 'Blessed are you when men reproach you and persecute you and, speaking falsely, say all manner of evil against you; for my sake rejoice and exult be-

74. CSEL 81:407; ACCS NT 6:317*.
75. PG 57:391; NPNF 1 10:221*; ACCS NT 1a:202*.

cause your reward is great in heaven' [Matt. 5:11-12; Luke 6:22-23]" (Gregory of Nyssa, On the Christian Mode of Life; Luke 6:20-26).[76]

We are to expect deception from those who are set upon resisting the coming kingdom.

> They shall scold you, Jesus says, as deceivers do, and try to mislead you. They shall separate you from others, even from their friendship and society. Let none of these things trouble you, he says. What harm will their intemperate tongue do to a well-established mind? The patient suffering of these things will not be without fruit, he says, especially for those who know how to endure confidently. These obstacles bear the hidden pledge of the highest happiness. To the faithful, nothing strange will happen to them. Even when suffering these things, they will serve for their benefit. On the contrary, they will resemble those before their time who bore to Israel the words that came from God above. These prophets were persecuted. They were sawn in two. They perished by the sword. They endured blame unjustly cast on them. But let all understand that these are the ones who shall be quiet partakers with those whose deeds they anticipated. (Cyril of Alexandria, Commentary on Luke, Homily 27; Luke 6:20-26)[77]

For those who love the Lord, all things are always working together for the good, despite external evidences.

### 2. The Enemy Within

Do not expect a flood of good wishes each time you make a hard decision requiring courage: "'Woe to you when all people speak well of you.' Notice how by the word 'woe' he revealed to us the extent of the punishment awaiting hypocrisy. This word 'woe,' after all, is an exclamation of lament, so that it is as if he is lamenting their fate when he says, 'Woe to you when all people speak well of you.' Notice too the precision in the expression: he didn't simply say 'people' but 'all people.' Be realistic! It is not possible for a virtuous person who travels by the straight and narrow path and follows

76. FC 58:156*; ACCS NT 3:106*.
77. CGSL 130**; ACCS NT 3:105-6*.

Christ's commands to enjoy the praise and admiration of all people, so strong is the impulse of evil and the resistance to virtue" (Chrysostom, Homilies on Genesis 23.8; Luke 6:20-26).[78] Getting compliments? Watch out.

Leo the Great understood that persecution involves not only an external battle, but an internal struggle. "Persecution is to be reckoned not only as that which is done against Christian godliness by the sword or fire or other physical torments. For the ravages of persecution are also inflicted by struggles of character, the perversity of the disobedient, and the barbs of slanderous tongues" (Leo the Great, Letters 167.1; 2 Tim. 3:12).[79] In speaking of persecution, the meaning is not limited to physical, but includes also verbal battering.

Put a bolt on your mouth to prevent wordiness, warned the Opus Imperfectum:

"If the head of the household had known the hour at which the thief would arrive, he would have been vigilant and would never have allowed his house to be burglarized." The head of the household represents the human soul. The thief is the devil. The house is the body. The doors are the mouth and ears, and the windows are the eyes. Like the thief who gains access through the doors and windows to despoil the householder, the devil also finds easy access to the soul of a man through his mouth, ears and eyes to take him captive. This is why Jeremiah wrote, "For death entered through our windows" [Jer. 9:21]. If you wish to be secure, install a bolt on your mouth, the door, which is to say, put the law of the fear of God in your mouth so that you can say with the psalmist, "I will guard my ways that I might not sin with my tongue. I will put a guard at my mouth" [Ps. 39:1 (38:1 LXX)]. (Opus Imperfectum in Matthaeum, Homily 51; Matt. 24:44)[80]

Righteousness lives by faith active in love. Jerome commented on Paul's metaphor of the breastplate of righteousness: "One who has put on a sturdy breastplate is difficult to wound. Especially well protected are those essential parts of the body upon which life depends. So put on the

---

78. FC 82:93-94**; ACCS NT 3:106*.
79. FC 34:290; ACCS NT 9:267*.
80. PG 56:924; ACCS NT 1b:210*.

breastplate. Strap it together by iron rings and insert the hooks in their place. One protected by such a breastplate of righteousness will not be like a vulnerable stag that receives the arrow in his liver" (Jerome, Epistle to the Ephesians 3; Eph. 6:14b).[81]

### 3. Persecution Visited upon Early Christians from All Sides

From the outset persecution has accompanied Christian witness. "We read that when Stephen was martyred a great persecution of the church broke out at Jerusalem and that they were all scattered across the countryside of Judea and Samaria, except for the apostles. James then wrote his letter to those who had been scattered because they had suffered persecution for the sake of righteousness" (Bede the Venerable, Concerning the Epistle of St. James; Jas. 1:1).[82] So it has been ever since.

Paul quoted Psalm 44:23: "For thy sake we are being killed all the day long" (Rom. 8:36a, RSV). Irenaeus commented: "The expression 'all the day long' means all the time in which we suffer persecution and are killed as sheep" (Irenaeus, Against Heresies 2.22.2; Rom. 8:36).[83] "Paul is exhorting his hearers to not be broken by persecution" (Augustine, Augustine on Romans 57; Rom. 8:35).[84]

The history of persecution shows how Jesus' warnings of troubled times would take vast and terrible dimensions. Jesus warned his followers of coming wars, turmoil, famines, and epidemics. "There will be terrors from heaven and great signs," wrote Cyril of Alexandria.

> Before all these things, he says, "They will lay their hands on you and persecute you, delivering you up to synagogues and to prisons and bringing you before kings and rulers for my name's sake. This will be for you a witness to you" [Luke 21:12-19]. Not long thereafter the land of the Jews was taken captive. The Roman armies overran it. They burned the temple, overthrew their national government, and stopped the means for legal temple worship. They no longer had sacrifices, now that

---

81. PL 26:550D-551A; cf. JTS 3:573; ACCS NT 8:210.
82. PL 93:10; ACCS NT 11:2.
83. ANF 1:390; ACCS NT 6:241.
84. AOR 20; ACCS NT 6:241.

the temple was destroyed. The whole country of the Jews together with Jerusalem itself was totally laid waste. Before these things happened, they had severely persecuted the blessed disciples. They imprisoned them and had a part in severe trials. They brought the disciples before judges and sent them to kings. Paul was sent to Rome to Caesar. . . . Christ promises, however, that he will deliver them certainly and completely. He says "not a hair of your head will perish." (Cyril of Alexandria, Commentary on Luke, Homily 139; Luke 21:12-19)[85]

## 4. Stand Firm

Standing firm through affliction tests confidence in God. Bede wrote: "Those who stand firm against the persecutions of unbelievers and the ridicule which comes from worldly people around them will have complete confidence when Christ comes again, because they know that the patience of the poor will not perish at the end. But anyone who is ashamed to stand up for Christ in this life or to do anything else which the Lord commands, or who in time of persecution is afraid to be known as a believer, will have no confidence at all when Christ returns, because he has not stuck to his profession of faith in this life" (Bede the Venerable, On 1 John; 1 John 2:28).[86] Confidence under conditions of persecution is deepened, if faith is secure.

Amid weariness, faith does not succumb, according to Severian of Gabala: "Paul is aware that we may grow weak with weariness, but amid this he says that we should not 'stoop down' or bow to persecutors" (Severian, quoted in Staab, Pauline Commentary from the Greek Church; 1 Thess. 3:3).[87]

The faithful grieve over those who lapse amid persecution: "I suffer with, I grieve with our fellow believers who, having lapsed and fallen by the impetus of persecution, drawing part of our hearts with them, have brought a like sorrow on us with their wounds" (Cyprian, Letters 17; 1 Cor. 12:26).[88]

85. CGSL 555-56*; ACCS NT 3:320-21*.
86. PL 93:97; ACCS NT 11:191.
87. NTA 15:329; ACCS NT 9:75*.
88. FC 51:49; ACCS NT 7:128.

Augustine understood that "Christ's passion profits none but those who follow in his footsteps" (Augustine, Sermons 304.2; 1 Pet. 2:21a).[89] Hilary of Arles summarized: "Those who suffer unjustly will find favor with God, because that is exactly what he did" (Hilary of Arles, Introductory Commentary on 1 Peter; 1 Pet. 2:19).[90]

### 5. To the End

It is written that "he who endures to the end will be saved" (Matt. 10:22b, RSV). "This is said because many begin but few reach the end," the Opus Imperfectum commented. "No one can endure with God '*to the end*' if he has not become a person who belongs wholly to God by means of grace" (Opus Imperfectum in Matthaeum, Homily 24, italics added; Matt. 10:22b).[91]

Regardless of how good a beginning might have seemed, the rehearsal of past moments of faith is no substitute for faith that endures to the end. "What is glorious is not to *begin* something good, but to reach the *end* of it in a good way. This is why the centerpiece of a good life is a good death. Firmness of heart can indeed reach the end. Fleshly desire often starts on some good purpose, but cannot reach the end except by the grace of God. So then, now that you have turned to God and begun to serve God and do the works of righteousness, never think back on your previous deeds. Think only about the end. The contemplation of our previous good service leads to pride, but the contemplation of our end leads to holy reverence" (Opus Imperfectum in Matthaeum, Homily 24, italics added; Matt. 10:22b).[92] The good death crowns the good life. Faith, insofar as it is enabled by persevering grace, remains faithful to the end.

God who gives life to the soul does not abandon the soul in death. Augustine drew this analogy: "Just as the soul itself is the life of the body, so in the same way God is the life of the soul. As the body dies when the soul that is its life abandons it, in the same way when God abandons the soul, it dies. To make sure, however, that God does not abandon the soul, it

---

89. WSA 3 8:316; ACCS NT 11:95.
90. PL *Suppl.* 3:92; ACCS NT 11:94*.
91. PG 56:760; ACCS NT 1a:202*.
92. PG 56:760; ACCS NT 1a:202*.

must always have enough faith not to fear death for God's sake. Then God does not abandon it, and it does not die" (Augustine, Sermon 273.1; Luke 21:12-19).[93] God does not abandon the faithful. Their faith is like a bulwark.

Persecution will be used by God for good. We are not to fear persecution, but hold it in perspective of end-time judgment. On this basis Jerome argued for the mobility and fearlessness of the Christian mission: "This is what the believers did in the first days: when persecution began in Jerusalem, they scattered throughout all Judaea. Their time of trial thus became a seed bed for the good news. . . . No matter how menacing the persecutor may be, he too must come before the judgment seat of the Savior" (Jerome, Commentary on Matthew 1; Matt. 10:23).[94]

### 6. What We Learn from the Mustard Seed

The kingdom of God is like a grain of mustard seed (Mark 4:30-32), the tiniest of seeds when sown, but it grows up and becomes the greatest of herbs. In this way faith grows in grace (2 Pet. 3:18). "A mustard seed looks so small," Augustine observed. "Nothing is less noteworthy to the sight. Nothing is stronger to the taste. What does that signify but the very great fervor and inner strength of faith in the church?" (Augustine, Sermon 246.3; Luke 17:5-6).[95] From the mustard seed we learn how faith can grow from small beginnings to powerful consequences.

Did the disciples ever move mountains? Yes, and much more, Chrysostom argued. "'If you have faith as a grain of mustard seed, you will say to this mountain: Move from here to there — and it will move. Nothing will be impossible to you.' But if you question, saying: 'Where did they ever really move a mountain?' I will say that they did things much greater than that in raising up innumerable dead. For moving a mountain and moving death from a body are not at all comparable. After them other saints far less blessed than the disciples are said to have moved mountains when necessity demanded. It is clear that the disciples also would have done so had necessity demanded. But if there was never need at that time, do not find fault with them" (Chrysostom, The Gospel of Matthew, Homily 57.4; Matt.

---

93. WSA 3 8:17**; ACCS NT 3:321.
94. CCL 77:69; ACCS NT 1a:202-3*.
95. WSA 3 7:104*; ACCS NT 3:267*.

17:20).[96] As challenges and necessities impinge, the possibilities of faith rise, not diminish. Church history furnishes ample demonstrations.

## F. Nothing Can Separate Us

"Who shall separate us from the love of Christ? Shall tribulation, or distress, or persecution, or famine, or nakedness, or peril or sword?" (Rom. 8:35, RSV). "Even though it is easy to make a list like this one," John Chrysostom noted, "each word contains thousands of lines of temptation. Tribulation, for instance, includes prisons and bonds, calumnies and banishments, and all other such hardships. A single word covers oceans of dangers and reveals to us all the evils which people encounter in life" (Chrysostom, Homilies on Romans 15; Rom. 8:35).[97] "No, in all these things we are more than conquerors through him who loved us. For I am sure that neither death, nor life, nor angels, nor principalities, nor things present, nor things to come, nor powers, nor height, nor depth, nor anything else in all creation, will be able to separate us from the love of God in Christ Jesus our Lord" (Rom. 8:37-39, RSV). The ancient church took great comfort in this text.

### 1. Gold Tested by Fire

Shortly before his own martyrdom, Cyprian wrote to the faithful of Carthage about the purpose of their terrible persecution: "None of these can separate believers; nothing can snatch away those clinging to Christ's body and blood. This persecution is for the examination and evaluation of our heart. God wanted us to be tried and proved, as he has always tried his own, and yet, in his trials, never at any time has his help failed believers [2 Cor. 12:9]" (Cyprian, Letters 11.5; Rom. 8:35).[98] Faith is tried because God wishes to make faith strong in a strength that death does not conquer.

Gregory the Great explained Paul's reasoning on suffering for the sake of witness: "I beg you, in all this recall to your mind what I believe you

96. PG 58:562; NPNF 1 10:355; ACCS NT 1b:62*.
97. NPNF 1 11:455-56; ACCS NT 6:241.
98. FC 51:32; ACCS NT 6:241.

must never forget: 'All who would live godly in Christ suffer persecution' [2 Tim. 3:12]. . . . The holy preacher [Paul] declared that his coming to the Thessalonians would have accomplished nothing *if he had not been shamefully treated.* . . . In this way adversity itself may increase significantly your desire for the love of God and your earnestness in good works. Similarly, the seeds planted for a future harvest germinate more fruitfully if they are covered over with frost. Likewise fire is increased by blowing on it that it may grow greater" (Gregory the Great, Letter 30 "To Narses," italics added; 1 Thess. 2:1).[99] The seed loves frost; fire loves wind.

Gold is tested by fire, as the Shepherd of Hermas explained: "Just as gold is tried by fire and becomes useful, so also you who live in the world are tried in it. So then, you who remain in it and pass through the flames will be purified. For just as gold casts off its dross, so also you will cast off all sorrow and tribulation, becoming pure and useful for the building of the tower" (Shepherd of Hermas, Visions 3.1; 1 Pet. 1:7).[100] So do not fear testing. "Because the saints saw that the divine fire would cleanse them and benefit them, they did not shrink back from or get discouraged by the trials which they faced. Rather than being hurt by what they went through, they grew and were made better, shining like gold that has been refined in a fire" (Athanasius, Festal Letters 10; 1 Pet. 1:7).[101]

### 2. The Greatness of God's Power Revealed in Trials

These challenges are permitted by God to enrich faith through the testing of the soul: "If none of these things ever happened, the greatness of God's power would never be revealed" (Theodoret, Commentary on the Second Epistle to the Corinthians 310; 2 Cor. 4:8).[102] John Chrysostom noted that these afflictions could come "not only from enemies, but even from our own households and friends. But these things are permitted by God, not for our defeat but for our discipline" (Chrysostom, Homilies on the Epistles of Paul to the Corinthians II.9.1; 2 Cor. 4:8).[103]

Wherever the faithful have stood as witnesses, they have always

99. NPNF 2 12:223*; ACCS NT 9:63.
100. FC 1:259; ACCS NT 11:71.
101. ARL 168; ACCS NT 11:71.
102. PG 82:402; ACCS NT 7:232.
103. NPNF 1 12:321; ACCS NT 7:232.

found that they are "persecuted but not forsaken" (2 Cor. 4:9a, KJV). "God was with them, like a shepherd, when they were in need. He looked after their interests, so that their enemies would not get the better of them" (Ambrosiaster, On Paul's Epistles to the Corinthians; 2 Cor. 4:9).[104]

Those who suffer for the truth are given special grace to face the challenge of persecution. Origen, who suffered torture and exile, wrote these poignant lines, not as a statement of human courage, but of God's grace: "As long as we rely on God's love, we suffer no feeling of pain. For his love, by which he loved us and drew us to him, makes us not feel the pain and crucifixion of the body. In all these things we are more than conquerors. The bride in the Song of Songs says something similar: 'I am wounded with love' [Song of Sol. 2:5]. In the same way our soul, once it has received Christ's wound of love, will not feel the wounds of the flesh, even if it gives the body over to the sword" (Origen, Commentary on the Epistle to the Romans; Rom. 8:37).[105]

### 3. All Historic Contingencies Are Viewed in End-Time Perspective

Neither death nor life can separate us from God's love: "'Death' here refers primarily to the death which separates the soul from the love of God, rather than what we usually think of as death, which merely separates the soul from the body. 'Life' here presumably refers to the life of sin which is constantly pressing to separate us from the love of God. 'Angels and principalities' refer to the devil and his hosts, against whom we have to struggle. 'Things present' are the desires of this world, and 'things to come' are the trials and temptations which may yet afflict us in this life" (Origen, Commentary on the Epistle to the Romans; Rom. 8:38).[106]

Paul prayed that "whether by life or by death" Christ would be "honored in my body" (Phil. 1:20b, RSV). John Chrysostom paraphrased Paul's intention: "'Whether I live or die,' Paul says, 'Christ will be magnified. How? Either through life, because he delivered me, or through death, because even death itself could not persuade me to deny him, since he has

---

104. CSEL 81:224; ACCS NT 7:233.
105. CER 4:116; ACCS NT 6:241-42.
106. CER 4:118; ACCS NT 6:242*.

given me such readiness that he has made me stronger than death. . . . So even death will bring me not shame but great gain. Why? Because I am not an immortal [angel] but I shall shine all the more brightly than if I were so. It is one thing for an immortal creature to despise death, another thing for one who is mortal. Thus it would be no shame to me if I died right now'" (Chrysostom, Homily on Philippians 4; Phil. 1:20a).[107] Chrysostom himself would face a severe crisis during his last days of exile, torture, sickness, and humiliation, yet his last writings reveal a securely faithful man.

Marius Victorinus proposed this paraphrase of Philippians 1:20: "'Christ is being magnified in my body, now as always, even my body, subjected to all punishments, bears them all and preaches Christ unceasingly, not terrified by punishments and not giving way under all the tribulations.' He explains the alternatives before him by adding, so to speak: 'Whether by life or by death: If I overcome my trials by endurance, Christ will be proclaimed. Or if I die under my punishments, he will be proclaimed all the more. All will recognize that I was not terrified by punishments or by death. In the Gospel I will either live out my life beyond these punishments or bear these punishments right up to death. In any case I will have persevered in the preaching of the Gospel" (Marius Victorinus, Epistle to the Philippians; Phil. 1:20b).[108]

Marius continued: "It is not death itself that is gain, but to die in Christ. Life is Christ. The one who has hope in him is always alive, both now and forever. . . . Therefore they achieve nothing, whether they hand me over to death or to tortures in life. Neither alternative harms me. Life under torments is no punishment for me, since Christ is my life. And if they kill me, that too is no punishment for me, since Christ for me is life and to die is gain" (Marius Victorinus, Epistle to the Philippians; Phil. 1:21).[109]

"What others had contrived for Paul's death proved to be life for him. This is life: if Christ is preached. He is fully prepared to meet death so that this can be accomplished. He knows that a great blessing will be given to him for his prayer and constancy. Human malice will continue to work against him in ignorance. To trample down the malevolence of those who were laying snares against his life under a covering of deceit, he bears pa-

---

107. IOEP 5:31; ACCS NT 8:227*.
108. BTMV 75 [1200A-B]; ACCS NT 8:227*.
109. BTMV 75-76 [1200B-D]; ACCS NT 8:227.

tient witness. He is fortified by the protection of God" (Ambrosiaster, On Paul's Epistle to the Philippians 1.21.1-2; Phil. 1:21).[110]

### 4. All Believers Share in the Suffering of Each

Any member of the body of Christ feels the suffering of each member of the body. If a fingernail is tender, the rest of the body is tender sympathetically. "When one member suffers, all the members suffer" (Basil, Letters 242 "To the Westerners"; 1 Cor. 12:26).[111]

The faithful do not turn their backs on those who suffer, as Augustine wrote: "Far be it from us to refuse to hear what is bitter and sad to those whom we love. It is not possible for one member to suffer without the other members suffering with it" (Augustine, Letters 99; 1 Cor. 12:26).[112]

### 5. A Word to All Who Desire a Godly Life

The apostle wrote to Timothy: "Indeed all who desire to live a godly life . . . will be persecuted" (2 Tim. 3:12, RSV). "Anyone who pursues the course of virtue should not expect to avoid grief, tribulation and temptations" (Chrysostom, Homilies on 2 Timothy 8; 2 Tim. 3:12).[113] So be prepared for inevitable trials, Augustine warned: "Some are afraid to offend. So they do not prepare them for the trials looming ahead. Rather they even promise them a pleasant world which God has not promised. What sort of teachers are these? . . . Rather, it is precisely because one is a Christian that he will suffer more in the world" (Augustine, Sermons 46.11; 2 Tim. 3:12).[114]

Theodoret of Cyr was not being perverse in realistically acknowledging what was so clearly understood by Paul: "In the present life he has promised us nothing pleasant or delightful, but rather trouble, toil, and peril and attacks of enemies" (Theodoret, Letters 109; 2 Tim. 3:12).[115]

110. CSEL 81.3:134-35; ACCS NT 8:227-28*.
111. FC 28:182*; ACCS NT 7:128.
112. FC 18:140; ACCS NT 7:128.
113. NPNF 1 13:506; ACCS NT 9:265.
114. WSA 3 2:269*; ACCS NT 9:266*.
115. NPNF 2 3:289*; ACCS NT 9:265.

"Persecution, therefore, will never be lacking," observed Augustine; "For, when our *enemies from without* leave off raging and there ensues a span of tranquility — even of genuine tranquility and great consolation at least to the weak — we are not without *enemies within.* . . . So it is that those who want to live godly lives in Christ must suffer the spiritual persecution of these and other aberrations in thought and morals, even when they are free from physical violence and vexation" (Augustine, The City of God 18.51.2, italics added; 2 Tim. 3:12).[116]

But "If the road is narrow and difficult," wondered Chrysostom, "how can it be said that 'My yoke is easy and my burden is light' [Matt. 11:30]? It is difficult because of the nature of the trials, but easy because of the willingness of the travelers. It is possible for even what is unendurable by nature to become light when we accept it with eagerness. Remember that the apostles who had been scourged returned rejoicing that they had been found worthy to be dishonored for the name of the Lord [cf. Acts 5:41]" (Chrysostom, On Lazarus and the Rich Man 3; 2 Tim. 3:12).[117] Whether the burden is light or easy depends upon who is bearing it, whether by the grit of our tenacity or by the uplifting power of God's grace.

### 6. Join the Battle

Athanasius called the worshiping community to join faith with godliness under conditions of persecution: "Just as brothers become strongly knit together when one helps another, so faith and godliness, coming from the same family, cohere together. A person who gives his attention to one of the two is strengthened by the other" (Athanasius, Festal Letters 9; 1 Tim. 6:12a).[118]

Caesarius of Arles urged constant vigilance in dealing with the Adversary. The faithful are "under attack from the enemy. For this reason, with Christ's help, everyone who travels the journey of this life should be armed unceasingly and always stand in camp. So if you want to be constantly vigilant so that you may know you serve in the Lord's camp, observe what the

---

116. FC 24:172-73; ACCS NT 9:265-66*.
117. COWP 67-68; ACCS NT 9:265*.
118. ARL 156; ACCS NT 9:217.

same apostle says, 'No one serving as God's soldier entangles himself in worldly affairs, that he may please him whose approval he has secured' [2 Tim. 2:4]" (Caesarius of Arles, Sermons 103.1; 2 Tim. 3:12).[119]

In a later sermon, Caesarius wrote: "Do not seek on the journey what is being kept for you in your fatherland. Because it is necessary for you to fight against the devil every day under the leadership of Christ, do not seek in the midst of battle the reward which is being saved for you in the kingdom. . . . Rather pay attention to what the apostle says . . . 'We must undergo many trials if we are to enter the reign of God' [Acts 14:22]" (Caesarius of Arles, Sermons 215.3; 2 Tim. 3:12).[120]

Be willing to fight for the persecuted in the way most consistent with faith, hope, and love. "If you see the faithful suffering anywhere, do not put harmony above truth. Make a noble stand, even to the point of death. And even then, do not be at war in your soul or of an adverse temper, but concentrate on the things themselves" (Chrysostom, Homilies on Romans 22; Rom. 12:17).[121] But do not attempt to repay evil (Rom. 12:17). Of this Tertullian remarked tersely: "This precept is absolute" (Tertullian, On Patience 10; Rom. 12:17).[122]

### 7. Let Your Forbearance Be Known

Paul instructed the church to "let everyone know your forbearance" (Phil. 4:5a, RSV*) in order that God's own forbearance will be made known. But what is meant by forbearance? Marius Victorinus wrote: "Forbearance is individual patience that observes due measure without straining beyond its station. When we live among strangers and live in a way commensurate with our lowliness, God will lift us up. So it is here that we do well to recognize our lowliness. 'Therefore let your forbearance be known to all.' Why does he tell us this? So that we may make a pleasing show here? No. Rather that when Christ comes he may raise up our lowliness and exalt our moderation" (Marius Victorinus, Epistle to the Philippians 4; Phil. 4:5a).[123]

119. FC 47:108-9; ACCS NT 9:266.
120. FC 66:115; ACCS NT 9:266.
121. NPNF 1 11:508; ACCS NT 9:319*.
122. ANF 3:713; ACCS NT 9:319.
123. BTMV 113 [1228D-29A]; ACCS NT 8:281*.

Do not prevent others from being edified by your patience: "Paul wants all to profit by good examples. When their forbearance becomes apparent as their regular way of life, their works will shine forth. Then there will be nothing absent. Others will imitate their virtue. They will be blessed not only from doing good deeds but also by inspiring good deeds in others" (Ambrosiaster, On Paul's Epistle to the Philippians 4.7.1; Phil. 4:5a).[124] The blessing of forbearance comes not only from the good that it is in itself, but from the good it elicits in others.

## 8. Summing Up the Forbearing Motif

The ancient church was engaged in intentional ongoing ministries to the imprisoned and persecuted. There were many in prison precisely because of their faith. To visit the imprisoned is not merely to come to see, but to attend and care for. Being completely helpless and isolated, the imprisoned and persecuted are especially in need of care and comfort and above all hope.

In Part Four we have examined good works in relation to those who face coercive acts, especially imprisonment and political persecution. Dignity amid coercion is a persistent theme of Christian good works. Our fundamental dignity as human beings made in God's image is not diminished by external conditions of imprisonment or persecution.

The central pattern in the Christian life for these liberating and comforting works of love is God's own work of outreaching love on our behalf, all the way to the cross. As Jesus brought freedom to those bound up, so are we called to do in whatever ways contextually feasible.

The task of redeeming the prisoner is best seen in the light of human creation, the fall, redemption, and final human destiny. Failure to understand this salvation-history context results in a failure to understand the central motivation of faith's concern for good works.

We have been asking how the ancient church understood their daily ministries to the persecuted and imprisoned. The answer we have found not only in their letters, poetry, hymnody, and homilies, but also in their explicit exegesis of scripture texts on persecution, trial, suffering, and forbearance.

124. CSEL 81.3:159; ACCS NT 8:281*.

It is within the range of every believer to practice these simple good works: showing mercy toward the prisoner, the maltreated, the ignored, the alienated. It does not require special education or abilities. It only needs a will to do good, which no one can acquire without grace.

## PART FIVE

# THE LEAST OF THESE

Classic Christian teaching pays special attention to "the littlest." "Nothing is littler than the 'littlest,'" wrote Hilary. "Nonetheless he commands us to fulfill our commission to the littlest" (Hilary of Poitiers, On Matthew 10.29; Matt. 10:42).[1] Why give greatest consideration to what is so small?

We have shown how good works reach out for the marginalized, the disabled, the addicted, the imprisoned, and the persecuted (in Part Four). The key verbs of good works have been found in the parable of the last judgment:

    feed
    assuage
    clothe
    welcome
    visit

All of these needy neighbors — the hungry, thirsty, naked, stranger, and imprisoned — are already designated as among *the least of these* through whose need the risen Christ becomes present to us.

We have now come full circle to those closest to us — our *children*. Being completely dependent and defenseless, children are those most directly in need of our constant care. We are asking, guided by the ancient Christian writers, why the lowliness of the child is so central to our highest calling.

1. SCH 1:251; ACCS NT 1a:214*.

What are the relational qualities that characterize highest treatment of the littlest? In caring for the least of these, we are called to embody integrity, and guilelessness, put away bitterness, disarm anger, and learn empathy.

The pattern in the Christian life for caring compassionately for those least able to defend themselves is pictured in the way in which Jesus himself reached out for the lowly, the little ones. This is seen from the outset in the way in which he himself as incarnate Lord voluntarily became a little child, obedient to his parents and to law, subject to suffering, hungering, sweating, thirsting, facing human limitations, even unto death. The incarnate Lord himself came into the world *as* "the least of these," as a defenseless infant, born in poverty, hunted, persecuted, displaced, homeless.

## A. The Child

Nowhere is the quality of our good works more decisive than in relation to children. The greatest privilege and task is raising our children wisely. In this way the greatest of all good works comes down to the least of these.

### 1. Thinking Small about Good Works

The greatest attention in Christianity is given to the smallest. The smaller they are, the higher they seem to rank in God's claim upon our responsibilities.

The child is a leading concern of faith's good works. We do not enter the kingdom of God until we become like little children (Matt. 18:3). This is typical of the way that usual priorities are reversed in the light of God's coming reign.

Why all this attention to "the least of these"? They are those who are most vulnerable, least able to care for themselves — the unborn, the child, the widowed mother, the fatherless, and especially children who are defenseless and destitute. It is these who most urgently need relief. They need, demand, and morally deserve more attention than the healthy, wealthy, and wise. Good works are especially focused on their well-being. We are asking about how these littlest of God's people fit into God's mighty plan for us, and how God's greatest gifts come to us through them.

The little ones are in the fullest sense persons, even if small. For the human person, created in God's image, is "worth more than many sparrows" (Matt. 10:31b, NIV), "more than the birds" (Luke 12:24b, TEV/GN*), "more than sheep" (Matt. 12:12a, TEV/GN*). They are on our heels every day. Even when they are grown they still are there. They never quit being our children.

## 2. Who Is the Greatest?

Jesus taught, "He who is least among you all is the one who is great" (Luke 9:48b, RSV). This is why children are the greatest, as Origen wrote, "like an angel worthy of looking upon the face of God" (Origen, Commentary on Matthew 13.29; Matt. 18:10).[2]

The icons of early Christianity frequently portray infants and children. They frequently accompany angels. They are portrayed as angels. They reveal the promise of God. They have not fallen so deeply into sin. They are beautiful.

The icons show Jesus receiving and blessing little children. When you are dealing with a child, he said, you are dealing with me. To receive a child is to receive me. John Chrysostom sharpened this point: "'Whoever receives one such child, receives me,' but 'whoever causes one of these to sin' will suffer the worst fate. And he was not even satisfied with the example of the millstone, but he also added his curse and told us to cut off such people, even as though they are like a hand or an eye to us. These little ones are guided by the angels, and that shows how highly we are to value them — just as God has valued them" (Chrysostom, The Gospel of Matthew, Homily 59.4; Matt. 18:13).[3] In meeting the child, you are meeting the incognito Christ.

The Fathers were not naïve. They understood that every child is an inheritor of the weighty history of sin. They knew that in due time each one would inevitably contribute his own willing acts to it. They understood original sin, but rejoiced at the proportional innocence of children who have not distorted free will as irretrievably as adults.

Children play no small part in God's saving purpose. They are the future. When we view the nations of the world from the vantage point of

2. GCSO 11:259; ANF 9:492; ACCS NT 1b:74*.
3. PG 58:579; NPNF 1 10:368; ACCS NT 1b:75*.

Zion in Jerusalem, the "least of these" are the Gentiles. It is upon them that God is pouring out his truth and love, in the Christian dispensation. Jesus' welcoming of children prefigures the future promise of the Gentiles living by simple faith. "The children here prefigure the Gentiles, to whom salvation is given through faith and the simplest word" (Hilary of Poitiers, On Matthew 19.3; Matt. 19:13).[4]

### 3. What Children Know That Adults Have Tended to Forget

Epiphanius the Latin pondered what it meant to "become like a child." They come giving blessings. Why? "A child does not know how to hold resentment or to smolder in hatred. He does not know how to repay evil for evil. He does not think base thoughts. He does not commit adultery or arson or murder. He is utterly ignorant of theft or brawling or all the things that will draw him to sin. He does not know how to disparage, how to blaspheme, how to hurt, how to lie. . . . Therefore what children are in their simplicity, let us become through a holy way of life, as children innocent of sin. And quite rightly, one who has become a child innocent of sin in this way is great in the kingdom of heaven. And whoever receives such a person will be receiving Christ himself" (Epiphanius the Latin, Interpretation of the Gospels 27; Matt. 18:5).[5] For an adult to become more like a child is to reenter a sphere of a more innocent, less adulterated life.

The child teaches the adult *simplicity*. It is only when "we ourselves assume this habit and will in all our affections, that we are shown the passageway to the heavens. We must therefore return to the simplicity of children, because with it we shall embrace the beauty of the Lord's humility" (Hilary of Poitiers, On Matthew 18.1; Matt. 18:4).[6] Each parent has the opportunity to learn this every day. It is especially evident in the very small child.

The reader may be saying, "Where do such children exist? I've never seen any like that." The Fathers say: Where do they not exist? This is how children are. Maybe not in pure form, but somewhere at the hidden center of their being they are blessed. Give them a closer look.

4. SCH 2:90; ACCS NT 1b:95*.
5. PL *Suppl.* 3:867; ACCS NT 1b:68-69*.
6. SCH 2:74; ACCS NT 1b:68*.

Among the "least of these" were the children of Galilee who came to Jesus and were blessed by him. They were blessed simply by his presence. They connected quickly with his own lowliness, kindness, and simplicity. They are by common grace blessed, wrote Hilary, because — look at the ways — "children follow their father, love their mother, do not know how to wish ill on their neighbor, show no concern for wealth, are not proud, do not hate, do not lie, believe what has been said and hold what they hear as truth" (Hilary of Poitiers, On Matthew 18.1; Matt. 18:4).[7]

In the episode of Jesus blessing children, Jerome imagined that he was in effect saying to adults: "Just as this child whose example I show you does not persist in anger, does not long remember injury suffered, does not chase after beautiful women, does not think one thing and say another, so you too, unless you have similar innocence and purity of mind, will not be able to enter the kingdom of heaven" (Jerome, Commentary on Matthew 3; Matt. 18:4).[8] The vestiges of purity of heart in the human condition are still there in our children, and waiting to be drawn out. Eden is soon forgotten, but never completely.

### 4. Learning Guilelessness

Children, thought Ambrose, "do not know spitefulness, have not learned to deceive, dare not strike back [1 Pet. 2:22-23]. They neglect to search for wealth, and do not work after honor and ambition. . . . Mature goodness comes close to childlike simplicity [1 Cor. 4:20]. It is not a virtue to be unable to sin, but to be unwilling to do so and to retain perseverance of will, so that the will imitates childhood and the person imitates nature" (Ambrose, Exposition of the Gospel of Luke 8.57; Luke 18:15-17).[9] Nature is viewed here in its unfallen sense, not its fallen sense.

"For those qualities which the child has by nature, God wishes us to have by choice: simplicity, forgetfulness of wrongs done to us, love of our parents, even if struck by them" (Apollinaris, Fragment 96; Matt. 19:15).[10]

What children are by nature, adults may become by grace. They are

---

7. SCH 2:75-76; ACCS NT 1b:68.
8. CCL 77:157; ACCS NT 1b:68*.
9. EHG 354*; ACCS NT 3:281-82*.
10. MKGK 31-32; ACCS NT 1b:96.

blessed in their ignorance. They "are ignorant of wickedness. They do not know how to return evil for evil or how to do someone an injury. They do not know how to be lustful or to fornicate or to rob. What they hear, they believe. They love their parents with complete affection. Therefore, beloved, the Lord instructs us that what they are by the gift of nature, we should become by the fear of God, a holy way of life and love of the heavenly kingdom" (Epiphanius the Latin, Interpretation of the Gospels 25; Matt. 19:14).[11]

Jesus had great affection for "the least of these" — those who are most like a child. "He made the child a representation of an innocent and humble life. The mind of a child is empty of fraud, and his heart is sincere. His thoughts are simple. He does not covet rank and does not know what is meant by one man being higher than another is," wrote Cyril of Alexandria. "Jesus showed the child as if in an object lesson, showing that he accepts and loves those who are like the child. He thinks they are worthy of standing at his side, as being like-minded with him and ready to walk in his steps" (Cyril of Alexandria, Commentary on Luke, Homily 54; Luke 9:46-50).[12] The Christian life teaches us to value our children in the same way that God values them.

We are called to an innocent, guileless, gentle life. This means, insofar as possible, never coming close enough to temptation to be willingly drawn further into it. "Knowing very little or nothing at all, the baby lacks those behaviors that we associate with the weightier charges of depravity and wickedness. It is also our duty to attempt to be like them in the very same way. We must entirely put away from us habits of ungodliness, that we also may be people who do not even recognize the path that leads to deception. Unconscious of spite and fraud, we must live in a simple and innocent manner, practicing gentleness and a priceless humility and readily avoiding wrath and spitefulness. These very qualities are found in those who are still babies" (Cyril of Alexandria, Commentary on Luke, Homily 121; Luke 18:15-17).[13] In willing the good for the child, the adult meets anew this guilelessness. What the newborn baby has in great measure, the embryo has in even greater measure. From conception the least of these is highly valued by believers.

---

11. PL *Suppl.* 3:862: ACCS NT 1b:95-96.
12. CGSL 237-38**; ACCS NT 3:165*.
13. CGSL 484**; ACCS NT 3:281*.

## 5. Relearning Lowliness

Lowliness of mind reflects the reality of God who himself has become lowly for us in the incarnation. "Christ calls him least whom lowly things please and who from modesty does not think highly of himself. This person pleases Christ. It is written that 'every one that exalts himself shall be humbled, and he that humbles himself shall be exalted' [Luke 14:11]. . . . Being simpleminded, as befits saints, we will be with Christ who honors simplicity" (Cyril of Alexandria, Commentary on Luke, Homily 54; Luke 9:46-50).[14]

Human reasoning about power is reversed in the coming kingdom, as Jesus taught: "If any one would be first, he must be last of all and servant of all" (Mark 9:35b, RSV). John Chrysostom commented: "If you are in love with precedence and the highest honor, you most of all must pursue the things in last place, being the least valued of all, being the lowliest of all, being the smallest of all, placing yourselves behind others" (Chrysostom, The Gospel of Matthew, Homily 58; Mark 9:35).[15]

What strikes the modern reader about these ancient Christian interpretations of children is their strong affirmation of the child, and the pattern of simplicity that those who are reborn must relearn. This runs counter to our expectations that classic Christian teaching would focus more on the patterns of original sin that are already embedded in children. As we encounter our children, we discover how decisive is the Gospel's call to the complete reversal of our way of looking at the world. The child radiates simple faith, innocence of evil, and trust of others.

## B. God Works through Human Limitations

When we complain that we cannot do good works because we are not prepared, or because we are not smart enough, or because we do not have enough education, we do well to remember the lowly characters whom Jesus chose to accomplish his mission.

---

14. CGSL 238-39**; ACCS NT 3:165*.
15. NPNF 1 10:359; ACCS NT 2:127*.

### 1. Jesus Chose the Least of the Unlettered to Accomplish His Mission

The "least of these" is seen in those ordinary fishermen Jesus called to an extraordinary worldwide teaching mission. "Reflect on the nature and grandeur of the one Almighty God," wrote Eusebius,

> who could associate himself with the poor of the lowly fisherman's class. To use them to carry out God's mission baffles all rationality. For having conceived the intention, which no one ever before had done, of spreading his own commands and teachings to all nations, and of revealing himself as the revealer of the one Almighty God to all humanity, he thought preferable to use the most unsophisticated and common people as ministers of his own design. Maybe God just wanted to work in the most unlikely way. For how could inarticulate folk be made able to teach, even if they were merely appointed tutors to a single person, much less to a great multitude? How could those without education instruct the nations? . . . When he had thus called them as his followers, he breathed into them his divine power, and filled them with strength and courage. As God himself he spoke his true word to them in his own way, enabling them to do great wonders, and made them instructors of rational and thinking souls. He empowered them, saying: "Come, follow me, and I will make you fish for people" [Mark 1:17; Matt. 4:19]. With this empowerment God sent them forth to be workers and teachers of holiness to all the nations, declaring them heralds of his own Word. (Eusebius, The Proof of the Gospel 3.7; Mark 1:16) [16]

The larger pattern of God's good work is cast on a world historical scale. Through human weakness his strength is made known.

Why did Jesus choose those so ill-prepared to demonstrate divine grace? Chromatius of Aquileia proposes this reason: To exalt the lowly, and to show that God's power is greater than our weakness.

> Oh, blessed are those fishermen whom the Lord chose from among so many doctors of the law and scribes, from among so many sages of the world, for the task of divine preaching and the grace of the apostolate!

16. TLG 2018.005, 3.7.5-8, 10-11; POG 1:156**; ACCS NT 2:18-19*.

Worthy of our Lord, indeed, and appropriate for his preaching was that choice, so that in the preaching of his name all the greater might be the wonder of praise as the humble and lowly of the age preached his word. They were not pretending to capture the world through the world's wisdom, but that they might free the human race from the sting of death through the simple preaching of the faith, or as the apostle says: "That your faith may not be in the wisdom of men, but in the power of God" [1 Cor. 2:5]. And in another place: "But the foolish things of the world has God chosen to put to shame the wise, and the weak things of the world has God chosen to put to shame the strong. The base things of the world and the despised God has chosen, even the things that are not, to bring to nothing the things that are" [1 Cor. 1:27-28]. Therefore, God has not chosen the noble of the world or the rich, lest their preaching be suspect. He has not chosen the wise of the world, lest people believe that they persuaded the human race with their wisdom. Rather he chose illiterate, unskilled and untutored fishermen, so that the Savior's grace might be made clear. (Chromatius, Tractate on Matthew 16.1; Matt. 4:21) [17]

God's power shows best through human limitations.

Eusebius thought the disciples might reasonably have protested that they were entirely unprepared for their task. "'How can we preach to Romans? How can we argue with Egyptians? We are brought up to use the Syrian[18] tongue only. What language shall we speak to Greeks? How shall we persuade Persians, Armenians, Chaldeans, Scythians, Indians and other scattered nations to give up their ancestral gods and worship the Creator of all? What abilities in speaking do we have in attempting such work as this? What hope of success can we have if we dare to proclaim laws directly opposed to the laws about their own gods that have been established for ages among all nations? By what power shall we ever survive our daring attempt?'" (Eusebius, The Proof of the Gospel 3.7; Mark 1:17).[19] What is impossible for men is possible with God.

God has chosen the most foolish things of the world to make his wisdom known. Ambrosiaster's most evident examples: "*The two most foolish*

17. CCL 9a:263; ACCS NT 1a:72*.
18. In the form of Aramaic.
19. TLG 2018.005, 3.7.10; POG 1:157*; ACCS NT 2:19*.

*things of the world* are in particular the virgin birth of Christ and his resurrection from the dead. The wise remain confounded because it is evident that what a few of them deny, many profess to be true. The profession of the many deserves a fair hearing from the few. Likewise, those who are mighty in this world can easily see the so-called weak things of Christ overturning demons and performing miracles. To the world the injuries and sufferings of the Savior are weak things, because the world does not understand that they have become the source of power through Christ who submitted to suffering in order to overcome death" (Ambrosiaster, On Paul's Epistles to the Corinthians, italics added; 1 Cor. 1:27).[20] Contrary to the world, God uses the weakest vessel to bear his power.

## 2. Providence Works through Limitations

Origen thought it persuasive evidence of divine providence that God chose the weak to teach the strong: "Now we can see how in a short time this religion has grown up, making progress through the persecution and death of its adherents and through their endurance of confiscation of property and every kind of bodily torture. And this is particularly remarkable since the teachers themselves were neither very skillful nor very numerous. Yet in spite of all, this word is being 'preached in all the world' [Matt. 24:14], so that Greeks and barbarians, wise and foolish now are adopting the Christian faith [cf. Rom. 1:14]. Hence there can be no doubt that it is not by human strength or resources that the word of Christ comes to prevail with all authority and convincing power in the minds and hearts of all humanity" (Origen, First Principles 4.1.2; Mark 1:17).[21] History itself proves that God uses our imperfections to cast into bold relief the divine perfections.

Divine providence attests God's strength by working precisely through human weaknesses. "In human terms, it was not possible for fishers to get the better of philosophers, but that is what actually happened by the power of God's grace" (Chrysostom, Homilies on the Epistles of Paul to the Corinthians I.5.5; 1 Cor. 1:27).[22]

Christian teaching does not depend upon rhetorical flourish, but

20. CSEL 81.19; ACCS NT 7:17*.
21. OFP 259; ACCS NT 2:19*.
22. NPNF 1 12:25; ACCS NT 7:17*.

God's active power to awaken and redeem: "If our Scriptures had persuaded people to believe because they had been written with rhetorical brilliance, there would remain the thought that our faith would be said to depend on the art of words and on human wisdom rather than on the power of God" (Origen, On First Principles 4.1.7; 1 Cor. 2:4).[23] God saw to it that the charge had to be implausible that the preaching of the Gospel depends upon the power of human rhetoric.

### 3. The Greater Value of Lesser Things

It is a fact of the salvation history remembered in Christian worship that God works through human weakness, surprising us constantly. He chooses Bethlehem, the least in Judah, out of which the Messiah shall come (Matt. 2:6). "God has chosen the foolish things of the world to shame the wise, and God has chosen the weak things of the world to shame the things which are strong, and the base things of the world and the despised God has chosen, the things that are not, so that he may nullify the things that are" (1 Cor. 1:27-28, NAS).

God chooses the lowly to convey the height and depth of his love. "God chose ignoble and contemptible things to raise up. It is not that they are really ignoble and contemptible. This is merely how the world sees them. By believing in Christ they have overturned worldly reasoning. God did this in order to destroy things which are really ignoble and contemptible, because those who judged were more deserving of judgment and condemnation. Their teaching was asserted in mere words but not demonstrated in power. So it was destroyed. Our teaching is proved true not only by words but by power as well" (Ambrosiaster, On Paul's Epistles to the Corinthians; 1 Cor. 1:28).[24]

The will, powerful as it appears to be, is unable to perform the slightest good work without grace. The Fathers were ever attentive to those sacred texts that showed that God chooses the weak things of the world to confound the things that are mighty (1 Cor. 1:27). All temporal powers are relativized in relation to the One source and ground of powers. What is meant in the world by great and small, inferior and superior, is turned up-

23. CWSO 177; ACCS NT 7:20*.
24. CSEL 81.19; ACCS NT 7:17*.

THE GOOD WORKS READER

side down in relation to the Gospel. Christ was crucified in weakness (2 Cor. 13:4). "The weakness of God is stronger than men" (1 Cor. 1:25b, NAS). God's greatness is greater than whatever importance the world may pretend to have. "For he who is in you is greater than he who is in the world" (1 John 4:4b, RSV).

As the sculptor selects the wood for what it can become, not what it is, so too the Lord chooses the faithful not for their already-existing good works or competencies, but according to their willingness to allow God's power to shine through their weakness. "An artist sees precious, not rough-hewn, stones, and chooses them — not because of what they are but because of what they can become. Like the sensitive artist who does not spurn the unshaped good — so too the Lord, upon seeing believers, does not choose their works but their hearts" (Opus Imperfectum in Matthaeum, Homily 7; Matt. 4:20).[25]

### 4. The Body Needs Hands and Feet

The living body of Christ needs hands as much as eyes. The body of Christ has the eyes of "teachers and leaders who see in sacred Scripture the mysteries of God," wrote Jerome, but "it also has hands, effective persons who are not eyes but hands. Do they plumb the mysteries of sacred Scripture? No, but they are powerful in works. The church has feet: those who make official journeys of all kinds. The foot runs that the hand may find the work it is to do. The eye does not scorn the hand, nor do these three scorn the belly as if it were idle and unemployed" (Jerome, Homily 85 on Matthew 18:7-9; 1 Cor. 12:21).[26]

The weaker means are favored by God to accomplish the greater ends. "What is lower than the foot? Or what is more honorable or necessary than the head? But the head, however important it is, is not self-sufficient, nor can it do everything by itself. If that were so, there would be no need to have feet" (Chrysostom, Homilies on the Epistles of Paul to the Corinthians I.31.1; 1 Cor. 12:21).[27] God's way is to make weak things the vessels of his power.

25. PG 56:674; ACCS NT 1a:72*.
26. FC 57:197*; ACCS NT 7:126.
27. NPNF 1 12:181; ACCS NT 7:126.

The greater cannot do without the lesser. "For there are things which a humbler person can do which an exalted one cannot, just as iron can do things which gold cannot. Because of this, the feet perform an honorable function for the head" (Ambrosiaster, On Paul's Epistles to the Corinthians; 1 Cor. 12:21).[28]

God gives great things to the small. "Both the greatness of the things given, and the weakness of them that receive, reveal the power of God, who not only gave great things, but gave them to those who are little. He used the term 'earthen' as an allusion to the frailty of our mortal nature, and to declare the weakness of our flesh. For it is like earthenware, which is soon damaged. It is soon destroyed by death by means of disease, climatic and natural changes. The power of God is most conspicuous when it performs mighty works by using base and lowly things" (Chrysostom, Homilies on the Epistles of Paul to the Corinthians II.8.3; 2 Cor. 4:7b).[29] The imperative for good works: Become hands and feet for the body of Christ.

### 5. The Day of Small Things

We are not to despise the day of small things (Zech. 4:10). Meekness is one of the fruits of the Spirit (Gal. 5:22-23). The powerful are the most skeptical about the idea that the meek inherit the earth. James noted how great a fire a little flame kindles, and how the tongue, a small member, may do great things (Jas. 3:5).

The Fathers pondered these scriptural ironies. The meek have a gentle strength and do not have to resort to power plays in order to feel secure. Moses was meek (Num. 12:3). The coming Anointed one, as Isaiah prophesied, would stand as a sheep before her shearers, and would be dumb, opening not his mouth (Isa. 53:7). Each one should esteem the other better than oneself in lowliness of mind (Phil. 2:3). When reviled, they do not revile again (1 Pet. 2:23).

What is the moral imperative that follows from this? Support the weak. Be patient to all (1 Thess. 3:14). Do not glory in yourself. Be aware of your own limitations (2 Cor. 12:3). Do not give the weak an occasion to fall. Do not put a stumbling block in their way (Rom. 14:13). Take care that your

28. CSEL 81.138; ACCS NT 7:126.
29. NPNF 1 12:320; ACCS NT 7:232*.

liberty does not become a stumbling block to the weak (1 Cor. 8:9). Paul says, "Who is weak without my being weak? Who is led into sin without my intense concern?" (2 Cor. 11:29, NAS).

The act that best symbolized the motif of lowliness was, according to Ambrose, the washing of feet:

> The church washes the feet of Christ, wipes them with her hair, anoints them with oil, and pours ointment on them. She not only cares for the wounded and caresses the weary, but she also moistens them with the sweet perfume of grace. She pours this grace not only on the rich and powerful but also on those of lowly birth. She weighs all in an equal balance. She receives all into the same bosom. She caresses all in the same embrace. Christ died once. He was buried once. Nevertheless he wants ointment to be poured on his feet each day. What are the feet of Christ on which we pour ointment? They are the feet of Christ of whom he himself says, "What you have done for one of the least of these, you have done to me" [Matt. 25:40]. The woman in the Gospel refreshes these feet. She moistens them with her tears when sin is forgiven of the lowest of persons, guilt is washed away, and pardon is granted. (Ambrose, Letter 62; Luke 7:44-48) [30]

In caring for the lowly and least, the church is participating in the service that Christ rendered to humanity. What the church is doing, in her best moments, is just what Christ did as if a servant washing feet.

### 6. The Foolishness of God

"When Paul speaks of the 'foolishness of God,' he is not implying that God is foolish. Rather he is saying that since God's way of reasoning is in accord with things of the spirit, it confounds the reasoning of the wise by what is wiser than reasoning. . . . What seems like the weakness of God is not really weak at all. Christ appeared to be defeated when he was killed, but he emerged as the victor and turned the reproof back on his persecutors" (Ambrosiaster, On Paul's Epistles to the Corinthians; 1 Cor. 1:25).[31]

30. FC 26:393-94*; ACCS NT 3:128-29.
31. CSEL 81.17; ACCS NT 7:16*.

God chose the least of these because they are more open to the truth, and less confident of their own righteousness and competencies. "A little learning is a dangerous thing because it may make those who have it less willing to learn more. The unlearned are more open to conviction, because they are not so foolish as to think that they are wise" (Chrysostom, Homilies on the Epistles of Paul to the Corinthians I.5.2; 1 Cor. 1:26).[32] Learning tempts exaggerated imagination.

Among nations Israel seemed to be the smallest and fewest of all people (Deut. 7:7), even a byword among stronger people (1 Kings 9:7), an outcast (Jer. 30:17). Israel seemed like a joke among the heathen, who shook their heads at their weakness (Ps. 44:14). But their weakness was crucial to their discipline, chastisement, and maturation.

By choosing the weak, God places his strength in bold relief. Jesus "began . . . in Bethlehem with a manger, in Jerusalem with a donkey" (Ephrem the Syrian, Commentary on Tatian's Diatessaron 18.1; Luke 19:29-36).[33] He was crucified in weakness, yet lives by the power of God (2 Cor. 13:4). He was willing to suffer "outside the gate" (Heb. 13:12a, RSV), which meant to go beyond the city walls, out into the waste places outside the city.

## 7. Searching for the Lost Sheep

The lost sheep of Jesus' parable epitomizes the "least of these." "When he said, 'See that you do not despise one of these little ones,' he is calling us to be merciful. Then he adds the parable of the ninety-nine sheep left in the mountains and the one stray that because of its great weakness could not walk. The good shepherd carried it on his shoulders to the rest of the flock" (Jerome, Commentary on Matthew 3; Matt. 18:12).[34]

The Lord actively pursues the lost sheep — the least of these. "It does not please the Father that anyone is lost. The shepherd leaves the ones that have been saved and seeks out the one lost. When he finds the one that has gone astray, he rejoices greatly at its discovery and at its safety" (Chrysostom, The Gospel of Matthew, Homily 59.4; Matt. 18:13).[35]

---

32. NPNF 1 12:23**; ACCS NT 7:17*.
33. ECTD 269; ACCS NT 3:297*.
34. CCL 77:160; ACCS NT 1b:74.
35. PG 58:579; NPNF 1 10:368; ACCS NT 1b:75.

The logic of the Gospel is laid bare in the one lost sheep. "This one sheep is the man Adam, whom in the beginning the Lord had created in his image and likeness. This one strayed from the company of the angels by sinning, and through him the entire human race strayed from God. Our Lord seeks to recall all humanity from death to life. For it was for us that he went to death, so that he might make us alive, we who had died. For he rejoiced even more over the hundredth sheep that was lost than over the ninety and nine" (Epiphanius the Latin, Interpretation of the Gospels 27; Matt. 18:13).[36] This is the logic of "the least of these."

## C. Works of Mercy

### 1. How the Merciful Bless and Are Blessed

Let acts of mercy be bound around your neck and written on the table of your heart, for they are intrinsic to the righteous life (Prov. 3:3). They are fruits of the life of good works.

Mercy is active. In saying "blessed are the merciful," Jesus "speaks here not only of those who show mercy by giving worldly goods, but also of those who demonstrate mercy in their actions" (Chrysostom, The Gospel of Matthew, Homily 15.6; Matt. 5:7).[37] Those who act mercifully do not wait for opportunities for mercy. They look for them actively.

Mercy "breaks chains, dispels darkness, extinguishes fire, kills the worm, and takes away the gnashing of teeth (cf. Mark 9:44-48). By it the gates of heaven open with the greatest of ease. In short, mercy is a queen who elevates humanity toward God" (Chrysostom, quoted in Cramer, Catena in Epistolas Catholicas; Jas. 2:13).[38] Showers of blessings come to humanity through quiet acts of mercy.

Mercy is like an anointing oil. "Just as oil enables athletes to escape the hands of their opponents, so mercy prepares those who practice it to avoid and escape the demonic powers" (Hesychius, quoted in Cramer, Catena in Epistolas Catholicas; Jas. 2:13).[39] No demonic power can hold in

---

36. PL *Suppl.* 3:867-68; ACCS NT 1b:75.
37. PG 57:227; NPNF 1 10:94; ACCS NT 1a:85.
38. CEC 13; ACCS NT 11:25*.
39. CEC 13; ACCS NT 11:26*.

its clutches one who acts mercifully. The merciful are blessed. They know they are already receiving God's mercy (Matt. 5:7). They know it will be fully enjoyed in eternal life.

The reward for showing mercy is already beginning to appear in the merciful act itself. "What reward can people expect if they obey the command to show mercy? 'They obtain mercy.' The reward at first glance appears to be an equal reimbursement, but actually the reward from God is much greater than human acts of goodness. For we ourselves are showing mercy as human beings are able. But we are obtaining mercy from the God of all. Human mercy and God's mercy are not the same. As wide as the interval is between corrupted and perfect goodness, so far is human mercy distinguished from divine mercy" (Chrysostom, The Gospel of Matthew, Homily 15.6; Matt. 5:7).[40] God's mercy adds infinite value to our acts of human mercy.

### 2. Show Mercy as You Have Received Mercy

Peter asked how many times we are to forgive. Jesus answered by the parable of the unmerciful servant, which the early exegetes studied deeply.

> When Peter asked this, the Lord taught to forgive not seven times but seventy times seven. He then added the parable of the unmerciful servant, which hinges on an analogy between a kind king and an unkind servant. The servant, though unworthy, had received such mercy from his master that even his immense debt was forgiven him. But he himself refused to show mercy to a fellow servant for a small debt. So, quite rightly, he was handed over to the jailers and received the just punishment of condemnation. For what would such a wretched wrongdoer not deserve to suffer? Though he had experienced such pity from his master, he was himself unjust and cruel to his fellow servant. By this example, we are clearly instructed and cautioned that if we do not forgive our fellow servants (the brothers who sin against us) of the debt of their sins, we will be condemned with a punishment like that which we pronounce. And though the comparison may seem to have been introduced for a particular occasion, the parable itself has within it an

---

40. PG 57:227; NPNF 1:10:94; ACCS NT 1a:85*.

eternal truth and obvious logic. (Chromatius, Tractate on Matthew 59.4; Matt. 18:30) [41]

Forgive as you have been forgiven — infinitely.

The unmerciful servant "did not even respect the very words through which he had himself been saved. With these words he himself had been freed from a debt of ten thousand talents! He did not even recognize the harbor by means of which he had barely escaped a shipwreck. Even the gesture of supplication did not remind him of his master's kindness. Casting all these out of his mind in his greed, cruelty and rancor, he was even more brutal than a wild beast in seizing his fellow servant by the throat. What are you doing, my beloved? Do you not see that you are bringing on a similar judgment upon yourself? You are not only deceiving yourself; you are thrusting a sword into yourself! You are revoking both the sentence and the gift" (Chrysostom, The Gospel of Matthew, Homily 61.4; Matt. 18:31-33).[42] We are in effect revoking voluntarily God's forgiveness of us by not forgiving our brother. God's gift intends to be received.

### 3. The Faithful Are Brought into the Sphere of God's Mercy by Themselves Becoming Agents of Mercy

We are brought ever nearer to the mercy of God in the measure by which we show mercy to others. Our tainted motives begin to be cleansed when we live out of God's holy love, according to Ambrose: "Compassion cleanses us. The Word of God cleanses us, according to what it is written: 'Now you are clean by reason of the word that I have spoken to you' [John 15:3]. Not only in this passage but also in others you have revealed how great grace is, and what scripture (LXX) means when it says: 'Alms delivers from death' [Tob. 12:9], and 'store up alms in the heart of the poor, and it shall obtain help for you on the evil day' [Sir. 29:12]" (Ambrose, Exposition of the Gospel of Luke 7.101; Luke 11:39-41).[43] Does this mean that our works save, or that God's work on our behalf elicits our good works?

41. CCL 9a:495; ACCS NT 1b:86**.
42. PG 58:593; NPNF 1 10:379; ACCS NT 1b:87*.
43. EHG 273**; ACCS NT 3:199*.

THE LEAST OF THESE

Clearly the latter, viewed in relation to all that Ambrose says elsewhere about the sole efficacy of grace for salvation.

Almsgiving, in Augustine's view, includes all acts of mercy. "Our Lord says, 'Give to the poor, and behold, all things are clean to you' [Luke 11:41]. This text does not apply just to the one who gives food to the hungry, drink to the thirsty, clothing to the naked, hospitality to the wayfarer or refuge to the fugitive. It applies to all acts of mercy. It applies to one who visits the sick and the prisoner, redeems the captive, bears the burdens of the weak, leads the blind, comforts the sorrowful, heals the sick, shows those on the wrong path the right way, gives clear counsel to the perplexed, and does whatever is needful for the needy. One who forgives trespasses is also giving alms. . . . There are many kinds of alms. In giving them, we are being helped by grace to receive the forgiveness of our own sins" (Augustine, Enchiridion 19.72; Luke 11:39-41).[44] No alms as such save without grace, but grace elicits alms.

If God showed mercy even to a persecutor of the church such as Paul himself was, he argued that God would show mercy to anyone willing to trust his Word. "I received mercy because I had acted ignorantly in unbelief, and the grace of our Lord overflowed for me with the faith and love that are in Christ Jesus" (1 Tim. 1:13b-14, RSV).

The whole of the Christian walk through time is penetrated by this sense of the lively assurance of God's mercy. It is this goodness and mercy of God that follows the faithful all the days of their lives (Ps. 23:6). Mercy sustains the community of faith daily. That is evident from the common benedictions and salutations of scripture (1 Tim. 1:2; 2 John 3; Jude 2; Gal. 6:16). The Lord's mercies are new every morning (Lam. 3:22-23).

## 4. Following the Way of God's Mercy

Mercy belongs to the very character of God. It is a divine attribute — a characteristic feature of God's very life. God's own attribute of incomparable mercy is approximately refracted by grace through human acts of mercy. The mercy of the Lord is from everlasting to everlasting upon those who hold him in awe (Ps. 103:17). Nowhere does God's mercy show itself more decisively than in the Son's atoning work on the cross (Heb. 2:17).

44. LCC 7:382**; ACCS NT 3:199*.

To be made in the image of God is to be capable of refracting divine mercy even under the broken conditions of the history of sin. "The traces of the divine image are more clearly recognized through acts of goodness than by physical likeness. We see the divine image in its righteousness, temperance, courage, wisdom, discipline, and through the entire chorus of virtues that are present quintessentially in God. These can become reflected in people through effort and imitation of God, as also the Lord points out in the Gospel when he says, 'Be merciful, even as your Father is merciful' [Luke 6:36]" (Origen, On First Principles 4.10; Luke 6:35-36).[45]

Guileless acts of mercy draw us ever nearer to the incomparable mercy of God. "Mercy is practiced when two things happen: vengeance is sacrificed and compassion is shown. The Lord included both of these in his brief sentence: 'Forgive, and you shall be forgiven; give, and it shall be given to you.' Acts of mercy have the effect of cleansing the heart, so that, even under the limitations of this life, we are enabled with purer mind to see the immutable reality of God" (Augustine, Letter 171a; Luke 6:37-38).[46] Through mercy, affections are purified. Aggression is moderated.

Therefore, "Should you not have had mercy on your fellow servant, as I had mercy on you?" (Matt. 18:33, RSV). Cyril of Alexandria extolled mercy as "a most excelling characteristic, and very pleasing to God, and in the highest degree fitting for the earnest soul. Imprint this upon your mind: compassion is an attribute of the divine nature" (Cyril of Alexandria, Commentary on Luke, Homily 29; Luke 6:35-36).[47]

## 5. Giving and Forgiving

Prayer rises to God and soars upward by two wings — forgiving and giving, according to Augustine: "'Forgive, and you will be forgiven.' 'Give, and it will be given you.' These are the two wings of prayer, on which it flies to God. So pardon the offender of what has been committed, and give to the person in need" (Augustine, Sermon 205.3; Luke 6:37-38).[48]

"What do you want from the Lord? Mercy. Give, and it shall be given

45. CWSO 216*; ACCS NT 3:109**.
46. FC 30:70*; ACCS NT 3:110*.
47. CGSL 133**; ACCS NT 3:109*.
48. WSA 3 6:105; ACCS NT 3:110*.

to you. What do you want from the Lord? Pardon. Forgive, and you will be forgiven" (Augustine, Sermon 179a.1; Luke 6:37-38).[49] Lacking mercy and pardon your prayers will ring hollow. So participate in divine forgiveness by forgiving. Receive God's gift by giving. Works of mercy deepen by forgiving "others the sins which they have committed against us and by giving alms to the poor and needy among us. But if, on the other hand, we are not well disposed toward those around us, we shall receive the condemnation handed out to the unmerciful servant, along with the retribution that is mentioned in the Lord's Prayer. For there we ask God to forgive us as we forgive those who have sinned against us [Matt. 6:12], but if we do not forgive them, we shall not be forgiven either" (Oecumenius, Commentary on James; Jas. 2:13).[50] To pretend to receive God's forgiveness without passing it along is to not receive it.

## 6. Mercy Bears Its Fruit in Good Works

Even when not observed by human eyes, God honors works of mercy. Their value does not depend upon being recognized: "Although the spite of some people does not grow gentle with any kindness, nevertheless the works of mercy are not fruitless, and kindness never becomes nothing even when offered to the ungrateful. May no one, dearly beloved, make themselves strangers to good works. . . . No mercy is worthless before God. No compassion is fruitless" (Leo the Great, Sermon 20.3.1; Luke 21:1-4).[51] Even small and quiet works of mercy bear fruit in due season, overcoming barriers, melting resistance.

Fruitless branches are pruned. They are useless except as fuel (Ezek. 15:2-8). The fruits of the spirit are like trees that produce in due time, even if slowly (Ps. 1:3). Even in old age they continue to flourish (Ps. 92:14). The righteous man is "like a tree planted by the water, that extends its roots by a stream and will not fear when the heat comes" (Jer. 17:8a, NAS). Wherever Israel is being restored, the Spirit is being poured out and the land is becoming fruitful (Isa. 32:15-16; Job 2:18-32; Prov. 12:12). The will of God is bearing fruit through human freedom when we act mercifully as God is merciful.

49. WSA 3 5:306; ACCS NT 3:110-11.
50. PG 119:476-67; ACCS NT 11:26*.
51. FC 93:74*; ACCS NT 3:316-17.

*7. Showing Mercy*

In the Bible, God's mercy is known in specific, historical actions (Isa. 30:18-26; Neh. 9:27-28; Jer. 33:24-26). We know what God's mercy is because we have experienced God acting mercifully. It is in fact most characteristic of God to act mercifully. It is on this basis that we have a confidence to call upon him for deliverance in present need because we have a historical memory of his merciful acts.

God shows divine mercy not through talk but through deeds (1 Kings 8:23; Deut. 7:9). God does not just feel pity for the human condition, without acting. God acts in merciful deeds by caring for humanity. Good works in scripture are characterized by acts, deeds, and behaviors, not by emotive states as such.

Human acts of mercy are refractions of God's merciful actions made known in history. Though enacted in time, these acts share in eternal divine mercy. This mercy endures forever (Pss. 100:5; 106:1; 107:1; 118:1).

God expects his covenant people to show mercy to one another because he has taught them how to act mercifully in time. He taught them through the events that reveal his character as merciful. This mercy is anticipated already in the narratives of Abraham (Gen. 24:12-14), Jacob (Gen. 32:10), and Moses with the people of Israel (Exod. 15:13). Actions done today show where the heart is and has been. When the heart has been touched by God's mercy, the suffering of the neighbor becomes more recognizable.

No one who closes his heart to his brother's need really grasps God's love (1 John 3:17). Just as God's mercy extends to the alien, the stranger, and the rejected, so does our mercy reach out to the broken edges of human suffering. When the next needy neighbor crosses our path, we already know that the Lord through the least of these is immediately addressing us through him. "No one is ready to receive God's compassion unless he himself is also compassionate" (Chromatius, Tractate on Matthew 17.6.1-2; Matt. 5:7).[52]

## D. The Gentle Touch

Gentleness characterizes the works of love. The mercy we have just discussed is closely related to corresponding personal qualities — kindness,

---

52. CCL 9a:274; ACCS NT 1a:85*.

forgiveness, meekness, forbearance — none separable, all interrelated. The gentleness that characterizes the Christian life has its pattern in the non-coercive gentleness of the Spirit, who manifests the spirit of Christ in human history. This gentleness is expressed precisely amid the hazardous conditions of the history of sin. In this way mercy becomes wise to the ways of the world.

### 1. Be Wise as Serpents, Harmless as Doves

Those who have been sent out "as sheep in the midst of wolves," says Jesus, must "be wise as serpents and innocent as doves" (Matt. 10:16, RSV). This phrase implies that we are to be "innocent as doves that we may not harm anyone, and cautious as serpents that we may be careful of letting anyone harm us" (Augustine, Sermons, Sermon 64a.2; Matt. 10:20).[53] Both sides of this equilibrium are to be kept in constant tension. Being like a dove does not mean being ignorant of deceptive motives. Being wise to the real world does not imply that we accommodate to its ungodliness.

"Beware of men; for they will deliver you up to councils, and flog you in their synagogues" (Matt. 10:17, RSV). John Chrysostom argued that God is preparing the faithful for a "new sort of combat: They are given grace to suffer wrong, and willingly permit others to inflict punishment upon them. This is meant to teach them that the victory is in suffering evil for the sake of good. By this means their eternal trophies are being prepared. He does not instruct them to fight and resist those who would persecute them. All he promises them is that they will suffer with him the utmost ills" (Chrysostom, The Gospel of Matthew, Homily 33.4; Matt. 10:17).[54] No one should set his foot on the narrow path without knowing how narrow it is.

Grace guides the footsteps along the path, teaching prudence and candor. "Wisdom even promises to give cleverness to the simple and the beginning of sense and understanding to the young [Prov. 1:4]. . . . Simplicity and cleverness are not inconsistent, as the Savior explains to us elsewhere in saying, 'Be clever as serpents and simple as doves' [Matt. 10:16]" (Cyril of Alexandria, Commentary on Luke, Homily 121; Luke 18:15-17).[55]

---

53. AMA 1:311-12; WSA 3 3:189; ACCS NT 1a:201*.
54. PG 57:391; NPNF 1 10:221**; ACCS NT 1a:199*.
55. CGSL 483-84**; ACCS NT 3:281*.

"No one can hurt you if you are determined to do only what is right. Blessed are you if you have to suffer for being upright. Have no dread of them; have no fear. Simply proclaim the Lord Christ holy in your hearts" (1 Pet. 3:13-15a, NJB). "Always be prepared to make a defense to any one who calls you to account for the hope that is in you" (1 Pet. 3:15b, RSV). "Peter is speaking here of things like abuse, damage and bodily injury which come to us from our enemies. These and similar things are the common lot of believers, both because they are good imitators of Christ and because they know that such things, far from doing them any harm, actually bring glory to those who endure them with patience" (Bede the Venerable, On 1 Peter; 1 Pet. 3:13).[56]

### 2. Be Gentle, Like a Dove

The gentleness that characterizes the works of love is typified by the dove, always a friendly sign in the sacred text. "A dove is a tame, innocent and simple bird. We are taught to copy the innocence of doves" (Origen, Homilies on Luke, Homily 27; Mark 1:10).[57]

The dove symbolizes guilelessness, according to Bede: "The dove is a stranger to malice. So may all bitterness, anger and indignation be taken away from us, together with all malice. The dove injures nothing with its mouth or talons, nor does it nourish itself or its young on tiny mice or grubs, as do almost all smaller birds. Let us see that our teeth are not weapons and arrows [Ps. 57:4 (LXX 56:5)]" (Bede the Venerable, Homilies on the Gospels 1.12; Mark 1:10).[58]

Works of love are altogether lacking in gall and aggressiveness, as is the dove, thought Tertullian: "The Holy Spirit came in the form of a dove in order that the nature of the Holy Spirit might be made plain by means of a creature of utter simplicity and innocence. For the dove's body has no gall in it. So after the deluge, by which the iniquity of the old world was purged away, after, so to speak, the baptism of the world, the dove as herald proclaimed to the earth the tempering of the wrath of heaven — sent forth from the ark and returning with an olive branch [cf. Gen. 8:11], which is a

56. PL 93:56; ACCS NT 11:103-4.
57. AEG 1:307; ACCS NT 2:13*.
58. Cetedoc 1367, 1.12.197; CSBH 1:120**; ACCS NT 2:14.

sign of peace among the nations" (Tertullian, On Baptism 8; Mark 1:10).[59] The dove prefigures peace.

Those who look toward nature for a pattern of gentleness in good works find that pattern in the dove. God's kindness, which we are to imitate, descends upon us like a dove, the gentlest of creatures, wrote John Chrysostom: "But why in the form of a dove? The dove is a gentle and pure creature. The Spirit, too, is 'a Spirit of gentleness' [cf. Gal. 5:22]. He appears in the form of a dove, reminding us of Noah, to whom, when once a common disaster had overtaken the whole world and humanity was in danger of perishing, the dove appeared as a sign of deliverance from the tempest and, bearing an olive branch, published the good tidings of a serene presence over the whole world [cf. Gen. 8:11]. All these things were given as a type of things to come. . . . The dove appeared, not bearing an olive branch, but pointing to our Deliverer from all evils, bringing hope filled with grace. For this dove does not simply lead one family out of an ark, but the whole world toward heaven" (Chrysostom, The Gospel of Matthew 12.3; Mark 1:10).[60]

This is why Mosaic law allowed that "a pair of pigeons or of turtledoves," could be "offered for any sin. The meekness of such gentle birds and their guilelessness and forgetfulness of injury is very acceptable to God. So he is instructing us to offer a sacrifice bearing the character of that against which we have offended" (Clement of Alexandria, Christ the Educator 1.5.14; Lev. 5:7).[61]

"Why," Augustine mused, "did the Son of God appear as a man and the Holy Spirit as a dove [Matt. 3:16; Mark 1:10; Luke 3:22; John 1:32]? Because the Son of God came to show humanity a pattern for excellent living, whereas the Holy Spirit bestows the gift which enables excellent living [cf. Rom. 8:2, 10; Gal. 6:8]" (Augustine, Questions, Question 43; Mark 1:10).[62] The pattern of good works is the obedience of the Son; the gift he brings comes by the power of the Spirit.

---

59. Cetedoc 0008, 8.17; AEG 1:304*; ACCS NT 2:13.
60. NPNF 1 10:77**; cf. TLG 2062.152 ad loc.; GMI 15; ACCS NT 2:13.
61. FC 23:15; ACCS OT 3:168*.
62. Cetedoc 0250, 1.26.96; FC 70:74**; ACCS NT 2:13-14*.

## 3. Restore the Brother in a Spirit of Gentleness

Gentleness and mercy are especially needed when one is counseling, admonishing, and restoring a wayward believer. Paul pled with the Galatians to restore the fallen "in a spirit of gentleness" (Gal. 6:1b, RSV). Ambrosiaster explained, "Now Paul speaks to those who were spiritually stronger, lest by becoming proud in their own good life they should think it right to despise and reject one who had perhaps been overtaken by sin. And so they must be told that people struggling with sin are to be spurred toward reform with kindness. If they were to be more harshly punished with coercive authority they would not accept reproof. They would begin to defend themselves against seeming to be base and worse. If you protect a person from strife and arrogance he will become meek in relation to you, since humility tends to make even the proud humble" (Ambrosiaster, On Paul's Epistle to the Galatians 6.2.1-2; Gal. 6:1b).[63] While harshness elicits defensiveness, gentleness engenders trust.

"Paul does not say 'punish' or 'pass judgment' but *restore*. Nor did he even stop there, but showing that he strongly desired them to be patient with those who stumbled he adds 'in a spirit of gentleness.' He does not say 'in gentleness' but 'in a spirit of gentleness,' showing that this also is the will of the Spirit and that the capacity to correct another's faults is a spiritual gift" (Chrysostom, Homily on Galatians, 3; Gal. 6:1b).[64]

Jerome, who is among the most acerbic of all the Fathers, nonetheless urged that correction be gentle: "The Spirit-led person should correct a sinner gently and meekly. He must not be inflexible, angry or aggrieved in his desire to correct him. He should stir him up with the promise of salvation, promising remission and bringing forth the testimony of Christ" (Jerome, Epistle to the Galatians 3.6.1; Gal. 6:1b).[65] A gentle Jerome? Hear him out: "Paul wants us to be gentle, approachable people, people who have left anger, bitterness, wrath and slander behind. If we are merciful and serene, taking the initiative in reaching out to others, our very approachability will overcome the shyness and fear of those for whom we reach out" (Jerome, Epistle to the Ephesians 3.5.1; Eph. 4:32).[66]

---

63. CSEL 81.3:62; ACCS NT 8:92.
64. IOEP 4:91; ACCS NT 8:92.
65. PL 26:425B-25C [518]; ACCS NT 8:92-93.
66. PL 26:517C-17D [637-38]; ACCS NT 8:181.

"There is no surer test of the spiritual person than his treatment of another's sin," Augustine observed. "Note how he takes care to deliver the sinner rather than triumph over him, to help him rather than punish him and, so far as lies in his capacity, to support him" (Augustine, Epistle to the Galatians 56; Gal. 6:1b).[67]

This gentleness is a fruit of the spirit (Gal. 5:22). The shepherd gently leads those that are with young (Isa. 40:11). Gentleness accompanies kindness. Paul calls the Ephesians to forbear one another in love (Eph. 4:2). "Be kind to one another, tenderhearted, forgiving each other, just as God in Christ also has forgiven you" (Eph. 4:32, NAS). These three behavioral patterns are closely interwoven: kindness, tenderheartedness, and forgiveness.

The Second Letter of Peter draws together these correlations in one packed sentence that pertains to every good work: "For this very reason, make every effort to add to your faith goodness; and to goodness, knowledge; and to knowledge, self-control; and to self-control, perseverance; and to perseverance, godliness; and to godliness, brotherly kindness; and to brotherly kindness, love. For if you possess these qualities in increasing measure, they will keep you from being ineffective and unproductive in your knowledge of our Lord Jesus Christ" (2 Pet. 1:5-8a, NAS).

### 4. The Daily Practice of Kindness

An essential quality of any good work is kindness. Kindness is kindled by love (1 Cor. 13:4). Love is patient, love is kind, it does not envy, it does not boast, it is not proud, it is not rude, it is not self-seeking, it is not easily angered, it keeps no record of wrongs. Acts of kindness are without any dissimulation (Rom. 12:9).

An act of kindness pours out of an overflowing sense of grateful good will. It wishes to share goodness with the neighbor. It does not act out of any other motivation. It does not calculate its profits and losses. It simply gives, doing what it can do to help, responding promptly, becoming eyes to the blind, feet to the lame (Job 29:15).

The wisdom that is from above is pure, peaceable, gentle, easily entreated, full of mercy (Jas. 3:17). This gentleness is born of holy love. It is strongest when pure, when it expresses a singleness of will to love God, and

---

67. PL 35:214; ACCS NT 8:93.

to love the neighbor in God. Out of this singleness of will flows peace, concord, and readiness to do the good.

## E. Put Away Bitterness

Anger and bitterness stand in the way of doing what is needed. They interrupt the gentle flow of love.

The pattern in the Christian life for overcoming anger and reconciling embittered enemies is seen in the way in which Jesus himself dealt with his adversaries. The Fathers explored and defined classic Christian reflection on how to transform bitterness into constructive action.

### 1. Do Not Return Bitterness with Bitterness

It is better patiently to submit to an unjust denunciation than to allow oneself to become embittered. Tertullian, writing under conditions of persecution, wrote: "If, with slight forbearance, I hear some bitter or evil remark directed against me, I may return it, and then I shall inevitably become bitter myself. Either that, or I shall be tormented by my unexpressed resentment. If I retaliate when cursed, how shall I be found to have followed the teaching of our Lord?" (Tertullian, On Patience 8; Mark 7:15).[68] The cycle of bitterness is broken by grace.

When we have pulled out the weeds of bitterness by the roots, we are to plant seeds that are "kind, tenderhearted, forgiving" (Eph. 4:32a, NAS). "Tell me what good it is to weed a garden if we do not plant good seed?" asked John Chrysostom. "Sow good habits and dispositions. To be free from a bad habit does not mean we have formed a good one. We need to take the further step of forming good habits and dispositions to replace what we have left behind" (Chrysostom, Homily on Ephesians, 16; Eph. 4:32).[69]

"All this bitterness is not merely to be cleansed but to be 'put away' altogether. Why should anyone try to contain it or hold it in? Why keep the beast of anger around so as to have to watch it constantly? It is possible to

---

68. Cetedoc 0009, 8.5; FC 40:207*; ACCS NT 2:99.
69. IOEP 4:265; ACCS NT 8:180.

banish it, to expel it and drive it off to some mountain place" (Chrysostom, Homily on Ephesians 15; Eph. 4:31a).[70] Those who nurse little corners of anger and allow them to remain uncleansed invite them to turn sour and pollute. Christian conversion and baptism intend to clean house completely.

The faithful are called to "put away bitterness, wrath, anger, clamor and slander, and all kinds of malice" (Eph. 4:31, RSV*). Marius Victorinus distinguished these terms: "He first uses these five terms — 'bitterness, wrath, anger, clamor, blasphemy.' Then at the end he has added the summarizing phrase *'with all malice.'* *Bitterness* consists in envying and speaking ill of others and similar actions. *Wrath* consists in the lust for vengeance and punishment. *Anger* is the impulse of a mind boiling over and upheaving of what is reasonable. *Clamor* is a kind of insane, uncontrolled utterance. And *blasphemy* is wicked thought or speech that attacks God and is primarily directed against God" (Marius Victorinus, Epistle to the Ephesians 2; Eph. 4:31a).[71] The strength of malice ends as each of these are being put away.

Do not put a face of external peace on internal discord. This is self-deceptive. Repression is counter-productive. It allows the bitterness to grow silently into a monster more vicious. "Some repress anger and clamor yet still remain mischievous. Paul therefore adds that these should be entirely done away, along with all malice. Such mischief consists not only in blasphemy but in putting on a face of peace while holding on to discord within the soul" (Ambrosiaster, On Paul's Epistle to the Ephesians; Eph. 4:31b).[72]

## 2. Relieving Burdens

Inordinate zealotry "binds heavy burdens" on others (Matt. 23:4a, RSV*). The person of faith makes allowances as needed, relieves burdens, responds to contingencies.

Zealots seldom want the harsh strictures they apply to others to apply to themselves. "First they require great and extreme strictness of life, without any indulgence, from those over whom they rule. Yet they are

---

70. IOEP 4:255; ACCS NT 8:180.
71. BTMV 189 [1282]; ACCS NT 8:180*.
72. CSEL 81.3:109; ACCS NT 8:180.

much less stringent with themselves. This is opposite from what the truly good leader ought to do. He ought to be a rigorous and severe judge especially in things that concern himself. But in the matters of those whom he directs, he ought to be gentle and ready to make allowances" (Chrysostom, The Gospel of Matthew, Homily 72.2; Matt. 23:4).[73]

Be the first to lend a hand to others in difficulty. Commenting on Matthew 23:4, Origen wrote: "Some lay heavy burdens upon the shoulders of others, but won't even lift a finger to help. These are the ones the Savior is talking about when he says, 'Whoever then relaxes one of the least of these commandments and teaches men so, shall be called least in the kingdom of God' [Matt. 5:19]. There are others, however, who hold responsible offices, whose actions precede their speech, who speak wisely, and who act with restraint on those who are disordered. They place merciful burdens on the shoulders of others. They themselves are the first to lift the heavy burden, for the exhortation of other listeners" (Origen, Commentary on Matthew 9; Matt. 23:4).[74]

The only teacher worth following is one who practices what he teaches. "Now therefore why do you make trial of God by putting a yoke upon the neck of the disciples which neither our fathers nor we have been able to bear?" (Acts 15:10, RSV). "For the Pharisees and scribes did not fulfill these duties in any moderation. That is to say, they did not do so with full strength nor even with a moderate effort, in fact not even lifting a finger. Consequently, leaders who are responsible for ordering justice among their people, but who themselves do not serve moderately, are surely not just in doing so, although they may appear to be just teachers. Such are they who impose heavy burdens on those coming to repentance, who preach but do not practice" (Opus Imperfectum in Matthaeum, Homily 43; Matt. 23:4).[75]

It is in the actual face-to-face meeting with the neighbor — the next one that comes into our path — that we are given an opportunity to embody God's love. At that moment, do not ask about the neighbor's worthiness. Put away bitterness. Augustine wrote: "It is the very law of Christ that we bear one another's burdens. Moreover, by loving Christ we easily bear the weakness of another, even him whom we do not yet love for the sake of

73. PG 58:668; NPNF 1 10:436-37**; ACCS NT 1b:165*.
74. GCSO 10.2:16-17; ACCS NT 1b:165*.
75. PG 56:878; ACCS NT 1b:165*.

his own good qualities. We realize that the one whom we love is someone for whom the Lord has died" (Augustine, Questions 71; 1 Cor. 8:12).[76]

## F. Learning Empathy with the Sufferer

God's own empathy for humanity is made known on the cross. This forms the pattern for Christian empathy. Listen carefully to the Fathers, and glimpse the richness of classic Christian reflection on empathic interpersonal relations.

The ancient Christian writers were engaged in what we today would call a primitive form of empathy, congruence, and unconditional acceptance. These are conditions that many today hold to be essential to constructive behavioral change. The Fathers commended acceptance, honesty, and love long before modern psychotherapeutic practices became professionalized.

### 1. Empathy Requires Actively Reaching Out for Others

But how deeply did the Fathers grasp empathy? Jerome understood empathic engagement as becoming as if one were oneself the sufferer: "A person who nurses a sick man becomes, in a sense, sick himself, not by pretending to have a fever but by thinking inwardly how he would like to be treated if he were sick himself" (Jerome, Letter 75 [From Jerome to Augustine]; 1 Cor. 9:20).[77] In an act of empathy, I enter voluntarily into the arena of the other's suffering. Empathy is a way of thinking *into* another's inward frame of reference, as if I were there myself. I ask how I would like to be understood and treated if I were there in that place. I put myself in another's place. The substitutionary understanding of atonement on the cross is the prototype.

I come into the other's consciousness not only as an act of imagination, but of participation. I am actually "being there" with the other, as deeply as possible. This act occurs "by compassion, not by dissimulation. For each one becomes like him whom he wants to help when such great

76. FC 70:184; ACCS NT 7:79*.
77. FC 12:354; ACCS NT 7:86*.

mercy prevails *as that which each one would wish for himself if he were in the same misery.* And so he becomes like the other — not by deceiving him but by putting himself in the other's place" (Augustine, Against Lying 12, italics added; 1 Cor. 9:20).[78]

This is arguably a more radical grasp of empathy (as participation) than are many modern views of empathy (as understanding). To seek to understand another's feelings is not as deep as to truly enter into the suffering of the other. The hard edges of lonely suffering are softened when this takes place. "It is always a great comfort, when we are suffering, to have someone near us who can share it with us" (Ambrosiaster, On Paul's Epistles to the Corinthians; 2 Cor. 7:6).[79]

Your first-hand experience of how you have suffered is the premise upon which you by analogy may choose to enter into the sphere of another's suffering. "Therefore do not say, 'The fellow is a smith, a cobbler, a farmer; he is stupid,' so that you despise him. If you suffer in some similar way, see in how many ways the Lord urges you to be moderate and enjoins you to care for these little ones" (Chrysostom, The Gospel of Matthew, Homily 59.4; Matt. 18:13).[80] The premise of empathy underlies the golden rule: Do to others as you would have them do to you. No such doing can take place without grasping what you would have them do to you under similar circumstance.

### 2. God's Empathy with Human Suffering

Reaching out for others in their suffering entails taking the inward risk of becoming aware of the neighbor's actual hurt. This means voluntarily putting oneself in touch with another's vulnerability, however painful. It requires an entry into the internal world of others who are different from ourselves. This is what God has done in the incarnation.

The incarnation is the astonishing pattern of empathy in the Bible. In reflection on Paul's phrase, "becoming all to all," Cyril of Jerusalem grasped that it is the Savior himself who "everywhere becomes 'all things to all men.' To the hungry, bread; to the thirsty, water; to the dead, resur-

---

78. FC 16:159*; ACCS NT 7:86*.
79. CSEL 81:251; ACCS NT 7:265.
80. PG 58:579; NPNF 1 10:368; ACCS NT 1b:74-75*.

rection; to the sick, a physician; to sinners, redemption" (Cyril of Jerusalem, Sermon on the Paralytic 10; 1 Cor. 9:22b).[81]

The incarnate Lord freely took upon himself our alienated human condition: "He who did not think it robbery to be equal with God took the nature of a slave. He became all things to all men to bring salvation to all. Paul, an imitator of him, lived as if freed from the law while remaining accountable to the law. He spent his life for the advantage of those he wished to win. He willingly became weak for the weak in order to strengthen them. He ran the race to overtake them" (Ambrose, Letters to Priests 54, "To Simplicianus"; 1 Cor. 9:22b).[82]

We grieve the Holy Spirit when we ignore the needs of the suffering neighbor. Ambrosiaster wrote: "The Holy Spirit rejoices in our salvation not for himself, since he has no lack of blessedness. But if we have disobeyed the Spirit, we have grieved the Spirit. His work in us is cut short, just when he wishes us to belong to life" (Ambrosiaster, On Paul's Epistle to the Ephesians; Eph. 4:30a).[83]


## 3. Crying Out to God from the Heart

God empathizes with our bleeding. "God knows how to hear even the blood of a just man, to which no tongue is attached and of which no voice pierces the air. The presence of good works is a loud voice before God" (Basil the Great, Exegetic Homilies 22; Exod. 14:15).[84] It does not require a literal tongue to be heard by God from these inward depths. Our works speak volumes even when we are inarticulate.

God has no problem understanding our inward motivations. God hears the cry of the human heart, according to Jerome: "The word 'cry' in Scripture does not refer to the cry of the voice but to the cry of the heart. In fact, the Lord says to Moses, 'Why are you crying out to me?' when Moses had not muttered any cry at all" (Jerome, Homilies on the Psalms 2; Exod. 14:15).[85] The speech of the heart is the subject of empathy, God's empathy toward us, and our empathy toward our fellow human being.

81. FC 64:215; ACCS NT 7:86-87*.
82. FC 26:295*; ACCS NT 7:87*.
83. CSEL 81.3:108; ACCS NT 8:179.
84. FC 46:353; ACCS OT 3:73.
85. FC 48:16; ACCS OT 3:73.

So do not hesitate to speak from the heart to God: "The heart reveals its silent longing, to which the triune God listens more than to the most thundering voices of nations" (Cassiodorus, Exposition of the Psalms 26.8; Exod. 14:15).[86]

### 4. Do Not Close Your Heart

Those who coldly turn away from the neighbor in need are compared to those who have a burned-out moral sense, or a "conscience seared." Theodoret of Cyr wrote: "'Conscience seared' refers to its absolute numbing, the deadening of the conscience" (Theodoret, Interpretation of the First Letter to Timothy; 1 Tim. 4:2).[87] Theodore of Mopsuestia explained: "'Having their consciences seared' means not having a whole conscience, for they live the opposite of what they themselves teach," and know to be right (Theodore of Mopsuestia, Commentary on 1 Timothy; 1 Tim. 4:2).[88]

People are responsible for their own callousness, says Chrysostom: "If the cause of their licentiousness is ignorance, why reproach them? Why not just inform them? For the one who is ignorant should not be punished or reproached but taught what he does not know. But how quickly Paul takes away from them this easy excuse: 'They have become callous and given themselves up to licentiousness, greedy to practice every kind of uncleanness'. . . . He shows here that the cause of their hardening was their own voluntary way of life. Their way of life arose freely out of their own laxity and lack of remorse" (Chrysostom, Homily on Ephesians 13; Eph. 4:19).[89] In turning incrementally away from the neighbor's need, step by step, we are making a choice to harden our hearts. The imperative: at each step do not close your heart to the other's need (1 John 3:17). "When you see someone in need, do not run away," wrote Chrysostom, "but think to yourself, if that were you, would you want to be treated like that?" (Chrysostom, quoted in Cramer, Catena in Epistolas Catholicas; 1 John 3:17).[90]

Admitting that you cannot exhaustively change the very conditions of limitation under which your neighbor lives — at least do something,

86. ACWCa 1:267; ACCS OT 3:73*.
87. PG 82:811; ACCS NT 9:183.
88. TEM 2:141; ACCS NT 9:183*.
89. IOEP 4:235; ACCS NT 8:171*.
90. CEC 128; ACCS NT 11:203.

says Augustine: "If you are not yet able to die for your brother, at least show him your ability to give him of your goods. Let love be stirring your inmost heart to do it, not for display but out of the very marrow of compassion, thinking only of the brother and his need" (Augustine, Ten Homilies on 1 John, 5.12; 1 John 3:17).[91]

## 5. Jesus' Identification with Outsiders

As an act of empathy, Jesus freely came into the houses of sinners. To make clear his identification with the tax collector, the prostitute, the alienated, the marginalized, and the rejected, Jesus welcomed all these to his table. "As he sat at table in the house, behold, many tax collectors and sinners came and sat down with Jesus and his disciples" (Matt. 9:10, RSV).

John Chrysostom described this scene:

What a gathering of ignoble characters! Matthew, rejoicing in the coming of Messiah, had called together all his tax-collector cronies. Here we see Christ employing every sort of remedy for the human malaise. He not only is found making discourses, healing, and chiding his opponents in argument, but also sitting with sinners at table. He is often portrayed as being right in the middle of such situations among people who were in a bad way. In this way he is teaching us that every season serves its own opportunity and every situation offers some possibility of benefit. And yet it is clear that these were a bunch of rascals set before him, who had been long swallowed up in injustice and covetousness. But Christ did not refuse to sit with them or eat with them because the potential opportunity for change was so great. Instead he chose to become partaker at the same table and under the same roof with those who had committed such offenses. For such is the task of the physician: If he does not enter into the arena of sickness, he does not free them from sickness. (Chrysostom, The Gospel of Matthew, Homily 30.2; Matt. 9:12) [92]

Jesus' daily ministry invited both conviviality and personal encounter. When Jesus "sat at table" he had in mind "more than tax collecting,"

91. LCC 8:301*; ACCS NT 11:203.
92. PG 57:363-64; NPNF 1 10:199-200*; ACCS NT 1a:177**.

according to Peter Chrysologus. "He took sustenance not on food but on the return of the sinner, that he might bring back through dining, conviviality, fellow-feeling and pleasant conversation those whom he knew could be overwhelmed if necessary by the power of the Judge, smitten by dread of his majesty, and swept over by the sheer presence of God" (Peter Chrysologus, Sermons, 29:4; Matt. 9:10).[93] It was empathy rather than coercive power moves that characterized Jesus' way of communicating.

The incarnation forms the basis of Christian empathy, as Chrysologus understood: "He who wanted to be on a familiar basis with men comes incognito in a human body. He who wanted to assist the guilty hides the Judge in himself. He who did not turn a deaf ear to servants conceals his omniscience. He who desired the weakest to be surrounded by parental love covers his majesty in mercy" (Peter Chrysologus, Sermons, 29:4; Matt. 9:10).[94] The temporary obscuration of the divine omnipotence in the incarnation is a constant theme of the Gospel narratives, and a moving expression of divine empathy.

When his disciples were asked *why* — "Why does your teacher eat with tax collectors and sinners?" (Matt. 9:11b, RSV), he answered that he had come to "give aid to the sick and medicine to those in need. For those who believed they were healthy, however, no cure was necessary," wrote Hilary. "Why does he say that he did not come for the righteous? He said that to show that if righteousness came from the law, forgiveness through grace would not be necessary" (Hilary of Poitiers, On Matthew 9.2; Matt. 9:11).[95]

## 6. His Sweat

No single episode of his history signified more deeply the engagement of the incarnate Lord in human suffering than his bloody sweat as he faced death for others (Luke 22:44-46). This was considered by the Fathers to be a physical indicator of the depths of his emotive engagement and compassion. The poetic mind of Ephrem the Syrian treated this passage typologically: "He sweated to heal Adam who was sick. 'It is by the sweat of your brow,' said God, 'that you will eat your bread' [Gen. 3:19]. He remained in prayer in this

---

93. CCL 24:171; ACCS NT 1a:178**.
94. CCL 24:171; ACCS NT 1a:178**.
95. SCH 1:204-6; ACCS NT 1a:178**.

garden to bring Adam back into his own garden again" (Ephrem the Syrian, Commentary on Tatian's Diatessaron 20.11; Luke 22:44-46).[96]

Justin Martyr, who willingly offered up his own life as a witness to truth, wrote: "In the recollection of the apostles and their successors, it is written that his perspiration poured out like drops of blood as he prayed and said, 'If it is possible, let this cup pass from me.' His bones were evidently quaking, and his heart was like wax melting in his belly. We therefore may understand that the Father wanted his Son to endure in reality these severe sufferings for us. Do not conclude from this that just because he was the Son of God he did not experience in any way the pain that was inflicted upon him in his humanity. The words 'my strength is dried up like a potsherd, and my tongue cleaves to my jaws' [Ps. 22:15] prophesied that he would remain silent through all this" (Justin Martyr, Dialogue with Trypho 103; Luke 22:44-46).[97] No one accompanied him in his struggle in the Garden.

Hippolytus viewed the sweat of Jesus as the surest signature of his true humanity. "Although he was God clearly revealed, he did not set aside what was human about himself. He is hungry and exhausted, weary and thirsty. He fears and flees. He is troubled when he prays. He sleeps on a pillow, yet as God he has a nature that never sleeps. He asks to be excused the suffering of the cup, yet he was present in the world for this very reason. In his agony, he sweats and an angel strengthens him, yet he strengthens those who believe in him" (Hippolytus, Against Noetus 18; Luke 22:44-46).[98]

### 7. His Death Shows the Full Extent of His Empathic Compassion for Sinners

The full range of his empathic participation in our human condition is not adequately grasped until his death. He was willing to become a curse for all. Cyril of Alexandria juxtaposes a devastating series of analogies:

He was 'numbered among the transgressors.'
For our sakes, he became a curse, accursed for us.
It is written again, 'cursed is every one that hangs on a tree.'

---

96. ECTD 297*; ACCS NT 3:344.
97. FC 6:310*; ACCS NT 3:344*.
98. ANF 5:230**; ACCS NT 3:343-44*.

His act did away with the curse that was on us.
We are *blessed* with him and because of him.
Knowing this, blessed David says,
"Blessed are we of the Lord, who made heaven and earth."
Blessings descend to us by his sufferings.
He *paid our debts* in our place.
He *bore our iniquities.*
He was *stricken* in our place, as it is written.
He *took our sins in his own body* on the tree.
*His bruises heal us.*
He also was *sick* because of our sins
That we might be *delivered from the sicknesses of our souls.*

(Cyril of Alexandria, Commentary on Luke,
Homily 153, italics and spacing added; Luke 23:33;
cf. Isa. 53:12; Deut. 21:23; Ps. 113:23 [LXX];
Isa. 53:6; 1 Pet. 2:24; Isa. 53:5)[99]

Each of these phrases is compounded, one upon the other, to demonstrate the extent to which God is willing to go to share in human suffering. In sum, according to Chrysostom: "God allowed his Son to suffer as a condemned sinner that we might be delivered from the penalty of our sins. . . . This is God's righteousness. So we are not justified by works — for then we would have to be perfect, which is impossible — but by grace, in which case all our sin is removed" (Chrysostom, Homilies on the Epistles of Paul to the Corinthians II.11.5; 2 Cor. 5:21).[100] God's righteousness is revealed in his suffering for us.

### 8. God Made Him to Be Sin for Us

Paul set forth the extent of Jesus' identification with the sufferer in this astonishing passage: "God made him who had no sin to be sin for us, so that in him we might become the righteousness of God" (2 Cor. 5:21, NIV).

The Fathers were intrigued by the deep ironies embedded in this passage. Ambrosiaster examined it layer by layer. Walk carefully with him

99. CGSL 609**; ACCS NT 3:360*.
100. NPNF 1:12:334*; ACCS NT 7:252*.

through this argument: "Christ did not have to be born as a man, but he freely became man because of man's sin. It was only because all flesh was subject to sin that he was made sin for us. In view of the fact that he was made an offering for sins, it is not wrong for him to be said to have been made 'sin,' because in the law the sacrifice that was offered for sins used to be called a 'sin.' After his death on the cross Christ descended to hell, because it was death, working through sin, which gave hell its power. Christ defeated death by his death, and brought such benefit to sinners that now death cannot hold those who are marked with the sign of the cross" (Ambrosiaster, On Paul's Epistles to the Corinthians; 2 Cor. 5:21).[101] He freely became sin for us in that he became an offering for sin, and by this defeated death, which gave hell its power. This power is defeated on the cross.

Theodoret of Cyr summarized: "Christ became what we are in order to call us to be what he is" (Theodoret, Commentary on the Second Epistle to the Corinthians, 318; 2 Cor. 5:21).[102] This is the event of revelation that most clearly forms the basis for our rejoicing with those who rejoice and weeping with those who weep (Rom. 12:15) — God's own incomparable empathy for human beings in their passions and struggles.

Just as he was born in a borrowed stable, Jesus was buried in a borrowed tomb. Maximus of Turin thought this detail significant: "Let us see why they placed the Savior in someone else's grave instead of his own. They placed him in another person's grave because he died *for* the salvation of others. They did not impose death on him. He endured death for us. Death did not just happen to him. It also benefited us. Why should he, who did not have his own death in himself, have his own grave? Why should he, whose dwelling remained in heaven, have a burial place on earth? Why should he have a grave? . . . He gives life to our death, that we may rise with him from the dead" (Maximus of Turin, Sermon 39.3, italics added; Luke 23:50-56).[103]

## 9. Summing Up the Nurturing Motif

What is the pattern in the Christian life for good works toward those least able to fend for themselves? It is the way in which Jesus himself identified

---

101. CSEL 81:238; ACCS NT 7:251-52*.
102. PG 82:411; ACCS NT 7:252*.
103. ACWM 95**; ACCS NT 3:371-72.

with the least. He himself as incarnate Lord voluntarily became a little child, powerless, dependent, obedient to his parents and to law, suffering, hungering, sweating, thirsting, facing human limitations, even unto death. The incarnate Lord came into the world as "the least of these," as a child, born in poverty, hunted, persecuted, displaced, homeless. The crucified Lord thoroughly understood our human infirmities.

Christian love reaches out in this way for the smallest, the least, the lowliest of persons, those least able to protect themselves. The little ones need what any infant needs: nurture, love, feeding, protection. This nurture and protection is a persistent theme of good works. Those who miss these gifts find themselves stunted, cut off. If such bad decisions are made in a child's early development, they are very hard to correct.

We have been asking how the ancient church understood their ministries to the least of these. The answers we have found not only in their letters, poetry, hymnody, and homilies, but also in their detailed reflections on scripture texts regarding children, guilelessness, growth, and empathy.

Our central motif in this Part has been *nurture,* and the gentle virtues required for its growth. Good works, acts of mercy, seek to provide conditions of growth, especially for those in early stages of their growing. Parents play the central role in guiding these little ones, enabling the conditions of their growth, defending them from harm.

The body of Christ looks out for the least of these. The good news speaks of God's attentiveness to the lost sheep, the broken life, the woman of Samaria, the least respected, the leper, the prostitute, the importunate widow. On a very personal one-on-one scale, Christianity reaches out one by one toward the whole world — all classes, all races, all generations, all societies, all languages. The outreach of Christian love extends to the lowliest, the least, the invisible, the neglected, and above all for the unborn child. All are human creatures less able to speak for themselves. In final judgment we at long last become aware that these small acts of kindness done to the lowliest and the least are done to Christ himself.

It is within the range of every believer to practice these simple good works: shepherding the flock, nurturing the littlest, finding the lost, going to the lowly. This does not require special education or abilities. It requires a good will, however, transformed by grace, rightly to do these good works in a way that glorifies God.

## PART SIX

# PHILANTHROPY

## A. The Difficulty of Being Rich

In merely having wealth one tends to love it inordinately, according to Augustine: "Such, O my soul, are the miseries that attend on riches. They are *gained* with toil and *kept* with fear. They are *enjoyed* with danger and *lost* with grief. It is hard to be saved if we have them; and impossible if we love them; and scarcely can we have them, but we shall love them inordinately. Teach us, O Lord, this difficult lesson: to manage conscientiously the goods we possess, and not covetously desire more than you give to us" (Augustine, Sermon 133, italics added; Mark 10:23).[1]

### 1. *The Problem Is Not Riches but Their Deceitfulness*

Early Christianity did not unambiguously condemn wealth as such. Rather more subtly, it pointed out that possessions may tend to corrupt in ways not worthy of our created nature.

Our luxuries themselves may become as thorns to us. Riches may choke the hearing of the Word, as John Chrysostom well knew. He had spent years in voluntary desert poverty, then to be called to deal with the most wealthy and powerful audience in the Roman Empire — the emperor, the court, and men of affairs at Constantinople. He argued: "When

---

1. GMI 247-48; ACCS NT 2:145.

the Word is choked, it is not merely due to the thorns as such, but to the negligence of those allowing them to spring up. There is a way, if there is a will, to hinder evil growth and use wealth appropriately. For this reason he warned not of 'the world' but of the 'care of the world'; not 'riches' as such but 'the deceitfulness of riches.' Let us not place the blame on what we possess, but on our own corrupt mind. For it is possible to be rich and not be deceived. It is possible to be in this world, and not be choked with its cares" (Chrysostom, The Gospel of Matthew, Homily 44.6; Mark 4:18).[2] Riches are deceitful not in themselves, but in how they promise more than they deliver. We are responsible for falling for these deceits, because they reside in our own inordinate loves.

We seldom stop to think of the moral disadvantages of luxury. In appearing to be friendly, wealth may become the enemy of our happiness. It brings two disadvantages: "Two contrary disadvantages accompany riches: First, our anxiety over them. They tend to wear us out, spreading darkness over us. The second is luxury, which makes us soft." Chrysostom continues: "Do not marvel at his calling our luxuries 'thorns.' One is in sound health which knows that luxury pricks sharper than any thorn. Luxury wastes the soul away even worse than anxiety. It causes more grievous pains both to body and soul." Why? "It brings on premature old age, dulls the senses, darkens our reasoning, blinds the keen-sighted mind, and makes the body flabby" (Chrysostom, The Gospel of Matthew, Homily 44.6-7; Mark 4:18).[3] Both anxiety and softness are enemies of happiness.

The currency of the moral economy is easily debased. Augustine argued: "A thing becomes defiled if it is mixed with a baser substance, even though that other substance is not vile in its own nature. Gold, for example, is debased by pure silver if mixed with it. So also is our mind defiled by a desire for the things of earth, although the earth itself is pure in its own class and in its own order. . . . We ought to fix our treasure and our heart on that which will abide forever and not on something which will pass away" (Augustine, Sermon on the Mount 2.13.44; Matt. 6:19 and 6:20).[4] The focus of Christian criticism is not upon the substance of wealth itself, but our relation to it, and whether we are valuing it in a fitting and proportional way.

The faithful are taught by the Fathers to recognize the subtle tempta-

---

2. NPNF 1 10:282; TLG 2062.152, 57.470.18-27; ACCS NT 2:57.
3. NPNF 1 10:282-83; ACCS NT 2:57*.
4. PL 34:1289; FC 11:152-53; ACCS NT 1a:141-42.

tions of wealth. In commenting on Esau's loss of his birthright, John Chrysostom observed:

> Never neglect the gifts from God. Never forfeit important things for worthless trifles. Why, tell me, should we be obsessed with a desire for money, when the kingdom of heaven and those ineffable blessings are within our grasp? Why prefer blessings that endure forever to those that are passing and scarcely last until evening? What could be worse than the folly of being deprived of the former through lust after the latter and never being able to enjoy their eternal blessing in a pure fashion? What good, after all, tell me, is such wealth? Are you not aware that acquisition of great wealth brings us nothing else than an increase in worry, anxiety, and sleeplessness? Do you not see that these people, in particular those possessing great wealth, are, so to say, everyone's slaves and day in day out are in fear even of shadows? This, you see, is the source of plotting, envy, deep hatred, and countless other evils. Often you would see the person with ten thousand talents of gold hidden away. He will call blessed the man behind the shop counter who prepares his own meals by hand. (Chrysostom, Homilies on Genesis 50.7; Gen. 25:34) [5]

The greater the wealth the greater the anxiety over losing wealth.

## 2. Excessive Luxury Makes One Dead While Still Alive

The acceleration of the compulsive desire for ever more pleasure is itself a kind of death — of consciousness and accountability. Adapting a metaphor from Plato, Jerome cautioned: "It is an idle pretense which some put forward that they can take their fill of pleasure with their faith and purity and mental uprightness unimpaired. . . . The bodily senses are like horses madly racing, but the soul like a charioteer holds the reins. And as the horses without a driver go at breakneck speed, so the body, if it be not governed by the reasonable soul, rushes to its own destruction" (Jerome, Against Jovinian 2.9-10; 1 Tim. 5:6).[6] Train your horses to go where you rationally would have them go.

5. FC 87:53**; ACCS OT 2:152*.
6. NPNF 2 6:395**; ACCS NT 9:198.

John Chrysostom warned of the special temptations and consequences of excessive luxury. "To live in luxury does not seem in itself to be a manifest and admitted crime. But then it brings forth in us great evils — drunkenness, violence, extortion and plunder. The prodigal who lives sumptuously, who bestows extravagant service on the belly, is often compelled to steal, and to seize the property of others and to use extortion and violence. If, then, you avoid luxurious living, you remove the foundation of extortion, and plunder, and drunkenness, and a thousand other evils, cutting away the root of iniquity from its extremity" (Chrysostom, Homilies Concerning the Statues 15.4; 1 Tim. 5:6).[7] To reform avarice is to save a person from many other forms of suffering.

Paul portrayed the self-indulgent as "dead even while still alive" (1 Tim. 5:6, RSV). "Such persons seize the property of another, are filled even to the point of vomiting with many delicacies, bury themselves in excessive drinking and store up for heaven little or nothing by way of charitable giving. Of these the apostle says they are 'dead while still living'" (Caesarius of Arles, Sermons 151.8; 1 Tim. 5:6).[8]

### 3. The Difficulty of the Rich Entering the Kingdom

Special grace is needed for the conversion and sanctification of the rich (Mark 10:23). John Chrysostom explained why it is not money as such, but the thorny and tempting relation to money that is potentially dangerous to the soul.

> What then did Christ say? "How difficult it will be for the rich to enter the kingdom of heaven." He was not criticizing money itself but the wills of those who are taken captive by it. If it will be difficult for the rich, how much more so for the avaricious! For if stinginess with one's own wealth is an impediment to gaining the kingdom, think how much fire is amassed for taking someone else's. But why does he say that it is hard for the rich man to enter the kingdom, to the disciples, who were poor and had nothing? He teaches them not to be ashamed of their poverty and, as it were, gives the reason why he did not allow them to possess anything.

7. NPNF 1 9:442; ACCS NT 9:198.
8. FC 47:332; ACCS NT 9:199*.

After saying it is hard, he also shows them that it is unachievable, and not simply unachievable but even in an exaggerated way impossible.[9] He shows this from the comparison of the camel and the needle: "It is easier for a camel to pass through the eye of a needle than for a rich man to enter the kingdom of heaven." Hence Christ demonstrates that there is a significant reward for the wealthy who can practice self-denial. He also said that this had to be the work of God, that he might show that great grace is needed for anyone who is going to receive it. (Chrysostom, The Gospel of Matthew, Homily 63.2; Matt. 19:25)[10]

Jerome added: "The Lord and Savior did not say that the rich would not enter the kingdom of heaven but that they will enter with difficulty" (Jerome, Homilies on the Psalms 16 [On Psalm 83 (84 LXX)]; Luke 19:2-4).[11]

### 4. Riches Are Not Evil as Such, but a Temptation to Evil

Wealth as such does not condemn, according to Caesarius of Arles: "Riches cannot *harm* a good person, because he spends them kindly. Likewise they cannot *help* an evil person as long as he possesses them avariciously or wastes them in dissipation" (Caesarius of Arles, Sermons 35.4, italics added; Jas. 5:2).[12]

The kingdom is hard to enter because the hearts of the rich are distracted elsewhere, according to Jerome. "This is why those who are rich find it hard to enter the kingdom of heaven [cf. Matt. 19:24; Mark 10:25; Luke 18:25]. For it is a kingdom that desires for its citizens a soul that soars aloft free from all ties and hindrances. 'Go your way,' the Lord said, 'and sell' not a part of your substance but 'all that you have, and give to the poor' [Matt. 19:21]; not to your friends or kinsfolk or relatives, nor to your wife or to your children." Spraying outrageous metaphors all about like buckshot, he adds: "When once you have put your hand to the plough you must not look back [Luke 9:62]. When once you stand on the housetop, you must think no more of your clothes within. To escape your Egyptian

---

9. Lacking special grace.
10. PG 58:605; NPNF 1 10:388-89; ACCS NT 1b:102*.
11. FC 48:119*; ACCS NT 3:290.
12. FC 31:175; ACCS NT 11:54*.

mistress [Gen. 39:12] you must abandon the cloak that belongs to this world. Even Elijah, in his quick translation to heaven could not take his mantle with him, but left in the world the garments of the world [2 Kings 2:11, 13]" (Jerome, Letters 118, To Julian; Mark 10:21a).[13] Jerome is pressing the edges of rhetorical exuberance to show how the whole range of canonical scripture flows together in illumining this single passage.

Seek a balance, advised Clement. Learn how to use possessions proportionally. Jesus sought to "teach the prosperous that they are not to neglect their own salvation, as if they had been already foredoomed, nor, on the other hand, to cast wealth into the sea, or condemn it as a traitor and an enemy to life, but learn in what way and how to use wealth and obtain life" (Clement of Alexandria, The Salvation of the Rich Man 26; Mark 10:23).[14]

## 5. The Rich Not Excluded from God's Mercy

Despite temptations it is still possible for the rich person to be a person of faith. Abraham was.

> The Savior by no means has excluded the rich on account of wealth itself, and the possession of property, nor fenced off salvation against them, if they are able and willing to submit their life to God's commandments, and prefer them to transitory things. Let them look to the Lord with steady eye, as those who look toward the slightest nod of a good helmsman, what he wishes, what he orders, what he indicates, what signal he gives his mariners, where and when he directs the ship's course. . . . *If* one is able in the midst of wealth to turn from its mystique, to entertain moderate desires, to exercise self-control, to seek God alone, and to breathe God and walk with God, such a man submits to the commandments, being free, unconquered, free of disease, unwounded by wealth. *But if not,* "sooner shall a camel enter through a needle's eye, than such a rich man reach the kingdom of God" [Mark 10:25; Luke 18:25]. (Clement of Alexandria, The Salvation of the Rich Man 26, italics added; Mark 10:25) [15]

13. Cetedoc 0620, 118.55.4.439.18; NPNF 2 6:222*; ACCS NT 2:142.
14. ANF 2:599*; TLG 0555.006, 26.6.4; ACCS NT 2:145.
15. ANF 2:598-99*; TLG 0555.006, 26.1.3-5; ACCS NT 2:145-46.

"There is no crime in possessions, but there is crime in those who do not know how to use possessions. For the foolish, wealth is a temptation to vice, but for the wise, it is a help to virtue" (Maximus of Turin, Sermons 95-96; Luke 19:5-8).[16]

## 6. The Transformation of Zacchaeus

Zacchaeus provides the biblical prototype of the conversion of the will in relation to wealth. He was not only rich, but filthy rich, and out of the worst of motives. "Zacchaeus was leader of the tax collectors, a man entirely abandoned to greed, whose only goal was the increase of his gains, a practice of tax collectors," wrote Cyril. Yet this very Zacchaeus "was counted worthy of mercy from Christ, who calls near those who are far away and gives light to those who are in darkness" (Cyril of Alexandria, Commentary on Luke, Homily 127; Luke 19:2-4).[17] Jesus took note of Zacchaeus in the sycamore tree.

From Zacchaeus we learn that the rich can be saved, but only by repentance that seeks serious restitution. "Come and let us see what was the method of Zacchaeus's conversion. He desired to see Jesus and therefore climbed into a sycamore tree, and so a seed of salvation sprouted within him. Christ saw this with the eyes of deity. Looking up, he also saw Zacchaeus with the eyes of humanity, and since it was his purpose for all to be saved, he extends his gentleness to him. To encourage him, he says, 'Come down quickly.' Zacchaeus searched to see Christ, but the multitude prevented him. What stood in the way was less the people than his own sins. He was short of stature, not merely from a bodily point of view but also spiritually. He could not see him unless he were raised up from the earth and climbed into the sycamore, by which Christ was about to pass" (Cyril of Alexandria, Commentary on Luke, Homily 127; Luke 19:2-4).[18] A short man with a large purse, he was seeking a glimpse of the anointed One.

In his conversion, Zacchaeus learned to value what is of greater value, his salvation, by making restitution for what is of lesser value, his ill-gotten gains. A change took place in his heart, from repentance to repara-

---

16. ACWM 219-20**; ACCS NT 3:291.
17. CGSL 505**; ACCS NT 3:289-90*.
18. CGSL 505-6**; ACCS NT 3:290*.

tion. Augustine observed: "The Lord, who had already welcomed Zacchaeus in his heart, was now ready to be welcomed by him in his house. He said, 'Zacchaeus, hurry up and come down, since I have to stay in your house.' He thought it was a marvelous piece of good luck to see Christ. While imagining it was a marvelous piece of luck quite beyond words to see him passing by, he was suddenly found worthy to have him in his house. Grace is poured out, and faith starts working through love. Zacchaeus says to Christ, 'Lord, half my goods I give to the poor, and if I have cheated anyone of anything, I am paying back four times over.' . . . There you are. That is really what welcoming Jesus means, welcoming him into your heart. Christ was already there. He was in Zacchaeus and spoke through him. The apostle says that this is what it means, 'For Christ to dwell in your hearts by faith' [Eph. 3:17]" (Augustine, Sermon 174.5; Luke 19:5-8).[19] Christ, who was already dwelling in his heart, is welcomed into his house.

Even though the wealthy are doubly reluctant to look foolish, Zacchaeus "climbed a sycamore tree, a tree of 'silly fruit,'" to teach us not to be afraid to do something foolish to glimpse Jesus. "The wise people of this world laugh at us about the cross of Christ and say, 'What sort of minds do you people have, who worship a crucified God?' What sort of minds do we have? They are certainly not your kind of mind. 'The wisdom of this world is folly with God' [1 Cor. 3:19]. No, we do not have your kind of mind. You call our minds foolish. Say what you like, but for our part, let us climb the sycamore tree and see Jesus. The reason you cannot see Jesus is that you are ashamed to climb the sycamore tree" (Augustine, Sermon 174.3; Luke 19:2-4).[20]

A ready and willing act of reparation showed the seriousness of his repentance, according to Ephrem the Syrian: "Seeing he knew his thoughts, Zacchaeus said, 'Just as he knows this, he knows also all that I have done.' He therefore said, 'All that I have unjustly received, I give back fourfold.' Jesus says to you: Hurry and come down from your fig tree. It is with you that I will be staying. The first fig tree of Adam will be forgotten, because of the last fig tree of the chief tax collector" (Ephrem the Syrian, Commentary on Tatian's Diatessaron 20; Luke 19:5-8).[21]

---

19. WSA 3 5:260-61**; ACCS NT 3:291.
20. WSA 3 5:259**; ACCS NT 3:290.
21. ECTD 240-41*; ACCS NT 3:291*.

Those who gladly receive new life are grateful to restore anything they may have unfairly taken from others in their old life. Ambrosiaster developed this theme: "Paul exhorts them not to return to their past vices and sins. He wants them to behave as new persons. What good is it to be called new if our evil deeds prove us to be still gripped by our old nature? The Christian is commanded not merely to avoid stealing but more so to care actively for the poor through his own hard work. Hence by commitment to good works he may restore what he formerly stole. We are not to be praised for refusing to steal. What makes one praiseworthy is to give of one's own resources to the needy" (Ambrosiaster, On Paul's Epistle to the Ephesians; Eph. 4:28c).[22]

## 7. Becoming Rich toward God

Let the person, whether rich or poor, become rich toward God through the love of virtue, wrote Cyril of Alexandria: "It is true that a person's life is not from one's possessions or because of having an overabundance. He who is rich toward God is very blessed and has glorious hope. Who is he? Evidently, one who does not love wealth but rather loves virtue, and to whom a few things are quite sufficient. It is one whose hand is open to the needs of the poor, comforting the sorrows of those in poverty according to his means and the utmost of his power. He gathers in the storehouses that are above and lays up treasures in heaven. Such a one shall find the interest of his virtue and the reward of his right and blameless life" (Cyril of Alexandria, Commentary on Luke, Homily 89; Luke 12:21).[23]

Virtue does not hinge on temporal gain. Ambrose wrote:

Although there are many charms of delights in riches, yet there are more profound incentives to practice virtue. Virtue does not require temporal assistance. Indeed the contribution of the poor person is more commended in scripture than the generosity of the rich. Yet with the authority of heavenly vision, Jesus condemned not those who have riches but those who do not know how to use them. The pauper is more praiseworthy who gives with eager compassion. He is not even

22. CSEL 81 3:107; ACCS NT 8:178*.
23. CGSL 362**; ACCS NT 3:208*.

intimidated by the prospect of looming scarcity. He thinks that he who has enough for natural survival does not lack. So the rich person is the more guilty who does not give thanks to God for what he has received, but vainly hides wealth given for the common use and conceals it in buried treasures [Matt. 25:18]. Then the offense consists not in the wealth but in the attitude. (Ambrose, Exposition of the Gospel of Luke 5.69; Luke 6:20-26)[24]

Wealth as such is not condemned, but failure to know how to use wealth for the common good.

Those who have conquered the vice of avarice have virtue as their own reward. "How happy is the man who has been able to cut out the root of vices, avarice. Surely he will not dread the recovery of balance. Avarice generally dulls men's senses and corrupts their judgments, so that they think of piety in terms of some worldly gain, and money as a reward for sagacity" (Ambrose, Letters 15; 1 Tim. 6:10).[25]

## B. The Stewardship of Wealth

In the parable of the talents, the Lord takes the original investment away from the non-productive and gives it to the productive one: "Take the bag of gold from him and give it to the one who has ten bags" (Matt. 25:28, New Century). To those who receive the grace to possess goods responsibly, more grace shall be given. But for those who make no good use of resources, even that which they have will be taken away (Matt. 25:29).

### 1. The Calling of the Affluent to Good Works

Among Old Testament prototypes of those who remained faithful even amid their affluence were Abraham, Joseph, and Job. Among New Testament prototypes of the faithful rich are, in addition to Zacchaeus, Matthew, Joseph of Arimathea, and Barnabas.

24. EHG 171-72**; ACCS NT 3:105*.
25. FC 26:83; ACCS NT 9:214-15*.

The patristic writers turned a searchlight on the moral use of property and the special vocation of those with abundant resources.

Whatever earthly treasures one may have, they are a trust from God and not to be left idle. "You know that many high-standing people renege on repayment of a loan," wrote John Chrysostom. Why wouldn't it be better to make temporal resources available to the needy now? For "in the future, what excuse will we have if we are negligent and fail to gain a hundredfold in place of the little we have, the future in place of the present, the eternal in place of the temporary? What excuse will we have if we heedlessly lock our money behind doors and barricades, and prefer to leave it lying idle? Instead, we should make it available to the needy now, so that in the future we may count on their affirmation" (Chrysostom, Homilies on Genesis 3.21; Luke 16:9-13).[26]

## 2. The Pattern

The pattern in the Christian life for the use of riches is the incarnate Lord, who though he was rich, voluntarily became poor for us, facing human limitations, hunger, and an unjust death. His message to those who have wealth is evident in biblical narratives that treat the wealthy not with contempt but respect, and challenge them to total accountability before the Giver of all creation's gifts. They do well to listen carefully to the Fathers on the right use of justly acquired wealth.

Jesus reached out not only for the poor but also for the rich. He called them to repent and have faith and to enter freely into the coming kingdom, guiding them toward compassion toward those who suffer.

Speaking honestly to the rich about their special moral responsibilities requires an attitude of candor, and at times fearless encounter, and a clever ability to penetrate defensive ploys. It also requires resisting the simplification that all property is intrinsically evil. This leads to cynicism about serious, though mundane, moral issues: prudent savings, financial planning, temporal accountability, and resource management.

26. FC 74:49-50**; ACCS NT 3:255-56*.

### 3. Philanthropy

Deuteronomic law stated: To anyone in need "you shall open your hand wide" (Deut. 15:8a, NKJV). God's free gifts invite our own open-handedness: "For all things come from thee, and of thine own have we given you" (1 Chron. 29:14, RSV*).

The root meaning of philanthropy is love of humanity. It is an attitude as much as an action. The philanthropic person is ready to give. Philanthropy is a desire to help humanity, and is manifested in acts of charity. As commonly used, it is the act of making economic provision for the less fortunate in society. The biblical term is almsgiving.

Withholding alms to the poor bears a close analogy with theft, according to Augustine. "The Christian soul understands how far removed he should be from theft of another's goods when he realizes that failure to share his surplus with the needy is like theft. The Lord says, 'Give, and it shall be given to you. Forgive, and you shall be forgiven.' Let us graciously and fervently perform these two types of almsgiving, that is, giving and forgiving, for we in turn pray the Lord to give us good things and not to repay our evil deeds" (Augustine, Sermon 206.2; Luke 6:37-38).[27]

Love to God is expressed by rendering service to man. One who loves God will love his brother also (1 John 4:21). "The end of the commandment is charity out of a pure heart" (1 Tim. 1:5a, KJV).

Jesus taught the blessedness of giving, that "it is more blessed to give than to receive" (Acts 20:35b, KJV). "Much is required from the person to whom much is given; much more is required from the person to whom much more is given" (Luke 12:48b, TEV/GN).

"God loves a cheerful giver," wrote Paul (2 Cor. 9:7b, RSV). "The apostle wants us to be sympathetic and merciful so that we might feel obliged to give to the poor and to do good works with a willing heart. Whoever hopes for mercy from God must be merciful, in order to indicate that he has some reason for his hope. For if a man is merciful, how much more is God!" (Ambrosiaster, On Paul's Epistle to the Romans; Rom. 15:27).[28]

In giving, one does not lose what is given. "Give alms, my brothers and sisters, and you won't lose what you give. Trust God. . . . You won't lose

27. FC 38:87; ACCS NT 3:110.
28. CSEL 81:473; ACCS NT 6:366*.

what you do for the poor. . . . Come now, let's see if you can cheer the poor up today. You be their granaries, so that God may give to you what you can give to them" (Augustine, Sermon 376a.3; Luke 6:37-38).[29] Let God's mercy flow through you directly to those most in need. The gift of God grows through our passing it along to another.

### 4. Treasures on Earth

Worldly wealth is best assessed in relation to eternity. Let your resources bring you closer to the real meaning of your own personal existence in time. John Chrysostom spoke well for the common Christian tradition on this point:

> Let us plan for what is needful. Do not remain anxious to bedeck your-selves with the trappings of wealth. Rather pay central attention simply to doing good. After all, our being will not come to an end with this present life, nor shall we be always in exile. Instead, before long we shall reach our true homeland. So let us do everything in the hope of not being found wanting there. What good is it to leave behind great wealth in foreign parts while starving for bare necessities in our true eternal country? Consequently, let us strive, dearly beloved, while there is still time, to transfer to there what we own in this country. Although, in fact, the distance may be great, nevertheless, the transfer is quite easy. Some are ready to make the transfer, and to travel there safely. They have deposited in a secure treasury whatever they were able to send ahead. The hands of the poor are working to lay up treasures in heaven through what is given them by the affluent. Since, then, the ease and security of this is so great, why do we delay? Why not rather act with all haste, so that we will have those things at our disposal in the place where we most have need of them? (Chrysostom, Homilies on Genesis 48.6; Gen. 28:20)[30]

Learn from those who despairingly sought to build the tower of Ba-bel. "There are many even today who in imitation of them want to be re-

---

29. WSA 3 10:350; ACCS NT 3:111.
30. FC 87:28; ACCS OT 2:119*.

membered for such achievements — by building splendid homes, baths, porches and avenues. If you were to ask each of them why they toil and labor and lay out such great expense for such purposes, you would hear mostly rationalizations. They would be seeking to ensure that their memory survives in perpetuity. They would like to have it said that 'this is the house belonging to so-and-so,' 'this is the property of so-and-so,'" Chrysostom noted. "But if you are hoping for a durable reputation, I will show you the way to succeed. You will be remembered in the age to come for the best you have done. You will enjoy an excellent name, and provide yourself with enduring confidence. How then will you manage both to be remembered day after day and also become the recipient of tributes even after passing from one life to the next? Only if you are ready to give away these goods of yours into the hands of the poor, letting go of precious stones, magnificent homes, properties and baths" (Chrysostom, Homilies on Genesis 30.7; Gen. 11:9).[31]

Piling wealth upon children may not be to their advantage. Salvian warned that "There is no compelling necessity for you to store up large earthly treasures for your children. You would do better to make your offspring treasures of God than make them richer in worldly goods" (Salvian, The Four Books of Timothy to the Church 1.4; Mark 10:25).[32]

### 5. Avoid Unfair Acquisition

Abraham was the model of faith. His relation to his worldly goods expressed this faith. In all his dealings he was remembered as one with a good will: "Notice, however, how this good man instructs his companions with his characteristic good common sense, through his very actions, by forbearing to take possession of a tomb for his wife before paying a just price," Chrysostom recalled.

> This is the man who was so famous and respected, who enjoyed such confidence with God and was the object of such admiration from everyone. Even the Hittites called him king. Yet he owned not even one square foot of land. Hence blessed Paul also celebrated this good man's

31. FC 82:224; ACCS OT 1:169-70*.
32. FC 3:277**; ACCS NT 2:146.

virtue in writing these words: "By faith Abraham dwelt in the land of promise, like a foreigner living in tents with Isaac and Jacob, coheirs of the same promise." Then to teach us how it was through faith that he dwelt there, he added, "He looked forward, you see, to the city built on foundations of which the builder and creator was God" [Heb. 11:10]. In the hope of things to come, Paul is saying, Abraham let present realities pass without inordinate notice. In the expectation of greater things to come, he set less store in passing things. He clung to this hope even before the law was given or the age of grace came. So what excuse will we have, tell me, who despite such wonderful promises and guarantees of ineffable blessings still hanker for present luxuries, buying up property, forever concerned about our own image, amassing all these possessions out of greed and avarice, and fulfilling in practice just what the blessed prophet said in his lament, "Woe to those who pile house on house and add property to property for the purpose of robbing their neighbor of something" [Isa. 5:8]. Do we not see this happening each day — widows being robbed, orphans despoiled, and the weak oppressed by the strong? This good man, Abraham, on the contrary, did not behave in that way. Instead he insisted on buying the tomb at a fair price, and, when he saw those from whom he sought it ready and willing to hand it over, he could not bring himself to accept it before he paid the right price. (Chrysostom, Homilies on Genesis 48.3-4; Gen. 23:13)[33]

To seek a fair price is more rewarding than to take advantage.

The significance of Abraham's purchase was not missed by John Chrysostom:

Sarah's death was the occasion for the patriarch's first instance of acquiring land. Sacred Scripture in fact shows us in every case the patriarch's virtue. He passed all his time as an alien and a nomad. It mentions this item that we might learn that the man who enjoyed so much assistance from on high, who had become so famous and whose family had increased in number to such a vast multitude, still could not call a place his own. This is unlike many today who still give all their attention to acquiring land, whole towns and great wealth beyond telling.

33. FC 87:26-27; ACCS OT 2:118*.

Abraham, however, had sufficient riches in his own soul. He put no store in accumulating other things. Some are prone, in the twinkling of an eye, to take to themselves every conceivable property, and, so to speak, stretch out in all directions their passion for avarice. Let them now imitate the patriarch who did not even own a place to inter Sarah's remains until, under pressure of the very necessity, he bought the field and cave from the Hittites. (Chrysostom, Homilies on Genesis 48.2; Gen. 23:6)[34]

Since Abraham had the promise, he had no desperate need to acquire land for himself.

## 6. Psychological Evasions of Covetousness

Paterius described the psychological dynamics of the divided minds of those who desperately desire ever-increasing worldly power and influence:

There are some in the church who can't stand being "the least of these." Even where humility should prevail, they hardly ever cease to be grand in their own eyes. You can see them being exalted with honors, enjoying pleasures, being entertained by the sheer number of things. Often they seek nothing except being in command of others. They enjoy being feared by many. They fail to live upright lives, yet desire to be known as upright. They seek out flatterers. They swell up with the admiration shown to them. Since they are eager for things in the present life, they do not seek the joys to come. When complex business challenges them, they have difficulty concentrating since they are absent even from themselves. But if a temptation against faith arises — for in this area they are quite restrained — they defend the faith by words and labors. They defend the heavenly patrimony, but they do not love it. (Paterius, Exposition of the Old and New Testament, Numbers 23; Num. 32:4)[35]

---

34. FC 87:25-26*; ACCS OT 2:117*.
35. PL 79:773, cf. Gregory the Great, Moral Interpretation of Job 27.13.24-25; ACCS OT 3:261*.

These affluent persons may "own many cattle yet refuse to cross the Jordan. Those who have many entanglements in this world do not seek a dwelling in the heavenly fatherland. Those entanglements hold them by their appearance. . . . Thus God says to them through Moses, 'Will your brethren go to battle, and you will sit here? Why do you undermine the hearts of the children of Israel?' [Num. 32:7]. . . . Many people, although they are believers, are occupied with present cares, as if they were feeding flocks across the Jordan. Contrary to the faith they professed in baptism, they serve perishable things with their whole minds and all their desires. . . . They do not know how clear the eternal light is, because they are blinded by transitory concerns. When they take pride in earthly things, they shut the door to heavenly light" (Paterius, Exposition of the Old and New Testament, Numbers 23; Num. 32:4).[36]

Augustine understood the compulsive aspect of reinforced coveting. "Don't covet. Don't go up and down in front of that country house belonging to someone else and sigh because it's such a fine one. Do not covet your neighbor's property. 'The Lord's is the earth and its fullness' [Ps. 24:1]. What haven't you acquired, if you have got hold of God?" (Augustine, Sermon 252a.6; Exod. 20:17).[37]

The rationalizing evasions of the covetous are best encountered with candor. Do not just brood over the needy. Give them a hand — now. "Whenever we talk about disregard for riches, some rich man replies to me: 'I have learned not to hope in the uncertainty of riches. I do not want to be rich, lest I fall into temptation. But since I am rich already, what am I to do with the possessions which I now happen to have?' The apostle intervenes: 'Let them give readily, sharing with the needy.' What does it mean to share with the needy? To share what you have with those who have nothing. Therefore, if you begin freely to share with others, you will not be playing the part of that plunderer and robber who broods in despair over the wants of the poor, as if brooding over the property of another" (Caesarius of Arles, Sermons 182.2; 1 Tim. 6:18).[38] Do not torture yourself over the resource gap between what belongs to you and another in need. Just act now; give readily.

---

36. PL 79:774; ACCS OT 3:261-62.
37. WSA 3 7:145-46; ACCS OT 3:108.
38. FC 47:468; ACCS NT 9:225*.

## C. The Love of Money

Creaturely goods present themselves as greater goods than they actually are. We test their value. We make decisions about their value. We are responsible for these decisions.

A god or idol is a creaturely value elevated to the center of values. It is a value by which we judge other values to be valuable. We decide to make creatures into gods. Our gods increase our temptation to mistakenly value what is properly valuable. Temptation portrays a limited good as a greater good, even the greatest good. We are tricked by our idolatries into doing evil while imagining that they are seeking some good.

Temptation comes shrouded in deceptions: moral ambiguities, half-truths, smoke and mirrors. "The tree, then, from which comes this fruit of mixed knowledge is among those things which are forbidden. Its fruit is combined of opposite qualities, and for this reason the serpent can exploit it. For the evil is not exposed in its nakedness, thereby appearing in its own proper nature. Wickedness would surely fail of its effect were it not decked with some fair color to entice to the desire of it him whom it deceives. The nature of evil is in this way ambiguous. It is like a snare concealing its hook while *displaying some phantom of good in the deceitfulness of its exterior.* The beauty of the bait always appears good to those who love money" (Gregory of Nyssa, On the Making of Man 20.2, italics added; 1 Tim. 6:10).[39] The snare is baited with honey.

### 1. The Deceptiveness of Riches

To avoid falling into this snare, the worm of avarice must be resisted, according to Valerian. "Therefore, dearly beloved, the rust is that worm which seeks alone to possess the recesses of the human heart. The worm is envy and avarice. But the thief is the devil. Believe this. To lay his plots against good deeds, he flatters us with the pomp of the world. To keep a man from sharing in the heavenly kingdom, he puts gold in his hands, silver before his eyes, and gems about his neck. In this way he nourishes pride and by the goad of covetousness enkindles the desires of the flesh" (Valerian, Homilies 7.3; 1 Tim. 6:9b).[40] The wise see through this deception.

39. NPNF 2 5:410*; ACCS NT 9:215*.
40. FC 17:346; ACCS NT 9:214*.

Paul warned that "People who want to get rich fall into temptation and a trap and into many foolish and harmful desires that plunge men into ruin and destruction" (1 Tim. 6:9). Augustine commented: "He did not say: Those who are rich. He said: *People who want to get rich.* . . . The name of riches is, as it were, sweet sounding to the ear. But, 'many vain and harmful desires' does not sound all that sweet. To be 'involved in many troubles' does not sound so sweet. So do not be so misled by one false good that you will thereby cling to many real evils" (Augustine, Sermons 11.3, italics added; 1 Tim. 6:9c).[41] To gain one apparent good for many undesirable consequences is not a good trade.

We have a battle on our hands in resisting our own readiness to consent to desires that lead to death. "See what a fight we have with our 'dead' sins, as that active soldier of Christ and faithful teacher of the church shows. For how is sin dead when it works many things in us while we struggle against it? What are these many things except foolish and harmful desires which plunge into death and destruction those who consent to them? And to bear them patiently and not to consent to them is a struggle, a conflict, a battle" (Augustine, Against Julian 2.9.32; 1 Tim. 6:9c).[42]

### 2. The Souls of the Greedy

Our own souls are diminished just as we think we are adding to them. Cyprian showed how worldly goods increase anxieties: "You are afraid that your wealth may fail. You may have begun to do some good generously from it, yet you do not know, in your wretchedness, that your very life itself may fail, and your salvation as well. While you are anxious lest any of your possessions be diminished, you do not take notice that you yourself, a lover of mammon rather than of your soul, are being diminished. While you are afraid lest for your own sake you lose your estate, you yourself are perishing for the sake of your estate" (Cyprian, Works and Almsgiving 10; 1 Tim. 6:9a).[43]

Coveting is like a fatal disease which, to be treated, must be rightly diagnosed. "Do you see the skill of physicians, who besides health are sup-

---

41. FC 11:359*; ACCS NT 9:214*.
42. FC 35:95; ACCS NT 9:214.
43. FC 36:236-37; ACCS NT 9:214*.

plying you also with the riches of wisdom? Sit down therefore with them, and learn from them the nature of your disease. For instance, do you love wealth and greedy gain, like those with a fever love water? Listen. It is just as when the physician says to you, 'If you wish only to gratify your desire, you will perish and undergo this or that consequence'" (Chrysostom, Homilies on Matthew 74.4; 1 Tim. 6:9a).[44]

The greediest are poorest of all, Chrysostom taught. They "destroy themselves, not you. For while they rob you of your money, they strip themselves of God's favor and help. For the one who bases his life on greed and gathers all the wealth of the world around him is in fact the poorest of all" (Chrysostom, quoted in Cramer, Catena in Epistolas Catholicas; Jas. 2:6).[45]

Oecumenius caught the irony: "James calls the rich man both proud and humble at the same time, because what puffs him up also brings him down. The rich man is said to fade away even while he goes about his business, because anyone engaged in business knows that it can always take an unexpected turn for the worse" (Oecumenius, Commentary on James; Jas. 1:11).[46]

Ponder the dialectical brilliance of Augustine: "Those who have given liberally of their riches have had great gains to compensate them for light losses. Their joy at what they assured for themselves more securely by readiness to give outweighed their sadness at the surrender of possessions that they more easily lost insofar as they clung to them with fear." (Augustine, The City of God 1.10; 1 Tim. 6:18).[47]

When the interests of wealth and nobility overlap, they taint each other, as Salvian wrote: "Do the nobility think that they are immune from his warnings, because he [James] referred only to the rich and not to the nobility as well? But there is so great an overlap between these two groups in practice that it makes little difference which one of them the apostle was speaking about. His words certainly apply to both" (Salvian the Presbyter, On the Governance of God 3.10; Jas. 2:5).[48]

---

44. NPNF 1 10:448-49*; ACCS NT 9:214*.
45. CEC 11; ACCS NT 11:23.
46. PG 119:461; ACCS NT 11:10.
47. ACG 18; NPNF 1 2:8; ACCS NT 9:225*.
48. FC 3:86; ACCS NT 11:23*.

### 3. The Fleeting Nature of Riches

Temporal goods will eventually prove themselves temporal by passing away. "The flower of the field is pretty and its smell is pleasant for a while, but it soon loses the attraction of its beauty and charm. The present happiness of the ungodly is exactly the same — it lasts for a day or two and then vanishes into nothing" (Bede the Venerable, Concerning the Epistle of St. James; Jas. 1:11).[49] "The rich man will see the wealth in which he gloried, and with which he used to despise the poor in this world, come to an end" (Bede the Venerable, Concerning the Epistle of St. James; Jas. 1:10).[50] "The rich must repent while there is still time for them to do so" (Hilary of Arles, Introductory Tractate on the Letter of James; Jas. 5:1).[51]

Death comes to all. We enter life "by the narrow way. How long will luxury last? How long will there be licentiousness? Have not the heedless among us been warned? What about the mockers and the procrastinators? Will not their banquets and gluttony and self-satisfaction, not to mention their wealth, their possessions and their property all disappear? What reward have they got? Death. And what will their end be? Dust and ashes, urns and worms" (Chrysostom, quoted in Cramer, Catena in Epistolas Catholicas; Jas. 5:3).[52]

These warnings "should terrify us very much, but we should not despair of the mercy of God. Those of us who have been careless up to now can, with God's help, correct ourselves." But penitent faith will then be ready to show "that we are willing to dispense more generously those alms which we have given sparingly up to now" (Caesarius of Arles, Sermons 199.5; Jas. 5:5).[53]

### 4. No One Can Serve Two Masters

Serving two masters is one too many. The Second Letter of Clement commented: "If we want to serve both God and money, it will do us no good. 'What good does it do a man to gain the whole world and forfeit his life?'

49. PL 93:12; ACCS NT 11:10.
50. PL 93:12; ACCS NT 11:11.
51. PL Suppl. 3:80; ACCS NT 11:54.
52. CEC 33; ACCS NT 11:54.
53. FC 66:56; ACCS NT 11:55.

[Matt. 16:26; Mark 8:36; Luke 9:25]. This world and the world to come are in conflict. This one tempts us to adultery, corruption, greed and deceit, while the other gives them up. We cannot be friends of both. To get the one, we must give the other up" (Pseudo-Clement of Rome, 2 Clement 6.2-5; Luke 16:9-13).[54]

Mammon does not have a proper claim to be the master of our human dignity and freedom. Recalling what the Lord said: "No servant can serve two masters" (Luke 16:13, KJV), Ambrose observed: "This is so not because there are two masters finally. The Lord is One. Although there are those who serve mammon, mammon does not possess any rights to any sovereignty. So his servants impose upon themselves the chains of slavery" (Ambrose, Exposition of the Gospel of Luke 7.244; Luke 16:9-13).[55]

### 5. By Desiring More, Pride Becomes Less

Loving the whole is greater than loving the part. Slavery to money is like slavery to lust. Augustine explained: "When the soul loves its own power, it slips from the common whole to its own particular part. Had the soul followed God as its ruler in the universal creation, it could have been most excellently governed by his laws. But in that apostatizing pride, which is called 'the beginning of sin' [Sir. 10:15], it sought for something more than the whole; and while it struggled to govern it by its own laws, it was thrust into caring for a part, since there is nothing more than the whole. So by desiring something more, it becomes less, and for this reason covetousness is called 'the root of all evils'" (Augustine, On the Trinity 12.9.14; 1 Tim. 6:10).[56] The whole is God. The part is some form of creation. To get these confused is to bring upon ourselves avoidable suffering.

Candor is increased when we view the relative as relative and the absolute as absolute. To live by grace is to possess nothing as if it were everything. That means to regard no worldly possession as the final source of happiness. "The man who possesses nothing as if he had everything disdains all. He is very outspoken with officials, and rulers, and the sovereign. By despising possessions and advancing step by step, he will scorn even

54. LCC 1:195*; ACCS NT 3:256*.
55. EHG 328**; ACCS NT 3:256*.
56. FC 45:356; ACCS NT 9:215-16*.

death with ease. Since he is above these things, he will speak openly with everyone and tremble with fear before no one. But the man who has devoted himself to money is a slave to it and also to his reputation, honor, the present life, in short, to all human concerns. This is why Paul has called it the root of all evil" (Chrysostom, On Virginity 81; 1 Tim. 6:10).[57] Why make yourself a slave?

It is possible for the rich to remain humble, but it is never easy. "Praise to the rich if they remain humble. Praise to the rich for becoming lowly. The one who writes to Timothy wants them to be like that, when he says, 'Order the rich of this world not to be haughty in mind.' I know what I am saying. Tell them this: The riches have been whispering persuasively to them to be proud. The riches they have make it all the more hard for them to be humble" (Augustine, Sermons 14.2; 1 Tim. 6:17a).[58]

Not riches as such, but pride is the tempter underneath riches: "It wasn't riches he was in dread of, but the disease of riches. The disease of riches is great pride. A person large of soul in the midst of riches is not prone to this disease, having a spirit greater than riches, surpassing them not by desiring but by putting them in proper order" (Augustine, Sermons 36.2; 1 Tim. 6:17a).[59]

## 6. Money and the Love of Money

The excessive passion, the *love* of money, brings with it a train of unnecessary suffering. The costs are high. Its path is replete with disaster. "What evils does it not cause! What fraudulent practices, what robberies! What miseries, enmities, contentions, battles! Does it not stretch forth its hand even to the dead, even to fathers and brothers? Do not they who are possessed by this passion violate the laws of nature and the commandments of God? In short does it not affect everything? Is it not this that renders our courts of justice necessary? Take away therefore the love of money, and you put an end to war, to battle, to enmity, to strife and contention" (Chrysostom, Homilies on 1 Timothy 17; 1 Tim. 6:10).[60]

57. COV 122; ACCS NT 9:215*.
58. WSA 3 1:317; ACCS NT 9:224*.
59. WSA 3 2:174-75; ACCS NT 9:224*.
60. NPNF 1 13:469; ACCS NT 9:215*.

The greater blessings of nature are offered to rich and poor alike. "God gives all things with liberality that are more necessary than riches: the air, the water, the fire, the sun — all things necessary to life. The rich man is not able to say that he enjoys more of the sunbeams than the poor man. He is not able to say that he breathes more plenteous air. These are offered to all alike. It is the greater and more necessary blessings, and those which maintain our life, that God has given to all in common. It is only the smaller and less valuable things are found unequally in the human condition" (Chrysostom, Homilies Concerning the Statues 2.6; 1 Tim. 6:17b).[61]

Faith is content with what God provides. "Therefore the man of good counsel says, 'I have learned in whatever state I am to be content' [Phil. 4:11]. For he knew that the root of all evils is the love of money. Therefore he was content with what he had, without seeking for what was another's. Sufficient for me, he says, is what I have. Whether I have little or much, to me it is much" (Ambrose, Duties of the Clergy 2.17.89; 1 Tim. 6:10).[62]

Paul learned to be content whatever the circumstances. He had known what it is to be in need, what it is to have plenty, and amid it all he has learned the secret of being content in any and every situation — whether well fed or hungry, whether living in plenty or in want. He knew he could do everything called for through the One who gives him strength (Phil. 4:10).

### 7. What Needs to Be Guarded

The possessions most worthy of being protected are not physical assets. "Note what possessions he especially orders us to guard: faith, fear of God, modesty, holiness, and discipline. Nothing earthly, nothing base, nothing perishable or transitory" (Salvian, The Four Books of Timothy to the Church 1.4; Mark 10:23).[63]

Cling to that which can never be taken away. "Riches are understood in a threefold way in holy Scripture — bad, good and indifferent. . . . The indifferent are those which can be either good or bad, since they can tend either way depending on the desire and the character of those who use

61. NPNF 1 9:351*; ACCS NT 9:225*.
62. NPNF 2 10:57; ACCS NT 9:215.
63. FC 3:276**; ACCS NT 2:145.

them. The blessed apostle says with regard to these, 'Charge the rich of this world not to be haughty, nor to set their hopes on uncertain riches but on God who richly furnishes us with everything to enjoy.' . . . Nothing is ours except this one thing, which is possessed by the heart, which clings to the soul and which can never be taken away by anyone" (John Cassian, Conferences I.3.9.1, 3; I.3.10.1; 1 Tim. 6:17a).[64]

## D. Cheerful Giving

### 1. The Collection for the Saints

Paul concentrated major energies on collecting contributions for needy Christians in Jerusalem (Rom. 15:25-28; 1 Cor. 16:1-4; 2 Cor. 8; cf. Jas. 1:27). In this collection for the saints, he urged believers to set aside a sum of money on the first day of every week, proportional to income, as a collection to the poor (1 Cor. 16:2). This was to be done in an orderly fashion. Representatives were selected from the various churches to return the funds to the poor of Jerusalem (Acts 11:27-30; Gal. 2:10). The apostle provided rules for the funds to be carefully administered (2 Cor. 18:21). It was a privilege to be able to share this almsdeed — to "remember the poor" (Gal. 2:10, RSV).

These were Gentile gifts to Jewish Christians. Since the Jews had given Gentiles spiritual blessings, so the Gentiles owed it to the Jews to share with them their material blessings (Rom. 15:27). So he began the collection in Galatia, Derbe, Lystra, Macedonia, Berea, Philippi — all around the churches of Anatolia and Greece.

The collection for the relief of the poor in Jerusalem made it all the more clear to Christians everywhere that there is one Lord, one baptism, one church, one God and Father of us all, one Gospel. By means of these collections, the unity of the church worldwide was beginning to be manifested. Every member of this body is related to every other member and to the head. The unity of the extended church was being experienced concretely by Gentiles showing their gratitude for the Jewish Christians in Judea, thereby demonstrating their thanksgiving for the covenant people.

---

64. ACWCas 128-29; NPNF 2 11:324; ACCS NT 9:224.

## 2. The Poor in Jerusalem

Why did the church of Jerusalem need this relief? Having suffered persecution and marginalization, they were poor. There were many visitors in Jerusalem on pilgrimage. This may have created a financial burden for that community. There also appeared to be many widows there (Acts 6:1-7). Perhaps at times there were serious shortages of food (Acts 11:27).

The church of Jerusalem had already provided the rest of the Christian world with a powerful model of the faithful community (Acts 4:32–5:11). There was a precedent in Jewish tradition for bringing to Jerusalem a temple tax and that was, in a sense, adapted and transformed in the Christian community. Just as the diaspora Jews supported Jerusalem's temple by sending an annual two-drachma tax, so did Christians provide relief for the poor of Jerusalem.

Who were these "poor in Jerusalem" who occupied so much of Paul's attention? Jerome explained: "The holy poor, care of whom was specially committed to Paul and Barnabas by the apostles, are those believers in Judea who brought the price of their possessions to the feet of the apostles [Acts 4:32-37] to be given to the needy, or because they were incurring hatred and punishment from their kin, family and parents, charged with being deserters of the law and believers in a crucified man. Paul's letters bear witness to the constant labor the holy apostle expended in ministering to them. He pleaded their case in Corinth, Thessaloniki, and in all the churches of the Gentiles. All were asked to prepare this offering to be taken to Jerusalem through himself or others, to 'remember the poor,' which he 'was eager to do'" (Jerome, Epistle to the Galatians 1.2.10; Gal. 2:10b).[65] Stewardship was an expression of faith from the very beginning.

The needs of the church in Jerusalem were particularly urgent: "Many believers of Jewish origin in Palestine had been robbed of all their goods and were being persecuted on all sides," John Chrysostom pointed out. "Those who had been converted from Greek backgrounds did not suffer such antagonism from those who had remained Greek as much as the believers of Jewish origin had suffered from their own people. Therefore he takes great pains that they should receive all assistance, as also when writing to the Romans and Corinthians [Rom. 15:25-29; 1 Cor. 16:1-4]"

---

65. PL 26:337C-38A [405]; ACCS NT 8:24-25*.

(Chrysostom, Homily on Galatians 2.10; Gal. 2:10a).[66] The relief went where the immediate needs were greatest.

### 3. Paul Pled for Generosity on Behalf of the Poor

The generous heart is open handed. "We should not be mean and calculating with what we have, but give with a generous hand. Look at how much people give to players and dancers — why not give just half as much to Christ?" (Chrysostom, Homilies on the Epistles of Paul to the Corinthians II.19.2-3; 2 Cor. 9:9).[67]

Do not sow sparingly. "Paul is referring to misers when he talks about people who sow sparingly. He says this here because the Corinthians had promised to send something and had subsequently backtracked" (Ambrosiaster, On Paul's Epistles to the Corinthians; 2 Cor. 9:6).[68] Paul called believers to the habits of regular financial accountability.

"The other apostles labored, but not as much as Paul. He used to earn his living with his own hands, from early morning until about eleven o'clock, and from then until four in the afternoon he would engage in public disputation with such energy that he would usually persuade those who spoke in opposition to him" (Ambrosiaster, On Paul's Epistles to the Corinthians; 2 Cor. 11:23).[69]

Let those who need more than enough think more about what is enough. "Note how Paul does not pray for riches or abundance, but only for enough to live on. Nor is this the only thing he should be admired for, because he asks the same thing of the Corinthians. . . . He wants them to have enough of this world's goods, but an overflowing abundance of spiritual blessings" (Chrysostom, Homilies on the Epistles of Paul to the Corinthians II.19.2; 2 Cor. 9:8).[70]

A grudging gift reserves a layer of bitterness. "People who give reluctantly or under compulsion present a blemished sacrifice which should not be accepted" (Basil the Great, The Long Rules; 2 Cor. 9:7).[71]

---

66. IOEP 4:40; cf. Jerome, PL 26:337; ACCS NT 8:24.
67. NPNF 1 12:369; ACCS NT 7:281.
68. CSEL 81:267; ACCS NT 7:279.
69. CSEL 81:292-93; ACCS NT 7:297.
70. NPNF 1 12:369*; ACCS NT 7:281*.
71. FC 9:292; ACCS NT 7:280.

The New Testament is persistent in encouraging the faithful to be open and generous.

## 4. The Cheerful Heart

"Each one should give what he has decided in his heart to give, not reluctantly or under compulsion, for God loves a cheerful giver" (2 Cor. 9:7, NIV*). "Paul is teaching them that if they give with a cheerful heart they will be storing up treasure for future use in heaven" (Ambrosiaster, On Paul's Epistles to the Corinthians; 2 Cor. 9:7).[72] Faith is demonstrated through generosity. "Under the test of this service, you will glorify God because of your obedience in acknowledging the Gospel of Christ, and by the generosity of your contribution for them and for others" (2 Cor. 9:13, RSV*). This obedience is intrinsic to our confession of the Gospel, not separable from it.

One who refreshes others will himself be refreshed (Prov. 11:25). You who do this will be like "a well-watered garden, like a spring whose waters never fail" (Isa. 58:11b, NIV), if you spend yourself on behalf of the hungry. The Lord is going to satisfy your needs in a sun-scorched land and strengthen your frame, if you satisfy the needs of the oppressed. Your night will be noonday, your light will rise in the darkness, if you care for the poor (Isa. 58:10-11; cf. Matt. 9:41).

"Paul praises [the church of Corinth] because they gave thanks even for things which were given to others . . . in spite of their own poverty. . . . Who is, understandably, more envious than the poor? But these people were free of that passion, so much so that they were able to rejoice in the blessings given to others" (Chrysostom, Homilies on the Epistles of Paul to the Corinthians II.20.2; 2 Cor. 9:14).[73]

Our gifts reflect God's gift to us. "'Gift' refers either to all the blessings which come from almsgiving, both to those who receive and to those who give, or to the inexpressible gift which Christ bestowed liberally on the whole world by his incarnation" (Chrysostom, Homilies on the Epistles of Paul to the Corinthians II.20.2; 2 Cor. 9:15).[74]

72. CSEL 81:267; ACCS NT 7:280.
73. NPNF 1 12:373*; ACCS NT 7:282*.
74. NPNF 1 12:373; ACCS NT 7:282*.

Generosity will be returned manifold. "The person who gives his wealth to the poor does not lose it but finds it more fully. This is why the Preacher said: 'Cast your bread upon the waters' [Eccles. 11:1], that is, upon the apparent corruption and decadence of this world. It will not be lost, but rather it will come back manifold and preserve us from destruction" (Oecumenius, Commentary on James; Jas. 5:1).[75]

## E. The Final Judgment: "Depart from Me"

It is a starkly dreadful note on which the parable of the sheep and goats ends. Final judgment awaits those who ignore "the least of these," who take good works flippantly: "Truly I say to you, to the extent that you did not do it to one of the least of these, you did not do it to Me. These will go away into eternal punishment, but the righteous into eternal life" (Matt. 25:45-46, NAS).

Gregory the Great spoke of the dire consequences of a life that does not bear the fruit of good works: "The axe is now laid at the root of the tree because, although [the final Judge] is waiting patiently, what he will do is nonetheless apparent. Every tree that does not bear good fruit will be cut down and thrown into the fire. Every wicked person, refusing to bear the fruit of good works in this life, will find the fires of hell all the more swiftly prepared" (Gregory the Great, Forty Gospel Homilies 6; Luke 3:7-9).[76] The judge awaits.

Put simply: "One who judges without mercy will be judged without mercy" (Augustine, Letter 102.4; Jas. 2:13).[77]

### 1. The Impenitent in Final Judgment

The unrepentant are making it extremely difficult on themselves on the last day, according to John Chrysostom:

It is not possible, not possible at all, for those who enjoy an easy life and freedom from want in this world, who continually indulge them-

75. PG 119:502-4; ACCS NT 11:54*.
76. CSGF 42; ACCS NT 3:61-62*.
77. FC 18:168; ACCS NT 11:25*.

selves in every way, who live randomly and foolishly, to enjoy honor in the other world. For if poverty does not trouble them, still their own desires trouble them. They are afflicted by their own excessive passions, which bring more than a little pain. If disease does not threaten them, still their temper grows hot, and it requires more than an ordinary struggle to overcome anger. If trials do not come to test them, still evil thoughts may continually undermine them. It is no small task to bridle foolish desire, to stop vainglory, to restrain presumption, to refrain from excess, and to persevere in modesty. Those who do not do these things, and others like them, will not enter the kingdom. (Chrysostom, On Lazarus and the Rich Man 3; 1 Tim. 5:6)[78]

The residues of the narcissistic life are fit to be burned.

Paul does not hesitate to use the harsh and final term "death" to describe one who lives always and only for immediate pleasure: "The body is not only said to be about to die on account of the departure of the soul, which will come to pass, but, in certain passages it is even spoken of as already dead on account of the great weakness of flesh and blood, as where the apostle says, 'The body, it is true, is dead on account of sin' [Rom. 8:10]" (Augustine, On the Trinity 4.3.5; 1 Tim. 5:6).[79]

### 2. Judgment Mitigated by Compassion

Where there are signs of compassion, God's clemency is promised. Leo the Great wrote: "Since mercy will be exalted over condemnation and the gifts of clemency will override a strictly just compensation, all the lives led by mortals and all their different kinds of actions will be appraised under the aspect of a single rule: love. No charges will be brought up where works of compassion have been found in acknowledgment of the Creator" (Leo the Great, Sermons 11.1; Jas. 2:16).[80]

Suppose one willingly persists in a life of self-absorption, even after conversion, faith, and baptism. The author of Hebrews declares: "No sacrifice for sins is left, but only a fearful expectation of judgment of raging fire

---

78. COWP 67; ACCS NT 9:198*.
79. FC 45:136; ACCS NT 9:199.
80. FC 93:47; ACCS NT 11:29*.

that will consume the enemies of God" (Heb. 10:26b-27, NIV). Isaiah pronounced woe upon the obstinate who heap sin upon sin (Isa. 30:1). Those who stubbornly refuse to live out the Christian life cannot expect to receive mercy in the end. "How can you believe if you accept praise from one another and yet make no effort to obtain the praise that comes from the only God?" (John 5:44, NIV).

Hence Ephrem warned: "Do not judge unjustly, so that you may not be judged according to your own injustice. With the judgment that you judge shall you be judged [Matt. 7:2]. This is like the phrase 'Forgive, and it will be forgiven you.' For once someone has judged in accordance with justice, he should forgive in accordance with grace, so that when he himself is judged in accordance with justice, he may be ready to receive forgiveness through grace" (Ephrem the Syrian, Commentary on Tatian's Diatessaron 6.18b; Luke 6:37-38).[81]

### 3. Summing Up the Stewardship Motif

The incarnate Lord knew what it was to be rich, incomparably so, but he came into the world as the poor, the child, the outcast, the refugee. He showed humanity the path of self-denial. The crucified Lord shared our human weakness, even unto death. He sent the Holy Spirit to help us grow to full maturity as persons. He calls each of us to use rightly the gifts we have received.

We have been asking how the ancient church understood the ministries to the affluent that they were actually offering. The answer we found not only in their letters, poetry, hymnody, and homilies, but also in their detailed exegesis of scripture texts on wealth, coveting, temptation, philanthropy, the fleeting value of worldly goods, reparations, and generous giving. Christianity has been engaged in this challenging dialogue with the affluent for two millennia.

Jesus' message to those who have wealth is evident in narratives that treat the wealthy not with contempt but respect, yet challenge them to total accountability in relation to their eternal destiny. The rich can be saved, but special difficulties lie in the way. Speaking honestly to the rich about their moral responsibilities requires a strong hold on one's identity, an atti-

---

81. ECTD 122*; ACCS NT 3:110*.

tude of candor, and the willingness to penetrate defensive dodges. A key evidence of the Christian life is intentional, orderly stewardship. Those who possess resources are called to use them for good purposes, to be ready to give cheerfully. It is within the range of every believer to practice these simple good works: stewardship of resources, willingness to live the simple life, being content with what one has, giving generously.

The pattern in the Christian life for the rich is seen in Jesus' own ministry to them. He was willing to confront them, to penetrate their evasions, to call them to repent, to press them for accountability, and to teach them how to become meek. The good news has always been challenging to our self-sufficiency.

Simple acts of fiscal accountability are best understood in relation to God's own taking responsibility for humanity amid the history of sin. All temporal wealth is viewed in relation to God's final judgment. Failure to understand this salvation-history context results in a failure to grasp the vitality underlying the vast arena of Christian philanthropy.

PART SEVEN

# DEEDS NOT WORDS

## A. Faith Active in Love

Classic Christianity teaches that everyone *already knows how they prefer to be treated by others*. We know this because it is intrinsic to our very consciousness to know how we wish to be treated. This is not acquired knowledge but belongs to our ordinary human consciousness. We are fully conscious of the difference between others treating us well or badly. Everyone knows that difference.

### 1. We Already Know What We
### Ought to Do — The Golden Rule

Jesus' "golden rule" is: "So whatever you wish that men would do to you, do so to them; for this is the law and the prophets" (Matt. 7:12, RSV*). The rule is clear: *Since you already know what you would wish others to do to you, you already know what you ought to do for others.* This rule is stated in scripture, but available to common human reasoning even apart from the history of salvation.

This command is clear, is understandable, and does not allow anyone to plead ignorance. Kant did not invent this categorical imperative. The ancient Christian exegetes understood it well: "In this statement Jesus briefly sums up all that is required. He shows that the definition of virtue is short and easy and *known already to all*," according to John Chrysostom.

321

"Note that he did not say, 'Whatever things that you want God to do for you, do these things to your neighbor.' Thus you do not have the excuse of saying, 'How is that even possible? God is God and I am a human being!' Instead, he said, 'Anything you want your neighbor to do to you, you yourself also will be doing for your neighbor.' What is less of a burden than this? What is more just? This, said Jesus, 'is the Law and the Prophets.' From this it is clear that knowing the good is in accord with our very created nature. So we all know within ourselves what our duties are. We cannot ever again find refuge in ignorance [Rom. 1:19-21]" (Chrysostom, The Gospel of Matthew, Homily 23.6, italics added; Matt. 7:12).[1]

Simply do the good you would want done to you. You know already what this is. You do not want the good merely to be conceptualized for you. You want it done in a timely way. This is the good that we all already know. It is not only understandable, but is built into our very consciousness of ourselves. This is an eminently reasonable requirement. We know that it is reasonable, because we know how we want others to treat us. In this way we are called to overcome evil with good (Rom. 12:21). "Therefore as we have opportunity, let us do good to all" (Gal. 6:10, NKJV). This decisive opportunity is constantly presenting itself to us. This is how the believer "holds fast to that which is good" (1 Thess. 5:21, NAS) — by doing it. All else can be set aside in comparison to this rule. "I want you to be wise in what is good and innocent in what is evil" (Rom. 16:19, NAS).

### 2. The Single Intention of a Good Work

All the works of love have a single intention — to do for others exactly what you would wish they would do for you. Nothing about this is ambiguous. It is all too clear, according to Augustine, and we would much prefer to evade its evident clarity: "There might be reason to fear that a person may have a double heart toward another, since the matters of the heart are hidden. But it is hard to imagine anyone who would wish that others would deal in a duplicitous manner with themselves" (Augustine, Sermon on the Mount, 2.22 [75]; Matt. 7:12).[2]

We know that it is not good for us to deceive ourselves. We already

---

1. PG 57:314; NPNF 1 10:161-62; ACCS NT 1a:151*.
2. PL 34:1304; FC 11:186**; ACCS NT 1a:151.

know what it means to be treated by others in a way that looks for no special or unfair advantage. It is just in this way that I know already *what* I should do for the neighbor, and even *how* we should do it. The believer "is called to love the neighbor as himself to the limit of his ability. In doing so he pours out his love in a way that others may love God as well" (Augustine, Letters 167.16, italics added; Rom. 13:9).[3]

Hence "the beginning and the end of virtue is love," wrote John Chrysostom. "Paul is not looking merely for any sort of love. He wants love to be an intense, single-minded love. For he does not say merely: 'Love your neighbor,' but adds: 'as yourself.' Christ himself said that the law and the prophets hang upon this [Matt. 22:39-40]" (Chrysostom, Homilies on Romans 23; Rom. 13:9).[4]

### 3. Deeds Not Words

Words do not feed the hungry. Bede the Venerable observed: "It is obvious that words alone are not going to help someone who is naked and hungry. One whose faith does not go beyond words is useless. Such faith is dead without works of Christian love which alone can bring it back to life" (Bede the Venerable, Concerning the Epistle of St. James; Jas. 2:15).[5]

A million words do not substitute for a single deed for the neighbor's good. It is in the actual living of life, not merely in pleasant words, that good works are done. Bede wrote: "Those who are wise and self-disciplined, or who at least seek to be such, demonstrate that fact by living out what they profess. This actual 'living out' is far more decisive than simply teaching others concepts. For someone who lives in a humble and wise way will give more evidence of God's power than any number of words could ever do" (Bede the Venerable, Concerning the Epistle of St. James; Jas. 3:13).[6]

Jesus taught by body language of the most radical sort: "Words will never be enough unless examples are made visible. Think of it: How, precisely did Jesus teach us, brothers and sisters? He was hanging on the

3. FC 30:46; CSEL 44:604; ACCS NT 6:331*.
4. NPNF 1 11:514; ACCS NT 6:331*.
5. PL 93:21; ACCS NT 11:28*.
6. PL 93:30; ACCS NT 11:42*.

cross!" (Augustine, Sermon 284.6; 1 Pet. 2:21b).[7] Jesus taught not by writing on ethics, but by embodying his teaching.

The good work is not a good speech. "Merely verbal mercy is detestable. Who does not react negatively to this sort of empty talk? It is idle piety that flatters the sick with elegant language when fruitless tears are offered to heaven. What does it profit to bewail another man's shipwreck if you take no care of his body which is suffering from exposure? What good does it do to torture your soul with grief over another's wound if you refuse him a health-giving cup?" (Valerian of Cimiez, Homily 7.5; Jas. 2:16).[8] Love cares actively about the hungering body as well as the hungering soul.

The power of God to transform human life is best grasped by following this body language of love. Do not just look at the deeds of those who are responding fully to God's own active goodness — do them. The truth of Christian teaching is confirmed when God empowers love through actions, wrote Ambrosiaster: "Even though what is taught may seem incredible to the world, it is made credible by deeds" (Ambrosiaster, On Paul's Epistle to the Romans; Rom. 1:5).[9]

### 4. Offering Food and Clothing for the Body Are Elementary Tests of the Readiness of Faith to Serve

James wrote: "If a brother or sister is ill-clad and in lack of daily food, and one of you says to them, 'Go in peace, be warmed and filled,' *without giving them the things needed for the body,* what does it profit?" (Jas. 2:15-16, RSV, italics added). Provide what is needed for the body as a confirmation of your faith, which alone saves without any works of merit. "True love cares both about help for the body and help for the soul. Here James concentrates on the first of these because he is speaking especially to those who are rich" (Hilary of Arles, Introductory Tractate on the Letter of James; Jas. 2:15).[10]

Confession occurs not simply with the mouth. It must be embodied. Only right living validates right teaching, according to John Chrysostom:

7. WSA 3 8:91; ACCS NT 11:95*.
8. FC 17:349; ACCS NT 11:28-29*.
9. CSEL 81:16-17; ACCS NT 6:12*.
10. PL *Suppl.* 3:71; ACCS NT 11:28*.

"Even if somebody believes rightly in the Father and the Son, as well as in the Holy Spirit, if he does not lead the right kind of life, his supposed 'faith' will not be real faith, nor will it benefit him at all as far as his salvation is concerned. Jesus said: 'This is eternal life, to know you, the only true God' [John 17:3]. But we must not think that merely uttering the words is enough to save us. For our life and behavior must correspond as well" (Chrysostom, quoted in Cramer, Catena in Epistolas Catholicas; Jas. 2:18).[11] The law of love, wrote Augustine, "is not written on tables of stone [cf. 2 Cor. 3:3] but is shed abroad in our hearts through the Holy Spirit who is given to us" (Augustine, The Spirit and the Letter 29; Rom. 13:19).[12]

God is pleased with good works elicited by faith, according to John Chrysostom: "God's mission was not to save people in order that they may remain barren or inert. For Scripture says that faith has saved us. God desired that it be this way. Now in what case, tell me, does faith save without doing anything at all? Faith's workings themselves are a gift of God, lest anyone should boast. What then is Paul saying? *Not that God has forbidden works but that he has forbidden us to be justified by works.* No one, Paul says, is justified by works, precisely in order that the grace and benevolence of God may become apparent!" (Chrysostom, Homily on Ephesians 4.2.9, italics added; Eph. 2:9a).[13]

## B. The Timing of Good Works

### 1. The Opportunity to Do Good Is Time-Limited

We are not given an infinite number of moments in which faith has the unique opportunity to share God's goodness: "This should be the careful consideration of wise people, that since the days of this life are short and the time uncertain, death should never be unexpected for those who are to die. Those who know that they are mortal should not come to an unprepared end" (Leo the Great, Sermon 90.4.1; Luke 12:16-20).[14] "Why, you do not even know what will happen tomorrow," says James. "What is your

11. CEC 15; ACCS NT 11:29-30*.
12. LCC 8:217; ACCS NT 6:331.
13. IOEP 2:140; ACCS NT 8:134*.
14. FC 93:382; ACCS NT 3:208.

life? You are a mist that appears for a little while and then vanishes" (Jas. 4:14, NIV).

Fleeting moments of opportunity to care for people in need may pass quickly and irreversibly. Caesarius of Arles taught that if at that moment you are "dead" to what is happening, you cannot later cry out for mercy: "'O you cry out, now that you are dead and in the power of another, for when you had opportunities and saw me in the person of the poor, you were blind'" (Caesarius of Arles, Sermons 31.4; Jas. 2:16).[15] Do not put on blinders at the unique moment of meeting the Lord in the person of the neighbor.

Each moment that passes ends an opportunity to share God's love with another. We have only the day to work in because the night is coming. Diodore commented on Romans 13:12: "'The day' is the time of this life which remains to us, in which we can do good works. 'The night' is the future, in which it will no longer be possible to work. Then we shall lie in the darkness, having lost the chance to do good works" (Diodore, quoted in Staab, Pauline Commentary from the Greek Church; Rom. 13:12).[16]

Augustine's life was turned upside down when he was unexpectedly read this passage in Paul as a call to decision: "Let us conduct ourselves becomingly as in the day, not in reveling and drunkenness, not in debauchery and licentiousness, not in quarreling and jealousy. But put on the Lord Jesus Christ, and make no provision for the flesh, to gratify its desires" (Rom. 13:13-14, RSV). Paul challenged Augustine to a transformed way befitting life in Christ.

## 2. Be Ready for an Immediate Response

A man falls among thieves. He is stripped of his clothing and wounded. He is bypassed by the religious professionals. A Samaritan sees him on the road and without delay binds up his wounds (Luke 10:30-34).

The promptness of his response is an expression of the life that is lived in attentiveness, through decisive and immediate responsiveness to the mercy of God, who himself was wounded for our transgressions (Isa. 53:55), who heals our wounds (Jer. 30:17), and who does so in a timely way (Rom. 5:6).

15. FC 31:157; ACCS NT 11:29*.
16. NTA 15:109; ACCS NT 6:333-34.

Of the travelers on the road, the Samaritan alone had mercy for the wounded, and immediately acted in a merciful way (Luke 10:33). The Samaritan could have turned away like the priest and the Levite, but he did not. He instantly empathized with the one who was hurt, broken, attacked, and wounded. Such compassion reflects God's own compassion amid human brokenness.

### 3. Becoming Aware: Attentive Empathy

To reach out spontaneously for sufferers is to become totally awake to their immediate situation of need. Empathy grasps both the inward feelings of the neighbor and the outward consequences of neglect.

This personal attentiveness is commended in one of the earliest writings following the New Testament, in the Didache. It calls the believer to be ready, be on guard, to "'watch' over your life. Do not let 'your lamps' go out, and do not keep 'your loins unbelted,' but 'be ready,' for 'you do not know the hour when our Lord is coming.' Meet together frequently in your effort to see what is good for your souls. A lifetime of faith will be of no advantage[17] to you unless you prove to be fully responsive to the very end" (Didache 16.1-2; Luke 12:35).[18]

The same intense quality of complete attentiveness is commended by Basil as characteristic of the Christian life, wherein every now is viewed in relation to eternity: "What is the mark of a Christian? It is to watch daily and hourly and to stand prepared in that state of total readiness to respond in a way pleasing to God, knowing that the Lord will come at an hour that we do not expect" (Basil the Great, The Morals 22; Luke 12:36-40).[19]

Empathy is like waking up to the neighbor's need, not sleeping through it. Cyril of Alexandria wrote: "We say that the human mind is awake when it repels any tendency to slumber off into that carelessness that often brings one into bondage. When sunk in stupor, the heavenly light within the mind is vulnerable to being clouded. It is already in danger from a violent and impetuous blast of wind. Christ commands us to be

---

17. Cf. Letter of Barnabas 4:9 (an allegorical/typological interpretation of the Old Testament, grouped with other early writings of the Apostolic Fathers).

18. LCC 1:178-79**; ACCS NT 3:214*.

19. FC 9:205*; ACCS NT 3:214*.

awake. To this end his disciple also arouses us by saying, 'Be awake. Be watchful' [1 Pet. 5:8]" (Cyril of Alexandria, Commentary on the Gospel of St. Luke, Homily 92; Luke 12:35).[20]

### 4. The Temporal Deed of Mercy Is Accountable in Relation to Eternity

The time of our death is not revealed to us — mercifully. This mystery is intended to sharpen our alertness to God's requirement at any time. This command occurs concretely in and through the neighbor. That meeting is decisive for the final judgment.

Tomorrow is not the time for acts of mercy — only today. Tomorrow is obscured. Tomorrow belongs to the realm of possibility. Only today are we actually given the live opportunity to help the neighbor in need. To act in love now is to connect with eternity, according to Augustine:

> With a single heart, therefore, and exclusively for the sake of the kingdom of heaven, we ought to do good to all. In this well-doing we ought not to think about temporal rewards. These temporal rewards bear no comparison to the kingdom of God. For it is with reference to all these temporal things that the Lord used the word, "tomorrow," when he said: "Do not think about tomorrow." For that word is not used except in the realm of time, where the future succeeds the past. When we perform any good deed, let us pay no heed to the temporal, but stand in relation to the eternal. Then, our deed will be not only good but also perfect. "For tomorrow," says he, "will have anxieties of its own." By this he means that you are to take food or drink or clothing when it is fitting that you do so. When the need for them is pressing, these things will be at hand. Our Father knows that we need all these things. "Sufficient for the day," he says, "is its own evil." In other words, when the presenting need is great, you will have sufficient reason to act. (Augustine, Sermon on the Mount 2.17 [56]; Matt. 6:34)[21]

The divine address through the neighbor is always now, not in time future.

The author of the Opus Imperfectum asked: "Why is the date of an

---

20. CGSL 370**; ACCS NT 3:213*.
21. PL 34:1294; FC 11:164-65*; ACCS NT 1a:145-46*.

individual's death hidden from him? Clearly it is so that he might always do good. He lives as though he might die at any moment. The date of Christ's second advent is withheld from the world for the same reason, namely, so that every generation might live in the expectation of Christ's return. This is why when his disciples asked him, 'Lord, will you restore the kingdom to Israel at this time?' Jesus replied, 'It is not for you to know the times and the seasons which the Father has established by his authority' [Acts 1:6-7]" (Opus Imperfectum in Matthaeum, Homily 51; Matt. 24:44).[22]

## C. Grace Works through Faith Active in Love

Whatever is good in good works is good insofar as enabled by grace. There is no exception. The major patristic writers understood this and became the pattern for the Reformers' teaching of justification, a thousand years before Luther. No one is ever saved by good works. Rather than put words in their mouths, we let them speak for themselves.

### 1. Works That Are Good Are Enabled by Grace

Grace alone empowers works, according to Augustine: "*Grace is given not because we have done good works but in order that we may have power to do them,* not because we have fulfilled the law but in order that we may be able to fulfill it" (Augustine, The Spirit and the Letter 16, italics added; Rom. 11:6).[23]

Since God's grace is not cheap, but given at great cost — the death of his only Son — it is not to be received as if without cost. Caesarius of Arles warned against accepting God's grace cheaply, or "in vain": "What does it mean to receive the grace of God in vain except to be unwilling to perform good works even with the help of his grace?" (Caesarius of Arles, Sermon 126.5; 2 Cor. 6:1).[24]

Works of love are not performed under the requirement of law, but by the power of grace (Rom. 6:14). The faithful remain unworthy of all the

22. PG 56:924; ACCS NT 1b:210*.
23. LCC 8:206; ACCS NT 6:287.
24. FC 47:219; ACCS NT 7:254*.

loving-kindness God has shown to us in nature and history (Pss. 8:1-4; 144:2-4). They know themselves to be recipients of his unmerited mercy, and crowned with his loving-kindness (Ps. 103:4; Luke 1:25). The point in time where grace and truth come closest to us within human history is Jesus Christ (John 1:14, 17). From his fullness we all receive grace upon grace (John 1:16). This grace is sufficient for our salvation (2 Cor. 12:9), which bears the fruit of good works.

### 2. What Law Requires, Grace Enables

Grace is received by faith. "Without faith, no good work is ever begun or completed" (Caesarius of Arles, Sermon 12.1; Mark 9:24).[25] The grace that enables works of love lives in our hearts by faith. It is born when we respond trustingly to God's unmerited grace revealed on the cross. It is not our doing but the gift of God.

John Chrysostom commented: "For 'by grace you are saved,' [Paul] says, 'through faith.' Then, so as to do no injury to free will, he allots a role to us, then takes it away again, saying *and this not of ourselves*. . . . Even faith, he says, is not from us. For if the Lord had not come, if he had not called us, how should we have been able to believe?" (Chrysostom, Homily on Ephesians, italics added; Eph. 2:8b).[26]

We are "God's workmanship, created in Christ Jesus for good works" (Eph. 2:10a, RSV*). Jerome commented: "We are his creation. This means that it is from him that we live, breathe, understand and are able to believe" (Jerome, Epistle to the Ephesians 1; Eph. 2:10a).[27]

Good works are not "accomplished" by an act of will, but flow freely as a response to grace. This is so even when the source of grace is unrecognized. Bede taught that even our most compassionate responses happen only by grace. They are not self-initiated. "Your place in the kingdom of heaven is ready, your room in the Father's house is prepared, your salvation in heaven awaits you. All you have to do, if you want to receive them, is to make yourself ready. But since no one can do this by his own efforts, Peter reminds us that we are kept in the power of God by faith. Nobody

25. FC 31:67; ACCS NT 2:124*.
26. IOEP 2:160; ACCS NT 8:134.
27. PL 26:470B-70C [577]; ACCS NT 8:134.

can keep doing good works in the strength of his own free will. So we must all ask God to help us, so that we may be brought to perfection by the One who made it possible for us to do good works in the first place" (Bede the Venerable, On 1 Peter; 1 Pet. 1:5b).[28]

Since we have fallen into sin — indeed, into a long history of sin — only God's creation of a new humanity can restore our original capacity for good works. Cyril of Alexandria wrote: "Human beings choose their own way of life and are entrusted with the reins of their own intelligence, so as to follow whatever course they wish, either toward the good or toward the contrary. But our created nature has implanted in us a zealous desire for whatever is good and the will to concern itself with goodness and righteousness. For this is what we mean by saying that humanity is 'in the image and likeness of God' [cf. Gen. 1:26] — that the unfallen creature is naturally disposed to what is good and right" (Cyril of Alexandria, Doctrinal Questions and Answers 2; Eph. 2:10b).[29] We are not unfallen creatures. But some remnant of the unfallen disposition lives in us by grace (not law — the law only reveals our fallenness).

We are made able by grace to rise from the death of our bondage to sin, according to Theodore of Mopsuestia: "We are re-created by the resurrection. Completely unable as we are to mend our ways by our own decision on account of the natural weakness that frustrates us, we are made able to come newly alive without pain and with great ease by the grace of the One who re-creates us for this purpose" (Theodore of Mopsuestia, Epistle to the Ephesians, quoted in Cramer, Catenae in Sancti Pauli Epistolas; Eph. 2:10b).[30]

### 3. Faith Lives by Participating in God's Righteousness

If faith is genuine, love will accompany it. This commonplace of Christian teaching is well stated by Caesarius of Arles: "John immediately joined love to faith, because *without love faith is empty.* Faith belongs to Christians when it overflows with love. But without love faith belongs to the demons" (Caesarius of Arles, Sermons 186.1, italics added; 1 John 5:1).[31]

---

28. PL 93:43; ACCS NT 11:70-71.
29. CASL 188; ACCS NT 8:135*.
30. CSPE 6:142; ACCS NT 8:135*.
31. FC 47:490; ACCS NT 11:221*.

One of the earliest Latin writers to grasp clearly Paul's view of the relation of faith and grace was Marius Victorinus: "Faith lives in righteousness. Faith remains the fountain of all the virtues, as Paul has often stated. . . . *Faith is proven to be true faith when we live righteously.* Then faith is seen to be useful to us, as the righteousness that accompanies faith is useful" (Marius Victorinus, Epistle to the Ephesians 2, italics added; Eph. 6:14b).[32]

"Righteousness comes from faith, which means that it too is a gift of God. For since this righteousness belongs to God, it is an unmerited gift. And the gifts of God greatly exceed any achievements of our own zeal" (Chrysostom, Homily on Philippians 12; Phil. 3:9b).[33]

Remembering the poor is not to be confused with seeking righteousness by works, which would claim these works as means of salvation. The patristic writers were emphatic on this point. Salvation comes by God's free sovereign grace. Remembering the poor flows out of that gift. Marius Victorinus reviewed the difference:

> When Paul and Barnabas were having those discussions with John and Peter and James, the Gospel was accepted and established in the way that Paul describes. The only thing that they did not hear willingly in this dispute was that works were not part of salvation. Their sole injunction, however, was that they should be mindful of the poor. Thus they agree on this point also, that the hope of salvation does not reside in the activity of doing works for the poor, but they simply enjoin — what? — that they be *mindful* of the poor. Not that we should spend all our efforts on it but that we should share with those who have not what we are able to have. We are instructed simply that we should be mindful of the poor, not that we should place our care and thought upon our own capacity to *possess our salvation by this means.* This is how Paul was instructed and guided in this matter. But this is not all Paul says [to the Galatians]. "That we should be mindful," he says, not "that we should do this" but that we should "keep them in mind." This is different from presenting our work as if meritorious. The Gospel Paul preached required him to be mindful of the poor and to bestow upon them whatever he could. In truth, indeed, no one is poor if, sim-

32. BTMV 201 [1290D-91A]; ACCS NT 8:210.
33. IOEP 5:125; ACCS NT 8:270.

ply keeping faith and trusting in God, he awaits the riches of his salvation. (Marius Victorinus, Epistle to the Galatians 1, some italics added; Gal. 2:10a)[34]

### 4. Faith Is Made Stronger, Not Weaker, through Works of Love

Faith is made stronger, not weaker, through works of love. And faith is weakened by the neglect of good works: "Faith then causes one to abstain from evil and to do good works. The more you abstain from evil and follow the good, the stronger you will make your faith. The less you abstain from evil, however, and the more you neglect good works, the weaker your faith will become" (Opus Imperfectum in Matthaeum, Homily 39; Matt. 21:22).[35]

The way from faith to practice takes time and is refined through experience. To have faith does not always lead to an immediate understanding of what faith does in a given situation. This discernment may come only gradually as faith is tested in experience. We learn more about how to manifest the works of love by practicing the works of love, according to Diodore: "When we realized what the advantages of good works are, the message of salvation is more powerful than it was when we first believed. For when we first believed in Christ we did not immediately acquire an exact understanding of what we should be doing, nor was it clear to us what we should stop doing and what we should continue doing" (Diodore, quoted in Staab, Pauline Commentary from the Greek Church; Rom. 13:11).[36] That became clear through practice.

### D. What Faith Does When Faith Is Working

Faith is still immature if it fails to *do what faith characteristically does*. But just what does faith typically *do* when it is working? When faith is *working*, what is faith actually *doing*?

---

34. BTMV 21-22 [1161B-61C]; ACCS NT 8:24*.
35. PG 56:846-47; ACCS NT 1b:133.
36. NTA 15:108; ACCS NT 6:332*.

In the Justification Reader we have spoken about *what faith is*. In the Good Works Reader we have set forth a detailed picture of *what faith does*.

Our issue has been not whether works save us by grace alone through faith alone — that is already settled, and all too clear in scripture to miss. Rather the question is: What are those works that express faith?

### 1. Faith Works through Love

The ancient Christian writers thought deeply through this question. Their key text came not from James (where one might have expected) but straight from Paul himself, who answers concisely: "Faith works through love" (Gal. 5:6, RSV*). This is a central linchpin of both biblical and patristic reasoning on the relation of faith and love, of doctrine and ethics.

The love in which faith becomes active is God's own love, the love of the Father through the Son, addressed by the Spirit to all humanity. Marius Victorinus wisely grasped this dynamic: "*Through this faith comes works fitting to salvation.* This comes about through the love that we have for Christ and God and thus toward every human being. For it is these two relationships above all that set life straight and fulfill the whole sense of the law. They contain all the commands in the Decalogue — if it follows necessarily that he who keeps faith will also keep love, since these two fulfill all the precepts of the law of Christ" (Marius Victorinus, Epistle to the Galatians 2, italics added; Gal. 5:6).[37]

To keep faith is to keep on loving. Had the Galatians abided in love, they would not have weakened their faith, a point nailed down by John Chrysostom: "It is the failure of the Galatians to become rooted in love that has given entrance to their forgetfulness of grace. Not just bare faith but *faith abiding in love* — that is what we are looking for. It is as though he said, 'Had you loved Christ as you ought, you would not have gone voluntarily into slavery, you would not have insulted your deliverer'" (Chrysostom, Homily on Galatians, italics added; Gal. 5:6-7).[38]

---

37. BTMV 60-61 [1189D-90A]; ACCS NT 8:76-77.
38. IOEP 4:80; ACCS NT 8:77*.

## 2. Whether Genuine Faith Can Be without Any Works

The believer gives evidence of belief "by working in a way worthy of faith," wrote Bede. "If you think that faith in his divinity and a profession of that faith are enough by themselves, read on!" (Bede the Venerable, On 1 John; 1 John 5:5).[39] This does not imply that the evidence of faith (the works of love) itself contributes to our justification. For our justification is already an accomplished fact on the cross, awaiting our faith's confirmation. To confirm it is to share in the love that is manifested there.

Love is the prevailing expression in the mirror of justifying faith. There can be no face in a mirror if the face itself is absent. To mirror is to mirror something. It is precisely in this close interconnection that faith shows through deeds. Faith reflects God's love in actions, according to Symeon the New Theologian: "Faith is shown by deeds like the features of the face in a mirror" (Symeon, Discourses 29.4; Jas. 2:18).[40]

Conscience provides a God-given check against self-deception. If you think you have faith, but continue to practice evil, you are confused, according to Augustine: "Lest believers imagine that they might be saved by *inactive faith,* even if they continue to practice these evils, God has put fear in their hearts" (Augustine, On Continence 14.13, italics added; Jas. 2:14).[41]

## 3. Faith without Works Is Dead

The other apostle who most plainly grasped the relationship was James, who asked: "What does it profit, my brethren, if a man says he has faith but has not works?" (Jas. 2:14a, RSV). Lacking all actions of faith, faith is, so to speak, dead. *"While faith provides the basis for works, the strength of faith comes out only in works"* (Leo the Great, Sermons 10.3, italics added; Jas. 2:17).[42] Luther's *On Good Works* makes the same point.

The faith that neglects to bear the fruit of love is not genuine faith, hence a dead faith. Only faith in God's mercy justifies. Faith, to be real, must

39. PL 93:113; ACCS NT 11:222*.
40. CWSS 312; ACCS NT 11:30.
41. FC 16:228-29; ACCS NT 11:28*.
42. FC 93:45; ACCS NT 11:29.

be a living, active faith, bearing fruit in works of love. John Chrysostom stated concisely the two sides of classic Christian ethics: "*'Faith without works is dead'* [Jas. 2:26b] *and works without faith are dead also.* For if we have sound doctrine but fail in living it out, the doctrine is of no use to us" (Chrysostom, Sermons on Genesis 2.14, italics added; Jas. 2:26b).[43]

Works of the law, which amount finally to works of the flesh, are those works performed without faith in the saving grace of God (Heb. 6:1, 9:14), detached from the living Word of grace. They are therefore dead works. These dead works (works of death, darkness, works of the flesh, works of the law), are sharply distinguished from good works — evidences of a faith that is becoming active in love.

A working faith is life giving, according to Hilary of Arles: "Works give life to faith, faith gives life to the soul, and the soul gives life to the body" (Hilary of Arles, Introductory Tractate on the Letter of James; Jas. 2:17).[44] Lacking soul there is no living body. Lacking works there is no living faith.


### 4. Active Faith Lives through Good Works

Works attest faith. Salvian the Presbyter wrote: "Good works are witnesses to the Christian faith, because otherwise a Christian cannot demonstrate that he has that faith. If he cannot show it, it may as well be completely nonexistent" (Salvian, On the Governance of God 4.1; Jas. 2:19).[45]

Good works do not work against faith, but manifest faith. Grace alone saves through faith alone. Faith lives by doing what faith does, becoming active in love, according to Didymus the Blind, who brought to bear this profound body-spirit analogy:

> Just as the spirit joins itself to the body and by doing so brings the latter to life, so works, joined to faith, give life to it as well. Furthermore, it is to be understood that *faith without works is not faith at all, just as a dead man is not really a human being.* But how can some say that, because the spirit which gives life to the body is more honorable than the

43. FC 74:37; ACCS NT 11:34*.
44. PL *Suppl.* 3:72; ACCS NT 11:29.
45. FC 3:92; ACCS NT 11:30*.

body, therefore works are more honorable than faith? I have looked into this matter in some detail and shall try to explain my position on this. It is undoubtedly true that the spirit is nobler than the body, but this does not mean that works can be put before faith, because a person is saved by grace, not by works but by faith. There should be no doubt but that *faith saves and then lives by doing its own works, so that the works which provide evidence of salvation by faith are not those of the law but of grace* — a different kind of thing altogether. (Didymus, Commentary on James, italics added; Jas. 2:26a; cf. Luther, Calvin).[46]

## 4. The "Supposed" Faith of Demons

The good confession of faith is made false by lacking faith's good works. Such are accounted as if dead, as death-laden as the very demons who confessed Christ in the Gospel, according to Augustine: "Those who believe and act according to true faith do live and are not dead, but those who do not believe, or else who believe like the demons, trembling but living evilly, proclaiming the Son of God but not having love, must rather be accounted dead" (Augustine, Tractates 22.7.2; Jas. 2:19).[47] Thus "the apostle [James] says that a man who believes and does not act has the faith of demons. If that is true, imagine the fate of a man who does not believe at all" (Caesarius of Arles, Sermons 12.5; Jas. 2:19).[48]

A supposed faith that lacks love represents a demonic pretense: "You can at one level believe what God says, and at another level you can believe that God exists. But can you believe in him so as to love him so much that you want to *do* what he tells you? There are many evil people around who can manage the first two of these. They believe that God means what he says, and they are quite prepared to accept that he exists. But it takes someone who is not just a nominal Christian, but . . . one in deed and word, who lives to love God, to do what faith requires. *Faith with love is Christian; . . . faith without love is demonic*" (Bede the Venerable, Concerning the Epistle of St. James, italics added; Jas. 2:19).[49]

---

46. PG 39:1732; ACCS NT 11:34*.
47. FC 79:203; ACCS NT 11:30.
48. FC 31:72; ACCS NT 11:30*.
49. PL 93:22; ACCS NT 11:30*.

"You believe that God is one; you do well." So what? "Even the demons believe — and shudder" (Jas. 2:19, RSV). Here James is pointing out that even the demonic powers exhibit a limited sort of faith. They may accurately recognize the Son of God, but still lack love. This is not the faith that works by love, according to Augustine: "The 'faith that works by love' [Gal. 5:6], is not the same faith that demons have. For 'the devils also believe and tremble' [Jas. 2:19]. But do they love? If they had not believed, they would not have said: 'You are the holy one of God' [Luke 4:34] or 'You are the Son of God' [Mark 3:11; Luke 4:41]. But if they had loved, they would not have said: 'What have we to do with you?' [Matt. 8:29; cf. Mark 5:7; Luke 8:28]" (Augustine, Letter 194, "To Sixtus"; Mark 3:11).[50] The demons show that it is possible to have a bare and dead faith without love, which is quite different from the living faith that becomes active in love.

The demonic powers themselves may give lip service to faith, yet lack the only faith that makes a difference — the faith that becomes active in love: "James gives us the example of the devils, saying that those who profess faith with their lips only are really no better than they are. For even they believe that Christ is the Son of God, that he is the Holy One of God and that he has authority over them" (Andreas, quoted in Cramer, Catena in Epistolas Catholicas; Jas. 2:19).[51]

As Luther would argue later, so the Latin writer Marius Victorinus wrote earlier that faith "contains all the other virtues and brings them all to fulfillment. Unless we are armed with this shield we will not have the strength to battle courageously and resist all these deadly powers. But with the protection of faith we repel all these blows and whatever attacks come from the whole host of powers" (Marius Victorinus, Epistle to the Ephesians 2; Eph. 6:16).[52]

The faith that works through love is, according to Augustine, "the faith that separates the righteous from the unclean demons, for they too, as the apostle James says, 'believe and tremble' [Jas. 2:19] but their actions are not good. Therefore they do not have that faith by which 'the righteous live' [Gal. 3:11]" (Augustine, On Grace and Free Will 18; Gal. 5:6).[53] Even though one might argue that the demonic powers in a marginal sense "be-

50. FC 30:308-9*; ACCS NT 3:40.
51. CEC 14-15; ACCS NT 11:30.
52. BTMV 202 [1291C]; ACCS NT 8:211. See T. Oden, *The Transforming Power of Grace* (Nashville: Abingdon, 1993).
53. PL 44:892; ACCS NT 8:77.

lieve," and even tremble because of their dreadful recognition of God, "Only those who are pure of heart will see God, and who would say that the devils are pure of heart? Nevertheless, they believe and tremble" (Augustine, Commentary on the Sermon on the Mount 53.10; Jas. 2:19).[54]

## 6. The Johannine Integration of Faith and Works

The integral relation of faith and works is found not only in Paul and James, but also prominently in the Johannine writings. The Fathers meditated deeply upon 1 John 5:4, "Whatever is born of God overcomes the world" (1 John 5:4, RSV). Bede showed that this overcoming is not by our efforts without grace: "The commandments of God are not burdensome. All those who are bound to keep them with true devotion, despite the adversities of this world, regard its temptations with equanimity, even to the point of readiness for death, because it is the gateway to the heavenly country. And lest anyone should think that we can somehow achieve all this by our own efforts, John adds that the substance of our victory is our faith, not our works" (Bede the Venerable, On 1 John; 1 John 5:4).[55]

"It is not faith in the abstract that overcomes the world," wrote Oecumenius, who wrote the earliest extant Greek commentary on the Revelation to John: "It must be faith in Jesus Christ, as John makes plain" (Oecumenius, Commentary on 1 John; 1 John 5:5).[56] Theophylact joined him on this point: "Once you have become brothers and sisters in love, you must go on to the next stage, which is to overcome the world. For those who have been born again in God must expel every kind of unbelief from their midst" (Theophylact, Commentary on 1 John; 1 John 5:4).[57] Faith does what faith believes.

## 7. Good News and Good Works

To misunderstand the relation of faith and works is to proclaim "a different gospel" (Gal. 1:6, NIV), contrary to the Gospel of Jesus Christ (Gal. 1:6-9; cf. Gal. 2:7; 1 Tim. 1:3; 6:3). Those who view good works as detachable

54. FC 11:219; ACCS NT 11:30*.
55. PL 93:113; ACCS NT 11:222*.
56. PG 119:676; ACCS NT 11:222-23.
57. PG 126:57; ACCS NT 11:222.

from God's good news are, in Paul's view, preaching a gospel different from "the one we preached to you" (Gal. 1:8, NIV).

The Gospel, or "euangelion," is good news or glad tidings of God's saving action in Jesus (1 Pet. 1:12; Heb. 4:2, 6). God's good news elicits good deeds. The Gospel kindles good works in grateful response to God's action.

Wherever this good news is proclaimed, it calls forth good works in response to the saving action of God in the death and resurrection of Jesus Christ. There is thus a close relationship between good news and good works. As God's redeeming love is given freely, even at great cost, so our good works are offered up in response to the free, self-giving grace of God, not as an obligation, not as a duty primarily, but as an act of gratitude for the good news.

The Gospel itself is the "pattern of sound teaching" (2 Tim. 1:13, NIV). In Jude 3, it is called "the faith." Good works depend upon hearing the good news, hearing the pattern of sound teaching that emerges out of the faith once delivered to the saints. Faith lives under a new dispensation, the "doctrine according to godliness" (1 Tim. 6:3, KJV*). The Gospel is "the new covenant" (Heb. 12:24, KJV; cf. 7:22; 8:6-13; 9:8-15), a dispensation of grace (Eph. 3:2).

Jesus sent his disciples to preach the Gospel in the villages (Luke 9:2, 6). In his week of passion, Jesus preached good news in the temple at Jerusalem (Luke 20:1). The good news is promised to be preached in all the world before the end of history (Matt. 24:14; Mark 13:10). Paul was called to testify to the Gospel of the grace of God (Acts 20:24; Rom. 1:1). All hearers of the Gospel are called to become accountable to this testimony of grace. The Gospel is God's power unto salvation for all who believe (Rom. 1:16). It manifests the righteousness of God (Rom. 1:17).

## 8. Defining Good Works

Good works are those acts performed in response to the grace and mercy made known in history. A work (Greek *ergon*) is defined as an act or deed, a purposeful activity, an undertaking. God is capable of doing works — always good. Man is capable of doing works — whether good or evil. Human acts may by grace share in the goodness of God's acts. Their goodness depends on whether they are responsive to the will of God.

Good works are fruits — acts of Christian responsiveness to grace, evidences of faith in God's coming to us, of our trust in God's embodied word to us. Good works are fruits grounded in the forgiveness received through the death of Christ. They are distinguished from attempting to accomplish self-initiated good works, according to the law. This can only become a curse to us if they pretend to be the basis of our justification. Good works grounded in God's good news are viewed not strictly as a law that is commanded, but the "law of liberty" (Jas. 1:25, RSV).

Works of the flesh are acts done in defiance of God's revealed grace. Fruits of the spirit are born out of God's good work for us. Works of the flesh are our works that are misplaced and out of touch with God's work for us. Among the works of the flesh are immorality, impurity, licentiousness, idolatry, sorcery, enmity, strife, jealousy, anger, selfishness, dissension, party-spirit, envy, drunkenness, carousing, and the like (Gal. 5:19-21). These works stand in sharp contrast with fruits of the spirit (Gal. 5:22-23). Those who live after the flesh (Rom. 8:12-13) perform their actions according to the flesh (Rom. 8:5-7). They are dominated by passions of the flesh (Eph. 2:3; Gal. 5:16; 1 Pet. 4:2). These are works of darkness, insofar as they fail to worship God and to demonstrate a life lived accountably in the presence of God's holy love. If the root is corrupted, the fruit will be corrupted — that is, if we do not live by faith, our works will be tainted.

### 9. God's Own Good Work on Behalf of Fallen Humanity

The Gospel is good news of God's willingness to come to us and do an incomparably good work on our behalf. It is a distortion to attempt to win God's favor on the basis of something good that we presumably do for God. These works are arrogant and fruitless, and hence not good works rooted in grace. We are justified — made able to stand in God's presence — by grace alone. Only God's mercy can upright our wrongs. Only when our faith trusts in God's good work do we find that our twisted lives are straightened out. Faith becomes active in good works, the works of love.

"Great are the works of the Lord. All who delight in them ponder them. . . . He has caused his wonders to be remembered . . . He has shown his people the power of his works" (Ps. 111:2, 4, 6, NIV). Simply to behold God's works motivates us, not simply to ponder, but to act in accordance with them.

341

Psalm 139:14 (NIV*) says, "I praise You because I am fearfully and wonderfully made. Your works are wonderful! I know this full well." This is not simply a statement of beholding, but of a beholding that transforms behavior.

In Ecclesiastes 3:11 (NIV*) the preacher exclaimed: "He has made everything beautiful in its time. He has also set eternity in the hearts of men, yet they cannot fathom what God has done from the beginning to end." Our beholding of the good works of God is seen both in time and in relation to eternity. But we can never grasp the whole because we do not have the same vision of the whole that God has.

### 10. God's Good Work in Creation

The entire work of creation is solely God's work. Creation is God's handiwork — everything conceivable — heaven and earth (Gen. 1:1, 11-25). Human history is played out on the theater of God's creation. Humanity is created good (Gen. 1:26-27, 31). Humanity is the crowning work of God's creation. Human fallenness is starkly visible in contrast to that original condition from which it is fallen.

God's good work in creation has become distorted by sin. Hence God graciously acted further to redeem what had become fallen in creation. God creates plants and animals and the physical order. Humanity is the special point in creation where God breathes into our bodies the breath of human life. This breath is in scripture called soul.

In Christian justification teaching that resists all works-righteousness, there is no implied aversion to working, doing, acting, and the performance of good deeds. Neither the prophets nor the apostles disdained energetic work. Even Jesus himself was described as a *tecton*, an artisan, a craftsman. Paul was a tentmaker, supporting himself by honest toil. Adam was ordained to work even before the fall — to tend the Garden (Gen. 1:28; 2:15). Prior to the fall, work is not a curse.

The central meaning of redeemed work in the Bible has to do with how our actions give truthful evidence of our faith. This is constantly attested in scripture: Matthew 5:16; Acts 9:36; Ephesians 2:10; Colossians 1:10; 2 Thessalonians 2:17; 1 Timothy 2:10; 5:10; 5:25; Titus 2:7, 14; Hebrews 10:24; 1 Peter 2:12.

## 11. Faith and Works

Our good works are never the basis for our salvation (Eph. 2:8-9). We do not need to seek God's favor on the basis of works of the law (Gal. 3:10-13), because Christ has come to fulfill the law for us by his death on the cross. So even the seemingly innocuous attempt to gain God's acceptance by doing works of the law becomes for conscience a curse (Gal. 2:16; 2:21; 3:10-14), since we never fulfill the law adequately.

The Christian life is empowered by the Spirit (Rom. 15:18-19; 1 Thess. 1:5). The Spirit seeks to elicit behaviors that are actively responsive to the good work of God (Col. 1:10). Good works are works that arise out of faith (1 Thess. 1:3; 2 Thess. 1:11).

The faithful are brought into the new covenant relationship to work in response to God's good work. They are not converted *by* works without God's good work. But they are given the command to: "Let your light shine before men in such a way that they may see your good works, and glorify your Father who is in heaven" (Matt. 5:16, NAS). Those who exhibit the life of good works, such as Dorcas (Acts 9:36) and Titus (Tit. 2:7), are commended among the saints.

Among the seven churches of Revelation, some are commended for their good works, and others admonished for works that are not worthy (Rev. 2:2, 5, 9). Why would the Lord call believers to "keep my commandments" (John 15:10, KJV) if they were purely superficial to the life of faith, asked Augustine? "If one is able to enter . . . life without observing the commandments, I do not understand why the Lord said, 'If you want to enter into eternal life, keep the commandments' (Matt. 19:17)" (Augustine, On Faith and Works 15.25; Jas. 2:17).[58]

The life of faith that elicits the fruits of good works will receive its heavenly reward finally as promised. Even if that reward is not fully evident in this life, it is given in eternal life. Any works that are not accountable to grace received by faith will not survive God's judgment (1 Cor. 3:10-15).

---

58. FC 27:252; ACCS NT 11:29*.

## E. Reconciling James and Paul

The question of faith and works is not an "either/or" — faith *or* works. Rather it is how faith becomes active in works.

It was taken for granted in classic Christianity that Paul and James could and must be reconciled. This "must" was due to the universally received premise that the Holy Spirit would not inspire attestations that were truly contrary to each other. But how did the Fathers reconcile these texts?

### 1. Reconciling James and Paul

James appealed to Abraham's faith, just as did Paul. "Do you want to be shown, you shallow man, that faith apart from works is barren? Was not Abraham our father justified by works, when he offered his son Isaac upon the altar?" (Jas. 2:20-21, RSV*).

The Fathers understood that James used the word "works" to refer to what Paul meant by "good works," that is, works flowing out of faith. For both Paul and James, the life of faith manifests itself in responsiveness to grace, which produces the fruits of the Spirit, good works.

Augustine argued that the "works of the law" of which Paul speaks are distinguishable from the "works of faith" of which James speaks. By the same Gospel we are freed from the former and accountable for the latter: "Holy Scripture should be interpreted in a way which is in complete agreement with those who first understood it and not in a way which seems to be inconsistent to those who are least familiar with it. *Paul said that a man is justified through faith without the works of the law, but not without those works of which James speaks*" (Augustine, On the Christian Life 13, italics added; Jas. 2:20).[59]

Paul and James are best seen as together, held in the closest correlation, in the opinion of Bede, to avoid temptations to license:

The apostle Paul preached that we are justified by faith without works. There are those who understand by this that it does not matter whether they live evil lives or do wicked and terrible things, as long as they believe in Christ, since Paul makes it clear that salvation is

59. FC 16:36; ACCS NT 11:30-31*.

through faith. Those who neglect works have made a great mistake. James here expounds how Paul's words ought to be understood. This is why *James uses the example of Abraham, who Paul also used as an example of faith, to show that the patriarch also did good works in the light of his faith.* It is therefore wrong to interpret Paul in such a way as to suggest that it did not matter whether Abraham put his faith into practice or not. What Paul meant was that no one obtains the gift of justification on the basis of merit derived from works performed beforehand, because the gift of justification comes only by grace through faith. (Bede the Venerable, Concerning the Epistle of St. James, italics added; Jas. 2:20)[60]

James refers to the works *of* faith, not works *prior to* faith, according to Bede: "The works mentioned here [in James] are works of faith. No one can have perfect works unless he has faith, but many have perfect faith without works, since they do not always have time to do them" (Bede the Venerable, Concerning the Epistle of St. James; Jas. 2:24).[61] To have perfect faith without works, as in the case of the thief on the cross, is possible only for those who are immediately dying, who have no time or opportunity for good works.

It is foolish to presume that one can believe without expressing that belief in any action whatever, argued Oecumenius. True faith is such that it elicits action: "Take note of what spiritual understanding really is. It is not enough to believe in a purely intellectual sense. For belief seeks to become effective in action. What James is saying here does not contradict the apostle Paul, who understood that both belief and action were a part of what he called 'faith'" (Oecumenius, Commentary on James; Jas. 2:14).[62]

James writes that faith by itself, when detached from any action, if it has no works, is like faith being dead (Jas. 2:14-17). The view of James is parallel to the view of Paul that Christian actions, the deeds and the behavior of the believer and the believing community, are finally accountable to the living God who acts in events (2 Cor. 8:7; Gal. 5:6; Col. 1:9-10). The Fathers were well instructed by Ephesians 2:10 and Titus 2:14, where Paul argues that Christians are saved in order to perform good works to glorify

60. PL 93:22; ACCS NT 11:31*.
61. PL 93:24; ACCS NT 11:33*.
62. PG 119:477; ACCS NT 11:28*.

God. So the basis of good works is never simply human moral initiative, but it is response to God's grace (2 Cor. 9:8; 2 Thess. 2:17).

## 2. *Distinguishing Faith before and after Baptism*

Andrew of Crete found another way of resolving the seeming discrepancy between Paul and James. It hinged on the decisive distinction between faith before and faith after baptism. Pre-baptismal faith does not of itself require works but only confession and the word of salvation, by which those who believe in Christ are justified. It is thus post-baptismal faith that is intrinsically conjoined with good works, according to Andreas:

> Now someone might object to this and say: "Did Paul not use Abraham as an example of someone who was justified by faith without works? And here James is using the very same Abraham as an example of someone who was justified, not by faith alone, but also by the actions that confirm that faith." What are we to say? How can Abraham be an example of faith without works, as well as of faith with works, at the same time? But the solution is ready to hand from the Scriptures. For the same Abraham is at different times an example of both kinds of faith. The first is *pre-baptismal* faith, which does not require works but only confession and the word of salvation, by which those who believe in Christ are justified. The second is *post-baptismal* faith, which is expressed in works. Understood in this way, the two apostles do not contradict one another, but one and the same Spirit is speaking through both of them. (Andrew of Crete, quoted in Cramer, Catena in Epistolas Catholicas, italics added; Jas. 2:21)[63]

Similarly Oecumenius argued that in James 2, the author was talking about faith after baptism. For a faith without works after baptism only makes all the more clear that we have received a talent but are not using it profitably. Oecumenius, like Andrew, distinguished between faith before baptism, which cannot bring any good works to God to claim merit for justification, and faith after baptism, which is freed to bring to God those acts that are pleasing to God: "James is talking here about faith after bap-

---

63. CEC 16; ACCS NT 11:32*.

tism, for a faith without works can only make us more guilty of sin, seeing that we have received a talent but are not using it profitably. The Lord himself demonstrated the need for works after baptism by going into the desert to do battle with the devil [Matt. 4:1-11]. Paul also exhorts those who have entered into the mystery of faith to 'strive to enter [God's] rest' [Heb. 4:11], as if bare inactive faith could not be enough. Holiness of life is also necessary, and for that, great efforts are required" (Oecumenius, Commentary on James; Jas. 2:26b).[64] No effort is required to receive grace. Great efforts are called for in responding daily to grace.

## 3. Abraham and Isaac Anticipate Christ

Both Paul and James knew that Abraham was as mature in his faith as he was in his works, according to Bede:

> James makes deft use of the example of Abraham in order to provoke those Jews who imagined that they were worthy followers of their great ancestor. In order to show them that they did not come up to the mark in times of trial and to test their faith by specific examples, James takes Abraham as his model. For what greater trial could there be than to demand that a man sacrifice his beloved son and heir? How much more would Abraham have preferred to give all the food and clothing he possessed to the poor than to be forced to make this supreme sacrifice at God's command? James is merely echoing what is said in Hebrews: "By faith Abraham, when he was tested, offered up Isaac, and he who had received the promises was ready to offer up his only son, of whom it was said, 'Through Isaac shall your descendants be named'" [Heb. 11:17-18]. *Looking at one and the same sacrifice, James praised the magnificence of Abraham's work, while Paul praised the constancy of his faith.* But in reality the two men are saying exactly the same thing, because they both knew that Abraham was perfect in his faith as well as in his works, and each one merely emphasized that aspect of the incident which his own audience was most in need of hearing. (Bede the Venerable, Concerning the Epistle of St. James, italics added; Jas. 2:21)[65]

64. PG 119:481; ACCS NT 11:34*.
65. PL 93:23; ACCS NT 11:31-32.

Abraham was faithful in a way that became active in his obedience to God even in the face of the loss of his only son. Isaac was an earthly type of Christ being offered up for us all, according to Hilary of Arles: "When Abraham went up the mountain to sacrifice Isaac, he took four things with him — a sword, fire, a heavy heart and a pile of wood. What does the fire stand for if not the suffering of Christ? What does the sword signify, if not death? What does the wood indicate, if not the cross? And what is the importance of Abraham's heavy heart, if it does not stand for the compassion of the Father and the angels as they beheld the death of Christ? Isaac was an earthly type of Christ and was offered up for us all. . . . The place where it happened was none other than the one which God would later choose for the site of his temple on Mount Zion, which is so called because Zion means 'mirror of life,' for it was there that Abraham saw as in a mirror the life which was to be revealed in the New Testament" (Hilary of Arles, Introductory Tractate on the Letter of James; Jas. 2:21).[66] It is this typic relation between Isaac and Christ that bridges the supposed gap between Paul and James. The wood, of course, is the cross. Using these corollary types, the gap is easily bridged.

### 4. The Abraham Narrative Resolves the Apparent Discrepancy

Using this same typology, Cyril of Alexandria offered a thoughtful and nuanced distinction to resolve the apparent dilemma between Paul and James, based on the coming resurrection: "On the one hand, the blessed James says that Abraham was justified by works when he bound Isaac his son on the altar, but on the other hand Paul says that he was justified by faith, which appears to be contradictory. However, this is to be understood as meaning that *Abraham had believed before he had Isaac. . . . Isaac was indeed given to him as a reward for his faith. Likewise, when he bound Isaac to the altar, he did not merely do the work which was required of him, but he did it with the faith that in Isaac his seed would be as numberless as the stars of heaven, believing that God could raise him from the dead* [Heb. 11:17-19]" (Cyril of Alexandria, quoted in Cramer, Catena in Epistolas Catholicas, italics added; Jas. 2:21).[67]

66. PL *Suppl.* 3:73; ACCS NT 11:31*.
67. CEC 17; ACCS NT 11:32*.

"You see that faith was active along with his works, and faith was completed by works," wrote James, "and the scripture was fulfilled which says, 'Abraham believed God, and it was reckoned to him as righteousness'; and he was called the friend of God" (Jas. 2:22-23, RSV). Only in this special sense is it then possible for James to argue, in a way quite consistent with Paul, "that a man is justified by works and not by faith alone" (Jas. 2:24, RSV).

Faith is ever ready to do whatever works God commands, according to Bede: "Abraham had such a vibrant faith in God that he was ready to *do* whatever God wanted him to. This is why his faith was reckoned to him as righteousness, and it was in order that we might know the full meaning of this that God ordered Abraham to sacrifice his son. *It was by his perfect accomplishment of God's command that the faith which he had in his heart was shown to be perfect*" (Bede the Venerable, Concerning the Epistle of St. James, italics added; Jas. 2:22).[68]

Abraham's deeds were perfected by faith, argued Cyril of Jerusalem: "Abraham was justified not by works but by faith. For although he had done many good things, *he was not called a friend of God until he believed, and every one of his deeds were perfected by faith*" (Cyril of Jerusalem, Catechetical Lectures 5.5, italics added; Jas. 2:23).[69] Augustine found further meaning in the same text: "That Abraham believed God deep in his heart is a matter of faith alone, but *that he took his son to sacrifice him . . . is not just a great act of faith but a great work as well*" (Augustine, Sermons 2.9, italics added; Jas. 2:23).[70]

"Abraham is the image of someone who is *justified by faith alone, since what he believed was credited to him as righteousness. But he is also approved because of his works, since he offered up his son Isaac on the altar* (Gen. 22:10-18). Of course he did not do this work by itself. In doing it, he remained firmly anchored in his faith, believing that through Isaac his seed would be multiplied until it was as numerous as the stars" (Oecumenius, Commentary on James, italics added; Jas. 2:23).[71]

68. PL 93:23-24; ACCS NT 11:32-33.
69. FC 61:141; ACCS NT 11:33.
70. WSA 3 1:181*; ACCS NT 11:33.
71. PG 119:481; ACCS NT 11:33.

## 5. Remembering Rahab

The Church Fathers were fascinated by the next analogy made by James, which is even more startling: "In the same way was not Rahab the harlot also justified by works when she received the messengers and sent them out another way? For as the body apart from the spirit is dead, so faith apart from works is dead" (Jas. 2:25-26, NAS*). How did faith work in the case of Rahab? By welcoming the stranger, "dealing kindly" (Josh. 2:12, NRSV*), and decisively helping the people of God in dire need, in response to God's revelation (Josh. 2:9-11).

Bede noted the irony that James, the leading advocate of faith's good works, commended Rahab the sinner as a woman of faith whose faith was active in love: "There must have been some people who would have argued that Abraham was a special case, since nobody would now be asked to make such a sacrifice, and that therefore his example does not really count. To answer this objection, James searches the Scriptures and comes up with the case of Rahab, a wicked woman and a foreigner to boot, who nevertheless was *justified by her faith because she performed works of mercy* and showed hospitality to members of God's people, even though her own life was thereby put in danger" (Bede the Venerable, Concerning the Epistle of St. James, italics added; Jas. 2:25).[72] Rahab's faith was not spoken, but embodied in actions.

Pachomius recognized candidly that "Rahab was a prostitute, but even so she was numbered among the saints" (Pachomius, Instruction 1.25; Jas. 2:25).[73] How? By her faith. Similarly Severian of Gabala wrote: "Listen to the testimony of Scripture. In the midst of prostitution there was a pearl, in the mire there was burnished gold, in the mud there was a flower blooming with godliness. A godly soul was concealed in a land of impiety" (Severian, quoted in Cramer, Catena in Epistolas Catholicas; Jas. 2:25).[74]

Active faith shines forth through works of righteousness, according to Cyril of Alexandria: "Just as faith without works is dead, so the reverse is also true. Therefore let integrity in faith shine forth along with the glories of upright living" (Cyril of Alexandria, Letters 55.2; Jas. 2:20).[75] "But some-

71. PL 93:24; ACCS NT 11:33-34*.
73. CSPK 3:23; ACCS NT 11:33.
74. CEC 18; ACCT NT 11:33.
75. FC 77:15; ACCS NT 11:31.

one will say, 'You have faith and I have works.' Show me your faith apart from your works, and I by my works will show you my faith" (Jas. 2:18, NRSV). The arguments are complementary.

## F. Faith Bears Fruit

### 1. Good Works according to Scripture

In scripture, good works are fruits of the Spirit, whereas evil works are works of the flesh. What is meant by "good"? In what way are works good? A work *is* good if it *does* good. The faithful are called to go about *doing* good, as Jesus did (Acts 10:38). This means doing good to all. God brings goodness to all, as the sun and the rain show (Matt. 5:45). The faithful learn an amazing truth, that in all things God works for good to those who love him (Rom. 8:28). We are to do good to those who hate us (Luke 6:27), and to bless those who persecute us (Rom. 12:14).

God's doing of the good is incomparably better than whatever we may do. But our works can participate in his works. In this sense it is said that "one who does good is of God" (3 John 11, RSV*). Apart from God, we do no good thing (Ps. 16:2). What we call good works is not separable from responsiveness to God's goodness. We are invited to participate in God's own goodness by doing good as God does good, after the singular pattern of God's goodness. The One who incomparably does good is incomparably good. No human is good precisely in the same way that God is good (Matt. 19:17; Mark 10:18), but only by participation and analogy.

God is in time bringing to his creatures the good that he has promised them (Jer. 32:42), first with the people of Israel (Ps. 73:1; Num. 10:29; Zech. 8:15), and through them to all humanity (Rom. 9:24-26). For those who walk uprightly, God does not withhold any good thing (Ps. 84:11).

When we behold that which most truly is, we see that it is good. Anything that is, is good, insofar as it participates in being, since being is good. The faithful enjoy "tasting and seeing that the Lord is good" (Ps. 34:8, KJV*). There can be no doubt that God is good (Ps. 100:5). So doing good deeds and enacting good works are the consequences of sharing in the life of the One who does good incomparably.

By looking at nature and history, any fair-minded observer can easily see how great is God's goodness (Ps. 31:19). God shows his goodness in all creation (Gen. 1). When creatures lapse into fallenness, God continues to show his goodness in the redemption of the history of sin, by entering into a covenant relationship with his people, redeeming them, taking care of them in the wilderness, giving them the land, teaching them the law, giving them the temple, offering forgiveness.

The new covenant promised by the prophets (Jer. 32:40) is fulfilled in Jesus Christ. This is good news. Those who respond in faith to this good news are given the great privilege of sharing in God's goodness, becoming "partakers of the Holy Spirit" (Heb. 6:4, NAS). Even though only God is good in the incomparable way that God is good, and though apart from God's goodness no one can do good (Rom. 3:12), nonetheless God calls all human creatures to do good to one another in the light of his common grace which is given in creation, and his redeeming grace which is given in the work of the Son, and finally in his sanctifying grace which is given in the work of the Holy Spirit leading toward consummation in the end of time.

So we are called to do good to one another (Luke 6:35) in the light of the good that God has done to us. Every fair-minded person is able, in some sense, to discern the difference between good and evil (Rom. 2:14-15; cf. Heb. 5:14). Due to conscience, the knowledge we have with ourselves, we cannot possibly not know something of the good. For despite our fallenness we are made to recognize the good for ourselves, and thereby to grasp what it might mean to the neighbor.

The fallen human will is permitted, allowed, and empowered by the Spirit of God to refract something of God's own goodness. We are to "cling to what is good" (Rom. 12:9, NIV). This requirement on reason and conscience is "holy, just, and good" (Rom. 7:12, KJV*). It calls us to seek justice (Amos 5:14-15), seek peace (Ps. 34:14), defend the weak (Isa. 1:17), and do justice, love kindness, and walk humbly with God (Mic. 6:8). What about this can we not understand, except as we desperately will not to understand it?

These good works are fruits of life with God, fruits that cannot be hid (1 Tim. 5:25; Matt. 5:16). They are a harvest that comes only out of good soil, the soil of faith (Matt. 13:8, 23). God's goodness bears fruit in actions (Jas. 3:17; cf. John 15:4-5). By responding to the goodness of God, we "learn to do well" (Isa. 1:17, Douay-Rheims).

## 2. Do Good Quietly

Faith bears fruit fitting to repentance and faith. This fruit grows quietly.

It is best to let your good works remain unheralded. Good works are destined in due time to be revealed, but not so much before human eyes as before God. We are instructed to let our works remain anonymous, and be hidden by us so as to be revealed in due time by God. Faith working in love allows God to bring a good work to light in God's own way and time.

Scripture teaches that God will reveal good works done in secret in God's own time.

> The Lord does not wish us to act in secret in order that our work may not be visible. For elsewhere he says, "Let your light shine so that men may see your good works, and they may glorify your Father who is in heaven" [Matt. 5:16]. But it is he who in due time will do the revealing. Every good thing becomes more pleasing when it is *hidden by us but revealed by God.* If you display yourself, there are few who will praise you, and few will understand, even if you should appear humble. If you do this, others are more likely to be bored by you . . . than to praise you. If, on the other hand, God reveals your work, no one will put you down, except perhaps a very evil man to whom any good work is distinctly displeasing. . . . It is impossible that the Lord would forever ignore the good work of a good person done in secret. God will make him known in this age, and glory in him in the future, because the glory is of God. (Opus Imperfectum in Matthaeum, Homily 13, italics added; Matt. 6:4)[76]

The faithful have no need to perform outward works in order to be seen by others, as some religious leaders did (as evidenced in Jesus' time by the Pharisee's phylacteries and the fringes of his garments). This "mad desire for glory" prompts him "to make a show in front of others who were watching," according to John Chrysostom. "He becomes preoccupied with *exhibiting whatever others want to see* . . . on calculating how to please those who are watching. If observers are noble, he makes a spectacle of devising conflicts. If his audience lacks enthusiasm, he . . . becomes downcast. If they delight in ridicule, he delights in ridicule — all in order to please

---

76. PG 56:708; ACCS NT 1a:125*.

those watching. If they are earnest and practice self-restraint, he tries to exhibit the same attitude, since this is the disposition of the one from whom he seeks praise. It is not that he does some things one way and some things in another way. No, he is far more predictable. He always acts with the spectator in mind, in all things absolutely" (Chrysostom, The Gospel of Matthew, Homily 72.2, italics added; Matt. 23:5).[77]

### 3. Good Works Are Beheld by God

The faithful do good works not in order to be praised, but to seek that which is worthy of praise. Augustine stated this principle: "Our good Master has taught us by his apostle not to live right and to do right *in order to be praised* by men, that is, not to make the praise of men our motive for doing right, yet for the sake of others we are to seek what is really worthy of being praised. Even when good men are praised, the benefit falls more on those who praise than on those who are praised. For, as far as the latter are concerned, it is enough for them that they are good. . . . Thus the apostle says in a certain passage: 'If I pleased men, I should not be the servant of Christ' [Gal. 1:10]" (Augustine, Letters 231.1.4; italics added; 1 Thess. 2:4).[78]

Do not even look for human praise, but rather for God to be praised through your actions. A disciple of Augustine, Fulgentius of Ruspe, developed this point: "In all good works, be careful lest you be stirred by desire for human praise. You ought to be praised in your good works, but insofar as you do them, you ought not to expect human praises. Even when the human tongue may praise you, you more desire praise from God alone. And thus it may come about that *while you do not seek human praise, God may be praised in your deeds.* . . . The apostle too avoided human glory in his works but sought God's glory. So he says, writing to the Thessalonians, 'Nor, indeed, did we ever appear with flattering speech, as you know, or with a pretext for greed — God is witness — nor did we seek praise from human beings, either from you or from others' [1 Thess. 2:5-6]" (Fulgentius of Ruspe, Letters 2.35, italics added; 1 Thess. 2:4).[79] Those justified by faith in God's grace do not need to seek merit with others.

---

77. PG 58:669; NPNF 1 10:437; ACCS NT 1b:166*.
78. FC 32:160-61; ACCS NT 9:64*.
79. FC 95:308; ACCS NT 9:64-65*.

It is sufficient to know that God beholds good works. So be content to let your good works be known by God. It is not necessary for them to be seen by men: "The disciples of Jesus did everything to be seen by God alone. The only ornaments they had . . . were good works. Meditating on divine teaching, they observed the divine commands, always applying them fittingly before the eyes of their souls. Their only tassel was the excellence of the pattern of the one whom they followed" (Origen, Commentary on Matthew 11; Matt. 23:5).[80]

## 4. Summing Up the Fruit-Bearing Motif

We all already know what we ought to do for others since we know what we wish others to do to and for us. We know this because it is intrinsic to our human consciousness to know how we wish to be dealt with. We are fully conscious of the difference between others treating us well or badly.

The opportunity to do good is time limited, and hence looks for those moments of opportunity when a good work is fitting to that time. Active faith shines forth through the works of love. Faith is made stronger, not weaker, through the works of love.

Since God is the source of all goods, no act is good without divine grace. Any good we do is enabled by grace. Whatever is good in our good works is only good insofar as it responds to God's own goodness.

No one is ever saved by good works. Salvation is by grace alone. Works are not empowered by law, but by the power of grace.

The point in time where grace and truth come closest to us within human history is Jesus Christ. This grace alone is sufficient for our salvation, which bears the fruit of good works. The focal activity in Christian good works is faith's response to grace. Indeed this is the central premise of all Christian teaching on virtue, love, responsibility, law, and all other requirements of the moral life.

Faith is always at work, always looking to do what faith does when it sees human need. Grace enables the faith that bears fruit in good works. This is distinguished from faith without works (antinomianism) and from works without faith (legalism).

The Fathers go much deeper than commending the perfunctory per-

---

80. GCSO 10.2:22; ACCS NT 1b:166*.

formance of good works. Rather they seek to understand them in relation to God's own good works for humanity amid the history of sin. All work of human hands is thus viewed in the light of the larger narrative of human creation, the fall, redemption, and final human destiny. Failure to understand this salvation-history context results in a failure to grasp the vitality underlying the concern for good works in Christian community.

It is within the range of every believer to practice these simple good works: showing mercy to those outcast, hospitality, stewardship, enabling, reaching out to the alienated and the lost. It does not require special education or abilities. It requires a good will, however, transformed by grace, rightly to do these good works in a way that is glorifying to God.

## G. Summary Review of Classic Christian Teaching on Good Works

### 1. Seven Motifs

Here is a summary sketch of the seven motifs we have explored in this Reader: provision, relief, inclusion, forbearance, growth, stewardship, and grace. In sum, good works may be examined in terms of these biblical metaphors: supplying, enabling, including, forbearing, nurturing, giving, and fruit-bearing. These good works address distinguishable human dilemmas: poverty, suffering, exclusion, coercion, neglect, loss of value, and works-righteousness. Among the needy helped by these good works are: the poor, the hungry, the outcasts, the imprisoned, the defenseless, the victims of waste, and the self-righteous.

The Christian teaching of good works is at every point grounded in the Gospel itself, the good news of God's own coming within human history. Anyone who might prematurely conclude that salvation depends on our good works will find the classic texts resisting this fiercely.

Christians of all times and cultures do not differ substantially on defining good works. There is a stable, explicit, consensual textual tradition of exposition of the biblical teaching of good works. Classic Christianity's master teachers show us how to think clearly about how faith works. Any action may be assessed through the lens of these ancient Christian interpreters of good works. All good works stem from justification by grace alone through faith alone. This wisdom was firmly established in the earliest generations of biblical interpretation, as we have shown, long before Luther or Calvin or the debates of Augsburg and Trent.

*The Justification Reader* focused on classic Christianity's struggle against works-righteousness — *works without faith. The Good Works Reader* has focused on the opposite error — cheap grace, *faith without works* of love.

The texts we have utilized are those on which there is substantial agreement between traditions of East and West, Catholic, Protestant, and Orthodox as to their evangelical importance and ecumenical authority. We have learned from these texts to think biblically about all crucial acts of good works — toward the poor, the hungry, the vulnerable, the needy, the widow, the fatherless, the sick and the imprisoned, and children, the least of these.

These scriptural interpretations are not primarily about public policy or ideology, but God's own way of mercifully caring for humanity amid pain, sorrow, and suffering. Hence the question of good works always thrusts us directly into the realm of profound reflection on the incarnation, the Messianic miracles, the binding up of demonic powers, and finally the cross.

## 2. Reprise

The poor are blessed and viewed in relation to the incarnate Lord, who became poor that we might become rich. We are not to show partiality to either the poor or the rich. The Gospel is good news to the poor, because of their readiness to believe. Where your heart is there will your treasure be also. How you treat the poor impinges on your eternal destiny. The problem is not property or wealth as such but avarice. The poor are more likely to be rich in faith. The faithful are called actively to seek out the neediest and provide them relief. The widow and fatherless are among those who in scripture are viewed as especially vulnerable and in need of care and support. In the pattern of the incarnation God chooses lowliness. God identifies with the "least of these" — the hungry, the thirsty, the naked, the sick, the imprisoned (these issues we have considered in Part One).

Jesus' parable of the sheep and goats on the last day is the pivotal scriptural reference for good works. Even the order for the consideration of good works is embedded textually in this parable. The good works of saving faith cited in Jesus' parable are prototypically: feeding the hungry, assuaging thirst, welcoming the stranger, clothing the naked, offering shelter for refugees, displaced persons, and the homeless, and nursing the sick (Part Two).

Since God the Father has reached out for us in the mission of the Son, the special calling of those who follow him is to reach out for the outcast, the marginalized, the leper, the handicapped, the blind, the deaf, those who cannot speak for themselves, the disabled, the paralyzed, the addicted. These acts are representative of works of love embodied by Jesus himself (Part Three).

The ancient Christian writers were engaged in ministries to the imprisoned and persecuted. To visit the imprisoned is not merely to come to see, but to attend and care for. Being completely helpless and isolated, the imprisoned and persecuted are especially in need of care and comfort and above all hope (Part Four).

The pattern in the Christian life for caring compassionately for those least able to defend themselves is the way in which Jesus himself reached out for the lowly, commending to the faithful their care. Even more so it is the way in which he himself as incarnate Lord voluntarily became a little child, obedient to his parents and to law, suffering, hungering, sweating, and thirsting, facing human limitations even unto death. The incarnate Lord came into the world as "the least of these," as a child, born in poverty, hunted, persecuted, displaced, homeless (Part Five).

For those blessed with worldly possessions, the pattern for the Christian life is the incarnate Lord, who though he was rich, voluntarily became poor for us, facing human limitations, hunger, and an unjust death. His message to those who have wealth is evident in narratives that treat the wealthy not with contempt but respect, and challenge them to total accountability in relation to their eternal destiny. The rich can be saved, but special difficulties lie in the way. Speaking honestly to the rich about their moral responsibilities requires an attitude of candor, and at times encounter to penetrate defensive maneuvers (Part Six).

We all already know what we ought to do for others since we know what we wish others to do to and for us. The opportunity to do good is time limited, and hence looks for those moments of opportunity when a good work is fitting to that time. Active faith shines forth through the works of love. Faith is made stronger, not weaker, through the works of love (Part Seven).

## H. Conclusion

We have seen laid out before us key texts of the Christian tradition on good works. We have bathed in its richness. We have heard the ancient Christian writers speak practically on modest good deeds. Anyone who reads these extracts carefully is likely to be stunned by the range and vitality of their wisdom.

But is this relevant today? That is left to the reader to ponder and decide. At the end of this journey, there are several conclusions that self-evidently emerge out of this journey.

Here is a short list of key conclusions:

1. The ancient Christian writers showed sustained, compassionate interest in the poor, the sufferer, the lowly, the sick, the prisoner, and the disabled. Never in the future will it be reasonable, if our textual evidence is correct, to lodge the charge that these concerns were ignored in classic Christianity.

2. The earliest and most consensual authoritative sources enjoy a substantial range of agreement on what the scriptures teach about good works. This is an imperfect but real consensus. Many points remain in debate, but the main thrust of the teaching is clear — all too clear — and some might wish that it might be more ambiguous.

3. By authoritative sources I mean primarily canonical scripture, but also (in a way that honors scripture as the decisive judge of all controversies) the ecumenical councils and the key Fathers and scripture commentators of both east and west who searched the scriptures and reflected extensively upon them. The conciliar decisions were premised on extensive debates and consensual judgments on what scripture says. So it is overly simple to pit scripture against conciliar tradition.

4. Orthodox, Catholics, classic Protestants, charismatics, and the heirs of evangelical revivalism today all have a right to appeal to the same ancient classic scriptural interpreters on good works. These are first of all the scriptures themselves, and secondarily the ecumenical decisions about scriptural truth, and thirdly the detailed exegesis of those major writers most widely viewed by the larger tradition of east and west as reliable and truthful in terms of the apostolic witness.

5. The Spirit's mission of eliciting proximate unity in the body of Christ is being concretely formed through all these Christian traditions, even amid their varieties. The classic scriptural interpreters of the first mil-

lennium achieved a plausible consensus on the pivotal issues long before many of the divisions of the church in the second millennium.

6. This consensus is especially compelling in the arena of good works, where cooperation has stunning practical consequences and immediate social significance. Divided modern Christianity is not fated to remain forever fixated on the polemics of defensiveness in offering acts of mercy. It appears that the Holy Spirit is actively at work to bring Christians of very different cultures together in concerted efforts to relieve human suffering. The classic exegetes provide the basis for cooperative ministries among Christians with very different ecclesiastical and liturgical memories. The proximate unity of orthodox, consensual Christian moral teaching in the first five centuries may be the most reliable basis for overcoming the antipathies of the last five centuries.

7. The texts here cited are not primarily dependent on European or western sources. These texts are pre-European, if Charlemagne (A.D. 800) marks the emergence of a distinctively European consciousness. Northern European hegemony (north of the Alps as a matured literary culture) did not exist when these patristic texts were being written. Pre-European texts that are not a scandal to the two-thirds world of Christians in Africa and Asia are thus available to global Christianity. These texts come chiefly from Asia and Africa. They may be appealed to without the excess baggage of either western European colonialism or modernity or capitalism.

In this series of Readers, we have attempted to present an orthodox model for integrating classical ecumenical theology, exegetical theology, and systematic theology on two complementary theological issues: the first, justification; the second, good works.